```
D1339686
```

DUKE · UNIVERSITY · PUBLICATIONS

THE

SENTIMENTAL NOVEL
IN AMERICA
1789-1860

The Sentimental Novel in America 1789-1860

BY HERBERT ROSS BROWN

OCTAGON BOOKS

A DIVISION OF FARRAR, STRAUS AND GIROUX

New York   1975

Reprinted 1975
by special arrangement with the Duke University Press

OCTAGON BOOKS
A DIVISION OF FARRAR, STRAUS & GIROUX, INC.
19 Union Square West
New York, N. Y. 10003

Library of Congress Cataloging in Publication Data

Brown, Herbert Ross, 1902-
        The sentimental novel in America, 1789-1860.

        Reprint of the ed. published by Duke University Press, Durham,
        N. C., in series: Duke University publications.

        Bibliography: p.
        Includes index.
        1. American fiction—19th century—History and criticism.   2.
        Sentimentalism in literature.   3. National characteristics, Amer-
        ican.   I. Title.
PS377.B7   1975   813'.03   74-31258
ISBN 0-374-91032-4

Manufactured by Braun-Brumfield, Inc.
Ann Arbor, Michigan

Printed in the United States of America

To

JAMES WADDELL TUPPER

PREFACE

THE HISTORIAN of American fiction may handle his subject in one of two ways. He may (as G. K. Chesterton has observed with respect to Victorian literature) divide it as one cuts a piece of currant cake, taking the currants as they come. Or he may divide it as one cuts wood—along the grain. In this history of the sentimental novel in America, from the beginning to the Civil War, I have attempted to follow the grain—to trace in popular fiction some manifestations of the sentimental mind.

As a means of presenting a cross-section of the national imagination as it is revealed in the abundant outpouring of sentimental novels, I have been primarily concerned with social trends, forces, creeds, movements, and literary fashions. The reflection of these streams of thought is, with a few exceptions, more significant than a chronological account of authors and novels. Many of the titles of these faded favorites, it is charitable to remark at the threshold of this book, deserve to appear on any list of the world's worst fiction. Collectively, however, they represent a wide level of taste, and they have had an enormous influence upon the lives of the American people. The familiar names of the giants of the period appear in this faintly perfumed world of sentimental fiction only when their novels offer striking contrasts to the prevailing mood, or when they reveal traces of the "handkerchiefly" feeling.

Although very few of these once popular novels are read today by critical readers with anything save an ironical appreciation, the secret of their wide appeal is not entirely obscured by their feverish sentiment. They provided a welcome compensation for the emotions, activities, and ideals which life denied to countless readers. They contained an amazing vitality which often transcended their preposterous plots. Frequently they voiced the genuine aspirations of their age.

In making the present study I have received hearty assistance from many friends who have had and have my best thanks. A generous sabbatical leave from my duties at Bowdoin College gave me leisure for much of the reading done in preparation for this book. For many courtesies I am grateful to Mr. Charles Adams, of the Columbia University Library; Miss Edith Hall Crowell, of the New York Society Library; Mr. James Alfred Eastman, of the New York Public Library; Miss Florence Garing, of the Mercantile Library Association, New York; Mr. Robert Hammond Haynes, of the Harvard College Library; Mr. V. Valta Parma, former Custodian of the Rare Book Room, Library of Congress; Mr. R. W. G. Vail, former Librarian of the American Antiquarian Society; Mr. Gerald Gardner Wilder, Librarian of Bowdoin College; and Mr. Lyle H. Wright, of the Henry E. Huntington Library and Art Gallery.

For a critical reading of the manuscript I wish to express my gratitude to Professors Jay Broadus Hubbell and Clarence Gohdes, of Duke University; George Sherburn, of Harvard University; and Harry Morgan Ayres, Oscar James Campbell, Jefferson Butler Fletcher, Emery Neff, Susanne Howe Nobbe, and Henry W. Wells, of Columbia University; and especially Ralph Leslie Rusk, to whom all students of American literature are deeply indebted. His wise suggestions and kindly interest deserve to bear fruit in a better book.

I am also grateful to the Duke University Press Centennial Prize Committee for the generous publication of this book as a part of the observance of the origins of Trinity College, now a part of Duke University. My thanks are also due to Mr. David Kelly Jackson, of the Duke Press, for his careful editing of the manuscript. Finally, I am thankful to Mr. and Mrs. Addison Mooney for providing a delightful sanctuary in New York during the composition of this study; and, last of all, my gratitude goes to the patient Griselda who prepared the Index without yielding to a swoon, and without dropping a tear.

H. R. B.

Bowdoin College
15 September 1940

CONTENTS

BOOK ONE

The Beginnings

1789-1820

An American novel is such a moral, sentimental thing,
that it is enough to give one the vapours to read one.
—Hannah Webster Foster,
The Boarding School, 1798.

I

THE TRIUMPH OF THE NOVEL

But *place aux dames* was his maxim, and all the ladies of New-York declared that the library of Mr. Caritat was charming. Its shelves could
scarcely sustain the weight of *Female Frailty*, the *Posthumous Daughter*,
and the *Cavern of Woe;* they required the aid of the carpenter to support
the burden of the *Cottage-on-the-Moor*, the *House of Tynian*, and the
Castles of Athlin and Dunbayne; or they groaned under the multiplied editions of the *Devil in Love*, *More Ghosts*, and *Rinaldo Rinaldini*. Novels
were called for by the young and the old; from the tender virgin of thirteen, whose little heart went pit-a-pat at the approach of a beau, to the
experienced matron of three score, who could not read without spectacles.

—John Davis, *Travels of Four
Years and a Half in the United
States of America* . . . , 1803.

THE NATURE of our ancestors' light reading is revealed both by
the lamentations of moralists who deplored fiction, and by the
delighted efforts of booksellers who helped to supply it. Until
the output of American novels began to achieve something like
ample proportions, opposition naturally was directed at the English fiction market. Even the great masters of the eighteenth-
century novel were welcomed only with grave reservations.
Richardson, who had taught the passions to move at the command of virtue, was not wholly acceptable to many critics who
feared that the charm of Lovelace might prove more attractive
than the virtue of Clarissa. Fielding's magnificent comic epic
in prose did not save him from frequent rebukes for his coarse-
ness and levity. Smollett, occasionally praised for his touches
of nature, shared the opprobrium of vulgarity heaped upon the
author of *Tom Jones*. Sterne, without Richardson's moral
earnestness, seemed a seductively pleasant philanderer with the
emotions, who threatened to substitute a watery benevolence
for the strict conscience cherished by the Puritans. Where the
giants of the century had failed to please, the swarms of imitators who filled with their wares those teeming "slop-shops of

literature," the circulating libraries, met with unqualified censure. Novel readers were often classed with frequenters of cock-fights and "stage-shews." Young women were warned against a taste for romances along with such inelegant breaches of female decorum as "sitting cross-legged, straddling, spitting, blowing noses, etc. etc."

Writing in 1824 when the novel had attained comparative respectability, James McHenry recalled with wonder the widespread hostility to fiction a generation before. "In those days," he remarked, "it was almost as disreputable to be detected reading a novel, as to be found betting at a cock-fight, or a gaming table. Those who had sons would have supposed them forever incapacitated for any useful pursuit in life, if they exhibited an inclination for novel reading; and those who had daughters who exhibited such an inclination, would have considered them as totally unfitted for ever becoming good wives or mothers. . . ."[1] It would be rash to assume that such suspicion checked appreciably the ardor with which eighteenth-century novels were devoured. Rather this hostility serves to indicate a growing passion for those romances which many good men believed to be heavily freighted with subtle temptations.

These evils appeared to be grave enough to demand the concern of prominent men of affairs. Thomas Jefferson saw in the "inordinate passion prevalent for novels" a national menace. "When this poison infects the mind," he wrote to Nathaniel Burwell, "it destroys its tone and revolts it against wholesome reading. . . . The result is a bloated imagination, sickly judgment, and disgust towards all the real businesses of life."[2] This "new-fangled taste for fiction" also alarmed Noah Webster. "A hundred volumes of modern novels may be read without acquiring a new idea," he protested in 1790. "At best novels may be considered as the toys of youth; the rattle boxes of sixteen."[3]

As early as 1772 John Trumbull was grieved to discover

---

[1] *American Monthly Magazine* (Philadelphia, 1824), II, 1-2.

[2] P. L. Ford (ed.), *The Writings of Thomas Jefferson* (New York and London, 1892-99), X, 104.

[3] *A Collection of Essays and Fugitive Writings* . . . (Boston, 1790), p. 29. Webster's remarks were reprinted with commendation in the *American Museum* for Nov., 1792.

that ladies poisoned their minds with novels and the "amorous follies of romances."[4] Timothy Dwight, another dominant figure of the established order in Connecticut, found to his disgust that "The Reading of girls is regularly lighter than that of boys." "Girls," he lamented, "sink down to songs, novels, and plays."[5] Educators were particularly concerned with the extent of novel reading by young women in boarding schools. In the first American edition of his popular *Lectures on Female Education,* John Burton issued due warning: "That course of reading must be unprofitable, which is confined to novels; and this, I am apprehensive, is too much the case. . . . Novels are the last books which should be read; instead of being almost the first, as is the too general practice. . . ."[6] Hannah Webster Foster did not allow her authorship of *The Coquette* in 1797 to deter her a year later from attacking the work of other novelists.[7] In *The Boarding School* she recorded her conviction that "Novels are the favourite, and the most dangerous kind of reading, now adopted by the generality of young ladies."[8] The Reverend Enos Hitchcock had the same complaint to make in his edifying *Memoirs of the Bloomsgrove Family.* "Nothing can have a worse effect . . . than the free use of those writings which are the offspring of modern novelists," he cautioned in 1790. "Their only tendency is to excite romantic notions, while they keep the mind devoid of ideas, and the heart destitute of sentiment."[9] The Boston *Weekly Magazine* found it necessary to remind "all who are concerned in *female* education" of the dangers of "those exaggerated expressions of tenderness, which are the characteristics of heroines in romance." The warning concluded with the observation that "Women, who have been much addicted to common novel-

[4] *The Poetical Works . . .* (Hartford, 1820), p. 76.
[5] *Travels in New-England and New-York* (New Haven, 1821-22), I, 515.
[6] *Lectures on Female Education and Manners* (New York, 1794), p. 132.
[7] Inconsistency of this kind was quite common. It was a favorite device to indicate that whatever evils lurked in the novels of fellow authors, one's own works were above reproach. See William Hill Brown's *The Power of Sympathy* in which Mr. Holmes is made to declare that "many fine girls have been ruined by reading novels."
[8] *The Boarding School* (Boston, 1798), p. 18.
[9] *Memoirs of the Bloomsgrove Family* (Boston, 1790), II, 82.

reading, are always acting in imitation of some Jemima, or Almeria, who never existed. . . ."[10] Susanna Rowson, who certainly was not without a share in contributing to the evils she deplored, also expressed her distrust of the value of an education in which "the female head" became "well stored with sensibility, and all the delicate feelings gleaned from a circulating library, the contents of which she has eagerly and indiscriminately perused. . . ."[11]

In the magazines there is abundant evidence of the current opposition to injudicious novel reading. Female readers of the *American Magazine* in 1788 were told that "your early studies are not always well directed—and you are permitted to devour a thousand volumes of fictitious nonsense, when a smaller number of books . . . would furnish you with more valuable treasures of knowledge."[12] Doctor Witherspoon joined the mounting chorus against fiction in the *United States Magazine* in 1794, in which he charged that "romances and fabulous narratives are a species of composition, from which the world hath received as little benefit, and as much hurt as any . . . excepting plays themselves. . . ."[13] Under the ominous caption of "Novel Reading, a Cause of Female Depravity," a moralist in the *Monthly Mirror* in 1797, after bemoaning the disappearance of "moderately stiff stays, covered elbows and concealed bosoms," concluded pointedly that "those who first made *novel-reading* an indispensable branch in forming the minds of young women, have a great deal to answer for."[14] Young ladies, presumably because they had more leisure than their brothers, became objects of tender concern. The editor of the *Universal Asylum* marveled at "the remissness of those parents and guardians, who suffer their daughters and wards to read, indiscriminately, the multiplicity of novels which are daily pub-

---

[10] *Weekly Magazine* (Boston, 1804), II, 145.

[11] *Mentoria* (Philadelphia, 1794), II, 87. Mrs. Rowson did not confine her strictures to this treatise on education. Confident of her invulnerability, she included in her own novel, *Sarah; or, The Exemplary Wife* (Boston, 1813), an account of one who read not wisely, but too well.

[12] *American Magazine* (New York, 1788), I, 244.

[13] *United States Magazine* (Newark, 1794), I, 245.

[14] Reprinted in the *New England Quarterly* (Boston, 1802), III, 172.

lished."[15] Mindful of its peculiar obligations to a feminine constituency, the *Lady's Magazine* in the opening volume in 1792 remarked that "Novels are a species of writing, which can scarcely be spoken of without being condemned. . . ."[16] In the first number, the editors printed a letter purporting to have come from a distressed mother who begged them "to caution the fair sex against reading improper books . . . and what you ought to be particularly severe against, are novels. . . . I have a family of three daughters, who are mad upon reading novels, and I can seldom prevail on them to read anything else."[17]

Scandalous reading of fiction by young ladies moved John Shippen, "a member of the Belles-Lettres Society" at Dickinson College, to publish a formidable monograph on the subject entitled *Observations on Novel Reading*.[18] In a review of the essay in the *Universal Asylum,* which usually contained its full share of fiction, a critic recommended the homily to "Such fair readers as inconsiderately trifle away the precious hours of youth in the indiscriminate perusal of novels," and concluded with the hope that they might find "some incentives to devote their attention to more useful studies."[19] There is the same oft-repeated advice in the first number of the *New York Magazine* in an essay dedicated to the "Fair Readers" of that periodical. "I would wish you to be careful in the choice of your books," the editor counseled, "never reading Novels or Romances, as there is seldom any good to be derived from them, and they often produce bad effects on the minds of young people. . . ."[20] According to an indictment in the *Weekly Magazine,* fiction tended to give young ladies "notions" which unfitted them for the stern realities of a life of childbearing and drab domestic routine. "Novels not only pollute the imaginations of young women," declared the critic, "but likewise give them false ideas of life, which too often make them

[15] *Universal Asylum and Columbian Magazine* (Philadelphia, 1792), II, 225.
[16] *Lady's Magazine* (Philadelphia, 1792), I, 296.
[17] *Ibid.,* I, 11.
[18] *Observations on Novel Reading* (Philadelphia, 1792).
[19] *Universal Asylum,* I, 262.
[20] *New York Magazine* (New York, 1790), I, 16.

act improperly; owing to the romantic turn of thinking they imbibe from their favourite studies."[21] The pollution of American womanhood commonly attributed to a taste for fiction inspired a humorist in Joseph Dennie's *Port Folio* to announce that affairs had reached such a sorry state that "if a man of sense has an inclination to chuse a rational woman for his wife, he reaches his grand climacteric before he can find a fair one to trust himself with—so universal is the corruption!— These are the fatal consequences of novels!"[22]

Editors and publishers of periodicals, confronted by a popular demand for fiction and heedful of the loud clamor against its evils, adroitly contrived an editorial policy calculated to maintain their circulation as well as their self-respect. This was achieved by neutralizing stories with sermons, and historiettes with homilies, often printed in parallel columns. There are few better examples of managing to hunt with the hounds and to run with the hares! The *New York Magazine,* which made its bow in 1790 with a scorching blast against novels and romances, also included in the first number a sufficiently lurid story, "The Fatal Effects of Seduction," which set the tone and mood for many later contributions.[23] At this profitable game of eating one's cake and having it, too, the *Massachusetts Magazine* became peculiarly adept. In its comparatively long existence, from 1789 to 1796, it served as a shrine for the worship of sentiment and sensibility; every issue bore witness to the influence of Richardson and Sterne. The editors saw to it, however, that readers who suffered contamination had only themselves to blame. The most rigid moralist could not have improved upon the warning contributed by Leander: "The sorrowful effects of reading novels and romances have been delineated by many, but one need not go far to be an eye

[21] *Weekly Magazine* (Philadelphia, 1798), I, 185. The same fear was expressed by Royall Tyler in *The Algerine Captive* (Walpole, 1797), I, x-xi. The pious Hannah Adams confessed late in her life that she "acquired false ideas of life" from novels read in her youth. See *A Memoir of Miss Hannah Adams* (Boston, 1832), p. 4.

[22] *Port Folio* (Philadelphia, 1802), II, 107.

[23] It was followed in the February issue by "Edmund and Harriot" in which a seducer's efforts are fully described. "The Country Squire's Revenge," the contents of which are amply indicated by the title, appeared in the June issue.

witness of the fatal consequences which result from such chimerical works; . . . they are written with an intent to captivate the feelings, and do in fact lead many on to the path of vice, from an idea that they are within the pale of gallantry."[24]

Faced with censure such as this in England earlier in the century, Samuel Richardson attempted to placate the opposition by introducing in *Pamela* "a new species of writing, that might possibly turn young people into a source of reading different from the pomp and parade of romance writing, and dismissing the improbable and marvelous with which novels generally abound, might tend to promote the cause of religion and virtue." Our early novelists took a leaf from the book of their master by including in their works the usual warnings against romances. To the charge that novels were lies, the authors answered with "Tales Founded upon Truth." To the objection that the hearth-side virtues were seldom found in fiction, the novelists replied with stories extolling Heaven, Home, and Mother. In answer to the indictment that novels were literary opiates, the writers cited their aim to improve the understanding and to inculcate lessons of prudence and virtue. "I am willing to flatter myself," wrote Mrs. Rowson in her Preface to *Trials of the Human Heart*, "that in offering this novel to the public, I am not preparing for my future life, either shame or repentance."[25]

A favorite device to gain respectability for the much maligned fiction was the novelist's insistence that his story was "Founded on Incidents in Real Life" or "Based upon Recent Facts." These claims of authenticity were frequently made on the title pages and re-enforced in the prefaces and advertisements of many early novels.[26] In their declarations of a factual

[24] *Massachusetts Magazine* (Boston, 1791), III, 662-664.

[25] *Trials of the Human Heart* (Philadelphia, 1795), I, xx.

[26] Among the tales for which was claimed authenticity, it is significant that *The Power of Sympathy*, the first American novel; *Charlotte Temple*, one of the most popular works of fiction ever published in this country; and *The Coquette*, the most convincingly told sentimental tale of the century, should each have had a basis in actual fact. For an account of the contemporary scandal included in *The Power of Sympathy*, see *Philenia: The Life and Works of Sarah Wentworth Morton, 1759-1846*, by Emily Pendleton and Milton Ellis (Orono, 1931); and "The Author of the First American Novel," by Ellis, in *American Literature*, IV, 359-368. Mrs. C. H.

warrant for their stories, authors often betrayed a nervous regard for the current prejudice against fiction as fiction. "However fond of novels and romances you may be," wrote Mrs.
Ann Bleecker in her "History of Maria Kittle," "the unfortunate adventures of one my neighbors, who died yesterday, will
make you despise that fiction, in which, knowing the subject
to be fabulous, we can never be so truly interested."[27] Superior
claims of truthfulness were advanced by James Butler in *Fortune's Foot-ball*. "Having been intimately acquainted with the
hero of the piece, in my juvenile days," he testified in the Preface, "I can with confidence vouch for the authenticity of the
narrative."[28] Even the most incredible episodes were solemnly
documented. Thus the author of *Margaretta* found sanction
for the amazing reconciliation between Warren and Matilda
and for the recovery of their long-lost daughter, not only in
"the ways of Providence," but "in actual life." A footnote as-
sures the skeptical reader that "It was such a circumstance"
which "suggested the subject of this volume. It was in the time
of the American Revolution."[29] A similar appeal to the
reader's love of truth was made by Mann in the Preface to his
Female Review. "The Female, who is the subject of the following Memoirs," he boasted, "does not only exist in theory and
imagination, but in reality."[30] The author of *Monima* promptly
disclaimed membership in "the honorable tribe of Novel-
Tinkers" and urged as the best recommendation for her own
work "that it is not utterly devoid of truth, as it is chiefly
founded on fact."[31] *Amelia* was warranted by the author as
having been based not only upon fact, but upon "Recent
Events" within the memory of readers, and therefore was

Dall's *The Romance of the Association* (Cambridge, 1875), and C. K. Bolton's *The
Elizabeth Whitman Mystery* (Peabody, 1912) discuss the incidents upon which Mrs.
Foster based *The Coquette*. See also my note in the Facsimile Text Society edition
of *The Coquette* (New York, 1939).

[27] *The Posthumous Works of Ann Eliza Bleecker in Prose and Verse* . . . (New
York, 1793), p. 19.

[28] *Fortune's Foot-ball* (Harrisburg, 1797), I, i.

[29] [Anon.,] *Margaretta; or, The Intricacies of the Heart* (Philadelphia, 1807), pp.
344-345.

[30] H. Mann, *The Female Review* (Dedham, 1797), pp. v-vi.

[31] Martha Read, *Monima; or, The Beggar Girl* (New York, 1802), p. v.

doubly deserving "from its authenticity, at least, an interest in the feeling heart."[32]

Ever alert for plausible means by which to convince readers of the "truth" of their fiction, novelists resorted to a wide variety of devices. The "editor" of the epistolary *Art of Courting* announced his readiness to produce the necessary proof upon demand of any doubting reader: "Several of the parties are now alive, and the original letters in the hands of the writer."[33] Although Mrs. Rowson was not quite willing to assert that her entire narrative in *Sarah* was taken from actual occurrences, she was careful to add that "Many of the scenes delineated in the following work are drawn from real life; some of them have occurred within my knowledge. . . ."[34] Other novelists occasionally cited the factual basis of their stories as the most compelling reason for granting their "consent" to allow the tales to appear in print. In "An Apology to the Public" prefixed to *Fidelity Rewarded* this ruse was employed by the author, "who at first, threw the following sheets together, without any further design than for his own amusement: But, as they are founded on truth . . . he now consents they may appear in public."[35] Charles Brockden Brown yielded to the popular demand for "authenticity" in his dedicatory inscription in *Ormond*. "You are desirous of hearing an authentic, and not a fictitious tale," he wrote to Rosenberg. "It will, therefore, be my duty to relate events in no artificial or elaborate order, and without that harmonious congruity and luminous amplification, which might justly be displayed in a tale flowing merely from pure invention."[36] Eliza Vicery relied upon the usual method of circumventing prejudice by frankly admitting that she shared the distrust felt by many critics upon the subject of fiction. After making this gesture of right thinking, she

---

[32] [Anon.,] *Amelia; or, The Faithless Briton* (Boston, 1798), p. 2. An edition in German was published at Baltimore in 1809.

[33] Ebenezer Bradford, *The Art of Courting* (Newburyport, 1795), pp. vii-viii.

[34] *Sarah; or, The Exemplary Wife* (Boston, 1813), p. iii. This novel appeared in weekly installments in the *Weekly Magazine* of Boston from June 4, 1803, to June 30, 1804, under the title, "Sincerity; a novel in a series of original letters."

[35] [Anon.,] *Fidelity Rewarded* (Boston, 1796), p. [3].

[36] *Ormond* (New York, 1799), p. iii.

promptly claimed exemption for her own work. "But those which are founded on interesting scenes in real life," she wrote in defense of *Emily Hamilton,* "may be calculated to afford moral instruction to the youthful mind, in the most pleasing manner."[37]

The nice distinction between romances and novels "founded on fact" was a difficult one to make. Two of Mrs. Rowson's heroines discussed the problem in *Trials of the Human Heart.* Meriel was confident that her father's prohibition of novels could not possibly include "true histories." "Perhaps these were the kind my father meant, when he talked about romances and novels," she wrote to Celia, "but yet that cannot be, as this is a real history, the characters drawn from life."[38] The convention was certainly abused. Editors flooded their periodicals with "pathetic fragments" and "affecting historiettes" vouchsafing their fidelity to truth.[39] The *Port Folio* finally was forced to rebuke its contributors. "'A Fact' may be very true, but is very dull," protested the editor after reading many "true stories" submitted by ambitious writers. "We may not tax the memory, and teaze the patience of our readers with a barren recital, as void of beauty as of use."[40] An aroused reader of the same magazine also objected to the sanctity of "truth" in fiction: "I do not always, especially in my vacant hours, neglect a novel," he wrote, "merely because I am told by a dull searcher for matters of fact, that it is not *legitimate* history. . . . A good story is the same, let it issue either from *knightly castles, or from ladies' bowers.*"[41]

With the cornerstone of our early fiction resting firmly upon truth, its artificers were equally anxious to point its spire in the direction of heaven. "If, from the perusal of these juvenile sentiments," wrote Samuel Relf in the "Advertise-

[37] *Emily Hamilton* (Worcester, 1803), p. iv.

[38] *Trials of the Human Heart,* I, 41-42.

[39] For a few examples, see: *Massachusetts Magazine,* I, 361, 648-649, 786-787; *New York Weekly Magazine,* I, 191, 212, 274; *Universal Asylum,* I, 374; *The Nightingale,* I, 196. Dr. Hitchcock in *The Farmer's Friend* (Boston, 1793) testified that "Stories, founded on fact, or on circumstances which might easily be supposed to happen in real life, may be made very useful in families."

[40] *Port Folio,* IV, 255.   [41] *Ibid.,* II, 138.

ment" to *Infidelity*, "one remiss husband be reclaimed to the due exercise of social virtue;—if it pluck from the bosom of one neglected wife, a single pang . . . the ambition of the Author will be accomplished; whatever may be the fate of his work at the awful bar of criticism."[42] Novelists recognized that their first task was to satisfy the moralist rather than the literary critic. "The drift of the subject is to show the preference of virtue, to riches and grandeur . . . ," declared the author of *Fidelity Rewarded*. "As the author aimed to inculcate virtue, and discourage vice, he hopes it will be kindly received."[43] In the absence of any well-formulated body of criticism for fiction, most reviewers contented themselves with a few general observations on the moral tendencies of the novels under consideration. A writer in the *Weekly Magazine* expressed the general attitude when he remarked in 1798: "To the story-telling moralist the United States is a new and untrodden field. . . . The value of such works lies without doubt in their moral tendency."[44] The prefaces to most novels of this period indicate how painfully aware the authors were of the judgment of the moralist. "The following sheets were written, chiefly with a view to exhibit the pernicious effects which result from a vitious education," George Watterston affirmed in his Preface to *The Lawyer*, "and thus to show the propriety of early instilling into the youthful mind principles of justice, of truth, and of honesty."[45] Mrs. Rowson also wrote with one eye to the approbation of the moral critic. "Heaven forbid," she prayed in *Trials of the Human Heart*, "I should suffer ought to escape my pen, that might call a blush to the cheek of innocence, or deserve a glance of displeasure from the eye of the most rigid moralist."[46] The lack of "sublimity" in the incidents in *Fortune's Foot-ball* was apologized for on the same grounds. "If the subjects are not sublime," Butler explained, "they have a manifest tendency to propagate sentiments of virtue—to stim-

[42] *Infidelity* (Philadelphia, 1797), p. 11.
[43] *Fidelity Rewarded*, p. [3].
[44] *Weekly Magazine* (Philadelphia, 1798), I, 202.
[45] *The Lawyer* (Pittsburgh, 1808), p. v.
[46] *Trials of the Human Heart*, I, xv.

ulate youth to an humble resignation to the dispensations of providence—and to discountenance vice."[47]

The assurance that most fiction readers were women conditioned many of the warnings and determined much of the advice with which these novels are larded. The moral of *Charlotte* was designed for the "American Fair." "If the following tale should save one hapless fair one from the errors which ruined poor Charlotte, or rescue from impending misery the heart of one anxious parent," wrote Mrs. Rowson, "I shall feel a much higher gratification in reflecting on this trifling performance, than could possibly result from the applause which might attend the most elegant, finished piece of literature whose tendency might deprave the heart or mislead the understanding."[48] The spectacular typographical display which helped to dedicate *The Power of Sympathy* to the daughters of Columbia was followed by a statement of the author's ambition to write a novel in which "the dangerous Consequences of Seduction are exposed, and the Advantages of Female Education set forth and recommended."[49] Occasionally characters were made to address their readers directly. Thus Eliza Wharton in *The Coquette* included a significant warning in her farewell to Sanford. "May my unhappy story serve as a beacon to warn the American fair," she declared to her betrayer, "of the dangerous tendency and destructive consequences of associating with men of your character, of destroying their time, and risking their reputations by the practice of coquetry and its attendant follies!"[50] The dedication of John Davis's *Wanderings of William* is pleasantly revealing of the feverish conditions under which many American girls devoured their fiction. "Avail yourself of the moment that offers to indulge in the perusal of this book," he counseled Flavia. "Take it, read it;

---

[47] *Fortune's Foot-ball*, I, i.
[48] *Charlotte: A Tale of Truth* (Philadelphia, 1794), I, vi. This celebrated novel was published in London in 1791, but it had its largest circulation in America under the more familiar title of *Charlotte Temple*. R. W. G. Vail has located 161 of the "well over 200 editions." See his *Susanna Haswell Rowson, The Author of Charlotte Temple: A Bibliographical Study* (Worcester, 1922).
[49] W. H. Brown, *The Power of Sympathy* (Boston, 1789), I, vi.
[50] H. W. Foster, *The Coquette* (Boston, 1797), p. 244.

there is nothing to fear. Your governess is gone out, and your mamma is not yet risen. Do you hesitate? *Werter* has been under your pillow, and the *Monk* has lain in your toilet."[51]

Of the fast growing popularity of the novel there is abundant evidence, not only in the strictures of the moralists, whose grave concern indicates the strength of the taste they deplored, but also in the gradual unbending of the Puritan antipathy to fiction and a corresponding change in public taste. Professor Harold Thompson has acutely described this change of temper in which "Sentiment takes the place of Conscience and Revelation; Æsthetics usurps the place of Theology. . . . Instead of Justice, Grace, Duty, Humility, and Fear, we are to hear of Benevolence, Pity, Beauty, and Feeling. As for the useful and ingenious Devil of Mather and Wodrow—*le diable est mort!*"[52] The triumph of fiction is depicted impressively in the increasing number of American reprints of foreign fiction. Between 1744, the date of the publication of *Pamela,* the first English novel to be printed in America, and 1789, which marked the appearance of the earliest native novel, fifty-six reprints of foreign fiction were sufficient to satisfy the popular demand. From 1789 to the turn of the century, American presses struck off upwards of three hundred and fifty titles of popular foreign novels, while the flourishing circulating libraries with their hundreds of importations became the delight of readers as they also became favorite targets for the shafts of the moralists.

There was always an undercurrent of interest in fiction. As early as 1755, Samuel Davies lamented that "Plays and Romances" were "more read than the History of the blessed Jesus."[53] Royall Tyler, after an absence of several years from this country, was quick to note upon his return in 1797 "the extreme avidity, with which books of mere amusement were purchased and perused by all ranks of his countrymen. . . . In our inland towns of consequence, social libraries had been instituted, composed of books, designed to amuse rather than to

[51] *The Wanderings of William* (Philadelphia, 1801), Dedication.
[52] *A Scottish Man of Feeling* . . . (Oxford, 1931), p. 16.
[53] *Religion and Patriotism: The Constituents of a Good Soldier* (Philadelphia, 1755), p. 29.

instruct; and country booksellers, fostering the new born taste of the people, had filled the whole land with modern Travels, and Novels almost as incredible. . . ."[54] The genial Parson Weems, who traveled through the South for Mathew Carey's Philadelphia publishing house, showered his employer with demands for more fiction. "I should have told you when talking about the Miscellaneous Books," he wrote from Dumfries, Virginia, on the last day of January in 1797, "that I can vend many more of the Novels than you probably possess."[55] There is the same message from Petersburg two months later: "Of fine Sentimental Novels, entertaining Histories, etc. etc. I could vend a vast many."[56] Amusing evidence of the change in taste from theology to less heavy fare is to be found in Weems's complaint to Carey in 1798 for "sending me scarcely anything but Sable colour'd Divinity" instead of "the pick and choice of fine Novels," for which there existed so profitable a demand.[57] If Divinity had to be sent, Weems advised sagely, "Let the Moral and Religious be as highly dulcified as possible."[58]

This avidity for novels is often reflected in the utterances of fictional characters. The heroine of *Ferdinand and Elizabeth* entreated her lover: "Could you get me some novels? The only book that I took with me into the country was an odd volume of Camilla, which I have almost got by heart."[59] Dolly Pringle in *Trials of the Human Heart* was also a tireless reader of fiction and went into raptures over "the divine history of Lady Frances and Lady Caroline, or the loves of Edward and Harriet."[60] Another fair enthusiast in the same novel thrilled over "the sorrows of *The Welsh Heiress.*" "I felt the most exquisite delight," wrote Harriet, "in the remembrance that there was an author, who in conjunction with a Burney and Lee would snatch the British novel from oblivion. . . ."[61] There is also

---

[54] *The Algerine Captive* (Walpole, 1797), I, v-vi.
[55] E. E. F. Skeel, *Mason Locke Weems: His Works and Ways* (New York, 1929), II, 74.   [56] *Ibid.,* II, 79.
[57] *Ibid.,* II, 98.   [58] *Ibid.,* II, 44.
[59] J. Davis, *The Original Letters of Ferdinand and Elizabeth* (New York, 1798), p. 8.
[60] Rowson, *Trials of the Human Heart,* I, 38.
[61] *Ibid.,* IV, 74.

praise for Miss Burney and two of her less gifted but equally popular contemporaries in *The Inquisitor.* "Oh, ye sweet tuneful sisters, may ye never forsake my mansion," caroled an ecstatic admirer, "but when on the wing to visit your favorites —Burney, Moore [*sic*] and Inchbald—stop for a moment, and dart a single ray of your sacred fire upon the humblest of your votaries. . . ."[62]

Further evidence of the increasing respectability of the novel may be found in the attitude of those writers whose first efforts were timidly offered to the public as books of conduct rather than as fiction. Mrs. Foster, who had garnished her work with melancholy examples of the corruption caused by novel reading, relented somewhat in 1798, although she still felt "great prudence is necessary to make a useful selection." "Some of them are fraught with sentiment," she admitted, while others "convey lessons for moral improvement; and exhibit striking pictures of virtue rewarded. . . ."[63] Dr. Enos Hitchcock, hardly a champion of the novel, had the estimable Mr. Worthy exclaim after a day in the fields: "How soothing then must a book of sentimental improvement and entertainment, be to one fatigued by labor."[64] "Didactic essays are not always capable of engaging the attention of young ladies," noted W. H. Brown in *The Power of Sympathy.* "We fly from the laboured precepts of the essayist, to the sprightly narrative of the novelist."[65] Fiction, it appears, had triumphed, and writers hastened to make the best of the situation by fashioning it to their own ends. Thus Henry Sherburne in *The Oriental Philanthropist* announced philosophically, "Since the tales of fiction are so greatly multiplied, so entertaining, and with such avidity perused; I would render them as harmless and useful as possible."[66] The moral freight with which most early American novels were burdened made them seem a bit heavy when compared with imported brands of fiction. Amelia Parr in

[62] Susanna Rowson, *The Inquisitor* (Philadelphia, 1794), II, 110. The first edition was published in 1793.   [63] *The Boarding School,* p. 23.

[64] *The Farmer's Friend* (Boston, 1793), p. 207.

[65] *The Power of Sympathy,* II, 4-5.

[66] *The Oriental Philanthropist* (Portsmouth, 1800), pp. 16-17.

The Boarding School found native novels little better than sermons, and insisted that her fiction bear London imprints. "Foreign to be sure," she wrote Miss Henley, "else it would not be worth attention. They have attained a far greater degree of refinement in the old world, than we have in the new; and are so perfectly acquainted with the passions, that there is something extremely amusing and gratifying in their plots and under-plots, operating in various ways, till the dear creatures are jumbled into matrimony in the prettiest manner that can be conceived."[67] It was in the satisfaction of this taste that the circulating libraries realized their opportunity to combine public pleasure with private profits. A captivating assortment of titles from a New York lending library was listed in *Ferdinand and Elizabeth:* "They possessed alluring, melting, irresistible titles: such, for instance, as *Delicate Embarrassments, Venial Trespasses, Misplaced Confidence, Female Frailties,* and *Excessive Sensibility.*"[68] Drugged with "literary opium" of this kind, volatile readers found the didacticism of American novels more fit for sermons than romances. *"We,* in this country," Amelia complained, "are too much in a state of nature to write good novels yet. An American novel is such a moral, sentimental thing, that it is enough to give one the vapours to read one."[69]

The fountainhead of those "greasy, combustible, duodecimos" so heartily abominated by moralists was the popular lending and circulating libraries.[70] Boston, Philadelphia, and New York were well provided with them, while residents of smaller towns were forced to depend upon the local stationer, who often combined with his printing business, trade in books, millinery, and patent medicines. The peregrinations of Parson Weems revealed a brisk market for novels in the South, while in New England, Royall Tyler had reported in 1797 that coun-

[67] Foster, *The Boarding School*, p. 156.
[68] Davis, *Ferdinand and Elizabeth*, p. 62.
[69] Foster, *The Boarding School*, pp. 156-157.
[70] For helpful discussions of early society and lending libraries, see A. B. Keep's *History of the New York Society Library* (New York, 1908), and C. K. Bolton's "Circulating Libraries in Boston, 1765-1865," *Publications of the Colonial Society of Massachusetts* (Boston, 1910), XI, 196-207.

try bookdealers were fostering the newborn taste by supplying farmers' libraries with more diverting fare than "some dreary somebody's Day of Doom. . . ."[71] Members of the small farming community of Hatboro, Pennsylvania, certainly beguiled their leisure hours with something besides Michael Wigglesworth and "Sable colour'd Divinity." An examination of the loan book of the Union Library from 1762 to 1774 reveals the popularity of fiction in what was, perhaps, a typical rural settlement.[72] Eliza Haywood's didactic and sentimental *The History of Betsy Thoughtless* led the list with forty-five withdrawals in the twelve-year period. It is heartening to find that the demand for *Tom Jones* equaled that for Brooke's *The Fool of Quality*. *Pamela, Sir Charles Grandison, Tristram Shandy, Humphry Clinker,* and *The Vicar of Wakefield* were also popular.[73] The fact that bookstores in the provinces were well stocked may be seen in the loss by fire of a collection of books valued at $3,320 suffered by A. C. Jordan, of Norfolk, one of Mathew Carey's Virginia customers.[74] Another of Carey's customers, a bookseller of Raleigh, North Carolina, begged the publisher to "be so obliging" as to send as many novels as possible. "It will be mutually our interest to keep a good collection," she wrote in 1801, "as the good folks here love *light* reading."[75] Proprietors were not slow in catering to this rapidly growing public. Plans for a circulating library in Charleston, South Carolina, were addressed to prospective subscribers as

[71] *The Algerine Captive,* I, vi.

[72] C. T. Hallenbeck, "A Colonial Reading List from the Union Library of Hatboro, Pennsylvania," *Pennsylvania Magazine of History and Biography,* LVI, 289-340. This scholar's forthcoming study of book distribution in the Colonies will throw much light upon reading tastes of the period.

[73] *Ibid.* A summary of the number of calls for fiction between 1762 and 1774 indicates that the taste of country readers did not differ essentially from that of their city cousins: *Betsy Thoughtless,* 45; *Tom Jones,* 43; *Fool of Quality,* 43; Chaigneau's *History of Jack Connor,* 25; Hill's *History of Charlotte Seymour,* 24; *Pamela,* 20; *Tristram Shandy,* 15; *Humphry Clinker,* 11; *Grandison,* 10; *The Vicar of Wakefield,* 8; and Hill's *Adventures of George Edwards, a Creole,* 7.

[74] A. Growoll, *Book Trade Bibliography in the United States in the XIXth Century* (New York, 1898), p. xiii.

[75] E. L. Bradsher, *Mathew Carey: Editor, Author, and Publisher* (New York, 1912), p. 33. Carey's shipment included Mackenzie's *Man of Feeling, Man of the World,* and *Julia de Roubigne;* Inchbald's *Simple Story;* and *Melissa & Narcia.* Other titles in the consignment reveal the vogue of Gothic and Oriental tales.

early as 1763.[76] There was, moreover, considerable publishing done by small-town establishments. Title pages of American novels before 1800 bear the imprints of such widely scattered communities as Hallowell and Harrisburg, and Portsmouth and Pittsburgh. Native fiction of the period was also published at Dedham, Leominster, and Walpole.

The rules governing Mein's circulating library near the British Coffee House on the north side of King Street in Boston reveal prosperity there in 1765. Customers were respectfully urged to make six or eight choices from the catalogue to avoid disappointment because of the heavy demand, while country readers were advised to pay double charges for the privilege of taking "two books at a time."[77] Mein's account with Longmans, his London dealer, showed purchases amounting to £2,099, which should have enabled him to make good his promise to "amuse the man of leisure" and "insinuate knowledge and instruction under the veil of entertainment to the Fair Sex."[78] Brisk novel reading was also reported by Martin's library, later enlarged and known as the "Boston Circulating Library." The *Independent Chronicle* of August 31, 1786, printed unmistakable evidence of the popularity of certain titles. An advertisement complained that *Clarissa* and several other works in constant demand were overdue "to the great disappointment of the Subscribers and disgrace of the establishment. . . ."[79] Other Boston booksellers and stationers found it to their advantage to maintain circulating libraries to accommodate the novel-reading public. Two years after he had taken over Battelle's Boston Bookstore, Benjamin Guild advertised a "constantly increasing Circulating Library" at 59 Cornhill, later moved to Washington Street.[80] Fiction naturally bulked large on the shelves of these libraries. Novels and romances constituted more than one third of the titles in the "Catalogue

[76] *South Carolina Gazette,* March 5-12, 1763. Garrat Noel advertised the opening of a circulating library in New York in the New York *Gazette* for Aug. 29, 1763.

[77] Bolton, *op. cit.,* p. 197.   [78] *Ibid.,* p. 199.

[79] *Independent Chronicle* (Boston, 1786), Aug. 31.

[80] *Ibid.,* May 10, 1787. W. P. Blake took over Guild's establishment at the latter's death in 1792. See Bolton, *op. cit.,* pp. 201-202.

of Books, for Sale or Circulation," offered by W. P. Blake in Boston in 1796.[81] Booksellers made special efforts to please the ladies who had more time for reading than men and who constituted the better half of the subscribers. Joshua Thomas advertised in 1793 "the newest and most approved Publications," and promised that "Great pains will be taken to render this Library worthy the patronage of the *Ladies* of *Boston,* and its vicinity."[82] Millinery and novels, synonymous to moralists as "the whipt syllabub of vanity" and "mere female flummery," proved a profitable combination to Miss Mary Sprague at her shop on Milk Street, Boston. That she was not unmindful of the usual criticisms directed at "circulating library trash" may be seen from the terms of her prudent notice: "In selecting volumes, she has not confined her choice to Romances and Magazines ... whatever instructs while it pleases, have portions of her shelves allotted to them."[83] The ladies of South Boston were to be similarly accommodated at the millinery shop of Kezia Butler whose constant study was to provide the latest thing in feathers and fiction.[84] Both, doubtless, were equally light and captivating.

The catalogue of William Pritchard's American Circulating Library on Market Street in Philadelphia listed one hundred novels for circulation in 1785.[85] Pritchard boasted that he was "Happy in the reflection, that the humble office of bookseller, is by no means without its utility with respect to the public," and saw in the cessation of hostilities with Great Britain new opportunities "to import mental instruction and entertainment for those who so generously countenanced his efforts during the war."[86] The prospectus for J. Osborn's library in Philadelphia illustrates the assiduity with which booksellers nurtured the increasing passion for novels. "The depart-

[81] The catalogue, offered to his customers gratis, listed 1,440 titles, of which 507 were novels. There is a copy in the New York Public Library.

[82] *Independent Chronicle,* June 27, 1793. Quoted by Bolton, *op. cit.,* p. 205.

[83] *Ibid.,* May 17, 1802. Quoted by Bolton, *op. cit.,* p. 205.

[84] *Columbian Centinel* (Boston, 1804), May 2. Quoted by Bolton, *op. cit.,* p. 205.

[85] *Catalogue of a Scarce and Valuable Collection of Books . . . now Selling by William Pritchard* (Philadelphia, 1785). Copy in New York Public Library.

[86] *Ibid.,* pp. 1-2.

ment of *Novels and Romances (as hitherto obtaining the most substantial patronage)* has been so copiously and so attentively supplied," the proprietor boasted in the *Port Folio,* "that scarcely a Novel or Romance not included in it can be named, from *That Ancient Most Fam'd Romance, Parthenissa* by the Earl of Orrery, to the latest of the productions of the London press, which have reached this country."[87]

Of New York's circulating libraries, Caritat's was easily the most famous. An English observer, who spent four years in the United States and had noted "the *vulgar* taste for romances" prevalent among all ranks of people, had high praise for Caritat's genius. "I would place the bust of Caritat among those of the Sosii of Horace, and the Trypho of Quintilian," the *Port Folio* quoted him as declaring. "His talents were not meanly cultivated by letters: he could tell a good book from a bad one, which few modern librarians can do."[88] Caritat's *Explanatory Catalogue* is a mine of information about the reading tastes of the time.[89] Of the 1,171 titles of fiction listed in the issue for 1799, more than one fourth, 331 titles, are recommended as having been written by "females." The vogue of letter fiction which had reached its climax in England a decade earlier, may be found in the 143 novels denominated as epistolary. The growing favor enjoyed by the Gothic tales of the "Monk" Lewis and Mrs. Radcliffe school of agreeable terror is evident in the 45 titles described as "Gothic." One hundred and thirty-five tales are conciliatingly labeled "didactic," while 98 are listed as "sentimental." The rage for Oriental stories fostered by many of the contemporary magazines is shown in 23 of Caritat's offerings. The terrific odds against which native novelists were compelled to struggle is to be seen in the exploitation of foreign authors by American publishers. Of the 1,171 titles cited in this issue of Caritat's catalogue, only 18 were written by native authors.

The novel-reading public, however, regarded the nationality

[87] *Port Folio,* V, 277.   [88] *Ibid.,* III, 367.

[89] *Explanatory Catalogue: Caritat's General and Increasing Circulating Library* (New York, 1799). This is but one of a number of issues published by Caritat. For a thorough analysis of Caritat's offerings, see George Gates Raddin, Jr., *An Early New York Library of Fiction* (New York, 1940).

of the author as of little consequence; it was the story in which the average reader was interested. Catalogues of less popular New York lending libraries also bear witness to the demand for fiction. Novels had an important place among the several thousand "choice books" advertised by Garrat Noel in the New York *Gazette* for August 24, 1763. Samuel Loudon thanked his subscribers in 1774 for their flattering patronage and announced that he "found it necessary to publish a new catalogue . . . having enlarged his collection to upwards of a thousand volumes."[90] In a later advertisement in Holt's *New York Journal* for February 23, 1775, Loudon boasted of a further increase in stock and a greater variety of novels. Hugh Gaine's "Catalogue of Books, lately imported from England, Ireland, and Scotland," shows that this enterprising publisher offered more titles in fiction than in any one of his other departments which included Divinity, History, Physics, Surgery, Philosophy, and Classics.[91] The number of novels in the New York Society Library also kept pace with the ever-increasing calls for fiction. The 75 novels listed in the catalogue of 1789 were increased by 41 titles in 1791, and by the addition of 46 more in the following year. By 1800 there were 279 titles which constantly received additions in the first years of the nineteenth century until fiction became the department with the most startling growth in the entire collection.[92]

Patronage of the circulating libraries by ladies was a familiar commonplace of moralists. Samuel Loudon proclaimed proudly "that the ladies are his best customers, and shew becoming delicacy of taste in their choice of books."[93] But he was tactful enough to toss in a sop for his male patrons: "Neither are the gentlemen deficient in shewing the ladies a laudable example in this respect."[94] The regulations governing the conduct of these libraries indicate the female taste for novel read-

[90] New York *Gazette*, Nov. 21, 1774.
[91] A copy of Hugh Gaine's catalogue is in the New York Public Library. Novels also outnumbered "Classical Authors" in the catalogue published by Henry Knox for his bookstore in Cornhill, Boston, in 1773. A copy of this issue may also be found in the New York Public Library.
[92] Keep, *op. cit.* Copies of the 1789 catalogue and later supplements are preserved in the New York Public Library.
[93] New York *Gazette*, Nov. 21, 1774.   [94] *Ibid.*

ing was not an inexpensive one. A yearly subscription at Caritat's cost six dollars with the privilege of withdrawing "at least two books at a time, and never more than four." Subscribers living in the country were permitted six volumes at one withdrawal.[95] Blake's Boston Bookstore charged subscribers two dollars each quarter with an allowance of two books at a time "and no more—to change them as often as the subscriber pleases—and no book to be retained longer than one month."[96] Samuel Berrian's Chatham Street "Increasing and Circulating Library" in New York made provision for monthly subscriptions at fifty cents. The annual dues of four dollars and fifty cents might be increased if the patron desired a more generous allowance of books.[97] Blake's library welcomed nonsubscribers who paid *"five-pence* per week for each duodecimo volume of the size of a common testament or under."[98] The popularity of these institutions made strict rules necessary to insure the prompt return of books. The proprietor of ·Martin's complained in the *Chronicle* in 1786 about "those Ladies and Gentlemen who have kept Books beyond the limited time, and still do so, that such delay is a great injury to his business, both as to the accommodation of his *good* customers, and the profit to himself; it tends to frustrate the very establishment, and instead of a *Circulating,* to render it a *Stagnated* Library."[99] Loudon begged his customers to exchange books frequently: "The Library is open from morning to eight at night, and the readers may have a book·exchanged, if they please, every day, by their humble servant, Samuel Loudon."[100]

The need of keeping the shelves of lending libraries well stocked with new titles led inevitably to the production of novels which were as poor as works of art as they were popular as forms of amusement.[101] Critics had much to say about the

[95] Caritat's *Explanatory Catalogue,* p. 1.

[96] Blake's *Catalogue of Books* (Boston, 1796), p. 1.

[97] *Catalogue: Samuel Berrian's Increasing and Circulating Library* (New York, 1803). Copy in the New York Public Library.

[98] Blake's *Catalogue of Books,* p. 1.

[99] *Independent Chronicle* (Boston, 1786), May 25. Quoted by Bolton, *op. cit.,* pp. 200-201.

[100] Holt's *New York Journal; or General Advertiser,* Feb. 23, 1775.

[101] There is an admirable account of the wares of English circulating libraries in

shopworn plots and stock characters to be found in "by far the greater number of those novels, which crowd the teeming catalogue of a circulating library." "They are sought out with such avidity, and run through with such delight," continued a writer in the *Port Folio,* "by all those (a considerable part of my fellow citizens), who cannot resist the impulse of curiosity, or withstand the allurements of a title page."[102] "I wonder that the novel readers are not tired of reading one story so many times," exclaimed Mrs. Rowson, whose own practice in this respect did not make her an invulnerable critic, "with only the variation of its being told different ways."[103] In *Charlotte* she bewailed the disrepute into which the trash of circulating libraries had brought the novelist. A writer of fiction, she declared, "at a time when such a variety of works are ushered into the world under that name, stands but a poor chance for fame in the annals of literature. . . ."[104] Authors of novels, however, were reaping the more immediate rewards of popularity. The vogue of fashionable Memoirs was particularly obnoxious to the critics who charged that books of this sort tended to deprive "vice of its grossness . . . by uniting it with the engaging qualities of the heart." Books of this description, wrote an essayist in the *Port Folio,* "make no small part of the literature of the day." "They fill our circulating libraries, are recommended to the public in advertisements, and soon become soiled by constant use."[105]

Fully aware of the nature of much of this criticism, proprietors of lending libraries strove in various ways to offset its force. Osborn's "Prospectus," which was printed in the *Port Folio,* was designed to conciliate those who were alarmed at the mania for novels. "Enough has been said, it is hoped, to convince those of their error who imagine that Novels and Romances constitute the principal part of this collection," ran the Advertisement, "and who, but for the prejudice which they entertain against this kind of reading, would willingly sub-

---

J. M. S. Tompkins's *The Popular Novel in England, 1770-1800* (London, 1932), pp. 1-33.

[102] *Port Folio,* II, 142.   [103] Rowson, *The Inquisitor,* III, 189.
[104] *Charlotte,* I, vi.   [105] *Port Folio,* III, 28.

scribe to a library, from which their families might be supplied with books of instruction and rational amusement."[106] The ingenious Caritat often emphasized the moral tendencies of books in short squibs in his catalogue. Thus *Favourites of Felicity* was puffed as coming from the pen of "the respected Mr. Potter, who in this work undertakes to remove the prejudices against novels."[107] Minds of a superior order were invited to try *Affected Indifference,* described by Caritat as "a sentimental novel."[108] The emotionally elect were urged to borrow *Hermit of the Rock,* which was praised as suitable only for those who "have not learned to despise the refinements and delicacies of a sentimental attachment."[109] Regina Maria Roche's *Children of the Abbey* was warranted to gratify the most strait-laced reader: "Every page is replete with the most exalted sentiments, favourable to religion, morality, and virtue."[110]

The rise in popularity of the circulating libraries marked the climax in the triumph of the novel.[111] "To the writer of fiction," conceded a contributor to the *Port Folio* in 1803, "alone every ear is open, and every tongue lavish of applause; curiosity sparkles in every eye, and every bosom is throbbing with concern."[112] "This is a novel-reading age," admitted the editor of the *New York Magazine* in 1797, "all descriptions fly for amusement to them. . . ."[113] In his weekly essay in the *Port Folio,* "The Lounger" yielded to the trend of the times. "Much has been said of the pernicious effects of novels," he wrote in 1804, "but I am not inclined to join in the popular clamour against these elegant offsprings of the imagination. I would suffer all young persons, nay encourage them, in reading novels. . . ."[114] Even the moralists surrendered to the seductive

---

[106] *Ibid.,* V, 277.   [107] *Explanatory Catalogue,* p. 153.
[108] *Ibid.,* p. 126.   [109] *Ibid.,* p. 165.
[110] *Ibid.,* p. 138. An American reprint of this popular novel was published in Philadelphia in 1798. "Few novels have been read with more avidity, and few are more deserving an attentive perusal," according to Caritat's blurb.
[111] The triumph, of course, was a qualified one. It was not until the advent of Scott and Cooper that the old antagonism lost most of its effectiveness. See G. H. Orians, "Censure of Fiction in American Romances and Magazines: 1789-1810," *Publications of the Modern Language Association,* LII, 195-214.
[112] III, 171.   [113] *New York Magazine,* II (N. S.), 398.
[114] *Port Folio,* IV, 201.

fascinations of fiction. Dr. Aiken confessed that, despite his better judgment, he was unable to resist the invitation of a title page. "I have frequently felt it with regard to our modern novels," he acknowledged shamefully, "which, if lying on my table, and taken up in an idle hour, have led me through the most tedious and disgusting pages, while, like Pistol eating his leek, I have swallowed and execrated to the end."[115]

The work of Judith Sargent Murray reveals how an essayist with a deep-seated distrust of fiction turned novel writer in spite of herself. As "the elegant Constantia," Mrs. Murray was one of the most admired members of the coterie of bluestockings whose effusions sweetened the pages of the *Massachusetts Magazine*. A foe of the "licentiously luxurious," she had been fond of exposing "the prejudices prepared in the hot-bed of novel reading."[116] Her children were permitted to read fiction only in their mother's presence, "hoping that she might, by her suggestions and observations, present an antidote to the poison, with which the pen of the novelist is too often fraught."[117] Her own "Story of Margaretta," which purls its sentimental way through thirty-three numbers of *The Gleaner,* was planned as a miscellany on education, manners, and morals. Mrs. Murray was well aware, however, that didactic essays had been superseded by fiction on the dressing tables of young ladies. The Margaretta narrative is virtually a novel. Into it went many of the most precious ingredients of sentimental, popular fiction. Here are to be found a heroine of sensibility who delighted to record every tremor of her feeling heart, and a sinister seducer who responded to an appeal to his "inborn goodness." Virtue was fittingly rewarded only after a series of feverish trials and romantic episodes dear to the patrons of the circulating libraries. Margaretta's story needed only to be pranked out with a captivating title and a neat binding to enable it to take its place beside those "combustible duodecimos" which the author had so frequently employed her pen to deplore.

[115] Quoted with approval in the *Port Folio,* III, 171.
[116] J. S. Murray, *The Gleaner* (Boston, 1798), I, 82.
[117] *Ibid.*, p. 70.

II

RICHARDSON AND SEDUCTION

Among all the writings, which unite sentiment with character, and present images of life, Richardson's perhaps, may be placed at the head of the list; of whom it has been justly said—"He taught the passions to move at the command of reason." His Clarissa has been considered, by good judges, as the most finished model of female excellence which has ever been offered for their imitation.

—Enos Hitchcock, *Memoirs of the Bloomsgrove Family*, 1790.

IT IS ONE OF the curiosities of our literary history that Benjamin Franklin's edition of *Pamela* in 1744 should have been the first English novel printed in America. Richardson would have been the first to approve that characteristic regard for public piety and private profit which induced the creator of Poor Richard to publish the famous story of a country serving-girl who kept her virtue so that her virtue might keep her. Pamela's rich reward had proved plainly enough that there were circumstances in which virtue, as well as honesty, was the best policy. Here was a dramatic example of the spirit of Franklin's own prudent proverbs which a trading, utilitarian, middle-class public might read with instruction and pleasure.

Richardson, moreover, had successfully anticipated many of the objections which had made English novelists unacceptable to American moralists. *Pamela* was truly "a new species of writing designed to turn young people into a course of reading different from the pomp and parade of romance-writing." In his postscript to *Clarissa,* the author had indignantly corrected those readers who had mistaken that "divine history" for "a mere *novel* or *romance.*" For Richardson, sentiment was deeply tinged with conscience. It had none of that vague, puttylike, indeterminate quality which moralists feared as a dangerous sanction for passionate impulse. When critics decried the word *sentimental* as savoring of Continental license rather than the solid English virtues of religion and morality, it was Laurence Sterne, not Richardson, of whom they were thinking. Although he was rarely praised without some reservations, Samuel Richardson enjoyed a peculiar immunity from the common prejudice. After summarizing the usual counts in the indictment against writers of fiction, a critic in the *Port Folio* hastened to add, "But no one, I imagine, who ever read Richardson, could dream for a moment that they are applicable to him; on the contrary . . . the palm is invariably bestowed by him on the social and domestic virtues, on piety, filial duty, humility, and charity. The good child, parent, consort, and friend, are the portraits on which this writer loves to dwell with complacency."[1] That he was read before the printing of the first American edition of *Pamela* may be inferred from William Bradford's advertisement in the *Pennsylvania Gazette* in 1742.[2] Franklin's edition in 1744 was not followed by other reprints until 1786, although the trickle of importations from London increased steadily as opposition to novel-reading relaxed. By the turn of the century there were at least twenty editions of Richardson's novels bearing imprints of native publishers, more than those of any other English novelist.

Richardson was a household name wherever novels were discussed in the Colonies. Dr. Alexander Hamilton noted that *Pamela* rivaled *The Marrow of Modern Divinity* in popularity at an auction of books in Boston in 1744 at which it was one of the five volumes most frequently called for at the sale.[3] The tradition that the pious Jonathan Edwards resolved to use *Clarissa* as a model for the improvement of his own style may have arisen from the fact that *Pamela* and *Clarissa* were among the titles of the books that he had listed for future reading.[4] Dr. Edwards's daughter Esther, although a bit irked by the

[1] *Port Folio*, II, 185.
[2] *Pennsylvania Gazette* (Philadelphia, 1742), Sept. 23. Franklin made much of the moral qualities of the work in his advertisements in the issues of Oct. 11 and 14.
[3] A. B. Hart (ed.), *Hamilton's Itinerarium* . . . (St. Louis, 1907), pp. 136-137.
[4] F. B. Dexter, "The Manuscripts of Jonathan Edwards," *Proceedings of the Massachusetts Historical Society* (Cambridge, 1901), XV (Second Series), 2-16.

length of *Pamela,* recorded her pleasure at having read it from cover to cover. "There is sertainly [*sic*] many excellent observations and rules laid down that I shall never repent my pains," she wrote in her diary in 1757.[5] Before his tenth birthday, in 1792, William Wirt had heard about the plot of *Clarissa* from a member of the family with whom he boarded while attending school in Maryland. "From her, too, I first heard the name of Clarissa Harlowe," he recalled in his autobiographical sketch quoted by Kennedy in the *Memoirs,* "and gave me, in her manner, a skeleton of the story."[6] The didactic elements in Richardson's novels had been discussed so often in Alexander Graydon's presence that he had come to believe "they were formal stuff, consisting chiefly of the dull chronicles relating to courtship and marriage, with which, superannuated aunts and grandmothers torment the young misses subject to their control." Upon actually reading *Clarissa,* however, he was moved to tears, and followed the heroine's adventures "with more interest than any tale had ever excited . . . before."[7] Graydon also confessed that he had patterned his conduct as a young man on the model of Lovelace: "I still affected the man of pleasure and dissipation; had a sovereign contempt for matrimony, and was even puppy enough, with shame I yet think of it, to ape the style of Lovelace, in some of my epistolary correspondencies."[8]

Most of Richardson's admirers were recruited from women readers. One of the most lyric of these in a panegyric contributed to the *American Magazine* in 1758, compared Richardson's printing press to an altar from which "hallow'd incense" sweetened the atmosphere, and likened his pages to "Virgin-Sheets" which "no prostitution stains."[9] There is abundant evidence that the novels played an important part in forming the minds of young ladies. In Trumbull's *The Progress of Dulness* there is an instance of the belief that Rich-

[5] J. Fisher, "The Journal of Esther Burr," *New England Quarterly,* III, 301.

[6] J. P. Kennedy (ed.), *Memoirs of the Life of William Wirt* (Philadelphia, 1850), I, 30.

[7] A. Graydon, *Memoirs of a Life* . . . (Harrisburg, 1811), pp. 85-86.

[8] *Ibid.,* p. 97.

[9] *American Magazine* (Philadelphia, 1758), I, 281-295.

ardson, as well as the less "moral" of the novelists, was sometimes responsible for imparting "notions" to giddy females—

> Thus HARRIET reads, and reading really
> Believes herself a young Pamela,
> The high-wrought whim, the tender strain
> Elate her mind and turn her brain.
> Before her glass, with smiling grace,
> She views the wonders of her face;
> There stands in admiration moveless,
> And hopes a Grandison or Lovelace.[10]

William Woodbridge, who conducted a school for girls in
New Haven in 1779-80 while completing his senior year at
Yale, testified that *Pamela* and *Clarissa,* along with Young's
Night Thoughts and a few other books, were significant factors
in the development of female character in America before the
establishment of seminaries for women.[11] Cox and Berry, Boston booksellers, had found it profitable to issue *Clarissa* and *Sir
Charles Grandison* abridged in "Little Books for the Instruction and Amusement of Children, adorn'd with a Variety of
Cuts, and bound in Gilt Paper."[12] Perhaps little Anna Winslow had been presented with a copy so prettily bound and so
mercifully abridged. On September 29, 1772, she entered in
her diary the record of her completion of *The Generous In-
constant,* and further noted, "have begun *Sir Charles Grandison.*[13] In 1772, Wilson Cary ordered handsomely lettered,
calfbound copies of all three of Richardson's novels for his
granddaughter Sarah in Virginia. With characteristic shrewd-
ness, Benjamin Franklin included an ounce of sour in his
pound of sweet by sending a French translation of *Pamela* to

[10] *The Poetical Works,* p. 77.
[11] M. S. Benson, *Women in Eighteenth Century America* (New York, 1935), p.
150.   [12] *Catalogue* (Boston, 1776), p. 39.
[13] A. M. Earle (ed.), *The Diary of Anna Green Winslow* (Boston, 1894), p. 70.
Fervid admirers of Richardson were scornful of abridgments for those who would not
spare the time "to note the various postures which the heart assumes during the suspense of a catastrophe." "For such weak hands," continued a scoffer, "some generous
person has provided a little abstract of *Clarissa;* just the recreation of an hour or two
for a sofa-lolling miss on a summer's afternoon . . ." (*Monthly Magazine and
American Review,* New York, 1800, III, 166-167).

his daughter Sally.[14] One may hope that she thus perfected her character and her irregular verbs with equal satisfaction to her father and to herself.

The novels of Richardson occupied a large portion of the time at Mrs. Foster's model seminary, Harmony Grove, described in *The Boarding School*. "What a surprising command has this great master of the passions over our feelings!" the preceptress remarked. "It is happy for his own and succeeding ages, that he embarked in the course of virtue. . . . Though I am not much of a novel reader, yet his pen has operated like magic on my fancy; and so extremely was I interested, that I could have dispensed with sleep or food for the pleasure I found in reading him."[15] Although Dr. Enos Hitchcock believed Richardson to be the first of writers, he tempered his praise with the admonition that he should be read "with caution and under the direction of a guide." For even "this great master in the science of human nature, has laid open scenes, which it would have been safer to have kept concealed; and has excited sentiments, which it would have been more advantageous to early virtue not to have admitted."[16] Moralists like Mrs. Foster and Dr. Hitchcock, who were chiefly concerned with the education of young ladies, found high authority for their approval of Richardson in the influential letters of Dr. John Bennett. Richardson's novels were the only ones excepted from Bennett's prohibition of fiction. "If, in short," he advised parents and teachers, "I wished a girl to be every thing that was *great,* I would have her continually study his Clarissa. If I was ambitious to make her every thing that was *lovely,* she should spend *her days and nights,* in contemplating his Byron."[17] If higher praise were possible, an admirer in the *Monthly Magazine* tried to bestow it. In her opinion, only the character of Jesus Christ was worthy to be compared with the author of *Grandison*. "I know no moderation in my love of

---

[14] A. H. Smythe (ed.), *The Writings of Benjamin Franklin* (New York and London, 1905), III, 422.   [15] *The Boarding School*, p. 160.

[16] *Memoirs of the Bloomsgrove Family*, II, 87.

[17] *Letters to a Young Lady on a Variety of Useful and Interesting Subjects . . .* (Hartford, 1791), II, 61.

Richardson . . . ," she declared truthfully enough in 1800. "I worship him already as the sublimest teacher of rectitude, and most irresistible conductor in that road which leads to happiness here, and to Heaven hereafter, that modern ages have produced."[18]

Richardson's enviable position in the regard of American critics may be seen in the somewhat grudging testimony of those whose approval of fiction was never very thoroughgoing. Mrs. Murray recalled her grandfather, who "indulged, perhaps to excess, an invincible aversion to novels. . . . Yet, the Holy Bible and *Clarissa Harlowe*, were the books in which he accustomed his daughters to read alternately. . . ."[19] Although "The Gleaner" in the *Massachusetts Magazine* rarely endorsed novels, she opened her column to an admirer of Richardson who held "that *Clarissa Harlowe* is the *first human production now extant*" and "hesitates not to place it, for *literary excellence, above the Iliad of Homer, or any other work, ancient or modern.*"[20] The luxuriance of Richardson's descriptions, "which so intimately blend the charms of virtue and the fascinations of vice," seemed dangerous to Mrs. Foster, yet she felt constrained to conclude, "so multifarious are his excellencies, that his faults appear but specks, which serve as foils to display his beauties to better advantage."[21] The circle of Richardson's admirers was further enlarged by many readers to whom the merest mention of Sterne was anathema. Propriety of conduct, not impulse, is at the core of *Pamela,* while in *Clarissa,* "enthusiasm" and excessive sensibility are mentioned only for rebuke. The ill-repute into which *sentiment* had fallen in the closing years of the eighteenth century, was not attributed to Richardson's example. "He must be strangely mistaken, who imagines that Richardson was what is vulgarly called a *sentimentalist,*" wrote a critic in 1802. "The inundation of froth and sentiment, in the form of novels, which cover, in this age, the shelves of our libraries, has taken place in direct

[18] *Monthly Magazine* (New York, 1800), III, 163-164.
[19] *The Gleaner,* II, 65.
[20] *Ibid.*   [21] *The Boarding School,* p. 161.

contempt and defiance of the precept and example of Richardson."[22]

It is to the subject matter of Richardson's novels, to his eternal preoccupation with problems of conduct and conscience, to which our early novelists looked for their inspiration, and upon which critics justified their approval. Although the epistolary form was widely imitated here as in England, particularly by beginners who found it a comparatively simple way in which to tell a story,[23] Richardson's *matter* rather than his *manner* had the more striking influence in American fiction.[24] From him were largely derived the stock figures of the seduced maiden, the mercenary parents, the captivating libertine, and the reformed rake. He is also in the main responsible for the idealistic portraiture of character as well as the emphasis upon a prudential morality and an elaborate system of rewards and punishments in many of our eighteenth-century novels.[25]

The title page of *Clarissa* promised that the story would comprehend "The most Important Concerns of Private Life. And particularly shewing, The Distresses that may attend the Misconduct Both of Parents and Children, in Relation to Marriage." One of the consequences of Richardson's vogue in America is the frequency with which this melancholy theme recurs in our fiction. Sorely disturbed at the plight of a favorite heroine who had been reduced to beggary "by her stubborn, ill-natured father because she loved Melmont," a female novel-addict is made to exclaim in *Monima:* "I hate almost all fathers in novels, because their poor daughters must suffer so much for their stubbornness."[26] That the theme of parental inter-

---

[22] *Port Folio,* II, 185.

[23] For an account of the zeal with which our early novelists seized upon this deceptively easy method, see Chapter III, "The Elegant Epistolarians," pp. 52-73.

[24] Almost the exact opposite is true of Sterne's influence. See Chapter IV, "Sterne and Sensibility," pp. 74-99. For Sternesque imitations in a representative contemporary periodical, see "Elements of Sensibility in *The Massachusetts Magazine*," *American Literature,* I, 286-296; and "Richardson and Sterne in *The Massachusetts Magazine*," *New England Quarterly,* V, 65-82.

[25] The mood and spirit of native American drama are often paralleled in the fiction. Dramatists as well as novelists turned to sentimental models for their inspiration. See "Sensibility in Eighteenth-Century American Drama," *American Literature,* IV, 47-60.   [26] Read, *Monima,* p. 255.

ference in marriage was popular with readers is shown in some of the blurbs used by Caritat to commend his wares to his patrons in 1799. Of *Secrecy; or, The Ruin on the Rock,* Caritat announced, "The principal object of this novel is to represent the mischievous effects of the tyranny of some parents over their children."[27] The same theme was used to puff *Denial; or, The Happy Retreat.* "This is a well written novel," according to the squib in the catalogue, "the moral purpose of which is to expose those parents who usurp an absolute authority over their children in respect to their matrimonial engagements."[28]

The familiar episode in *Clarissa* in which the heroine's father championed the suit of the repulsive Solmes because of his large estate is paralleled in many American stories. Thus Mr. Granville in *Fidelity Rewarded* advised his daughter Polly that "A large estate is all that you ought to look after . . . why need you care about his morals, as long as he has money enough?"[29] If the motives of mercenary fathers often bore close resemblance to those of Mr. Harlowe, the features of the ill-favored, splayfooted suitors suggest the unwelcome Solmes. Polly's description of Mr. Stapleton applies with equal fitness to Clarissa's awkward lover. "Now Mr. Stapleton is very wealthy, but he is quite ill-looking," the heroine wrote to her confidante who is an American cousin of Anna Howe. He "has very coarse features, and a dead-looking eye; with hollow cheeks, large irregular teeth, and a mouth no ways speaking approbation."[30] In *The Hapless Orphan* there is even a closer similarity between Caroline's suitor, Trevers, and Richardson's original, whose habit of "hemming up" irked Clary. "Half a dozen hems succeed every expression," Caroline wrote disdainfully. "He is impatient to become a married man."[31] Most of these persecuted heroines had by heart Clary's arguments against mercenary matches. Parents and suitors received them coldly, however, and accorded them the same severe treatment suffered by Richardson's celebrated victim.[32]

[27] *Explanatory Catalogue,* p. 199.   [28] *Ibid.,* p. 145.
[29] [Anon.,] *Fidelity Rewarded,* p. 42.   [30] *Ibid.,* p. 5.
[31] [Anon.,] *The Hapless Orphan* (Boston, 1793), II, 176.
[32] [Anon.,] *Fidelity Rewarded,* pp. 14, 17. "I am used with great severity by my

Charles Brockden Brown made use of this theme in *Edgar Huntly* where the happiness of Mrs. Lorimer had been frustrated by the avarice of her parents and the machinations of a jealous brother.[33] Even the parents of the liberal Constantia Dudley were tempted to interfere in the all-important concern of marriage. "Her parents were blemished with some of the frailties of that character," wrote Constantia's lover. "They held themselves entitled to prescribe in this article, but they forbore to exert their power."[34] Few parents showed such forbearance, however, and the hard-hearted father and mother became stock characters in the fiction of the period. The heroine of *Constantius and Pulchera* attributed her sufferings to parental ambition and avarice. "Ambition! Cruel ambition is the cause of our misfortune," she cried to her lover. "No man was ever better pleased with another than my father was with you until Monsieur le Monte, only son and heir to a rich nobleman in France, waited on him, and offered to make me his wife . . . the temptation was too great for him to withstand. . . ."[35] One of the many afflictions which Mrs. Rowson visited upon her characters was provided by Rainsforth's unfeeling father who strove to break Meriel's engagement to Frederic in order to have his son wed "a very amiable woman, possessing a fortune of twenty thousand pounds."[36] The author of *The Hapless Orphan*, who made tearful use of this conventional theme, protested against "connections which result from motives of convenience or interest" in "the grand article of marriage." "Marriages, formed upon the idea of protection or fortune, although the corruption of the present age may style them marriages of reason, in my view, are but legal prostitutions."[37] The miseries of a loveless, forced marriage darken many pages

---

parents who try all in their power to make me break with Mr. Danford, and favour Mr. Stapleton," Polly wrote to Sophia in Clary's vein.

[33] *Edgar Huntly* (Philadelphia, 1799), I, 102.

[34] Brown, *Ormond*, p. 25.

[35] [Anon.,] *The History of Constantius and Pulchera* (Leominster, 1797), p. 14. For her obduracy, Pulchera was imprisoned by her father in a tower "forty feet high." [First ed.; Salem, 1795]   [36] *Trials of the Human Heart*, II, 4.

[37] [Anon.,] *The Hapless Orphan*, I, 59.

in Relf's *Infidelity*. Caroline's letter to her sister on this subject is in the strain so much beloved by female epistolarians. "The silent ashes of that deluded father whose power coerced me to the deed," she wrote to Maria, "sleep over the endless torments which his rashness has produced!"[38] The mothers in these novels usually resemble Mrs. Harlowe in their reluctant but passive submission to their husbands' treatment of their willful daughters. An exception is to be found in the conduct of the flinty-hearted Mrs. Hammond in *Kelroy* who stopped at no villainy to prevent her daughter's marriage. Her favorite theme was the folly of "indulging romantic attachments," and she "ridiculed involuntary love unless the object of it were gifted with more solid recommendations than mere good qualities of mind. . . ."[39]

Parental avarice became a bogey which at times rivaled seduction in its train of evil consequences. John Davis declared that his *Ferdinand and Elizabeth* would not have been written in vain if it could "admonish parents and guardians to consult the hearts as well as the interest of their children in the sacred bond of marriage," and "exhibit a striking picture of the folly and imprudence of disuniting two young people whose breasts glow reciprocally with the passion of love."[40] Novelists were so intent upon depicting selfish parents that some critics feared for the effect upon the impressionable minds of young female readers. The *Weekly Magazine* objected that "In novels, parents are described as cruel and obdurate, thwarting the inclinations of their children; and those children are made to invent numberless ways of deceiving the watchful eyes of their real friends, in order to run to their ruin."[41] The robust common

[38] *Infidelity*, p. 18.
[39] Rebecca Rush, *Kelroy* (Philadelphia, 1812), p. 5.
[40] *Ferdinand and Elizabeth*, p. 141.
[41] *Weekly Magazine* (Philadelphia, 1798), I, 185. This general subject was a favorite topic for discussion in contemporary periodicals. See *Massachusetts Magazine*, II, 89, 299, 485; IV, 157; *New York Magazine*, I, 562, 619-621, 646-648; V, 49; VI, 43-44; VII, 99, 490-494, 518-523; *New York Weekly Magazine*, I, 254-255, 271; II, 235. A contributor to the *New York Magazine* had plenty of reason to exclaim in 1794: "With so many examples of this nature continually presented to them,

sense of Captain Farrago in Brackenridge's *Modern Chivalry* was outraged at the fact that in "the greater part of our romances" parents "are usually represented as old humdrum curmudgeons . . . whose taste, in affairs of love, as in their dress, is antiquated, unfashionable, and absurd; but the adventurers, and fortune hunters, are all possessed of taste and spirit, and gallantry, and carry off the damsel. . . ."[42] Farrago was well aware that the Lovelaces were made all the more attractive by the very measures usually employed to discourage their suits. "Ridicule is the only remedy," he concluded wisely.[43] Unfortunately, ridicule was not a cherished weapon of the sentimentalists.

A favorite article in the sentimental creed is the belief in the innate goodness of the heart. Richardson's Squire B., who certainly was not a conspicuously promising subject for reform, seemed to prove that under the influence of Pamela's terrific virtue, a libertine might be reclaimed. To the sentimental heroine few challenges were at once so fascinating and so dangerous as the prospect of reforming an attractive rake by the soft blandishments of her superior virtue. An exciting topic for debate was the possibility of Sophia's reform of that prince of philanderers, Tom Jones. That there was grave danger in it, moralists were not slow to point out. Mrs. Foster found it necessary to declare: "That reformed rakes make the best husbands, is a common, and I am sorry to say, a too generally received maxim. Yet I cannot conceive, that any lady, who values, or properly considers her own happiness, will venture on the dangerous experiment."[44] There is the same warning in Eliza Vicery's *Emily Hamilton*. Mary Carter scouted the old adage that reformed rakes make the best husbands. "I never could see the propriety of the assertion," she wrote indignantly

---

how is it possible to reconcile the infatuation of parents who are daily offering up the honour and happiness of their children at the shrine of interest and ambition."

[42] H. H. Brackenridge, *Modern Chivalry* (Pittsburgh, 1793), III, 86. This volume was the first literary work printed west of the Alleghenies. The first two volumes were published in 1792 in Philadelphia; the fourth volume was issued in Philadelphia in 1797.

[43] *Ibid.*, III, 85.   [44] *The Boarding School*, p. 103.

to Emily. "Might it not be said with equal justice, that if a certain description of females were reformed, they would make the best wives?"[45] To this query, the heroine had no convincing answer.

Most females, however, cherished the hope that their virtue might succeed in the perilous, but interesting, enterprise. Eliza Wharton in *The Coquette* was fascinated by the prospect of reforming Major Sanford. The warnings of her confidante, Lucy Freeman, were unable to shake the heroine's faith in the inherent goodness of the human heart. "But is it not an adage, generally received," she asked hopefully, "that *a reformed rake makes the best husband?*"[46] The rakes themselves, who knew that overtures of reform often became preludes to seduction, chuckled wickedly over this feminine "vanity and ignorance" which led the unwary "to anticipate the honor of reclaiming the libertine, and reforming the rake!"[47] Even those hapless victims of seduction who had the best reason to doubt the doctrine of man's perfectibility were often the most incorrigible champions of that theory. After she had been reduced to beggary by Courtland, who had robbed her of both honor and fortune, Miss Wellwould still believed in the villain's reclamation. "I said that Mr. Courtland was not naturally bad," she told Margaret, "and believe me, good young lady, I have in a thousand instances, observed the rectitude of his heart."[48] After she had borne her lover three children, Miss Wellwould's faith was appropriately rewarded at a wedding which was as elaborate as it was tardy. "The rites of the church were performed; not a single ceremony was omitted," the author wrote proudly. Courtland, to the delight of those present at the marriage, conducted himself as "*a happy and grateful bridegroom.*"[49]

Susanna Rowson was especially fond of the reformed rake theme. In *The Fille de Chambre,* the philandering Barton was

[45] *Emily Hamilton*, p. 108. Miss Carter had no sentimental illusions on this subject. "I never would run the hazard of marrying a reformed rake, if such a thing could be found," she wrote to Emily. "But I am rather inclined to think, that Phoenix like, there is only one in a century."

[46] Foster, *The Coquette*, p. 76.   [47] *Ibid.*, pp. 80-81.
[48] Murray, *The Gleaner*, I, 116.   [49] *Ibid.*, I, 123.

not only won over to virtue by the Griselda-like suffering of his wife, but cheerfully committed to her care the cast-off object of his illicit passion.[50] Quite equal to this peculiar responsibility, Mrs. Barton informed her admiring friends "that her husband was entirely reclaimed" and "that she was the happiest woman in the creation. . . ."[51] A lusty marquis in *Sarah; or, The Exemplary Wife* was moved to instant repentance by Sarah's heroic efforts to remain exemplary under trying conditions. "It melted me almost to childish weakness . . . ," the reformed roué confessed. "I endeavoured to repair my errors, the moment I discovered they were such."[52] It was not one of Mrs. Rowson's heroines, however, who achieved the most spectacular reform in eighteenth-century American fiction. This distinction was reserved for Mercutio, the hero of Butler's *Fortune's Foot-ball.* He proved that the good heart transcended all differences of creed and color by convincing the noble Kerim, sovereign of Persia, to release, not one, but "thirty and seven females of different nations, religions, sizes, features and complexions, arrayed in all the pomp of magnificent prostitution."[53] Although there are many instances of the conversion of rakes in the novels of the period, the most militant of the reforming heroines failed to bring about so wholesale a resignation of pleasure.

Other evidences of Richardson's influence are to be found in the unwholesome preoccupation with death which characterized the behavior of many American Clarissas. After Harriot had been seduced by Lee in *The Hapless Orphan,* she wasted away in a room which resembled that of Clarissa. "Upon her opening the door, every object filled me with horror," wrote a visitor. "The shutters were closed. At the sight of the emaciated, heartbroken girl, bolstered up in her bed, my resolution left me."[54] The appearance of decaying beauty invariably interested the feeling heart. "I never saw a

[50] *The Fille de Chambre* (Dublin, 1793), p. 152.
[51] *Ibid.,* p. 165.
[52] Rowson, *Sarah; or, The Exemplary Wife,* pp. 178-179.
[53] *Fortune's Foot-ball,* II, 100.
[54] [Anon.,] *The Hapless Orphan,* II, 16.

more interesting object," Emily Hamilton declared after her call to see the dying Sophia. "Her fine dark eyes are irradiated with more than usual lustre. Her complexion, naturally very fine, appears more dazzling white. . . ."[55] The same morbid interest is betrayed in the account of Mary's last moments in *Glencarn*. "A long veil hung suspended from her head, and flowed round her delicate frame," a witness of the dissolution observed. "Her figure was uncommonly interesting. She resembled the ethereal spirit of departed peace; an airy sylph-like delicacy marked her whole form. . . ."[56] Declining heroines often felt a melancholy satisfaction in composing their own epitaphs. It enabled them to share, as if from the grave itself, the sensations of their sorrowing friends. "Death, Maria, is a serious event," Caroline informed a friend in *The Hapless Orphan*. She then prepared an inscription to remind posterity that "The body here entombed, once possessed a mind warm with humanity, animated with friendship, and glowing with a religious hope."[57] The contemplation of a coffin which had comforted Clarissa's last hours was also enjoyed by Siderio as woe's supreme luxury. "Siderio then took my hand," wrote Asphelia, "and led me to a coffin at the other end of the room; the lid was off, and it empty. 'There Asphelia (said he) is my coffin; in a very few years at the furthest, perhaps in a few days, that small spot will contain your friend Siderio. . . . There is nothing frightful in this sight; I enjoy the most pleasing reflections when I look at it.' "[58]

To Richardson's example must also be ascribed in part that minute circumstantiality with which Pamela's American sisters counted their blessings, physical and spiritual. Thus Meriel spared no details in describing her "neat back room, where was a tent bed, of striped Manchester, with every necessary appurtenance, a case of drawers, a neat dressing case, and a small trunk. . . . On opening the trunk I found it contained a piece of grey lutestring, two pieces of dark chintz, each enough for a

[55] Vicery, *Emily Hamilton*, p. 14.
[56] George Watterston, *Glencarn* (Alexandria, 1810), II, 177.
[57] [Anon.,] *The Hapless Orphan*, II, 220-221.
[58] *Massachusetts Magazine*, I, 482.

gown, about ten yards of muslin, and a piece of fine linen."[59] Richardson's insistence upon the doctrine of "poetic justice" also had its counterpart in the merciless meting out of rewards and punishments in many of our novels. The libertine in *Amelia* died on the field of honor with the words of Lovelace on his lips. "Nobly done," cried Doliscus. as he fell. "It is the vengeance of Amelia; and oh! may it serve to expiate the crime of her betrayer."[60] Wrongdoers in *Glencarn* suffered uniformly infamous ends. No less than a long prison term, a suicide, and three hangings were required to dispose of the villains in a somewhat crowded day of judgment in the last chapter.[61] Poetic justice was enforced with similar relentlessness in *Charlotte*. Belcour, the seducer, died at the hands of Montraville;[62] while La Rue, the wicked French governess who paved the way for Charlotte's ruin, met a harrowing death in a squalid hospital, "where having lingered a few days, she died, a striking example that vice, however prosperous in the beginning, in the end leads only to misery and shame."[63] Mrs. Rowson also followed Richardson's lead by reserving a heavenly reward for the heroine of *Sarah*. "It may be objected that the example will lose its effect, as my heroine is not in the end rewarded for her exemplary patience, virtue, and forbearance," she explained in her Preface. "But it was because I wished to avoid every unnatural appearance, that I left Sarah to meet her reward in a better world."[64]

Punishment was sometimes made to fit the crime with the nicety achieved in "The Affecting Story of Maria Arnold." "I should have mentioned to you," the author added in a postscript, "that her eldest daughter, neglected and forsaken by her parents, was last year seduced by a lord; . . . the second ran away with a dancing master—and her third, with a hairdresser."[65] The complacent morality of *Pamela* is to be found in countless stories in periodicals as well as in full-length

[59] Rowson, *Trials of the Human Heart*, II, 43-44; see also, IV, 35.
[60] [Anon.,] *Amelia; or, The Faithless Briton* (Boston, 1798), p. 33.
[61] Watterston, *Glencarn*, II, 264-265.
[62] Rowson, *Charlotte*, II, 167.   [63] *Ibid.*, II, 169.
[64] *Sarah; or, The Exemplary Wife*, p. i.   [65] *New York Magazine*, VI, 565.

novels. Morality was viewed as a kind of insurance policy promising benefits conveniently payable before death. "Thus was honesty rewarded," wrote the author of "Perrin and Lucetta." "Let those who desire the reward, practice the virtue."[66] Richard Bumper, a reformed rake in "The Sentimental Libertine," arrived at a curiously comfortable conclusion after marrying his victim: "I have been married a week, and am convinced that virtue is its own reward."[67] An essayist in the *Massachusetts Magazine* commented upon the confusion between prudence and virtue, but ended his homily rather lamely with the unheroic advice: "Let us make it our constant aim to follow virtue, if not 'for virtue's sake,' at least on account of our own ease, convenience, and security."[68] In face of this facile disposal of the problem, it is pleasant to come upon at least one reader who found Richardson's neat system of rewards and punishments thoroughly obnoxious. Esther Burr recorded her conviction that Squire B. was a paltry prize with which to recompense genuine virtue. "Riches and honour are set up too much—can Money reward Virtue?" she asked. "If the author had left it to me to have entitled the Books, I think I should have chosen Virtue tryed instead of rewarded."[69] A few other dissonant voices were heard amid the general chorus of praise. The *Port Folio* poked fun at Clary's friend, Miss Howe, "that dragon of discretion, that bully of chastity, who makes such a hubbub in defense of her citadel; though amidst all her vollies we discern much more smoke than fire."[70] The same periodical also quoted with relish Crébillon's remark that Pamela "is very silly and awkward after her marriage; but I observe she never prays in bed, which I believe is the only piece of furniture in her house that does not afford matter for her pious ejaculations."[71]

[66] *Massachusetts Magazine*, IV, 492.
[67] *Ibid.*, II, 174.   [68] *Ibid.*, VI, 542.
[69] *New England Quarterly*, III, 301.   [70] III, 151.
[71] *Ibid.* Praise for Richardson was much more common than censure. See *Port Folio*, II, 183, for a typical tribute. Most critics were in agreement with a writer in 1802, who declared: "If by some strange alternative, the existence of the works of Richardson should become incompatible with that of the productions of all other moralists . . . I should not hesitate to say, 'Let Richardson remain, though all others

The most striking manifestation of Richardson's influence is to be seen in the appalling popularity of the seduction motif with its seemingly limitless possibilities for sentimental and sensational scenes. Here, in a more or less Americanized setting, are to be encountered all the famous Richardsonian episodes from Squire B.'s tricks of low cunning to the superior ruses of Lovelace. Repeated with wearisome monotony are the fatal elopement by carriage, the abduction of the heroine from a masquerade ball, the victim's last will and testament with tearful remembrances for her friends and soft impeachments for her foes, and, finally, the lingering death from a broken heart—all calculated to inspire that "handkerchiefly feeling" which had become a requisite of popular fiction.

As is well known, American fiction began its career somewhat apologetically with an attempt in *The Power of Sympathy* "to expose the dangerous consequences of seduction." No other theme was able to provoke more purple patches or to inspire more poetic flights. One of these excursions into the sublime was quoted in 1789 by the *Massachusetts Magazine* as a "beauty" from *The Power of Sympathy:* "Behold the youthful virgin arrayed in all the delightful charms of vivacity, modesty and sprightliness—Behold even while she is rising in beauty and dignity, like a lily of the valley, in the full bloom of her graces, she is cut off suddenly by the rude hand of the seducer."[72] Seduction darkens many pages of this novel. "Surely there is no human vice of so black a die—so fatal in its consequences—or which causes a more general calamity," wrote the author, "than that of *seducing* a female from the path of honour."[73] The hero was deterred from committing this deep sin only by a vision of Hell in which he saw the "miserable race of seducers" ostracized by the other accursed souls. "Even the damned look upon them with horrour, and thank fate that

---

perish.' " See also "Richardson and Sterne in *The Massachusetts Magazine," New England Quarterly*, V, 65-82.

[72] W. H. Brown, *The Power of Sympathy*, II, 53. See *Massachusetts Magazine*, I, 52, in which this passage was reprinted along with two other "beauties" from the same novel: "Sensibility" and "Suicide." The passage was also cited by the *New York Magazine*, VI, 687-688.   [73] *Ibid.*, I, 114.

their crimes are not of so deep a die."[74] Although Harrington was able to conquer his passion, Brown provided a sufficient number of incidental seductions to satisfy the popular taste. The catastrophe of one of these affairs included a suicide in its long train of misery for which even the poetic prose of William Hill Brown seemed inadequate—

> With thee, SEDUCTION! are ally'd
> HORROUR, DESPAIR and SUICIDE.[75]

Of all the seducers who devoted their days and nights to a study of the maxims of Chesterfield and the wiles of Lovelace, none is more convincing than Major Sanford, the author of Eliza Wharton's ruin in Mrs. Foster's *The Coquette*. With a sufficient fortune to procure him respect, and with manners captivating enough to make him a welcome figure at polite assemblies, he richly merited the titles of "a Chesterfieldian" and "a second Lovelace" which were bestowed upon him by Eliza's friends.[76] Sanford possessed more than the outward trappings of his notorious original. His was something of the joy and zest of the game which gave gusto to Lovelace's philanderings. "Not that I have any ill designs," he wrote to Deighton, "but only to play off her own artillery, by using a little unmeaning gallantry. And let her beware of the consequences."[77] When Eliza seemed to favor the suit of the priggish Boyer, Sanford's pride was touched. "I shall be the more interested," he exulted, "as I am likely to meet with difficulties; and it is the glory of a rake, as well as a chieftain to combat obstacles."[78] He was impelled upon his criminal course as much by a desire to satisfy his vanity as to gratify his passion.

[74] *Ibid.*, II, 105.
[75] *Ibid.*, I, 118. For an account of the suicide motif in our early fiction and its relation to Goethe's *Sorrows of Werther*, see Chapter V, "Werther-Fever and Suicide," pp. 155-165.
[76] *The Coquette*, p. 164. After studying Sanford's miniature, Julia Granby declared, "He looks to me like a Chesterfieldian." Warnings against "Chesterfieldian seducers" also appear in *The Power of Sympathy*, II, 5-6; *The Hapless Orphan*, II, 38; and in Susanna Rowson's *Reuben and Rachel*, I, 124. Periodicals were full of blasts against Chesterfield's ethics. See *Massachusetts Magazine*, II, 36-38; *New York Magazine*, VI, 564; and *Port Folio*, V, 273.
[77] *Ibid.*, p. 26.   [78] *Ibid.*, p. 48.

"I must own myself a little revengeful too in this affair," he confided to Deighton. "I wish to punish her friends, as she calls them, for their malice towards me; for their cold and negligent treatment of me whenever I go to the house. I know that to frustrate their designs of a connection between Mr. Boyer and Eliza would be a grievous disappointment."[79] It is this element of outraged pride which distinguishes the seducer of *The Coquette* from many of his wicked contemporaries in English as well as in American fiction. Eliza, too, has her moments of agonized self-revelation in which she becomes something more than another horrible example to frighten schoolgirls. Brief as are these glimpses of truth in Mrs. Foster's novel, they lend conviction and dignity to a theme too often profaned by sensationalism and sentimentality.

It was inevitable, of course, that the externalities of Richardson's art should have been those most frequently copied by beginners. The seducer became a cardboard figure to be distinguished only by name from his fellow rakes who worked their wiles in these novels. All the timeworn tricks to beguile the "unsuspecting fair" were repeated monotonously in story after story. Indeed, these stratagems were employed so often that the female deluded by any of them deserves more compassion for the lack of ordinary intelligence than tears for the loss of her virtue. B.'s device of female impersonation was attempted by the villain in *The Hapless Orphan*. Caroline was warned that "the person Mrs. Wilkins has in her service, is not of the sex her habit denotes; but a man, placed in that capacity, the more effectually to complete your ruin."[80] The ruse of a bogus wedding service which Pamela had some reason to believe might finally defeat her prudence, proved the downfall of Amelia and many others. "The marriage ceremony was privately repeated," chronicled the author sadly, "but how it will excite the indignation of the virtuous reader when he

---

[79] *Ibid.*, p. 81. For a brilliant analysis of *Clarissa* as a tragedy of pride, see J. W. Krutch, *Five Masters* (New York, 1930), pp. 107-173.

[80] [Anon.,] *The Hapless Orphan*, I, 130. Lucretia and Caroline enjoyed several narrow escapes. Upon an earlier occasion they "observed a person in the habit of a woman gaining fast upon us. The oddity of her dress and the peculiarity of her appearance instantly made us suspect it to be a man" (*ibid.*, I, 51-52).

understands, that the sacred character of the priest was personated by a soldier whom Doliscus had suborned for that iniquitous occasion!"[81] The seducer in *Trials of the Human Heart* tempted Meriel to elope with him to the metropolis where he had arranged for a "London wedding."[82] In the same novel, which fully merited its title, Howard assailed the heroine's honor by using a "potion" compounded to rob the victim of her consciousness.[83] The villain of "Rosetta" also found something besides morality in Richardson. "He had read the beautiful novel of *Clarissa*," the author confessed with shame, "in which the perfidious lover, after having in vain tried every art of seduction to ruin an amiable woman, prepares a liquor which at once lulls to sleep her strength and her virtue. . . . Such was the model Lormon chose for his imitation."[84] Lord Rossiter's trick of feigning serious illness to recall Rebecca in *The Fille de Chambre* resembles the same dodge used by B. to bring back the fleeing Pamela. Upon her return, he also "jailed" his victim after the manner of Pamela's persecutor.[85] It is a relief to encounter an occasional libertine who observed the terms of a sporting code and despised the shopworn tricks of Lovelace's unimaginative imitators. "In all my warfare with women," boasted this superior scamp, "I never considered myself as justified either to use violent force, intoxicating drugs, or to delude them by promising marriage, or by a mock representation of that ceremony."[86] Such high scruples were rare. The repertory of most rakes was accurately

[81] [Anon.,] *Amelia; or, The Faithless Briton*, p. 12. The same device was employed successfully by Lee in *The Hapless Orphan*, II, 11.

[82] Rowson, *Trials of the Human Heart*, I, 48.

[83] *Ibid.*, I, 72.

[84] *Massachusetts Magazine*, VIII, 391-392.

[85] Rowson, *The Fille de Chambre*, pp. 118, 123.

[86] *New York Magazine*, VI, 46. Tabitha Tenney burlesqued this overworked formula in *Female Quixotism* when she has Patrick beg the novel-crazed Dorcasina to elope by chaise: "This manner of proceeding was so conformable to many instances which she had read in her favourite authors, that she was on the point of giving her consent." See *Female Quixotism* (Boston, 1825), I, 96. Upon a later occasion, the wily Patrick almost prevailed by echoing Lovelace's appeal to Clarissa. "Let us fly," he urged, "let us improve the present moment. I will place you with a reputable family, till the knot is tied, which will bind us forever" (*ibid.*, I, 140). Miss Tenney's parody was first published in Boston in 1801.

described by an indignant friend of Amelia in *The Gamesters:* "Sham marriage; sham certificate; sham clergyman; all sham."[87]

The libertine whose weapons were the vanity and sensibility of his fair prey was the most insidious of all. Mrs. Rowson found him "like the scaley snake, who tries to draw to its devouring jaws the harmless bird that thoughtless hops from spray to spray; he twines about, shews all his gilded scales, basks in the sun, rears up his crested head, and courts the little songster to his snare."[88] John Blair Linn hit upon an equally startling image. The glittering betrayer of female innocence reminded him of "the polished and plated coffin," a thing lovely to look at. But peer beneath the lid, "And lo! a loathsome corpse appears."[89] When the seducer came in the guise of "a man of sense, delicacy, of polished manners, and insinuating address," no one appeared to be safe. Even the exemplary Sarah, whose virtue withstood excruciating temptations, seemed vulnerable to her closest friend and admirer. "In such a situation," she admitted uneasily, "I would not answer for the steadiness even of my virtuous Sarah."[90] Daughters were sent into the world advised to regard every man as a potential seducer. The valedictory of Rebecca's mother was typical of the counsel given to many heroines: "God bless you, my child, be careful, circumspect, and wary; suspect every one of a design on you till you are convinced of the contrary. You must think all men knaves, and all women treacherous, and then you will avoid many troubles. Trust no one. . . ."[91] Periodicals repeated these warnings in hundreds of essays, "fragments," and "historiettes."[92] Even academic groves resounded with gradua-

[87] C. M. Warren, *The Gamesters* (Boston, 1805), p. 145.
[88] *The Inquisitor,* I, 81.
[89] *Miscellaneous Works* (New York, 1795), p. 174.
[90] Rowson, *Sarah; or, The Exemplary Wife,* p. 161.
[91] Rowson, *The Fille de Chambre,* p. 25.
[92] For tales of seductions by slightly Americanized Lovelaces, and for reflections upon this doleful theme, see: *Royal American Magazine* (Boston, 1774), I, 378, 426; *New Jersey Magazine* (New Brunswick, 1787), I, 97; *American Magazine* (New York, 1788), I, 465; *Massachusetts Magazine,* I, 205, 403, 470; II, 366, 464, 544, 616; III, 561, 662-663, 678; IV, 179; V, 204, 485, 498; VI, 687; VII, 355; VIII, 11-13, 389; *New York Magazine,* I, 22, 86, 554, 597-602; III, 690-692; IV, 93;

tion "parts" on the great peril. A Columbia College commencement address in 1795 was devoted in part at least to a method of discomfiting the seducer![93] The picaresque *Modern Chivalry* also had its caution to offer ladies of sensibility upon this engrossing subject.[94] With so general an alarm sounded against the bugaboo of seduction, it is not difficult to share Julia's surprise in *The Boarding School* when she exclaimed, "So often . . . has the pen of the divine, the moralist, and the novelist been employed on the subject of female frailty and seduction . . . that I am astonished when I see those who have the best means of information, heedlessly sacrificing their reputation, to the specious arts of the libertine!"[95]

Indeed, the unceasing threat of the seducer is so imminent in these novels "founded on fact" that, as Carl Van Doren has observed, "modern readers might think that age one of the most illicit on record if they did not understand that Richardson's Lovelace is merely being repeated in different colors and proportions."[96] Jacob Duché's testimony offers support both for the American women and the vogue of Samuel Richardson. "Thank Heaven!" he wrote in 1774, "they still retain their honest attachment to religion and common sense. The arts of gallantry are little known, and less practised in these *last retreats* of persecuted virtue."[97] Brissot de Warville's tribute to the American fair was equally reassuring. "Their frank and tender hearts have nothing to fear from the perfidy of men," he concluded in 1792. "Examples of this perfidy are rare; the vows of love are believed; and love always respects them, or shame

V, 52-54, 159-166; VI, 39-46, 564, 687-688; *New York Weekly Magazine,* I, 315; II, 59, 132; *The Nightingale* (Boston, 1796), I, 196; *Literary Museum* (West Chester, 1797), I, 43; *Lady's Magazine* (Philadelphia, 1792), I, 62; *Weekly Magazine* (Philadelphia, 1798), I, 326-328.

[93] Reprinted in *New York Magazine,* VI, 297-305.

[94] *Modern Chivalry* (Philadelphia, 1792), II, 64.

[95] Foster, *The Boarding School,* p. 184. Clarinda spoke with the authority of sad experience when she declared: "Women would do well to forbear their declamations against the falsity and wickedness of men; the fault is theirs, to fall into such coarse-spun snares as are laid for them" (*ibid.,* p. 185).

[96] *The American Novel* (New York, 1921), p. 7.

[97] *Observations on a Variety of Subjects* . . . (Philadelphia, 1774), p. 49.

follows the guilty."[98] The *Travels* of Chastellux is also favorable to female virtue in America at a time when novels "founded on truth" were describing seductions in every hamlet: "Licentious manners, in fact, are so foreign in America, that the communication with young women, leads to nothing bad, and freedom itself there bears a character of modesty far beyond our affected bashfulness and false reserve."[99]

That our novelists, who could not have found Nature and Richardson everywhere the same, adjusted Nature to Richardson, receives interesting confirmation in the significant heightening of the facts which underlie Mrs. Foster's *The Coquette*. This novel, although not so popular as Mrs. Rowson's *Charlotte Temple,* is certainly the most memorable of its kind in eighteenth-century American fiction.[100] The *cause célèbre* upon which it was based, the tragic career of Elizabeth Whitman of Hartford, was widely known up and down the Connecticut River Valley. The author, moreover, was in a position to know the facts, for she had married a cousin of the victim. If Mrs. Foster knew the details of the famous affair, she deftly trimmed them to fit the popular pattern bequeathed by Richardson in *Clarissa*. The shades of Lovelace and Clarissa, as well as those of Elizabeth and her unknown betrayer, constantly hovered over the pages. The heroine, Clarissa-like, is depicted in the novel as being hurried away by chaise at night without the knowledge or consent of her friends and relatives. "In simple fact," wrote Mrs. Caroline Dall, who was in possession of certain of Elizabeth Whitman's letters, "she went away in the regular stage-coach at high noon, with everybody's warm approval."[101] A similar Richardsonian bias was also given to the character of Eliza's betrayer, who was aptly described in the novel as "a second Lovelace."[102] The letters in *The Co-*

[98] *New Travels in the United States of America* . . . (London, 1794), I, 72.

[99] François Jean de Chastellux, *Travels in North America* . . . (London, 1787), I, 15-16.

[100] Although C. Gaylord of Boston published a "thirtieth edition" in 1833, it was probably a misprint for the thirteenth. See R. L. Shurter, "Mrs. Hannah Webster Foster and the Early American Novel," *American Literature*, IV, 306-308.

[101] *The Romance of the Association* . . . , p. 68.

[102] *The Coquette*, p. 55. Efforts have been made to identify the seducer as Pierrepont Edwards, but the evidence seems inconclusive.

quette also reveal an imagination "heated by the reading of Richardson's novel." Mrs. Dall found their tone to be "wholly unlike that of the real letters. . . ." "I think, too," she wrote in *The Romance of the Association,* "that the influence of Richardson's story may be seen wherever the author departs from the truth."[103] It is perhaps appropriate to conclude this consideration of Richardson's influence upon our early fiction with *The Coquette.* Published in 1797, less than a decade after Eliza's death in the old Bell Tavern in Danvers, and written by a relative of the victim, the story might well have been, as indeed it was advertised, "A novel founded on fact." The mood of the story, however, did not arise from the facts to be found in the lives of Elizabeth Whitman and her friends who moved in the best circles of Connecticut society. It emanated, rather, from the mind of that celebrated Virtuous Tradesman in London's "agreeable surburbane North End," who half a century before, had taught the passions to move at the command of virtue.

[103] *The Romance of the Association* . . . , pp. 68-70.

III

THE ELEGANT EPISTOLARIANS

Really, Celia, these young ladies who write so much, and so prettily to each other, must be very amiable and lovely, for you must know the whole book is in letters, it is indeed a charming history; you cannot think how much I cried whilst reading.

—Susanna Rowson, *Trials of the Human Heart*, 1795.

SAMUEL RICHARDSON's legacy of the theme of seduction was not his only bequest to American novelists. He also provided a serviceable method of presenting a story. The vogue of epistolary fiction in England, begun by *Pamela* in 1740, reached its peak in 1788, the year before the appearance of *The Power of Sympathy*.[1] It was not an accident that Richardson's heroines, Pamela and Clarissa, were his most convincing letter-writers; nor was it mere chance which decreed that the titles of other epistolary novels popular in America, *Evelina* and *Héloïse*, should bear the Christian names of young ladies. The chatty quality of familiar correspondence had peculiar charms for the feminine mind, and a mastery of this art became one of the more polite accomplishments of the elegant female. Few were disposed to deny the observation of Dr. Hitchcock that "There is evidently a greater facility in females for letter writing than in our sex."[2] The letter form, moreover, with its minute, voluminous, and easy circumstantiality, its ample opportunities for didactic and sentimental appeal, and its comparative formlessness, made it a tempting model for beginners.

Mrs. Foster, who aimed in *The Boarding School* to improve the manners and characters of young ladies, had high praise for the virtues of epistolary correspondence. "But the species

---

[1] For an admirable discussion of English letter fiction, see F. G. Black, "The Technique of Letter Fiction in English from 1740 to 1800," *Harvard Studies and Notes in Philology and Literature*, XV, 291-312.

[2] *Memoirs of the Bloomsgrove Family*, II, 102-103.

of writing, which is open to every capacity, and ornamental to every station, is the epistolary," she counseled those on the verge of young womanhood.[3] The letters of the celebrated Mrs. Chapone, a member of Richardson's circle in London, were recommended by Mrs. Foster as "profitable and pleasing, both in youth and more advanced age," and cited as "a valuable treasure of information and advice."[4] The students at Harmony Grove were also urged to study "the generous and polite Fitzborne's letters" as models for their own compositions. "The justness of his sentiments, and the ease and elegance of his diction are at once interesting and improving."[5] Dr. Bennett's letters had sentiment as well as morality to commend them. "These letters," declared the preceptress, "are not scholastic and elaborate dissertations; they are addressed to the heart. . . ."[6] Epistolary exercises, which were required of all girls at Harmony Grove, did not cease with their graduation; but continued until death. They were urged to correspond regularly with their teacher, who treasured their letters as a "renewed experience of the truth of the observation, that next to the personal presence and conversation, is the epistolary correspondence of a friend."[7]

Testimony upon the advantages of letter writing came from all quarters. Eliza Wharton in *The Coquette* wrote her lover of the double duty performed by letters exchanged between the sexes: "The knowledge and masculine virtues of your sex may be softened, and rendered more diffusive by the inquisitiveness, vivacity, and docility of ours; drawn forth and exercised by each other."[8] Emilius, a model suitor in Bradford's *The Art of Courting,* halted his tender protestations to compliment Olivia upon her progress. "I am charmed," he wrote a trifle condescendingly for an impassioned lover, "with that rapid improvement you have made within the last six months in your hand-writing, and in composition. An improvement in these particulars is an advantage which attends friends and lovers

---

[3] *The Boarding School,* p. 31.
[5] *Ibid.,* p. 128.
[7] *Ibid.,* p. 175.
[4] *Ibid.,* p. 25.
[6] *Ibid.,* p. 179.
[8] Foster, *The Coquette,* p. 68.

residing at a distance from each other."[9] Mothers were enjoined to teach their children to open their hearts to their elders in letters, because "Persons when holding the pen, generally express themselves more freely than when engaged in conversation."[10] This advice of Mrs. Murray was followed by the mother of Margaretta with gratifying results. Thus the little girl was "properly and happily habituated to disclose, without a blush, each rising thought. . . ."[11] The female propensity for scribbling was at times so strong that it could not wait for the usual occasions for correspondence. London gossip had reported that Richardson frequently wrote to his daughters while they were all living together in the same house. Intramural activity of this kind was carried on by Margaretta. She submitted with infinite relish "to little self-imposed absences," her father wrote proudly, "when my boy Plato, being constituted courier betwixt the apartments of my wife and daughter, an epistolary correspondence was carried on between them, from which more than one important benefit derived. . . ."[12]

Not the least of these advantages for the sentimental heroine was the opportunity afforded for the minute analysis of the heart. Jane Talbot confessed, "I have always found an unaccountable pleasure in dissecting, as it were, my heart; uncovering, one by one, its many folds, and laying it before you, as a country is shewn in a map . . . what volumes have I talked to you on that bewitching theme. . . ."[13] Margaretta's letters to Miranda were devoted to the same fertile subject. "In that little page," she wrote complacently, "I have laid every vein of my heart open. . . ."[14] Strephon in *The Art of Courting* recommended constant exercise in self-revelation by letter. "It frequently serves to give vent to the tenderest emotions of the soul, and of course to soothe the anxious and melancholy heart," he advised. "I would not be without this means of happiness for both of the Indies."[15] It was the troubled heart,

[9] *The Art of Courting*, p. 102.   [10] Murray, *The Gleaner*, I, 71.
[11] *Ibid*.   [12] *Ibid*.
[13] C. B. Brown, *Jane Talbot* (Philadelphia, 1801), p. 130.
[14] [Anon.,] *Margaretta*, p. 112.
[15] Bradford, *The Art of Courting*, p. 41.

"bleeding at every pore," not the joyful one, which was regarded with most interest by the "feeling reader." Young ladies blessed with tolerant fathers and placid love affairs were the first to admit they were poor subjects for sentimental correspondence. Their duty in fiction was to receive and to make copies of the more compelling letters of their interesting friends. "So do not fail of writing," Sophia urged Polly, "and tell me all your trouble; not waiting for me to answer you; for I have not much to write about. But you have a good subject, or a bad one, to write from, and I want to hear all your story."[16] The balm of correspondence was dearly prized by the sufferer. "I have frequent recourse to my pen," wrote Caroline in *The Hapless Orphan*. "It is a luxury thus to unbosom my affliction."[17] The anxieties of such correspondence were necessarily rather trying for the recipients of these doleful missives. "At the arrival of every mail," Maria confessed with reason, "a sudden horror seizes my mind, apprehensive of the approach of some grievous intelligence."[18]

Many of these persecuted scribblers showed at least some consideration for the sensibilities of their friends. "I am unfit to write," Caroline apologized to Maria, "yet fly to my pen, for a mitigation of my harassed mind."[19] The heroine of Mrs. Rowson's *Trials of the Human Heart* was equally solicitous for Celia's fortitude, but begged her indulgence. "Farewell, my dear girl, methinks you must be weary," she wrote, "of a correspondent who writes only on melancholy themes.—Ah! my Celia, the miserable know no luxury equal to that of dwelling on their sorrows, and weeping over their source . . . it is a privilege I shall not easily forego."[20] Richardson's Anna Howe was the model emulated by these sympathetic friends, while the heroines had Clarissa's confidence that their letters would not go unread or unwept. "While my eyes are yet moist, and my heart is loaded with sympathy," wrote the heroine of

[16] [Anon.,] *Fidelity Rewarded*, p. 21.
[17] [Anon.,] *The Hapless Orphan*, II, 128.
[18] [Anon.,] *Fidelity Rewarded*, p. 131.
[19] [Anon.,] *The Hapless Orphan*, I, 156.
[20] *Trials of the Human Heart*, IV, 13.

Infidelity, "let me transmit to my dearest sister, the sad tale of persecuted innocence; at which, I am sure her tender bosom will sigh in unison with my own."[21] Polly was equally sure of her faithful Sophia's tender interest. "Accordingly, I shall make no further apology," she declared, "but write on as usual."[22]

Letter-writing afforded sentimentalists capital opportunities to indulge in their favorite game of picturing themselves in the midst of their own woes, of striking heroic attitudes, and of anticipating the effect of their dramatic predicaments upon those to whom they laid bare their inmost souls. The sorely-beset Meriel attained rare mastery of the art of keeping her confidante on the tenterhooks of suspense. Besieged on every side by would-be ravishers, she made Celia wait three long weeks before relieving her fears. "I judge of my dear Celia's impatience," she wrote with ill-concealed relish, "by what I should feel were she in the situation in which I was, when I concluded my last: I will not trifle with you, but proceed in my narrative."[23] Nor were these scribblers unaware of the dramatic possibilities in bulletins dispatched nervously from the field of action. "You cannot see me just now," Jane Talbot wrote to Colden, "but the palpitating heart infects my fingers and the unsteady pen will speak to you eloquently."[24] Meriel broke off tantalizingly at the moment perilous: "I found myself alone on the wreck, slightly fastened to it by a small cord, that was passed around my waist and tied to a ring on the remaining part of the deck. The terrors which at that moment took possession of my mind are still too fresh in my memory to suffer me to proceed."[25] Equally exasperating were the motion-picture serial tricks employed by Anne, who had a habit of stopping her narrative at the very moment when pursuit was hottest and escape least probable. "I know you are interested in this narrative," she wrote to Elenor, "but I must drop my

[21] Relf, *Infidelity,* pp. 36-37.   [22] [Anon.,] *Fidelity Rewarded,* p. 22.
[23] Rowson, *Trials of the Human Heart,* II, 101.
[24] C. B. Brown, *Jane Talbot,* p. 262.
[25] Rowson, *Trials of the Human Heart,* III, 154.

pen for the present."[26] Writers in possession of the details of the outcome of an adventure enjoyed teasing those who were impatient to be enlightened. "I have wonders to relate," wrote Anne in high spirits, "but you must take all in the order as they occurred to me."[27] Eliza Wharton also relished these epistolary delights of toying with a reader's curiosity. "But you are impatient I know for the conclusion. You have hastily perused the preceding lines, and are straining your eye forward . . ." she wrote to Lucy. "Well then, not to play too long with the curiosity, which I know to be excited, and actuated by real friendship, I will relieve it."[28]

A sigh-by-sigh, tear-by-tear account of the writer's last moments, ending ominously with an unfinished sentence or a sprinkling of feverish asterisks, was a device calculated to test the sensibilities of the most calloused soul. "Dear Pappa," wrote Pulchera, "From the center of a frozen wilderness, on the border of the grave, please to receive this last token from your only child—driven from home. I have been the sport of fortune, but fifteen minutes will put me out of her power."[29] True to an epistolary tradition which is reluctant to allow a single thrill to escape, Agnes chronicled her emotions to the bitter end. "Augustina, this is the last time I shall ever address you," predicted the heroine truthfully enough in this instance. "This night the wretched Agnes must lay her head upon the earth. . . . Oh! my children, Oh! my beloved Vieurville. . . . Adieu! If thou hast any children, tell them my story, and teach them to subdue their passions. . . . Oh! that I had never—."[30] Only the novice needs the solemn footnote inserted by the author to announce that the letter was found in the pocket of the dead girl. Sarah's letter to her brother came to him as a voice from the grave. "My brother, the world and I have done with each other," cried the dying girl, "the grave yawns, I stand shivering on its brink. . . ."[31] Harriot, who believed the

[26] Rowson, Sarah; or, The Exemplary Wife, p. 57.
[27] Ibid., p. 162. Elenor's relish as narrator appears many times. See ibid., pp. 21, 235.   [28] Foster, The Coquette, p. 40.
[29] [Anon.,] Constantius and Pulchera, p. 58.   [30] Rowson, Mentoria, I, 75.
[31] Rowson, Sarah; or, The Exemplary Wife, p. 257.

only way to give repentance to her lover and to wring his
bosom was to die, arranged to have a message delivered to Lee,
her seducer, after she "had winged her way to the realms of
eternal bliss."[32]

Death by suicide was the supreme luxury of the sentimentalist, and it claimed many victims in American fiction. The
device of the letter made it possible to exploit this subject
shamelessly. With loaded pistol in one hand and a moistened
pen in the other, the actor was enabled to record his quivering
feelings until the last split second of exquisite agony. "My
heart sinks within me—," Harrington wrote to Worthy just
before the fatal bullet stilled his pen forever, "the instrument of
death is before me—farewel! farewel!—My soul sighs to be
freed from its confinement—."[33] The same highly sensational
method was used by John Davis in his *Ferdinand and Elizabeth*
where the mournful story of the lovers is related in a series of
letters which were "Found in the room of Elizabeth, enclosed
in a sealed cover, and lying on a table near the bed on which
they were both discovered weltering in their blood."[34]

Although critics were unanimous in their agreement with
Blair that "The first and fundamental requisite of Epistolary
Writing, is, to be natural and simple . . . ,"[35] most writers employed a diction rarely found on sea or land. Instead of using
letters as an ordinary medium for the exchange of the commonplaces of life, as Richardson had intended, writers regarded them as exercises in refined phrasing and vied with
each other in quest of the exquisite epithet. Margaretta belonged to this cult of the elegant. "Morpheus held me close
confined in his easy fetters," she wrote casually to Elce Thorn-
ton, "till the heat of the day unshackled my limbs, and roused
me to a sense of my intricate state."[36] Amelia also enjoyed
highly figurative language: "I shrink from the thought of
uniting myself to Captain Onslow at the very moment, when
tears of real sorrow will dim the lustre of the hymenial

[32] [Anon.,] *The Hapless Orphan*, II, 18.
[33] W. H. Brown, *The Power of Sympathy*, II, 154.
[34] *Ferdinand and Elizabeth*, p. 135.
[35] *Massachusetts Magazine*, I, 72.   [36] [Anon.,] *Margaretta*, p. 201.

torch."[37] This enchanting "language of the soul" was not confined to letters written by women. Ferdinand's style caught the contagion. "Was it fancy, or did I behold the pearly drop glisten faintly in thy eye?" he asked Elizabeth. "It was not fancy—my lips convinced me of the reality as I kissed it away from its chrystal sluice. And can I forget those humid kisses?"[38] The elderly Franks in Relf's *Infidelity* called upon this artificial diction to describe the conduct of his young wife and her lover. "Sensual debasement is not yet perpetrated," he informed a sympathetic friend, "but . . . that their souls even now revel in the voluptuousness of lascivious sentiment, is undemonstrably evident in the amorous language of their love-fraught eyes!"[39] The tortured style of most of these letters makes it easy to endorse Mrs. Murray's opinion that authors found their models in popular fiction rather than in nature. "I have thought that many a complete letter writer has been produced from the school of the novelist," she remarked, "and hence, probably, it is, that females have acquired so palpable a superiority . . . in this elegant and useful art."[40] Although the letters were usually written by women, every American Lovelace had his Yankee Jack Belford to whom he might report the progress of his intrigues.[41] Sentimental heroes also frequently wrote to each other in the approved style. Any schoolgirl might have envied the epistolary graces revealed in the letters exchanged between Alfred and William Courtney in *Infidelity*. Their correspondence dated from "a juvenile engagement," so dear to misses in boarding schools, to make detailed disclosures to each other of "the first operations of Cupid on their hearts."[42] Novelists were at some pains to account for the industry necessary to pro-

[37] Rowson, *Trials of the Human Heart*, II, 137.

[38] Davis, *Ferdinand and Elizabeth*, p. 29.

[39] Relf, *Infidelity*, p. 127.   [40] *The Gleaner*, II, 63.

[41] The letters exchanged between Sanford and Deighton in *The Coquette* resemble those between Lovelace and Belford. See *The Coquette*, pp. 25-26, 32-33, 48-50, 80-82, 92-94, 103-104, 138-140, 171-174, 188-190, 211-214, 240-246, 252-255. There is the same exultation of triumph after the betrayal of the heroine; the same cry of repentance and warning at the end: "I am undone . . . shun the dangerous paths which I have trodden. . . ." The relationship between Somerton and Evander in C. M. Warren's *The Gamesters* is of the same sort.

[42] Relf, *Infidelity*, p. 30.

duce the voluminous and frequent letters needed to carry forward their narratives. "My desk is, of late, always open; my paper spread: my pen moist," declared the heroine of *Jane Talbot,* who naturally felt some comment was needed to explain how she could contrive to write seven letters totaling more than twenty-one thousand words in four days.[43] Margaretta abstained from sleep to achieve her epistolary triumphs: "And here I am, with the sun already at my fingers' ends, without having closed my eye-lids, to recount to you, dear Elce, the incidents of yesterday, which have been to me very interesting."[44] The letters in *Ormond* are scrupulously accounted for by an early understanding between Constantia Dudley and her friend, Sophia Westyn. "A mutual engagement was formed," Sophia explained, "to record every sentiment and relate every event that happened in the life of either, and no opportunity of communicating information, was to be omitted."[45] Clara Howard gave her friend, Frances Harris, due warning at the beginning of a letter of thirteen thousand words. "I am, indeed, in a mood, just now, extremely favourable to the telling of a long story," she wrote without overstatement.[46]

Novelists were forced to assume that the recipients of letters were never sated. "I will send you another letter," Polly promised her aunt in *Fidelity Rewarded.* "But perhaps I shall trespass on your patience. Yet, as it is to my second mamma; and, as you say, you love to read my scribbles, I will write on without further apology."[47] Upon occasion, even the author was moved to exclamations of wonder. Charles Brockden Brown admitted his surprise at the bulk of Huntly's epistolary memoirs: "On looking back I am surprised at the length to which my story has run . . . one page has insensibly been added to another till I have consumed weeks and filled volumes."[48]

[43] C. B. Brown, *Jane Talbot,* p. 69.

[44] [Anon.,] *Margaretta,* p. 200. In this willing self-sacrifice she had plenty of company. "It is past twelve o'clock," Mary Gray wrote to Emily Hamilton, "but not feeling any inclination to sleep, I devote myself to the pleasing amusement of writing to my Emily." See *Emily Hamilton,* p. 19.   [45] C. B. Brown, *Ormond,* p. 263.

[46] C. B. Brown, *Clara Howard* (Philadelphia, 1801), p. 63.

[47] [Anon.,] *Fidelity Rewarded,* p. 83. Polly also had misgivings about the length of her letters. "Well, if I don't conclude," she wrote after an interminable digression, "you will think I am going to write a packet, instead of a letter."

[48] *Edgar Huntly,* III, 168.

Jane Talbot's powers were a source of amazement even to those who knew her most intimately. "How you have made yourself so absolute a mistress of the goose-quill I can't imagine," marveled Colden, her betrothed. "How you can maintain the writing posture, and pursue the writing movement for ten hours together, without benumbed brain, or aching fingers, is beyond my comprehension."[49]

Letters enjoyed a position of peculiar sanctity in fiction. Except when the plot demanded it, they were never lost or mislaid. Copies were religiously made for private circulation within a privileged circle of intimates, abstracts were often taken for future study, and the precious originals were treasured carefully. Even the most insulting proposals, if made by letter, were saved from destruction. The exemplary Sarah was tempted to burn the base notes she received, but happily found a method of preserving the offensive letters as well as her self-respect. "You see the situation they are in," she reported to a friend, "I have wet them with indignant tears; I have trampled them under my feet; I would have torn the infamous scrawls to atoms, and scattered them to the winds of Heaven, or given them to the devouring flames, but I preserved them that you might see how low, how very low, your poor Sarah is fallen."[50] Letters kept at so great a sacrifice were naturally handled with care. The hero in *Clara Howard* sent directions for the prompt return of his letters. "The pacquet is a precious one," he warned, "you will find in it, a more lively and exact picture of my life, than it is possible, by any other means, to communicate. Preserve it, therefore, with care, and return it safely and entire as soon as you have read it."[51] Sarah's prized journal was also accompanied by explicit directions. "When you have perused," Anne wrote to Elenor, "you will be so good as to return it by the next post, as everything which bears the impression of Sarah's hand is invaluable to me."[52] Often the

[49] C. B. Brown, *Jane Talbot*, pp. 148-149.
[50] Rowson, *Sarah; or, The Exemplary Wife*, p. 148.
[51] C. B. Brown, *Clara Howard*, p. iv.
[52] Rowson, *Sarah; or, The Exemplary Wife*, p. 183. The way in which one letter found its way to many readers is illustrated in this novel. Anne, who had her letters

recipients of letters served as editors of the bulky correspondence; Huntly found the ordering of Waldegrave's papers a labor of love. He described his mixed emotions while "counting over my friend's letters, setting them apart from my own, and preparing them for that transcription from which I expected so high and yet so mournful a gratification."[53] Despite demands for the utmost secrecy and many protestations of the intimate nature of the contents of the letters, their authors were fully aware that they were writing for a large following. Even those who kept their private memoirs locked in secret closets were not without a hope that "unforeseen circumstances" would make them available for publication. "Every sentence was a treasury to moralists and painters," remarked the editor of Ormond's letters.[54] Constantia's correspondence was also designed for many readers. "It is not impossible," she wrote, "but that these letters may be communicated to the world at some future period."[55] Sentimental letter writers invariably wrote with an eye on the favorable verdict of posterity.

"The field of epistolary writing is unbounded," observed a critic in the *New York Magazine*.[56] Moralists seized upon the form as a convenient device for the inculcation of lessons for the guidance of life. The volatile Eliza Wharton protested that she found Lucy Freeman's letters a bit heavy. "I have received your letter; your moral lecture rather," she complained, "and be assured, my dear, your monitorial lessons and advice shall be attended to."[57] A selection of letters written by the girls at Harmony Grove covers a wide range of edifying subjects, including reflections upon the benefits of early rising and warnings against the "tawdry geegaws" of fashion.[58] Miss Henley's sober letters drew mild protests from a young correspondent. "Indeed, Harriot," she replied, "I open your letters with as much gravity as I would a sermon; you have such a knack of

---

directly from Sarah, made copies for Elenor. Elenor also had permission to make copies and abstracts for her own use.

[53] C. B. Brown, *Edgar Huntly*, II, 56-57.
[54] C. B. Brown, *Ormond*, p. 212.   [55] *Ibid.*, p. 31.
[56] *New York Magazine*, II, 447.   [57] Foster, *The Coquette*, p. 9.
[58] Foster, *The Boarding School*, pp. 115-117, 119.

moralizing on every event."[59] Mrs. Murray, who entertained grave doubts about the propriety of fiction, found the epistolary form a useful vehicle for moral remarks on such diverse topics as the conduct of foster mothers, the evils of slander, and "the proper way to think of persons and things."[60] She concluded her "Gleaner" essays with a series of letters on "Eminent Characters" written for "the improvement and felicity of the young proficient."[61]

Mrs. Rowson's *Mentoria* is a veritable correspondence-school course in social behavior, with letters on the value of chaperones and reputations, the beauty of filial duty, the impropriety of writing careless letters, the advantages of personal neatness after marriage, the ethics of second marriages, and the genuine inconveniences attending seduction. Many of these truths were brought home to the tender bosoms of fair readers by "entertaining tales apposite to the subjects. . . ."[62] Of this omnibus type is Dr. Hitchcock's *Memoirs of the Bloomsgrove Family*, written, the author declared, in answer to pressing requests for his "sentiments on a mode of domestic education, suited to the present state of society, government, and manners in this country."[63] The lives of the Bloomsgrove children serve only as a scanty framework for remarks on the desirability of exercise, punctuality, and cleanliness. The interests of the "American fair" may be gleaned from discussions of the servant problem, the proper upbringing of children, the physical effects of nursing upon the health and beauty of young mothers, and the need of domestic harmony. In his prefatory apology, the author acknowledged the heterogeneous character of the contents of his book. "It will not be in my power," he wrote acutely, "in the course of epistolary writing, to observe rigid order, on a subject which involves a great variety of transactions."[64]

The attempts at epistolary fiction in the formative period of the American novel fall readily into a number of the well-

[59] *Ibid.*, p. 136.　　　　　　[60] *The Gleaner*, II, 114.
[61] *Ibid.*, p. 207.　　　　　　[62] *Mentoria*, I, 20.
[63] *Memoirs of the Bloomsgrove Family*, I, 14.
[64] *Ibid.*, p. 18.

defined types prevalent in England. One of these forms, the least successful of all, is the attempt to pack the entire narrative into a single, long-winded letter. This is the artificial method essayed by Mrs. Ann Bleecker in her "History of Maria Kittle." The author was not unmindful of the difficulty of preserving the atmosphere of actual correspondence in a letter containing upwards of seventeen thousand words! After a breathless spurt of forty-two hundred words, the correspondent announced, "I am sorry, dear Susan, to quit Maria in this interesting part of her history; but order requires that we should now return to her spouse, whom we left on his way through the wood."[65] Mrs. Bleecker occasionally inserted friendly reminders to enable her readers to gather up the loose ends of the story. "But doubtless, my dear," she wrote considerately, "your generous sensibility is alarmed at my silence about Mrs. Kittle; I think we left her reposing under a tree. . . ."[66] Despite these attempts to gain some measure of conviction, the novel fails to invoke any illusion of reality.

A more popular method is that employed by Hitchcock in his *Memoirs of the Bloomsgrove Family,* by Mrs. Foster in *The Boarding School,* and by Mrs. Rowson in *Mentoria.* The thin narrative which meanders with a mazy motion through the didactic design in each book is only incidental to the all-important purpose of teaching a lesson.[67] The authors often spiced their precepts by including "affecting historiettes" and "pathetic interludes" at strategic points. Of this sort is Mrs. Rowson's story of Agnes told in seven "true" letters. "I have a collection of letters in my possession," wrote Mentoria, "which I think might well be termed a school for lovers, and will, I am certain, be of more effect in convincing you of the impropriety of clandestine marriages, than a whole sheet of dull precepts."[68] The give-and-take of familiar correspondence is

[65] Bleecker, *The Posthumous Works* . . . , p. 42.

[66] *Ibid.,* p. 48.

[67] For the same general design, see Hitchcock's *The Farmer's Friend* (Boston, 1793), chaps. i, iv, xii, xiv; and Bradford's *The Art of Courting* in which eight different kinds of courtship are described in letters.

[68] *Mentoria,* I, 49.

lacking in these manuals of behavior. Mrs. Rowson did not hesitate to omit the replies of the pupils to the letters of their preceptress. "I have avoided giving any of the young ladies' letters," she explained, "as they would only prove an interruption to the general design."[69]

A third form frequently used by authors of letter fiction is that in which a journal or diary was employed to carry forward the narrative.[70] Some such device was necessary, for so often were scribbling heroines imprisoned by avaricious fathers and would-be seducers that they found few opportunities for posting letters regularly. Thus Polly in *Fidelity Rewarded* confided her thoughts to a journal until she found a way to dispatch it to Sophia. "I went to my chamber, and spent the remainder of the day and evening in lamenting my great affliction," she noted, "and then wrote thus far, and shall still continue, writing, until I have an opportunity to send you what I have written."[71] Martinette's exile in *Ormond* was devoted to "composing her own memoirs" which at a later date she allowed her friends to read.[72] Much the same motive prompted Sarah to keep "a regular journal, if so it can be called, of every occurrence which took place . . . with a design should any event put a period to her existence, it might have been transmitted to me."[73] Another favorite device of the most tearful kind was a deathbed journal, written Clarissa-like, in justification of the victim's conduct. Thus Emily Hammond, with but a few days to live, "employed herself at intervals in composing a pathetic little narrative of her misfortunes."[74] The dying Leonora in Mrs. Wood's *Julia and the Illuminated Baron*, penned a sentimental history of her career as a warning against the miseries of seduction. "If ever you are tempted to swerve

---

[69] *Ibid.*, p. 20.

[70] This convention was not confined to fiction. Esther Burr, daughter of Jonathan Edwards, began a journal in 1754 which she sent in letter form to her friend, "Fidelia," who was Miss Sally Prince, daughter of the Reverend Thomas Prince, pastor of Old South Church, Boston. See J. Fisher (ed.), "The Journal of Esther Burr," *New England Quarterly*, III, 296-315.

[71] [Anon.,] *Fidelity Rewarded*, p. 33.   [72] C. B. Brown, *Ormond*, p. 240.

[73] Rowson, *Sarah; or, The Exemplary Wife*, p. 183 .

[74] Rush, *Kelroy*, pp. 293-294.

from the paths of virtue," she said as she committed her manuscript to Julia who was persecuted by the same villain, "read that paper, and while you read it, remember you have seen the wretched writer, deprived of these charms which rendered her an object of affection, upon the bed of death."[75] Sometimes heroines kept "memorials" of their lives for their friends and for posterity. This was the method employed by Caroline Wentworth in *The Step-Mother*, who apologized for including material with which her recipient was already familiar. ". . . as my history may be deposited in your cabinet for the inspection of your children," she explained, "I shall narrate as faithfully as if you were ignorant of every occurrence."[76] More often the journal was used as a convenient means of exposition to inform the reader of events antecedent to the opening of the novel. Thus Mrs. Hayman, the bosom friend of the heroine's mother in *Constantia Neville,* "Avoiding to communicate what had befallen herself since the death of her husband . . . promised to arrange some papers, containing the history of her life, which she had composed at various periods, and which she would soon present to Constantia for perusal."[77]

The journal device was used in a none too successful attempt to gain conviction for the astounding adventures of that American Robinson Crusoe, Unca Winkfield, in *The Female American.* The author announced his discovery of Unca's journal "among the papers of a deceased friend." "I found it both pleasing and instructive, not unworthy of the most sensible reader," he declared, "highly fit to be perused by the young of

[75] Sally Sayward Barrell Keating Wood, *Julia and the Illuminated Baron* (Portsmouth, 1800), p. 173.

[76] H. Wells, *The Step-Mother* (London, 1799), II, 182. Although the title page describes the author as "of Charlestown, South Carolina," it is likely that she was in England when this, and her other novel, *Constantia Neville* (London, 1800), were published. Helena Wells was the daughter of Robert Wells, who went to South Carolina in 1753 and settled in Charleston as a printer. His Loyalist sympathies, however, forced him to return to England, where he died in 1794. It is not impossible that Helena was born in Charleston, but the use of *America* on title pages of English novels may well have been to allure purchasers. See R. B. Heilman, *America in English Fiction: 1760-1800* (Baton Rouge, 1937), pp. 62 ff.

[77] Wells, *Contantia Neville,* II, 170. Mrs. Hayman's "history" is a narrative of almost one hundred pages, III, 178-275.

both sexes."[78] The journal was penned with a wealth of circumstantial detail after the manner of Defoe and Richardson. Confidence was expressed by the author that the narrative would "descend to late posterity, when most of its contemporaries, founded only in fiction, will have long been forgotten."[79] The journal was also used to heighten the sense of actuality of Captain Farrago's travels in *Modern Chivalry*. Here, as in *The Female American,* the author posed as an editor in possession of the manuscript. "I have occasionally made extracts," he wrote soberly, "and put them in the form of a continued history."[80] John Davis followed this convention in *Walter Kennedy* to chronicle the hero's idyllic married life on the shores of the Mississippi with his noble savage, Oosnooqua, to whom, appropriately enough, Kennedy gave lessons in penmanship![81] Unfortunately Oosnooqua's progress was not quite rapid enough to enable the author to include in his novel a sample of her epistolary style. Samuel Woodworth's *The Champions of Freedom,* an historical novel with a strong infusion of sentiment, also based its claim to authenticity upon a journal. Despite the loss of his right hand in the service of his country, Major Willoughby kept a faithful account of his exploits. "The writing a journal of his military career, was his morning amusement," Woodworth declared, ". . . and, since his misfortune, he had acquired the art of writing an elegant character with his left hand. It is to this journal that I am indebted for the facts here recorded."[82] "Extracts" from the diary of

[78] [Anon.,] *The Female American* (Newburyport, [1800 or 1801?]), I, [iii]. Wegelin dated the first American edition of this novel as early as 1790, but R. W. G. Vail, upon convincing evidence, believes it to be a decade later. The story was first published in London in 1767. There is no evidence to support the claim on the title page that this novel was written by an American. The anonymous author probably used the word *American* to exploit the popular interest in the New World.

[79] *The Female American,* I, [iii]. Dr. Tremaine McDowell has set forth the author's indebtedness to Defoe in "An American Robinson Crusoe," *American Literature,* I, 307-309.

[80] Brackenridge, *Modern Chivalry* (Philadelphia, 1792), I, 150.

[81] *Walter Kennedy* (London, 1805), pp. 159-192.

[82] *The Champions of Freedom* (New York, 1816), I, 14. Woodworth's novel is a good example of the way in which historical fiction was seasoned with sentiment. The author aimed "to soften the rough notes of the bugle by the gentler tones of the lyre . . . and to shift the scene occasionally from the hostile camp to the mansion of love."

Captain George Washington Willoughby, who inherited his father's pen as well as his sword, were also included.[83] The distinction between the letter and the journal is not always maintained in these novels and is not easy to define; usually it is a mere matter of length. Its utility, however, demonstrated expertly by Richardson, was readily exploited by American novelists.

Another type of epistolary novel consisted of letters written, not by the heroine herself, but by a friend in possession of the facts. This method of telling a story by one not immediately concerned in the adventures, provided excellent opportunities for comments upon the conduct of the principal actors. Mrs. Rowson's *Sarah* is an admirable example of this method by which the heroine's friend, Anne, kept her correspondent, Elenor, fully informed. At times she enclosed Sarah's own letters and journals; at others, she suppressed such letters which seemed to contain "no material incidents."[84] Edgar Huntly, in possession of the correspondence of the dead Waldegrave, also acted as epistolary editor. Fearful of the effect of the writer's liberal religious notions upon the mind of his young correspondent, Huntly found censorship necessary: "I resolved merely to select for thy perusal such as were narrative or descriptive."[85]

Pamela and *Clarissa* provided the models for the most popular and, on the whole, the most satisfactory means of presenting a story in epistolary form. Here the letters gain force and conviction by coming directly from the scene of action by the hand of the leading actor. Almost every American Clarissa had her Anna Howe for whom no detail was too minute or no letter too long. Of the seventy letters which comprise *Trials of the Human Heart*, fifty-one were penned by Meriel to her friend, Celia, who, in turn offered advice and consolation. *The Coquette* is perhaps the best example of this popular type. Eliza wrote to her confidante, Lucy, about the events con-

[83] *Ibid.*, II, 131-140, 253-265, 331-335.
[84] *Sarah; or, The Exemplary Wife*, p. 242.
[85] C. B. Brown, *Edgar Huntly*, II, 63.

temporary with her letters; while Deighton, who played the part of a Yankee Jack Belford to Sanford's Lovelace, was regularly informed of the successive stages of the rake's progress. Although letters by other hands appear from time to time, as in *Pamela* and *Clarissa,* the main narrative is carried on by the heroine's own letters. Often the confidante has a mild love affair of her own, as did Lucy, but her life is in the main uneventful. Indeed, anything less than leisure would have presented grave difficulties for one whose chief end in life was to offer advice, encouragement, and solace to her persecuted friend.

In stories told mainly by direct narration, letters often appear as convenient, but incidental, expository and narrative devices. Such partial dependence upon letters seemed to recommend itself to many writers as a less artificial and a more flexible way to carry forward their stories than the strictly epistolary form.[86] Although other novelists occasionally adopted the epistolary form as a mere convention, they made no effort to create an illusion of actual correspondence. Such a novel is Charles Brockden Brown's *Wieland.* The author paid so little attention to the mood of the familiar letter that most readers are quite unaware of the fact that they are supposed to be reading an epistolary novel and come upon Brown's note with

[86] For incidental uses of the letter, see: *The Fille de Chambre,* pp. 76-78, 135-142, 200-206, 216-226, 263-271; *Constantius and Pulchera,* pp. 58-59, 78, 87; *The Algerine Captive,* pp. 37, 38-43, 102-103; *Fortune's Foot-ball,* I, 44, 56-59, 85-87, 118-123, 126, 177; II, 161-163; *Amelia; or, The Faithless Briton,* pp. 14-15, 27-28; *Reuben and Rachel,* pp. 13-20, 25-34, 34-38, 38-40, 41-60, 248-249; *The Fortunate Discovery,* pp. 16-18, 27-37, 135-137; "Story of Margaretta" in *The Gleaner,* I, 76-80, 82-86, 92-96, 108-111, 111-114, 115-18, 119-121, 190-194, 194-199; *The Step-Mother,* I, 179-183; II, 87-95, 103-111, 114-120, 120-127, 128-138, 139-146, 153-157, 163-171, 172-175, 176-181, 188-194, 196-206, 207-210, 231-236; *Julia and the Illuminated Baron,* pp. 79-86, 129-136, 174-181, 241-244; *Constantia Neville,* I, 204-207, 340-348, 358-362; III, 42-46, 86-97, 316-321; *Amelia; or, The Influence of Virtue,* pp. 90-91, 95-97, 99-103, 123-126, 126-130; *Monima,* pp. 24, 26, 35-36, 93, 113-114, 115-116, 121-122, 159-162, 340-341; *Moreland Vale,* pp. 29-32, 33, 57, 61, 63-64; *The Gamesters,* pp. 28-29, 79-80, 82-84, 84-89, 100-103, 125, 129-133; *Glencarn,* I, 102; II, 200-205; *The Champions of Freedom,* I, 85-91, 109, 148-151, 152-162, 244-245, 248-264; II, 15-16, 16-26, 35-46, 71-78, 80-88, 89-94, 96-101, 113, 141-142, 166-173, 174-177, 186-187, 192-197, 201-205, 206-217, 226-234, 269-271, 281, 312-316, 317-326.

genuine surprise. "It will be necessary to add," he wrote, "that this narrative is addressed, in epistolary form, by the Lady whose story it contains, to a small number of friends, whose curiosity in regard to it, had been greatly awakened."[87] Jeremy Belknap's *The Foresters* was also cast in the form of letters, but the device served merely as a framework for the political allegory.[88] In neither of these novels was it more than a handy way of beginning the story.

The artificiality of epistolary fiction is apparent even in the expert hands of Richardson. Without their master's great psychological insight, imitators were led into gross absurdities. The vogue of epistolary fiction, moreover, was declining rapidly at the end of the century, and satirists enjoyed sporting with what appeared to be an overworked convention. The *Port Folio* printed a burlesque of the extravagant diction which embroidered many elegant letters, in an epistle from Isabella Clara Matilda to Sophia Saccharissa Myrtilla.˙ This effusion was solemnly referred "to the consideration of all boarding school misses."[89] Even Caritat, whose shelves groaned beneath so many epistolary novels, recommended to his subscribers a travesty on the letter form "to expose the spun-out superfluities of female chit-chat which is met with in some productions of the epistolary kind."[90] There is much the same sort of criticism in the *Port Folio* in 1802. "What effect such graceless raptures and broken periods may produce on untutored minds, let ten thousand boarding schools witness," a contributor exclaimed. "The taylor's daughter, talks now as familiarly to her confidante, Miss Polly Staytape, of swains and sentiments, as the accomplished dames of genteel life."[91] Parodists also made

---

[87] *Wieland* (New York, 1798), p. [i].

[88] The earlier form of Belknap's allegory as it appeared in the *Columbian Magazine* in 1787 was without the epistolary device. When the story appeared in book form in 1792, he yielded to the popular fashion.

[89] III, 371.

[90] *Explanatory Catalogue*, p. 135. In this issue of the catalogue in 1799 there are 143 titles described as epistolary.

[91] *Port Folio*, II, 107. Another critic discouraged "the unrestricted perusal of Richardson's novels . . . because in a class of young females, of his acquaintance, their conversation and letters, which they were continually transmitting to each other;

merry over the far-fetched ruses employed by persecuted maidens to correspond with their lovers. In "Memoirs of Eliza," the eye of the watchful father "was caught by the rinds of more than a hundred lemons, which lay scattered at his feet . . . and hastening to his daughter's chamber, he stole behind her, and surprised her in the moment of dipping the point of her bodkin into a lemon, for the purpose of tracing the dictates of a bleeding heart to the beloved Frederic, whom she had taught to call forth the latent characters, by exposing the paper to the fire."[92] The failure of most novelists to achieve any individuality in their letters led another satirist to compose a "stock letter" fully warranted to fit into any novel. "It is fraught with style, manner, and sentiment," he wrote maliciously "and the next worthy gentleman, who gives a three guinea novel in two volumes, is welcome to insert it in his work."[93]

Tabitha Tenney included elegant epistolarians among the extravagances of popular fiction at which she poked fun in *Female Quixotism*.[94] Dorcasina Sheldon, who had been nurtured upon an unwholesome diet of sentimental novels from her father's large library, became the laughingstock of the countryside when she emulated the models of behavior set forth in her favorite romances. She asserted she would have been unhappy "not to have had either a friend, to whom she could confide the secret of her love, or a maid who could be bribed by an enamorado, to place a letter in her way, and then confidentially assert that she knew not from whence it came."[95] Pleased with the transports of joy with which heroines usually greeted letters from their lovers, Dorcasina vowed she would not exchange her Patrick's epistles "for all the treasures of

were nothing but a studied attempt to imitate the sentimental idioms &c. of *Clarissa Harlowe*" (*ibid.*, II, 217).

[92] *Ibid.*, III, 307.   [93] *Ibid.*, II, 107.

[94] *Female Quixotism* (Boston, 1825). Miss Tenney's amusing satire had for its model *The Female Quixote; or, The Adventures of Arabella* by the American-born Charlotte Lennox. Mrs. Lennox had burlesqued English novels of sentiment. Her work appeared in London in 1752. Mrs. Lennox's claims to the title of the first American novelist are set forth by G. H. Maynadier in *The First American Novelist?* (Cambridge, Mass., 1940).   [95] *Ibid.*, I, 11.

Peru." "She had got them arranged in perfect order, tied with a silken string . . . ," wrote Miss Tenney. "Taking the first in order, she kissed the seal and super-scription; then, after opening it, and pressing the inside upon her heart, she read it three times over."[96] Lysander, a sensible suitor, was rejected indignantly because he had failed to master the sentimental style. "She compared it with various letters in her favourite authors; and found it so widely different in style and sentiment, that she abhorred the idea of a connexion with a person who could be the author of it."[97]

The marked decrease in the number of epistolary novels by the turn of the century may have been due in part to a recognition of the fact that the possibilities of the form had been exhausted. The essential artificiality of letter fiction had been further accentuated by the clumsiness of beginners. Tales of sentimental analysis were yielding in popularity to Gothic and historical novels which seemed less adaptable to the letter form. Epistolary novels, however, still appeared occasionally, and the individual letter proved a serviceable device, used incidentally, in fiction better suited to direct narration.

For most of the hesitating beginners who wrote our early novels, the letter fiction of Samuel Richardson and his followers in England rendered yeomanly service. To the moralist, it furnished a handy mold into which he could pour his homilies. To the educator, still slightly distrustful of romances, it offered many sugar-coated lessons on a wide variety of edifying subjects. To the sentimentalist, it provided an unrivaled means of depicting every tremor of the feeling heart. To the aspiring bluestocking, like Judith Sargent Murray, it seemed to promise, without long apprenticeship, an easy leap to literary fame. The escritoires of eighteenth-century females were bursting with chatty letters. All that seemed necessary to convert them into an elegant and improving novel was a little heightening here and there, a slight re-ordering of events, the addition of a few stock characters and striking situations easily borrowed from the popular lending libraries, and, before one was

[96] *Ibid.,* I, 151. [97] *Ibid.,* I, 19.

aware of it—the thing was done. And if the result happened to be an artless, go-as-you-please sort of narrative, without either depth of insight or distinction of form, the author's ample compensation was the assurance that in some bosom the tale invoked a responsive sigh, or that it guided the "sedulous aspirings" of the feeling heart.

IV

STERNE AND SENSIBILITY

Hail Sensibility! Ye eloquent *tears* of *beauty!* that add dignity to human
nature by correcting its foibles—it was *these* that corrected my faults when
recrimination would have failed of success—it was *these* that opened every
avenue of contrition in my heart, when *words* would have dammed up
every sluice of repentance.

—William Hill Brown, *The
Power of Sympathy,* 1789.

To PROCEED FROM the *sentimentalism* of Samuel Richardson to
the *sensibility* of Laurence Sterne is to move from the comfortable, if somewhat stuffy domestic circle, secure abode of all
the household virtues, to a moonlit garden where weeping willows encircle an interesting ruin, and an engaging softness
melts "the genial currents of the soul." Here in the transfigur-
ing mists, Justice dissolves to Benevolence, Puritan Duty is
meliorated to Pity, and stern Conscience becomes subtilized
until it bends gracefully to Inclination.

It was precisely this distinction between conscience and
impulse, between punctilio and ecstasy, which Richardson had
rigorously observed in his novels and which in turn commended them to respectable readers in England and America.
They had found in his sentimentalism familiar elements which
had appeared earlier in the century in the works of Steele and
Lillo. Sentiment took her accustomed place by the family
hearth and with a matronly air imparted friendly counsel of
prudence and circumspection. She would have shuddered with
horror at the extravagant lengths to which feeling had been
carried by writers in the decade following Richardson's death.
With them, sentiment lost her Philistine character and feeling
became an end in itself.

Laurence Sterne was high priest of the cult of sensibility.
This pleasant savorer of exquisite sensations was easily the first

of those forces responsible for the vogue of sensibility in American fiction. No other English writer whose influence is to be found in our early novels seemed at once so disquieting and so significant.[1] In the half-light of sensibility, benevolence seemed to blend with indulgence; even moralists found it a bit difficult to distinguish delicacy from looseness in the mysterious shades of the finer feelings.

Critics immediately perceived the seductive nature of this new menace. "I suppose few writers have done more injury to morals than Sterne," charged a contributor to the *New England Quarterly* in 1802. "Formerly, if a man felt a passion for the wife or mistress of his friend, he was conscious at least, that, if he persisted in the pursuit, he was acting wrong; and if the Novel Writer invented such a character, it was to hold him out as an object of detestation and punishment. Now this is so varnished over with delicate attachment and generous sensibility, that the most shocking acts of perfidy and seduction are committed not only without remorse, but with self-complacency. . . ."[2] The obscenity and vulgarity which Mrs. Foster had found objectionable in Jonathan Swift carried their own antidote and seemed to her "much less pernicious in their tendency than those of Sterne." "They are not so enchanting in their nature, nor so subtle in their effects," she complained in *The Boarding School,* as in Sterne's "noxious insinuations of licentious wit . . . concealed under the artful blandishments of sympathetic sensibility. . . ."[3] Although he admired Sterne's "pathetic and tender strokes," Jacob Duché had the same objection to offer. "But still I am not quite satisfied," he told an admirer of Yorick, "that the feelings he described are anything more than those we have in common with the brute creation,

---

[1] Sensibility also filtered into this country through the novels of Rousseau, Brooke, Griffith, Mackenzie, Goldsmith, and Pratt. There is an excellent summary of sensibility in early American fiction in Tremaine McDowell's "Sensibility in the Eighteenth Century American Novel," *Studies in Philology,* XXIV, 383-402. Dr. McDowell found "sensibility in some form in every novel of the century save *The Oriental Philanthropist. . . .*" This last novel, however, contains certain humanitarian interests with which sensibility is often blended.

[2] *New England Quarterly* (Boston, 1802), III, 84.

[3] *The Boarding School,* p. 205.

at least that there is anything heavenly in them . . . otherwise passion may get the name of virtue, and a finely tempered frame become the only Heaven we would wish for."[4] Sterne's popularity also alarmed a moralist in the *Massachusetts Magazine*. "But too many, especially persons of warm passions and tender feelings," he lamented, "are too apt to be captivated with everything which drops from his descriptive, though loose and unguarded pen, and, in swallowing the nectar, to swallow what is enflaming and poisonous."[5] The justice of much of this criticism was acknowledged in 1789 by the editor of *The Beauties of Sterne*. "The chaste part of the world complain so loudly of the obscenity which taints the writings of Sterne, and, indeed, with some reason," he admitted, "that those readers were not suffered to penetrate beyond the title page of his *Tristram Shandy*. . . ."[6] It was for such readers that only the most unexceptionable of Sterne's "Beauties" were published separately in a chaste anthology, "Selected for the Heart of Sensibility."[7]

Sensibility! No word will appear more frequently in the ensuing pages; no word was at once so sacred and so silly, so prone to invoke ecstatic rhapsody and callous parody. To define it one must learn not only to read between the lines, but between feverish asterisks, hectic exclamation points, and quivering dashes. Fully to sense its hallowed associations, the chords of one's own sensorium must vibrate sympathetically with those of the votaries of feeling. Its vocabulary was "the silent language of the eye" and "the elocution of the soul." Not to luxuriate in every connotation was to lose caste forever with the cult of the emotionally elect. Its range reached from sensual indulgence to angelic compassion, from "fiddling harmonics on the strings of sensualism" to the music of the

---

[4] *Observations on a Variety of Subjects*, pp. 208-209.

[5] *Massachusetts Magazine*, II, 329.

[6] *The Beauties of Sterne* (Philadelphia, 1789), p. iv.

[7] The editor of an edition of *The Beauties of Sterne* published in Boston in 1807 objected "that the dread of offending the ear of Chastity, so laudable in itself, has . . . been carried to an excess, thereby depriving us of many most laughable scenes . . . and that, upon the whole, the past compilers of Sterne . . . kept their eye rather upon his morality than his humour."

spheres. Novelists exhibited a becoming reverence as they approached the magic word. To define was to defile. The sensitive plant always shrank at the approach of the botanist. For the reader of true sensibility, definition was unnecessary; for the soul devoid of feeling, it was futile. If writers hesitated to define sensibility, they vied with each other in composing apostrophes to its sovereign powers. "Blest Sensibility! Exquisite meliorator of the mind! Touched by the magic of thy wand, the heart finds grief delicious!" Thus sang Davis in *Ferdinand and Elizabeth.*[8] "Hail *Sensibility!* Sweetener of the joys of life!" caroled the author of *The Power of Sympathy.* ". . . *Sensibility* is the good *Samaritan,* who taketh him by the hand, and consoleth him, and poureth wine and oil into his wounds. Thou art a pleasant companion—a grateful friend— and a *neighbour* to those who are destitute of shelter.—"[9] Thus was sensibility often associated with humanitarianism; it concerned itself with the misfortunes of old soldiers and slaves as well as with kindness to donkeys. The ready sympathies of Thomas Jefferson responded to the implications of the word, and, although he was a foe of fiction, he was moved to pronounce "The writings of Sterne . . . the best course of morality that ever was written."[10] Even that doughty Federalist, Joseph Dennie, who found few of Jefferson's ideas palatable, was in complete accord on this point. Sterne's sensibility, he wrote in 1796, was "worth a million cold homilies." He also endorsed Yorick's observation "that every time we smile, and still more every time we laugh, it adds something to the fragment of life."[11]

Although *sensibility* was used less comprehensively than *sentiment,* and usually lacked the moral connotations given the word by Richardson, to whom it was often synonymous with *sententiousness,* the meanings frequently overlapped. Sensibility even acquired a Platonic tinge when it was employed to describe Sterne's love of Eliza. ". . . had you, worthy lady,'

[8] *Ferdinand and Elizabeth,* p. 120.
[9] W. H. Brown, *The Power of Sympathy,* II, 32-33.
[10] Ford (ed.), *The Writings of Thomas Jefferson,* IV, 429.
[11] *The Lay Preacher* (Walpole, 1796), p. 40.

wrote Charles to Caroline in *Infidelity,* "only reverted to that sublime and disinterested passion for a married woman, which filled the sentimental bosom of Yorick, the model of my ambition;—you would, nay, could not have proved so ungenerous as to dash in my face, an offering so pure. . . ."[12] A belief in the unselfishness of sensibility may be inferred from the query of "Ethicus" in the *Port Folio.* "Is not an excess of sensibility," he asked, "of all things the farthest removed, from an excess of egotism?"[13] Undiscriminating readers professed to see little difference between sentiment and sensibility. Richardson and Sterne were lumped together by Letitia in *The Contrast* in order to account for the conduct of the heroine. "Why, she read Sir Charles Grandison, Clarissa Harlowe, Shenstone and the Sentimental Journal [*sic*]," she declared.[14] In the same comedy, Van Rough also identified sensibility with moral sentiment when he attributed Maria's conduct to her reading "your Charles Grandisons, your Sentimental Journals [*sic*] . . . and such other trumpery."[15]

Since the possession of sensibility became a requisite of emotional respectability, writers were at great pains to display its manifestations and to define its attributes. Indeed, the process of determining whether or not one was blessed with this highly prized quality was not unlike the methods employed by Calvinists seeking for signs of their spiritual salvation. The accompanying symptoms were certainly often the same. Swoons, trances, visions, languishings, ecstasies, and a variety of emotional delirium tremens were all welcomed as evidences of "election." Those interested in the component parts of a soul of sensibility were treated to an account of an autopsy of a man of superior delicacy. "Nature seems to have taken uncommon pains, to have used uncommonly refined and subtle materials,

---

[12] Relf, *Infidelity,* p. 91. The much debated relationship between Yorick and Eliza presented "a nice point" for moralists. Although one apologist defended it as the "closest union that purity could possibly admit of," there were others such as John Davis, who felt constrained to qualify his admiration with the reminder that "Yorick had a wife of his own." See *Ferdinand and Elizabeth,* p. 17; *Massachusetts Magazine,* I, 14, 99, 160, 638.   [13] V, 145.

[14] R. Tyler, *The Contrast* (Philadelphia, 1790), Act I, scene i, p. 4.

[15] *Ibid.,* Act I, scene ii, p. 11.

in the construction of his *sensorium*," reported the specialist in this new science of the soul, "and to have lined the passage from thence to the heart, with the most delicate texture. His passions are irresistible; they either melt the whole frame, almost to apparent dissolution, or strain every nerve to the highest point of tension. . . . His soul seems a pure ethereal flame, residing at all the avenues of sense."[16] With passions so strong and physique so fragile, it is not surprising that the autopsy should have revealed his nerves as "being as it were one continued sore from a peculiar delicacy of feeling."[17] Charles Brockden Brown might have cited this case as an instance of spontaneous combustion by excessive sensibility.

The best diagnosticians were in friendly disagreement upon the vexed question whether it was the heart or the soul from which sensibility emanated. By a happy compromise, the sensorium was selected as the seat of this exquisite element. Sensibility and soul were, however, closely related. "I feel *that I have a soul*—and every man of sensibility feels it within himself," maintained the hero of *The Power of Sympathy*.[18] "Indeed a man without sensibility," he added, "exhibits no sign of a soul."[19] Mrs. Rowson, on the other hand, was the leader of those who were convinced that "the heart was the seat of sensibility."[20] She was supported by a writer on "Anatomy" in the *Massachusetts Magazine*, who found the source to be the heart, "this nervous center . . . this plexus, the seat of sensibility!"[21] Margaretta's sensibility was discernible without microscopic analysis. "Hers is seated in her animated eye," wrote the author, "and but one glance of hers will convince you. . . ."[22] Wherever it was, all men agreed that there was a powerful and subtle bond between sensibility and physical well-being. In *Glencarn*, George Watterston tried to prove "that happiness is the result of a certain physical organization of the nerves, modified by habits of virtue."[23] There was no dissent from the

---

[16] *Massachusetts Magazine*, II, 47-48.   [17] *Ibid.*, II, 48.
[18] W. H. Brown, *The Power of Sympathy*, II, 29.
[19] *Ibid.*, II, 155.
[20] *The Inquisitor*, II, 88.   [21] *Massachusetts Magazine*, I, 20.
[22] [Anon.,] *Margaretta*, p. 33.   [23] *Glencarn*, I, 3.

conclusion reached by the author of *The Hapless Orphan* who decided, "There is an inexpressible sympathy between the mind and the body; they are mutually affected."[24]

Of all the cherished tokens of sensibility, the tear was at once the most common and the most precious. The eye became the chief seat of expression for all sons and daughters of feeling. "The most striking feature of the face, and that to which we most frequently direct our view, is *the eye*," corroborated an essayist in the *Port Folio*. "There is more in it, than shape, motion, or colour; there is thought and passion, there is life and soul; there is reason and speech."[25]   In this language of the eye, tears were the most eloquent pleaders. They were infallible signs of grace in the religion of the heart. "For ever honoured be the sacred drop of humanity," Susanna Rowson rhapsodized in *Charlotte*, "the angel of mercy shall record its source, and the soul from whence it sprang shall be immortal."[26]   Tears were the most acceptable tributes in courtship. "His countenance is expressive," Caroline wrote of Evremond, "his eyes beam with understanding and glisten with sensibility."[27]   Reuben's character was similarly enhanced in the estimation of Rebecca when she tested his sensibility by recounting a tale of delicate distress. He met the ordeal triumphantly, the heroine reported after the examination, for his "eyes glistened with the dew of sensibility."[28]   Eliza's suitor in *The Coquette* manifested his sensibility eloquently during his proposal of marriage. "He spoke with emphasis," she noted with approval. "The tear of sensibility sparkled in his eye."[29]   Eliza responded with a sympathetic shower of her own. "I flew with extacy to my mamma," she wrote later to a friend. "She was unable to speak. I was equally so. We therefore indulged, a moment, the pleasing emotions of sympathizing sensibility."[30]   Humble

[24] [Anon.,] *The Hapless Orphan*, I, 85.   [25] IV, 189.
[26] *Charlotte*, II, 93.
[27] [Anon.,] *The Hapless Orphan*, I, 69.
[28] S. H. Rowson, *Reuben and Rachel* (Boston, 1798), II, 272.
[29] Foster, *The Coquette*, p. 42. Tears also served Mr. Boyer when he severed the engagement. "I gave free scope to the sensibility of my heart," he wrote, "and the effeminate relief of tears materially lightened the load which oppressed me."
[30] *Ibid.*, p. 97.

maidens without a dowry learned that tears were riches enough. "If your bosom, lovely Rebecca, glows with sensibility," the noble Sir George assured her, "every obstacle is easily removed."[31] Rebecca, of course, lost little time in convincing Sir George by giving vent to "a hallowed flood" that drowned her eyes. Writers of sentimental fiction proceeded upon the assumption that tears, like murder, will always out. Thus Monima, a true votary of sensibility, endeavored to hide her feelings only to find that "the big drops would, in spite of herself, swell into her eyes, and discharge themselves on her agitated tucker."[32] Although sensibility was generally believed to have been a strictly modern virtue, an infallible sign of man's progress and perfectibility, Mrs. Rowson could not resist making over Christopher Columbus into a modern man of feeling. When the great voyager shed "scalding tears" in the presence of his Queen in *Reuben and Rachel,* we are told that "Isabelle rose from her seat, her own eyes glistening with the dew of sensibility...."[33]

Ordinary weeping was not enough to satisfy the more exquisite devotees of the cult of the "hanky" and the tear. Milkmaids were permitted to have out their cry and be comforted, but the refined daughters of sensibility shed tears which played fantastic tricks before high Heaven. Monima's had the distinction of vaporizing readily: "The compounded tear of adverse fate and sweet humanity rested on her cheek, whose warmth diffused it with gentlest exhalations, and they mounted as a sacrifice of innocence, and persecuted worth."[34] Tear-tracking became a popular pastime indulged in by the more privileged. Will de Burling resorted to this method of complimenting Margaretta. "The tear trickled down her cheek, and dropped on her hand," he wrote in triumph. "I bowed over her, and kissed it off."[35] Most sentimental lovers were adepts in this

[31] Rowson, *The Fille de Chambre,* pp. 81-82.
[32] Read, *Monima,* p. 29.
[33] *Reuben and Rachel,* I, 37. Columbus was also made to speak the language of sensibility: "If a tear does start at the thought of parting, I also know you will wipe it off unseen, lest it should unman the heart of your adoring Columbus."
[34] Read, *Monima,* p. 165.   [35] [Anon.,] *Margaretta,* p. 36.

curious technique. Mrs. Wood noted with satisfaction the adroit competence of Sir William in *Amelia:* "With his arm affectionately round her waist, he pressed her to his glowing bosom, and kissed off the tear, which trembled like the pearly dew-drop upon the rose of her lovely cheek."[36] Monima, who attained some skill at this game, rarely missed a tear. "As she sang, a tear of bitter remembrance glided over the furrowed cheek of her father. She did not observe it till she finished. One little tear glistened from the rays of Debby's lamp, about midway from his eye. Monima saw it, and kissed it off."[37]

To the uninitiated, tears, like the stars, might appear to be all alike. The connoisseur, however, found pleasure in distinguishing between their various glories. "There are tears of *pleasure* as well as tears of *distress!*" observed Keate in "The Family Picture." "The latter are excited by our *own sufferings;* the former are the involuntary tribute which *Sensibility* pays to *Virtue!*"[38] A more subtle distinction was drawn by a comforter in *The Inquisitor.* "A tear had fallen upon her cheek, another stood glittering in her eye," he observed carefully. "The first was a tear of suspense, the last of joy. I kissed them both away. . . ."[39] Especially sweet were lovers' tears. As one of Margaretta's fell upon the hand of Vernon, he met the soft challenge in the approved style. "If I could condense thee, little drop, to the hardness of a diamond," he cried, "I would place thee as a precious tribute from a precious heart, on my bosom, and neither prosperity nor adversity should tear thee hence."[40] Even without such condensation, Margaretta's tears seemed to possess unusual powers of endurance. After an absence of a fortnight from her mother's home, the daughter wrote, "The tear is still wet upon my cheek!"[41] An instance of less miraculous durability was recorded by a writer in the *Massachusetts Magazine.* "The crystal which stole forth in the morning from my eye lids," he testified, "holds its place at the

[36] S. S. B. K. Wood, *Amelia; or, The Influence of Virtue* (Portsmouth [1802?]), p. 228. The heroine replied appropriately: "I felt the impressions of his lips, which gathered my tears."   [37] Read, *Monima,* pp. 252-253.
[38] *Massachusetts Magazine,* I, 158.   [39] Rowson, *The Inquisitor,* I, 62.
[40] [Anon.,] *Margaretta,* p. 257.   [41] Murray, *The Gleaner,* I, 76.

midnight hour."[42] Monima's tears cavorted about strangely. "This tear did not assuage her sorrow," remarked the author, "it lingered about her heart, and trembled through her nerves."[43] Heaven without tears seemed inconceivable to Gray as he thought of his departed Sophia. "Ah! perhaps she now sees me; perhaps the tear of celestial pity trembles in her eye; if tears of pity can be shed in heaven, she sheds them for me."[44] Some heroines, supremely confident that it would not be unregarded, were content to drop a single tear; others were more prodigal. "I am reading the story of La Roche," wrote Sophia, who belonged to the school of copious weepers, "my tears fall on it like rain, I cannot see to go on."[45] The sons and daughters of sensibility dropped tears as fast as the Arabian trees their medicinable gum. Such constant showering forced authors to practice considerable ingenuity to avoid commonplace repetition. Novelists desperate for synonyms would have been well advised to subscribe for the Massachusetts Magazine. The numerous elegant variations of nomenclature resorted to by contributors to this popular periodical made it an admirable thesaurum lacrimarum for the cult of sensibility.[46]

Tears and sensibility were both highly contagious, and the soul of sensibility rarely failed to respond in the presence of grief or misfortune. "There is a principle in human nature," wrote the author of Monima, "that is creative of sympathy between souls of the same cast...."[47] Two such souls were those of Mrs. Virgillius and Miranda Stewart; their chords of sensibility vibrated in a delicious harmony. "Then a fresh flood came flowing, attended with the inmost sobbings of her heart," Miranda noted. "The chords of mine trembled; and I accompanied her sobs, with a tear."[48] A scene of contagious sensibil-

---

[42] Massachusetts Magazine, III, 95.   [43] Read, Monima, p. 312.
[44] Vicery, Emily Hamilton, p. 29.   [45] Watterston, Glencarn, II, 204.
[46] A few samples, ranging from the glisten to the sob, will indicate to what lengths writers went in quest of dainty variety: "Gush of rapture," "lucid emanation," "kindly showers," "dew of humanity," "silent streams," "watery petitioner," "hallowed floods," "melting language of the ever-speaking eye," "gems of the morning," "tenderest drops of affection," "dews of charity," "balm of compassion," "pure drops of celestial sensibility," "chrystal wanderer," "dropping clouds," "warm current of compassion," "humid drops," and "dew of angelick compassion."
[47] Read, Monima, p. 328.   [48] [Anon.,] Margaretta, p. 53.

ity was minutely described by the author of *Infidelity* in which the victim, "pressing a screaming infant to her breast, mingling with its milk the tears of her affliction," found that her "two elder children, leaning on each side, catched the bitter sighs of their mother with tender hearts which seemed to float in the water of their eyes."[49] Mercutio's feverish sensibility in *Fortune's Foot-ball* threatened to have serious consequences for the sympathetic Isabella, "whose heart, tender as the orb of sight, had caught the sweet infection . . . with a sudden tremor, which thrilled like lightning through the deepest, and most intricate recesses of it."[50] No one was immune at the reunion between Maria and Henry Kittle. "Meanwhile the spectators found themselves wonderfully affected," wrote Mrs. Bleecker. "The tender contagion ran from bosom to bosom—they wept aloud; and the house of joy seemed to be the house of lamentation."[51] James Butler yearned for the brush "of the immortal Raphael, to paint the emotions of the whole family" at the moment of separation. "Not an eye present but shed the tear of real affection!" he declared. "Not a heart but palpitated in perfect unison!"[52] An equally well-trained chorus of sensibility was described in "The Funeral." "The ceremony was begun: the corpse was deposited in its narrow cell," chronicled a witness of the scene. "Tears flowed more freely from the eyes of the mourners . . . the spectators dropped theirs in unison."[53]

Mrs. Rowson was confident she would be understood when she recorded an instance of contagious sensibility in *The Inquisitor*. "He attempted to speak, but was forced to stop— something rose in his throat—I felt the same in mine—but what that was," she concluded, "I will leave to the imagination of every reader of sensibility."[54] The force of the sweet contagion proved too much for Caroline's powers of resistance. "I continued insensibly silent," she wrote bravely, "until the load

<hr/>

[49] Relf, *Infidelity*, p. 121.   [50] Butler, *Fortune's Foot-ball*, I, 117.

[51] Bleecker, *The Posthumous Works*, p. 83. The happy couple responded to each other's moods with amazing speed: ". . . they wept—they smiled—they mourned, and rejoiced alternately, with an abrupt transition from one passion to another."

[52] *Fortune's Foot-ball*, I, 34.

[53] *New York Weekly Magazine*, II, 44.   [54] *The Inquisitor*, II, 98.

at my heart bursting from my eyes, afforded an alleviation by a torrent of tears. : . ."[55] Even the dumb animals were represented as matching sob for sob in sympathy with their masters' woes. "The only comfort I now have is in this little dog," asserted the sufferer in "The Lover's Grave." "Here, the live long day he attends me, and will often drop tear for tear with me."[56] Readers may consider this to be a burlesque only at the peril of forfeiting whatever claims they may possess to membership in the cult of sensibility. The *Port Folio* quoted from a letter by Sterne to an admirer who was interested in this subject of sympathetic sensibility. "A true feeler always brings half the entertainment along with him . . . ," Yorick explained, "and the vibrations in him so entirely correspond with those excited, it is like reading himself and not the book."[57] Fearful of the effects of too concentrated a sensibility in "true feelers" of this description, the editor of *The Beauties of Sterne* considerately inserted "breathers" between the more exquisite episodes. "I intended to have arranged them alphabetically," he pointed out in his Preface, "till I found the stories of *Le Fevre,* the *Monk* and *Maria,* would be too closely connected for the *feeling reader,* and would wound the bosom of *sensibility* too deeply: I therefore placed them at a proper distance from each other."[58]

If tears were presumptive evidence of the heart of sensibility, swoons were proof conclusive. Margaretta's picturesque fainting spells were proudly described by her mother, who wisely refused to worry about serious after-effects. "My daughter," she wrote, ". . . frequently changed colour; the lily and the rose seemed to chase each other upon her now mantling, and now pallid cheek. . . ."[59] Polly recovered from her not unwelcome swoon to find herself in the arms of her lover: " 'O, Mr. Danford,' said I. And indeed that was all I could say; for the interview was too much for my weak frame of body to bear; and I fainted in his arms, which greatly perplexed the

[55] Relf, *Infidelity,* p. 98.   [56] *New York Magazine,* VI, 652.

[57] *Port Folio,* III, 290. Quoted from a letter to "Dr. Eustace of North Carolina," who had written to express his enthusiasm about *Tristram Shandy.*

[58] *The Beauties of Sterne,* p. v.   [59] Murray, *The Gleaner,* I, 279.

company; but they soon recovered me again."[60] Heroines were not unaware of the strategic advantages of well-timed swooning. Margaretta's looks were improved by such experiences: ". . . an almost lifeless corse, her lips yet moved, and every charming feature received an extatic kind of ejaculatory impression."[61] It is to be feared that the egoism which taints sensibility was often responsible for these suspensions of consciousness. The practiced votary of sensibility could induce his chords of sympathy to vibrate almost at will, and thus achieve the desired trance by a form of emotional self-abuse. Monima certainly enjoyed the two-ply thrill of being mourned over as dead and receiving congratulations upon revival, although she played fast and loose with the feelings of her aged father. The author took full advantage of the scene: "The roses and lilies faded on her beauteous face, and made room for the yellow hue of death! Sunken and hollow became the countenance. . . . But for once Fate befriended the woe-worn man . . . Monima gave signs of returning life, and . . . blessed her father with a transcendent smile."[62] Sly puss, Monima! But not quite sly enough to hide in that "transcendent smile" the complacency of carrying off triumphantly a "strong scene" so popular with theatergoers and novel readers. Mrs. Rowson's Sarah felt something stronger than a mere swoon was needed to do complete justice to her condition when she saw Jessy with the Marquis. "The momentary suspension of my faculties could hardly be called a swoon . . . ," she wrote indignantly. "I seemed petrified . . . I remained above half an hour a mere passive machine in the hands of the housekeeper. . . ."[63] Fortunately for Sarah, a bona-fide *female* housekeeper!

The woes of men of feeling were a curious mixture of regret and rhetoric. Henry Kittle's outburst was too self-conscious to be indicative of anything more than his own egoism. "Stop here unhappy man!" he declaimed. "Here let the fibres of thy heart crack with excrutiating misery—let the

[60] [Anon.,] *Fidelity Rewarded*, p. 60.
[61] Murray, *The Gleaner*, I, 284.   [62] Read, *Monima*, p. 421.
[63] *Sarah; or, The Exemplary Wife*, p. 204.

cruel view of mangled wretches, so nearly allied to thee, extort drops of blood from thy cleaving bosom!" Even the author yielded to the rhythmic sway. "It did—it did," Mrs. Bleecker wrote as if in a trance. "Uttering a deep groan he fell insensible from his horse. . . ."[64] Rainforth was also guilty of shameless posturing at the news of his father's bankruptcy. "You never can be mine, Meriel: never!" he cried in heroic style. "Oh my heart, yet hold a little, burst not till I have told my gentle love, how much this resignment costs me."[65] Whatever the cost, this rhetorical display provided sweet compensation.

The effects of sensibility were at times violent enough to tax the strongest powers of description and to invoke strange images. Mrs. Bleecker could find nothing in all nature to do complete justice to the heaving bosom of Maria except "Ontario-Lake, when agitated by fierce winds."[66] Sarah's unusual manifestation of sensibility at her wedding ruined her happiness as well as her bridal gown. "Tears rose to my eyes; I endeavoured to chase them back to my swelling heart; I succeeded," she recalled sadly, "but the consequences were worse than had I suffered them to flow; for just as the clergyman pronounced us man and wife, my nose gushed out blood; my handkerchief and clothes were suffused with the crimson torrent. . . ."[67] Frightful results usually followed the drying of the wells of tears. "I have wept the fountains of my eyes dry, and now they burn and shoot," Sarah wrote, "while my heart that lately swelled and struggled even to agony, seems like an icicle in my bosom, as torpid and as cold."[68] The daughters of sensibility seemed to have almost infinite capacity for suffering. Sarah was sometimes embarrassed at the stoutness of her own heart. After bidding farewell to her brother in what she supposed was to have been her valedictory letter, she found it necessary to explain later that "the human heart is not so easily broken as is generally believed; oft may it be lacerated until it

[64] *The Posthumous Works,* p. 44.
[65] Rowson, *Trials of the Human Heart,* I, 143-144.
[66] *The Posthumous Works,* p. 33.
[67] Rowson, *Sarah; or, The Exemplary Wife,* p. 6.
[68] *Ibid.,* p. 203.

bleeds to the very quick; oft may it be wrung until every fibre cracks, and yet it will beat and supply the vital stream that nourishes existence."[69] Although Sarah ultimately succumbed to her woes, the resiliency which she described must have accounted for many of the surprising recoveries in these novels. "My heart dropped blood, the cold sweat of agony oozed out of every pore," wrote Glencarn of his sufferings.[70] Happily, he recovered, as did the father of Lucy who was seized by "a fever and a strong delirium." "I was for three weeks insensible to miseries almost beyond the strength of human nature to support . . . and my life was despaired of," he recollected in later years.[71] Made wary by so many "deathbed" recoveries, the calloused reader of sentimental fiction soon learns to regard the deathrattle itself with skepticism. Only at the sound of the earth being thrown over the coffin may one be reasonably certain.

Temporary suspension of the faculties was often serious enough, even though the victim bounced back into health. Jenny, seduced by the ruse of a false marriage in *The Fille de Chambre*, "became so violent, that she was unable to proceed. . . . For several days she was unable to give us any account of what had befallen her. She was feverish, sometimes delirious, and when any lucid intervals appeared, too weak and languid to be capable of speaking more than two or three words at a time."[72] Amelia, another hapless victim of a bogus marriage ceremony, "fell senseless to the ground. For a while, convulsive motion shook her frame, but gradually subsiding, the flame of life seemed to be extinct, and all her terrors at an end."[73] The more exquisite the sensibility, the greater the suffering. "I fear she will fall a victim to that exquisite sensibility she so largely possesses," Caroline predicted of a friend in *The Hapless Orphan*, "and sink with the weight of her affliction to the grave. Repose has fled her couch; her pillow is wet with the dew of

---

[69] *Ibid.*, p. 260.
[70] Watterston, *Glencarn*, II, 213.   [71] Rowson, *Charlotte*, I, 20.
[72] Rowson, *The Fille de Chambre*, p. 126.
[73] [Anon.,] *Amelia; or, The Faithless Briton*, p. 15.

sorrow. . . ."[74] Whatever claims to "modernity" may be made
for Charles Brockden Brown's heroine, Constantia Dudley, she
remained a true child of her time in yielding to the slightest
touch of emotion. The sound of the voice of a returned friend
sent her into a swoon. "The torrent of emotion was too abrupt
and too vehement," wrote a witness of the scene. "Her faculties
were overwhelmed, and she sunk upon the floor motionless
and without sense. . . ."[75]

Male sensibility was no less susceptible and extravagant.
Upon seeing the innocent Rachel in a compromising situation
which she could have explained easily in a moment, Hamden
and Courtney went into hysterics. The former "reeled against
a post, staggered and fell," while Courtney "attempted to
speak, but his voice failed him; he gasped, groaned, and fell
to the floor."[76] A meeting between Mercutio and Charles in
Fortune's Foot-ball threw the friends into a "mutual transport"
and "shackled their organs of speech for several minutes."
Mercutio described "the sudden shock, which, like the swift-
winged, vivid lightning, has penetrated to the very centre of
my soul—stunned my whole fabric—and unhinged all my
senses."[77] The extravagance of Henry Kittle's grief reveals the
relish for strong scenes which was frequently gratified in sentimental fiction. "Again, in the furious extravagance of passion," wrote Mrs. Bleecker, "he tore the hair from his head, and
casting himself prostrate on the ashes, he gathered the crumbling bones to his bosom, while the big drops of anguish issued
at every pore, till life, unable longer to sustain the mental conflict, suspended her powers, and once more deprived him of
sensation."[78]

Although sensibility is often to be seen under the stress of
catastrophic action, Sterne had taught that the merest trifle
might be freighted with exquisite sensations. "It is a matter of

---

[74] [Anon.,] *The Hapless Orphan*, II, 148. Caroline also languished from excessive
sensibility. To those who attempted to comfort her, she replied, "But medicine will
not heal a bleeding heart."

[75] *Ormond*, p. 257.

[76] Rowson, *Reuben and Rachel*, II, 333-334.

[77] Butler, *Fortune's Foot-ball*, I, 77-78.   [78] *The Posthumous Works*, p. 47.

associations," Dr. Tompkins remarked, "and the nerves respond to the least twitch on the spider-fine filaments of memory and pity."[79] Thus Worthy, who responded to the slightest feather-prick of the feelings, was thrilled by touching a piece of embroidery which Myra had worked upon as a little girl. "It shall yield more fragrance to my soul," he declared, "than all the *boquets* of the universe."[80] Mrs. Bloomsgrove also believed that the emotion itself, rather than its source, was the important consideration. She taught her children not to kill flies "for their presumption in invading the houses of mortals," but to usher them to the door gently, "saying, 'It is an innocent creature, my dear, do not hurt it; is not the world wide enough for you both?' "[81] Uncle Toby's liberation of the fly in *Tristram Shandy* inspired Russell to spare some robins in order "that the annals of benevolence may no longer record the Shandian ebulition as a solitary instance."[82] "Blest innocents!" he cried as he dropped his fowling piece, "go, warble in the ear of the maternal bird, and glad, by your sweet carols, the domestic nest; narrate, my little flutterers, how you have disarmed your enemy, and say, that against lives so unoffending, his hand shall never more be raised."[83]

Few of Richardson's admirers had anything to say about their master as a stylist. With Sterne, on the other hand, manner was everything. Readers of American periodicals soon learned to detect with sinking hearts the signs of an approaching Sternesque fragment. Sometimes the "pathetic morceau" was flanked by an elegant steel engraving with its inevitable representation of a marble urn and a sensitive plant to help induce the particular variety of trance needed to enable the reader

[79] *The Popular Novel in England: 1770-1800*, p. 96.

[80] W. H. Brown, *The Power of Sympathy*, I, 74.

[81] Hitchcock, *Memoirs of the Bloomsgrove Family*, I, 212. Uncle Toby has much to answer for in the numerous invocations to the fly in American novels. There is a typical instance in C. M. Warren's *The Gamesters:* "Leander was all sensibility. In childhood he had often wept at the sufferings of a fly, which his less susceptible playmates tortured for sport. . . . These delicate sensibilities were refined by education; and he still was 'tremblingly alive' to exquisite feeling."

[82] Murray, *The Gleaner*, II, 300.   [83] *Ibid.*, II, 299.

"to frisk and curvet through all the intricacies of sentiment."[84]
"It has been the fate of a great original writer in our own country," observed a critic in the *Port Folio* in 1803, "to be succeeded
by a crowd of unworthy imitators: I speak of the author of
Tristram Shandy. As his *manner* was extraordinary, this has
been the great object of imitation to the tribe of his copyists."[85]
Many of these imitators wrote under what they believed to be
an aura from their master's spirit. Thus an American Yorick
in the *Massachusetts Magazine* announced, "My spirits were
not enflamed, but softened, subtilized, and sublimated. In
short, I felt myself all over *Sternified*."[86] The essence of Sterne,
however, proved to be as elusive as had the elements of Richardson's true greatness, and imitators found that Yorick's cassock
was constantly slipping off as they gamboled about in what
was fondly hoped to be the true Shandian manner. After a
show of commendable patience, the *Port Folio* was finally compelled to declare an editorial moratorium on all Sternesque
fragments and "pieces after the manner of Sterne." "The style
of Sterne has provoked a host of imitators," bemoaned the
weary editor, "most of them vile enough, who have copied his
ribaldry, quaintness and obscurity, but have lost sight of his
simplicity and wit."[87] Sterne's style was the subject of admired
comment by almost every reader of imaginative literature.
Alexander Graydon wrote that he was not displeased that
"Tristram Shandy has no story at all. In a book I look for
the thought, sentiment, language...."[88] The youthful Thomas
Jefferson was also captivated by Sterne's style. He entered "a
fragment" in his commonplace book: "Everything presses on:
and every time I kiss thy hand to bid adieu, every absence
which follows it, are preludes to that eternal separation which

---

[84] For samples of Sternesque fragments, see: *Massachusetts Magazine,* I, 566-567;
II, 471-472, 522-523; III, 241-242, 269-270, 277, 420-421, 436-437, 532-533, 660-661,
741-742; IV, 417-420; V, 212-213; VII, 18-21; VIII, 312-313; *Weekly Magazine* (New
York, 1795-1797), I, 103, 111, 223, 228-229, 239; II, 84, 119, 271, 303, 324, 353;
New York Magazine (1793-1797), IV, 158; V, 52-54; VI, 559-561, 746-747, 756.
[85] III, 419. [86] VI, 231. [87] III, 83.
[88] Quoted by the Duyckincks in *Cyclopaedia of American Literature* (New York,
1856), I, 357.

we are shortly to make."[89] In manner and subject it was fully deserving of a place in the *Massachusetts Magazine*.

The question of the measure in which American life afforded parallels of the fevered emotionalism portrayed in our early fiction is one which constantly presents itself. Consideration should be given to the conventionalized extravagance of diction and bearing commonly used for the popular presentation of strong emotions. As has been pointed out with respect to the popular novel in England during this period, "Something must be allowed for the influence of the stage and of the emphatic style of acting developed in the large play-houses."[90] Letters and memoirs, however, present evidence that "the handkerchiefly feeling" was not confined to the pages of novels. In a document purporting to record the last words of Frances Apthorp, the "Ophelia" of *The Power of Sympathy*, Dr. McDowell found "more frantic passion and acute sensibility than are set down in any early American novel."[91] General Washington shed his distinguished tears in public at a New York production of Bicker-Staffe's *The Maid of the Mill* in 1792 and was frequently lauded for his acute sensibility.[92] The repression of feeling so highly prized by the cult of the casuals may have been successfully cultivated by the aristocracy, but it had hardly become an accepted code of behavior in the young Republic. "Who, that frequents the theatre," asked an observer in the *Port Folio*, "has not often seen men, inured to danger and distress, give themselves up to the scenic delusion, and big tears course steadily down their sun-burnt cheeks?"[93] The sources

[89] G. Chinard (ed.), *The Literary Bible of Thomas Jefferson* (Baltimore, 1928), p. 81.   [90] Tompkins, *op. cit.*, p. 106.

[91] T. McDowell, "Last Words of a Sentimental Heroine," *American Literature*, IV, 174.

[92] *Federal Gazette* (New York, 1792), Nov. 17. Quoted by P. L. Ford in *Washington and the Theatre* (New York, 1899), p. 36. Washington's conduct at the surrender of Cornwallis was also cited as evidence of his superior sensibility. "Tears trickled from his eyes during most of the scene," Mann testified in *The Female Review*, p. 155. His behavior in the Major André affair was defended in *The Traveller Returned*, reprinted in *The Gleaner* (Boston, 1798), III, 122-123. Dr. Benson in *Women in Eighteenth Century America* concludes that fiction and drama had little value as "a picture of feminine existence" because of their subservience to foreign literary models. See *ibid.*, pp. 188-222.

[93] II, 82.

of this exaggerated emotionalism, heightened altruism, and flamboyant expression which effloresced in our early literature has been a perennial topic for debate. Perhaps the possessors of a continent, with a Niagara and a Mississippi between two oceans, found the spirit of restraint somewhat uncongenial. A people who had just achieved their political independence by revolution were likely, moreover, to cherish the sentimental theory that men in general are actuated by altruistic motives. The "peculiar genius" of American political and social institutions seemed to demand superlatives. "Ought not the literature of a free people to be declamatory? Should it not exhort and animate?" asked Dr. Daniel Drake. "If cold, literal, and passionless, how could it act as the handmaid of improvement?"[94] In 1788 Henry Mackenzie tried to account for the popularity of a code of refined sensibility as the product of a newly introduced literature which had not completely allied itself with the employments and feelings of society. Although the Scottish man of feeling was thinking of Germany and Scotland, his biographer, Professor Thompson, believes it "applies equally well to the American literature which came in the following generation."[95]

Whatever the degree of emotionalism in America in the closing decades of the century may have been, it is difficult to attribute the artificial diction of most fictional characters to an attempt to echo actual conversation. It is scarcely conceivable that a Yankee lover would have greeted his lady in the enraptured style of Constantius as he embraced Pulchera: "O transcendently propitious heaven, thrice bountiful, inexhaustible, magnificent Providence! inexpressibly benevolent and superlatively beneficent Fates!"[96] Margaretta's rhetorical explosion when she learned that her husband was to be saved the necessity of a trip to Europe could hardly have had a counterpart, even in contemporary drama. "Then he shall not go," she shrieked. "Avaunt, ye brooding fiends, that hover round the

---

[94] *Discourse on the History, Character, and Prospects of the West* (Cincinnati, 1834), p. 32.   [95] Thompson, *op. cit.*, p. 288.
[96] [Anon.,] *Constantius and Pulchera*, p. 92.

land of murder!—ye shall not intercept the virtuous career of Hamilton—ye shall not presume to manacle those hands that have, a thousand times, been stretched forth to wipe the tear from the face of sorrow—Avaunt, ye hell-born fiends!—Algiers, united for his destruction, shall not detain him; for lo, a blessed father descends from heaven, to save his well near sinking Margaretta."[97] Humor and restraint were not conspicuous among the gifts of the sentimentalist. As Professor Pattee has remarked, "Whatever the cause, the fact remains that none of our literary creators, cultured or uncultured, felt wholly comfortable when he had called a spade merely a spade."[98]

It was inevitable that the diction of sensibility should have invited parody. The *Massachusetts Magazine* reprinted a mock-rhapsody beginning, "Alas, poor potatoe . . . " to poke fun at "these raving philosophers . . . who could find a resemblance between religion and a raddish . . . and squeeze morality for a dozen pages out of a green gooseberry."[99] Peter Plainman, who found himself bewildered by the smoky rhapsodies of Sterne's imitators, implored his betrothed to "Make a solemn vow never more to put your faith in *metaphors* and *comparisons,* two cursed things which have done more mischief to young women than libertinism itself."[100] Burlesque of affected sensibility appears in a "Lamentation over an Unfortunate Animalcule." "Belinda was always remarkably fond of pathetic novels, tragedies and elegies. Sterne's sentimental beauties were her peculiar favorites," wrote the satirist. "She had indeed contracted so great tenderness of sensibility from such reading . . . she actually fell into a fit on a gentleman's treading on her favorite cat's tail as he eagerly stooped to save her child from falling into the fire."[101] The ultrarefined must have winced at "The Sentimental Horse." This animal "stopped suddenly, hung his head, and presented an attitude so moving,

[97] Murray, *The Gleaner*, I, 285.
[98] F. L. Pattee, *The First Century of American Literature, 1770-1870* (New York, 1935), p. 123.
[99] *Massachusetts Magazine*, VIII, 523.
[100] *Ibid.*, VIII, 560.
[101] *Ibid.*, III, 447. See also *Port Folio*, II, 183.

and so pregnant with silent reproach, that Balaam's ass, with all his loquacity, would have suffered by the comparison."[102] Another satirist wrote mischievously, "Killed a flea that I caught under my arm pit; think it was a female, in circumstances; hope nobody observed me."[103] Sensibility and seduction, those familiar beauties so much admired by readers, were ridiculed in "Maria" in which the heroine slipped, and with a commendable dramatic economy, simultaneously lost her virtue and the contents of a pail of milk. A moment later, the same hapless fair, after pressing a robin to her bosom, "looked up to Heaven, then laid her head upon the earth—and expired."[104] The tear cult became a popular target for humorists. The *Port Folio* printed the "Prospectus" of a contemplated "History of Weeping" to appear in ten volumes including books on the "State of Tears before the Flood," and the "Rise of White Handkerchiefs." An entire volume was to have been devoted to "Novel Writing" with tears classified as to their *"genera and species*—Salt tears, bitter tears, sweet tears, sweet bitter tears, salt delicious tears, tears half delicious half agonizing, and other varieties manufactured and distilled in the writings of the new philosophers—On sentimental torrents, cataracts of sensibility, and water-falls of fine feeling. . . . The whole to be embellished by engravings by the first artists, of black eyes, blue eyes, and hazel eyes in all stages of crying from the *glisten* to the *sob*."[105]

More serious than these burlesques of exaggerated diction and extravagant gesture were the charges that sensibility relaxed the mind, and led to an unwholesome enjoyment of self-induced woe. The best of resolutions thus became sicklied over by a pale cast of feeling and lost the name of action. "In the enthusiasm of sentiment . . . ," warned the *Port Folio,* "there is

---

[102] *Ibid.,* VIII, 312.   [103] *Ibid.,* II, 418.

[104] *Ibid.,* III, 421. This periodical continued to the end of its long career as a shrine for the worship of sensibility. Although the critics became more numerous in the later years of its existence, they were always a small minority. See *ibid.,* VII, 574, "On the Death of a College Canary," and *ibid.,* VIII, 181, "Elegiac Lines occasioned by the Premature Death of a Dove, alias Pigeon. . . ."

[105] *Port Folio,* II, 222.

as much danger as in the enthusiasm of religion, in substituting certain impulsive feelings in place of practical duties; and the pupils of these refined sentimentalists are but too apt to talk of virtues they never practise; to pay in words what they owe in actions. . . ."[106] Novelists attempted to break the force of this criticism by insisting upon the soundness of their own brand of sensibility. In *The Inquisitor,* Mrs. Rowson probed the motives of her humanitarian hero. " 'Search your heart,' replies a soft voice, 'and see if it is not an unwarrantable curiosity, rather than a real wish to do good, that now inspires you.' "[107] Mrs. Foster assured her readers that seducers were quick to distinguish between false and true sensibility. "If a lady will consent to enter the lists against the antagonist of her honor, she may be sure of loosing [*sic*] the prize," chortled Major Sanford in *The Coquette.* "Besides, were her delicacy genuine, she would banish the man at once, who presumed to doubt, which he certainly does, who attempts to vanquish it!"[108] Readers of the *New York Magazine* were urged to emulate the true sensibility of Maria. "Maria wept not only at the tale of fiction, at the sufferings of injured beauty, or of graceful heroism," the author stated proudly, "her pity and her bounty were extended to the loathsome scenes of squalid poverty and pale disease."[109] The same qualities of desirable sensibility were praised by Judith Sargent Murray in her eulogy of Joseph Russell. "Doubtless he was a branch of the Shandian family," she wrote, *"the milk of human kindness,* with a never ebbing current, flowed in his veins; nor did any Le Fevre languish, within his knowledge, to whom he did not hasten to administer the oil and wine of consolation."[110] *The Gleaner* also warned against those sentimentalists whose actions rarely squared with their feelings. Lavinia noted uneasily how Alphonso swore eternal love, but shied away from the mention of a date for the wedding ceremony. His "passion is sentimental, precisely of that description which I wish," she confessed, ". . . and yet, strange to tell, his tongue has never uttered *a single*

[106] II, 169.
[107] *The Inquisitor,* I, 14.
[108] *The Coquette,* p. 212.
[109] *New York Magazine,* V, 160.
[110] *The Gleaner,* II, 298.

sentence, which announced what *his eyes were continually proclaiming. . . ."*[111]

Other critics remarked that the woes of sensibility outweighed its pleasures, and that a heart of exquisite tenderness was at best a dubious gift. Caroline's sufferings in *Infidelity* led her to the same conclusion. "Oh, that I were cased against sensibility," she exclaimed to her sister, "that thereby I might endure without a sigh these meditated marks of indifference. . . ."[112] Mrs. Rowson's heroines suffered with such intensity that their creator was moved to confess, "Oh! how blest the heart whose sensibility has never been awakened, who, though dead to all the joys of love and friendship, feels not the pang of disappointment, or the piercing sting of ingratitude!"[113] Sensitive plants did not flourish in the bracing air which still blows through the pages of *Modern Chivalry.* "Sensibility is irritable, unpersevering, desponding, extravagant," wrote Brackenridge, who recommended cool common sense as the best recipe for happiness, even in affairs of the heart. "The fond love of a refined mind," he concluded, "produces silliness, in proportion to the delicacy of the feelings. . . ."[114] Benjamin Franklin, appropriately enough, was represented in *The Asylum* as an arch foe of sensibility. "Examine the varied circles of society . . . ," counseled the great exemplar of the American age of prose and reason, "you will there perceive how few among the sentimentally refined are even apparently at ease. . . . Exquisite sensibilities are ever subject to exquisite inquietudes."[115]

[111] *Ibid.,* II, 53. [112] Relf, *Infidelity,* p. 72.
[113] *Trials of the Human Heart,* IV, 39-40.
[114] *Modern Chivalry,* III, 84.
[115] I. Mitchell, *The Asylum; or, Alonzo and Melissa* (Poughkeepsie, 1811), II, 182-183. Nothing in this bizarre novel is quite so preposterous as the curious literary fraud to which it gave rise. The story first appeared over Mitchell's signature as "Alonzo and Melissa, a Tale," in the *Political Barometer* of Poughkeepsie from June 5 to Oct. 30, 1804. Joseph Nelson, proprietor of the *Barometer,* secured a copyright for the publication of the novel in book form on Dec. 2, 1810, and advertised its appearance as "A new novel: the Asylum, or Alonzo and Melissa," on Sept. 25, 1811. In Plattsburg, N. Y., in the same year, there appeared a volume entitled "A short account of the courtship of Alonzo and Melissa. . . ." The title page bore the name of Daniel Jackson, jun., as author. Jackson appears to have followed the version which had appeared serially in the *Barometer* seven years before, in 1804. Mitchell's

Sensibility also lost caste by becoming identified with excesses of all kinds in politics and religion, as well as in social conduct. Confronted by strange enthusiasms in church and state, readers looked back with longing to the old-fashioned man of feeling. "We can easily imagine," charged a critic, "what sort of *wild beast* a new Man of Feeling would be, fresh from the mint of Mary Wollestonecraft and William Godwin, precious twins of Jacobinical birth. . . ."[116] William Hill Brown regretted in 1789 that even Laurence Sterne seemed outmoded to the bright young people of the new school. "Sentiment out of date—alas! poor *Yorick*," he cried in *The Power of Sympathy.* "May thy pages never be soiled by the fingers of prejudice."[117] The *Port Folio* admitted that "There may have existed, it is true, a cant of *sentiment* which was disgusting by its excess, but, in avoiding this, we have fallen into an opposite extreme."[118] Worthy was alarmed at those who objected to Sterne. "These anti-sentimentalists would banish thee from the society of all books!" he exclaimed bitterly. "Surely these *antis* have no more to do with thee, than the gods of the *Canaanites*—In character and understanding they are alike— eyes have *they,* but they see not—ears have *they,* but they hear not, neither is there any knowledge to be found in them."[119] Alas! poor Yorick! The high priest of sensibility was accused of hypocrisy. "As a proof among others," charged Samuel Curwen in 1782, "he suffered an aged mother, which but for the proof of it is hardly to be credited, to die in jail for want of money to discharge a debt of twenty pounds. The public ought to know the character of a writer who so ill in practice exemplified that which his pen so justly and beautifully describes."[120]

original novel was never reprinted, while Jackson's bold "steal" went into a second edition in 1824 and was republished at least eleven times between 1824 and 1876. There is an excellent summary of the history of the fraud in D. S. Rankin's biography of Mitchell in *Dictionary of American Biography,* XIII, 48-49.

[116] *Port Folio,* V, 244.

[117] *The Power of Sympathy,* I, 64.   [118] *Port Folio,* II, 49.

[119] W. H. Brown, *The Power of Sympathy,* I, 64-65.

[120] G. A. Ward (ed.), *Journal and Letters of the Late Samuel Curwen* (New York, 1842), pp. 357-358.

Alas! poor Yorick! Even the founder of the cult of the "hanky" and the tear had been accused of callously allowing his aged mother to die in a loathsome prison. And what of Eliza? What must the feeling heart think of a cleric who sported with the affections of a pure woman? And both married, too! And what of Henry Mackenzie, that great Scottish Man of Feeling? Was he not in private life the flintiest of Edinburgh solicitors, comfortably at home amid unfeeling laws as dead to pity as was Balaam's ass? "Oh Harry! Harry! you have feelings only on paper," protested Mrs. Mackenzie, who had faced her husband daily over toasted scones in the damp wintry mornings of the Athens of the North. If the gods had feet of clay, what of the minor deities less gifted in their powers? Were American men of feeling more successful in facing the merciless scrutiny of their wives?

And this fellow Rousseau! What about him and his madcap followers? "Where are your fine feelings now?" frightened men were asking everywhere. "The character of this New Man of Feeling," charged that bulwark of law and order, the *Port Folio,* "like his great prototype Rousseau, that eloquent lunatic, and splendid scoundrel, is benevolence to the whole species, and want of feeling to every individual . . . he melts with tenderness for Jackasses, Algerines and commonwealthsmen, and, without a pang, casts away as offal, all the charities of life."[121] With this blanket indictment by that levelheaded Addisonian, Joseph Dennie, we may leave for a time the sons and daughters of feeling. We shall soon meet them again, eagerly scanning the horizon for new stars of reform against the morning skies of the nineteenth century.

[121] V, 244-245.

V

SEX AND SENSIBILITY

I.

THE FEMALE NOVELISTS

Here the widely extended fields of literature court attention; and the American fair are invited to cull the flowers, and cultivate the expanding laurel.

—Hannah Webster Foster,
The Boarding School, 1798.

THE VIRILE bass notes of Hugh Henry Brackenridge's *Modern Chivalry* served only to bring into shrill relief the unmistakably feminine treble which dominated the opening chorus of American fiction. With glad assent, women quickly accepted their responsibility as a civilizing force in the early decades of the raw, young Republic. Few moralists, however, were willing to concede that woman was equal to man. Dr. Hitchcock had reasoned plausibly enough that since society must have a head, it was man's rightful duty to assume it. Woman's power was thought to reside more properly in her undoubted influence over masculine wills and affections. Hers was the grateful task of embellishing and refining society, and of forming the character of the rising generation.

In England, after the middle of the century, female genius was being vindicated by a rapidly increasing number of women writers. Dr. Hitchcock noted that "While the names of Mrs. Rowe, Chapone, Macauley [*sic*], Barbauld, Miss Burns, Moore [*sic*], and many others are remembered, the sprightliness, strength, and elegance of female genius must be acknowledged."[1] The literary lady did not emerge in America, however, until a generation after the emancipation of her sisters

[1] *Memoirs of the Bloomsgrove Family,* II, 15.

abroad. Brown observed in *The Power of Sympathy* in 1789,
"...it is a matter of regret that *American* literature boasts so few
productions from the pens of the ladies."[2] The novel in which
this lament appeared, however, was dedicated "to the Young
Ladies of United Columbia," and for some time was attributed
to one of them, Mrs. Sarah Wentworth Morton, "the divine
Philenia" of the *Massachusetts Magazine*.[3] This periodical was
the most successful of those publications in New England which
offered their chaste columns as "a *retreat in which feminine
delicacy may shelter itself*."[4] It had been preceded in 1784 by the
Gentleman's and Lady's Town and Country Magazine which
had promised to pay special attention to contributions from the
American fair, and was promptly followed in Philadelphia and
New York by other forerunners of *Godey's Lady's Book*. The
editors, wisely convinced that women liked to read what other
women had written, begged the Constantias, Euphelias, Be-
lindas, Charlottes, Almerines, and possessors of other elegant
aliases, "to appear in the two-fold robe of elegant prose and
highly wrought verse."[5] This invitation was answered by
scores of genteel offerings which lent their faint perfume to
the pages of our early magazines. "Don't you see Lucinda and
Constantia, Prudentia and Beatrice, and half a score more,
week after week, in the very front of the paper?" asked a contributor to the *Port Folio* in 1803.[6] The gradual widening of
woman's "proper sphere" may be seen in the appearance, between 1784 and 1860, of at least one hundred magazines chiefly
designed for women.[7]

Woman's place, as every schoolboy still knows, is the home.
Had not Governor Winthrop recorded in his *Journal* that
melancholy instance of the wife of "Mr. Hopkins, the governor
of Hartford ... who was fallen into a sad infirmity, the loss of
her understanding and reason ... by occasion of her giving

[2] *The Power of Sympathy*, II, 15.
[3] For an informative biography of Mrs. Morton, who was not only known as
"Philenia," but also as "the American Sappho" and "the Mrs. Montagu of America,"
see Emily Pendleton and Milton Ellis, *Philenia* (Orono, 1931).
[4] *Massachusetts Magazine*, I, 130.
[5] *Ibid.*, I, 705.   [6] III, 73.
[7] Bertha-Monica Stearns, "Before *Godey's*," *American Literature*, II, 248.

herself wholly to reading and writing, and had written many books."[8] Almost two centuries later, was not the Reverend Calvin Stowe, husband of the author of the most popular "female novel" of the time, justified in advising the young ladies of Bradford Academy to devote themselves to their families?[9] When female novelists made their appearance in America in the last decade of the eighteenth century, they came forward in the face of a popular prejudice which decreed that woman's place was over the washtub and cradle, not the writing desk. They advanced, not as writers, but as exemplary wives and mothers. Mrs. Sally Wood assured her readers in *Julia and the Illuminated Baron* "that not one social, or one domestic duty, have ever been sacrificed or postponed by her pen. . . ."[10] The same justification was presented in behalf of Mrs. Murray. "I have dined with this lady," wrote Colwort to his betrothed, "and pleased to find that her literary pursuits did not interfere with her domestic virtues; she is a most excellent wife, and one of the best of mothers, and the perfect order of her household declares her a complete house-wife."[11] Mrs. Foster was careful to point out in the dedication of *The Boarding School* that she spent only "a part of her leisure hours" with the pen, and that her sole aim in writing was "to improve the Manners, and form the Character of Young Ladies."

The atmosphere of the novel of domestic manners and morals, moreover, was one in which the genteel female felt thoroughly at home; she might attempt it without unduly extending her "proper sphere."[12] Mrs. Wood certainly exhibited disarming modesty. "Her abilities are too scanty," she apologized in her preface to *Julia*, "to allow her to understand

[8] J. K. Hosmer (ed.), *Winthrop's Journal: 1630-1649* (New York, 1908), II, 225.
[9] J. S. Pond, *Bradford, a New England Academy* (Boston, 1930), pp. 160-162.
[10] *Julia and the Illuminated Baron*, p. iv. In Mrs. Wood's *Dorval; or, The Speculator* (Portsmouth, 1801), the author protested: "I hope no one will suppose that I entertain ideas so fallacious as to imagine it necessary for a female to be a writer: far from it" (p. iv).   [11] *Ibid.*, p. 82.
[12] C. B. Brown's *Alcuin*, and Paine's *Reflections of Unhappy Marriage* both championed woman's rights, but did not command a large popular following. See A. G. Violette, *Economic Feminism in American Literature Prior to 1848* in "University of Maine Studies" (Second Series), XXVI (Orono, 1925).

either religious or philosophical subjects in others, much more inadequate to the attempting them herself; incapable of undertaking the labours of history, or of attaining the sublime heights of poetry; the only path which lay open, was that of Romance."[13] Such diffidence was grateful incense to those who found "female ambition" and "assurance" equally repugnant. In *Ferdinand and Elmira,* Mrs. Wood reminded her readers of the vast difference "between the ordinary day-labor of the common English novelist, who works for a living similar to a Mechanic, and has no other end in view than to bring forth a fashionable piece of Goods, that will suit the taste of the moment, and remunerate himself, and the Lady of refined sentiments and correct taste, who writes for the amusement of herself, her Friends and the Public."[14] A complete disavowal of any desire for literary distinction or selfish, unwomanly ambition was made by the author of *Adelaide.* "The authoress of the following pages is conscious of their inferiority to many recent European publications," she declared, "yet she flatters herself to find patronage among her country-women; many of whom, divested of prejudice, may not permit an American production to be consigned to oblivion, or criticized with rigour, on being assured that it is not presented as a candidate for literary fame."[15] Caroline Matilda Warren advanced a plea of moral zeal as justification for publishing *The Gamesters.* She insisted that she asked nothing "of the ill-judging and censorious hypercritic, who views with the jaundiced eye of prejudice 'every production from a *female pen,*'" but instead addressed those understanding readers who "approve the *intention,* though a want of merit should oblige them to censure the *execution of the work.*"[16] *Margaretta* was offered to readers

[13] *Julia and the Illuminated Baron,* p. iv.

[14] *Ferdinand and Elmira* (Baltimore, 1804), pp. iii-iv.

[15] Margaret Botsford, *Adelaide* (Philadelphia, 1816), p. iii.

[16] *The Gamesters,* p. vii. This novelist's regard for the approval of the moralist rather than for the literary critic is typical: "Though the writer is confident the work would not pass unscorched through the fiery ordeal of criticism; yet if it gain one soul to virtue, or lure one profligate from the arms of dissipation, or snatch from the precipice of ruin, one fair fabric of innocence, she will deem herself amply compensated. . . " (*ibid.,* p. v).

with the same plea. "I may not be blameless for offering [it] for the amusement or inspection of an intelligent public," admitted the author, "but meek-eyed benevolence will palliate those errors which spring from the head, when the intention of the heart is to promote virtue and morality."[17] The author of *The Fortunate Discovery* excused her temerity by humble reiterations of her high motive. "Of one point she is conscious," she stated in her petition to the public, "that a good intention has guided her pen—and as nothing will be found in it, militating against the most rigid principles of virtue, she hopes for indulgence at least. . . ."[18]

Although women entered it with a hesitancy becoming to their sex, the path of romance-writing which Mrs. Wood had declared to be open to females soon became a well-trodden thoroughfare. A few years after Brown's expression of concern over the scarcity of productions "from the female pen," Mrs. Foster was able to announce in *The Boarding School* that "Philenia's talents justly entitle her to a rank among the literary ornaments of Columbia."[19] In 1800 Henry Sherburne proudly observed that "it is indeed a most interesting circumstance, that female literary merit hath presented so brilliant an addition to our national glory."[20] So great was the popularity enjoyed by "female novelists" in 1801 that Tabitha Tenney was moved to write that "the ladies of late seem to have almost appropriated this department of writing."[21] The didactic-sentimental tale of domestic manners proved to be so congenial to female taste and talent that more than one third of the American novels published before the advent of Cooper's *Precaution* in 1820 were written by women. Nathaniel Hawthorne's classic explosion on this subject in 1855 indicates the extent of the inundation later in the nineteenth century when the prejudice against women's writing had relaxed. "America is now wholly given over to a d——d mob of scribbling women, and I should have no chance of success while the public taste is occupied

---

[17] [Anon.,] *Margaretta*, p. iii.
[18] [Anon.,] *The Fortunate Discovery* (New York, 1798), p. [i].
[19] *The Boarding School*, p. 201.
[20] *The Oriental Philanthropist*, p. v.   [21] *Female Quixotism*, I, 7.

with their trash . . . ," he complained to Ticknor.²² *Knicker-bocker's* was unable to report that the flood was receding, ". . . and the cry is, 'still they come,' " it announced irritably.²³

While these ancestors of Hawthorne's detested "ink-stained women" were blazing the way for their less timid sisters, the male novelists made constant appeals to female readers and to feminine interests. The first American novel had been inscribed to women, and few of its followers were sent forth to tempt fortune without an appeal to women's tastes and ideals. The author of *Constantius and Pulchera* permitted himself to hope that his novel would occupy a place in ladies' libraries "like a new planet in the Solar System."²⁴ Herman Mann assured hesitating purchasers of his *Female Review* that it had been written "with a diction softened and comported to the taste of the *virtuous* female." "I have studiously endeavored," he wrote, "to meliorate every circumstance, that might seem too much tinctured with the rougher, masculine virtues."²⁵ In his Advertisement, Samuel Relf expressed his wish that the generality of the readers of *Infidelity* would be "of the mild, the soft, and gentle formed of soul."²⁶ *Fidelity Rewarded* was commended to prospective feminine readers for its helpful dissertations upon "domestic regulations."²⁷ Other novelists, like Samuel Woodworth, were ever ready to praise woman for her civilizing function in society, and to hail her as "Heaven's last, best gift to man."²⁸

In novels written primarily for women, and very often by them, a limitation of scope to the comparatively narrow domestic interests was almost inevitable. For a taste of the same God's plenty which Henry Fielding bestowed with such rich prodigality in *Tom Jones,* the reader must turn to the picaresque *Modern Chivalry* rather than to these stuffy domestic tales.

²² C. Ticknor, *Hawthorne and His Publisher* (Boston, 1913), p. 141.
²³ *Knickerbocker's Magazine* (New York, 1855), XLV, 525.
²⁴ [Anon.,] *Constantius and Pulchera,* p. vi.
²⁵ *The Female Review,* pp. xii-xiii.
²⁶ *Infidelity,* p. ii. Among the subscribers were James Neal, "preceptor of a Young Ladies' Academy," and John Poor, "Principal of the Young Ladies' Academy of Philadelphia."
²⁷ [Anon.,] *Fidelity Rewarded,* p. [3]. ²⁸ *The Champions of Freedom,* II, 98.

The world of the genteel female of the eighteenth century was a severely circumscribed one with the home as all-important center. There were visits, of course, to the houses of friends; occasional parties, and if Steele or Lillo were to be performed, a trip or two to the theater. In the summertime there was the annual "retreat" to an elegant villa in the country. A composite setting of these novels immediately carries one indoors to a heavily carpeted, overheated parlor, that "home room of the house." In this woman's world, man enters primarily as suitor or husband, rarely as merchant or man-of-affairs. One seeks in vain for the gorgeous gallery of scamps and "originals" which Captain Farrago encountered in the highways and byways of the gaudy young Republic. The themes of these feminine novels suffer a similar constriction as a result of woman's limited experience. "The lives of women being commonly domestic," observed the author of *The Female American,* "the occurrences of them are generally pretty nearly of the same kind. . . ."[29] The nursery, the school, the sickroom, the chamber of death, and the various domestic relationships afforded heroines their opportunities for ministrations of mercy and of love. The threadbare theme of persecuted innocence was varied only as the reward alternated between husbands and Heaven. Hovering over all, and pervading every action was the prudential morality to which women were committed more strictly than men. God and man had entrusted to woman the high office of softening man's rougher instincts and of ennobling his character. For carrying out this lofty mission the novel seemed a convenient instrument. "Let us, my dear girls, to whom a propitious Providence has entrusted a considerable portion of his common bounty for the good of man," counseled Caroline Warren in *The Gamesters,* "let us be the faithful stewards of our Master."[30]

Faithful they proved to be, but the standards they upheld were conventional enough. Their principles lay safely within the well-established moral values. That women were "secon-

---

[29] [Anon.,] *The Female American,* p. 6.   [30] *The Gamesters,* p. 48.

dary objects in creation" was accepted as axiomatic. "Nor have we any right to require of superior man an example of the virtue to which he would train us," Constantia wrote in the *Port Folio*. "Our state of society is a dependent one, and it is ours to be good and amiable, whatever may be the conduct of the men to whom we are subjected."[31] Helena Wells, in *The Step-Mother,* heartily approved of the principles which led Charlotte "to think of *man* as a *lord* and *master,* from whose *will* there is no appeal."[32] Marriage was the goal of every respectable woman; the old maid and the bachelor were without decent status in a society which regarded the raising of a large family as a moral duty. "An old bachelor is a being which Nature never intended," wrote a contributor to the *New York Magazine*, ". . . what becomes of him after this life, God only knows!"[33] In feminine fiction, the old maid might be expected to receive more generous treatment, but she had few champions to present her motives with sympathy. Miss Norcliffe in *Constantia Neville* was drawn unfeelingly as "a tall meagre female, who had long been verging to fifty . . . an inimitable representation of a virago disappointed in the accomplishment of her favorite wish."[34] Even the usually sensible Harriot in *Female Quixotism* was not free of the prejudice which regarded every maiden lady as an object for merriment. "I would not be an old maid for all the world," she vowed.[35] Women novelists, usually alert for opportunities to dignify female character, neglected to add the lovable maiden aunt to their gallery of exemplary wives and model mothers.[36]

A feminine touch in these novels is to be discerned in their intense concern with marriage. Upon this sacred subject all compromise was taboo. Even the liberal Constantia Dudley,

---

[31] II, 137.   [32] *The Step-Mother,* II, 21-22.
[33] *New York Magazine*, II (N. S.), 474-475.
[34] *Constantia Neville*, II, 342.   [35] Tenney, *Female Quixotism*, II, 51.
[36] Mrs. Stanly's defense in *Female Quixotism* is an honorable exception: "I know several worthy and honorable women of that class, who live single rather than marry barely for the sake of having a husband. They are, in my opinion, much more respectable than women, who merely to avoid the imputation of being an old maid, will marry the first man who offers himself" (II, 52). For a further discussion of this subject in later domestic fiction, see Chapter IV, "Home, Sweet Home," pp. 285-287.

who tried to walk in the light of pure reason, shuddered at the suggestion of experimenting with the bonds of holy wedlock.[37] All women agreed in confounding the members of "the deistical tribe" who held polygamy to be a dictate of nature. "We say," solemnly affirmed the author of *The Art of Courting*, "that our God has told us, that *marriage is honourable in all*."[38] There were no dissenting voices. The female novelists also presented a solid front against the illuminati and the advocates of "the new philosophy" who scoffed at the old-fashioned virtues and proclaimed "the new woman." "That there should be advocates found for abolishing the law of marriage, and sanctioning that promiscuous intercourse between the sexes, at which human nature recoils," wrote Helena Wells, "would not excite surprise, were they only to be met with among the profligate."[39] The same author in a later novel warned readers they would find no newfangled notions about the emancipation of women in her story. "So my dear young ladies, if you go on, remember it is at your own risk," she cautioned plainly. "You must acquit me of any intention to trick you into a perusal of old-fashioned sentiments, and the incidents of common life."[40]

The female novelists made a modern ideal of the conduct of the patient Griselda. Their favorite role was that of the long-suffering, uncomplaining wife who bore her domestic cross with meekness and humility. Amelia in *The Gamesters* would have preferred death to the utterance of a single recrimination against her husband's callous treatment. Although treated with sottish brutality, "yet she bore all with patient meekness; sometimes a few starting tears would speak her injuries, and the plaintive melody of her guitar, more eloquent than language would 'speak feelingly' the pangs which rent her exquisitely feeling heart."[41] Mrs. Hayman, the domestic

---

[37] Charles Brockden Brown had more liberal views as may be seen in his first book, *Alcuin: A Dialogue*, in which he shows his interest in reforming the institution of marriage.

[38] Bradford, *The Art of Courting*, p. 14.

[39] *The Step-Mother*, II, 239-240.   [40] *Constantia Neville*, I, 172.

[41] Warren, *The Gamesters*, pp. 281-282.

saint in *Constantia Neville,* cheerfully welcomed each new instance of ill-usage by her husband as an opportunity to teach the world woman's seemingly infinite capacity for suffering. When Hayman brutally ordered her to nurse his illegitimate child, she was all complaisance. "If there is any child whom you wish to acknowledge as being your own offspring," she told her errant spouse, "I will receive it with thankfulness, and cherish it as my own. Indeed you may rely on my hearty acquiescence in such a plan."[42] Lady Stanly, Mrs. Wood's heroine in *Amelia,* also clasped her profligate husband's bastards to her breast as "dear little innocents." When Lady Barrymore, the wicked mistress, brazenly hinted that the nursery was likely to receive other additions, the wronged wife was patience on a monument. "Sir William's children, madam," she replied virtuously, "will always find a friend and protector in his wife, and an asylum in his house."[43] It is heartening to learn that passivity and patience had limits even in a Griselda, for Lady Stanly added a qualification to her generous offer. "I shall beg leave to decline," she hinted pointedly, "the honour of taking any one, who does not claim him as a parent."[44] Mrs. Wood knew that her heroine's conduct would have been condemned by the disciples of "the new philosophy" as base servility. "But Amelia was not a disciple or pupil of Mary Woolstonecraft [*sic*]," she noted with pride, "she was not a woman of fashion, nor a woman of spirit. She was an old-fashioned wife, and she meant to obey her husband: she meant to do her duty in the strictest sense of the word."[45]

To be an old-fashioned wife was to revel in the beauty of submission and to seek solace in patient resignation; the severest ill-usage was not sufficient justification for divorce. To know how to suffer was the first duty of virtuous wifehood. "Leaving a husband, is a serious undertaking," Caroline wrote to Maria in *The Hapless Orphan.* "I believe I may venture to assert, that, in few instances, has a separation ever removed the

---

[42] Wells, *Constantia Neville,* III, 216.
[43] Wood, *Amelia; or, The Influence of Virtue,* p. 143.
[44] *Ibid.,* pp. 143-144.   [45] *Ibid.,* p. 103.

cause of uneasiness, but rather increased the wretchedness. . . ."[46] When her friends suggested divorce, Amelia was
adamant. "There has always been something so degrading in
the idea of a divorced wife," she wrote to Sir William, "that
forgive me, if I say, I would prefer death or almost any other
wretchedness to it. . . ."[47] Marriages, no matter what they produced on earth, seemed to be made in Heaven; second attachments were viewed as profanations of a solemn vow. Caroline
Wentworth was overcome by the "delicacy" exhibited in the
will of her late husband. "No reference to a second marriage,
no change in the disposition of his fortune, should such an
event take place," she exclaimed. "To have called another by
that endearing appellation would have been the most effectual
way of proving I was unworthy of the first."[48] Few second
marriages are recorded in these novels. The Countess de Launa
in *Julia* was besieged by eligible suitors. "But she had steadily
refused every proposal of this kind," Mrs. Wood wrote with
approval. "Second marriages, she disliked from principle."[49]
Second attachments were equally repugnant. Major Willoughby's sister in *The Champions of Freedom* regarded her
plighted troth as sacred as marriage and resolutely spurned all
offers after her lover's death at Bunker Hill. "The idea of a
second engagement was sacrilege to her first and only love,"
wrote Woodworth, "and she therefore determined to remain a
vestal for life."[50] The men at times attempted to live up to
this fantastic ideal set by their gentle monitresses. Thus Edward
Glanville, repulsed by Caroline in *The Step-Mother,* would not
listen to the suggestion of another love. "No; I maintain it,"
he vowed, "twice in one's life it is utterly impossible to be so
attached. If I must relinquish the hope of obtaining your hand,
a life of celibacy is my determination."[51] A delicate point in
the ethics of widowhood was happily settled when Mrs. Noble

[46] [Anon.,] *The Hapless Orphan*, I, 211.
[47] Wood, *Amelia; or, The Influence of Virtue*, p. 100.
[48] Wells, *The Step-Mother*, I, 244-245.
[49] *Julia and the Illuminated Baron*, p. 28.
[50] *The Champions of Freedom*, I, 14.
[51] Wells, *The Step-Mother*, I, 172.

found herself in love with the brother of her deceased husband. In finally consenting to give him her hand, she laid the flattering unction to her soul that she did not profane, but merely "renewed her first marriage."[52]

Although they never condoned parental tyranny, the women novelists lent their weight to the authority of parents in ordering the lives of their children. There is a melancholy list of fatal results of the failure to heed the prudential advice of parents or guardians.[53] Passivity was held up as an ideal; independence was rarely urged. Clarissa's rebellion against her family was merely for the right to remain unmarried. Sophia's flight from Squire Western's roof was to avoid marriage with the obnoxious Blifil, not to elope with Tom Jones. Louisa's conduct in *The Fortunate Discovery* was regarded as exemplary in the much debated matter of parental control. Her "father had taught her to believe, that marriages without the sanction of Parents, would ever be unhappy." This principle she applied at the risk of losing her own happiness. When Captain Bellmore urged his welcome suit before consulting his own parents, Louisa was resolute. "O, Sir," she replied to her lover, "do not think you will ever be independent of the duty you owe your parents; I must not, I cannot, hear you any longer on this subject."[54] This passive ideal of conduct which never came within hailing distance of independence contradicts at every point the modern notions of feminine behavior. The most daring demands of these timid heroines were merely for negative boons. Thus Julia willingly offered her freedom for a "right" which was inalienably her own. "Oh save me from the worst of evils, and restore me to my friends," she implored the bad Baron, "or

<hr />

[52] [Anon.,] *The Hapless Orphan*, I, 9.

[53] Novelists frequently pointed their preachments with exempla of dutiful and undutiful daughters, and tearful interludes about good and bad apprentices with a neatly contrived scale of rewards and punishments to barb their conclusions. See the contrasting careers of Flavia and Prudelia in *The Boarding School*, pp. 82-83, 88. The story of Carewell and Claudius illustrates that prudence leads to happiness, and self-indulgence ends in ruin; see *The Gleaner*, II, 239-242. For other object lessons in narrative form, see *The Inquisitor*, III, 227-232; *The Hapless Orphan*, I, 214; and "Marian and Lydia" in *Mentoria* I, 76-106; II, 3-38.

[54] [Anon.,] *The Fortunate Discovery*, pp. 22-23.

if that is displeasing, immure me in a nunnery; confine me to a convent, but do not force me to a connexion that my soul abhors!"[55]

Meredith's Sir Willoughby Patterne was born to bask in the feminine world of the women novelists. In this cloudland of sentiment he would have met hundreds of unfaded Laetitias eager to feed his self-esteem. His overmastering possessiveness would have been flattered by an eternal devotion which shrank at the thought of a second attachment. His fastidious egoism would have been exquisitely gloved against the faintest feather-prick of independence. Here was to be found creamy purity linked with a subservience grateful for every condescending notice. In this Utopia of masculine complacency there were no dainty rogues in porcelain to tantalize and to perplex. All was self-effacing virtue, abject humility, and perfect complaisance.

2.

THE SENTIMENTAL HEROINE

> There is not a tale, we believe, in which there is not some wife or daughter, who is generous and gentle, and prudent and cheerful, and almost all the men who behave properly owe most of their good actions to the influence and suggestions of these lovely monitresses.
> —*Port Folio*, 1805.

PAMELA'S AMERICAN daughters had their work cut out for them. They found the heroine's lot far from being a sinecure in sentimental fiction, but proved themselves equal to every assignment. Delicate as dewdrops, they retained their freshness even while roasting over the slow fires of affliction, and survived to rear a race of hardy pioneers. "When oppressed by adversity or agonized by misfortune, who steps forth to tranquilize the mind, or calm the perturbations of feeling?" asked George Watterston in *Glencarn*. "Woman!" he promptly answered. "Amiable, angelical woman, beings on whom nature has stamped the image of perfection . . . to smooth the rugged paths of life, and enamel with flowers of never ending

[55] Wood, *Julia and the Illuminated Baron*, p. 211.

fragrance, the barren heaths of existence."[1] Samuel Woodworth's apostrophe is even more fervent: "Woman ever has
been, still is, and always will be, the main spring, the *primum
mobile* of every masculine achievement, from the hero to the
clown—from the man to the stripling; and whether she fire a
Troy, or excite emulation in a game of marbles; whether she
influence a court or rule in a dairy, the end, cause, and effect,
are still the same."[2]

These ecstatic tributes to the power of woman were appropriate for heroines whose slender shoulders were destined to
bear so many burdens. To refine and to spiritualize man and
through their soft influence upon him, to ennoble civilization
itself—this was the great mission of the lovely monitresses who
emerged in our first novels. Woman was the natural educator
with a divine injunction to teach the young idea how to shoot.
The genteel female was the sweet taskmaster to awe by her
holy beauty the wayward and the vicious. She was, to borrow
a familiar figure, a sensitive plant in a garden of noxious weeds.
Her place was in the sick chamber and in the squalid abodes of
poverty and suffering. She was the modern Griselda to reclaim
erring man by unexampled meekness in face of basest injuries.
She must, moreover, achieve her objects all sublime without being in the least "forward," but rather by an indirect influence
all the more powerful because it was self-effacing. If successful,
hers was the pleasant haven of a happy domestic circle with a
bevy of "cherubs of innocence" to lisp their gratitude, and an
adoring, reclaimed husband to crown her felicity. If her destiny
was to recall the sinner by an uncomplaining and a lingering
"decline," she gladly played her part to the end to teach the
world how Christian innocence should die.

For the manifold responsibilities of this high calling the
heroines received appropriate training. "Childhood and youth
may be considered as a term of apprenticeship in which they
are to be exercised in those employments whereby they are to
live," advised Dr. Hitchcock.[3] The burden of supervising such

[1] *Glencarn*, I, 112. [2] *The Champions of Freedom*, II, 99.
[3] *The Farmer's Friend* (Boston, 1793), p. 132.

education also fell to women. "Much, in this momentous department, depends upon *female administration,*" wrote Mrs. Murray, "and the mother, or the woman to whom she may delegate her office, will imprint on the opening mind, characters, ideas and conclusions, which time, in all its variety of vicissitudes, will never be able to erase."[4] Such an upbringing had the desired effect upon Margaretta. "A singularity of character had ever distinguished her from her little associates," wrote the author complacently. "When they would be at their gambols and plays, she would seldom join in their amusements; and though amidst all the alluring temptations of juvenile mirth, and laughing hilarity, she would either sit musing as a philosopher, or spend her leisure hours in reading."[5] The "reading" was likely to be somewhat heavy. Thus Louisa in *Constantia Neville* did not spend her days "in perusing fictitious narratives of true and faithful lovers, whose example she was emulating." "No!" the author declared emphatically. "She devoted a great portion of her time to reading the best works that have been written on the duties of the female sex."[6] Unca Winkfield, heroine of *The Female American,* had many occasions to be grateful for her youthful study of religious works which "was as methodical and exact as though I had been [trained] to be a divine."[7]

For this training, the home, not the boarding school, was regarded as the proper place. Although Mrs. Foster's model establishment, Harmony Grove, seemed harmless enough with its devotion to "every species of pastime, consistent with the decorum of the sex,"[8] most novelists viewed boarding schools with open alarm. Lady Glanville in *The Step-Mother* preferred private tutoring for Caroline. "I was unwilling," she stated, "such good natural parts, and so amiable a disposition . . . should run any risk of being destroyed or perverted, by the bad examples likely to occur among a great number of young people, indiscriminately collected together. . . ."[9] Parents had not forgotten

[4] *The Gleaner,* II, 6.
[5] *Margaretta,* pp. 32-33.
[6] Wells, *Constantia Neville,* I, 27.
[7] [Anon.,] *The Female American,* p. 35.
[8] *The Boarding School,* p. 10.
[9] Wells, *The Step-Mother,* I, 21-22.

that Charlotte Temple had been lured away from a boarding school through the connivance of a designing French governess. The absurdities as well as the evils of a boarding-school education became a popular target for satirists. Rebecca Rush described the effects of a fashionable course of training on the Gurnet children in *Kelroy*. "After remaining three years longer," she observed caustically, "and having each a parcel of smeared-looking drawings, and a piece of embroidery to display as their own work, although more than half of it was done by their tutoresses, they were taken home, and considered by their parents as completely educated."[10]

Heroines of a serious turn of mind were soon to discover, as did the erudite Constantia, "that superior intellectual endowments were in no degree necessary for ensuring a welcome in the *beau monde*."[11] Mrs. Williamson, who had little respect for bluestockings, was alarmed as she watched her ward "unpack her trunks, in which were collected as her greatest treasures, part of the library selected for her use by her father." An advocate of the opinion that feminine gentility consisted of knowing little and doing nothing, she remarked pointedly "that a book-worm was her aversion; that women who read much were always sure to have a great many enemies; and that, in her idea, her own sex could not be too highly *accomplished*, but it was ridiculous for any of them to attempt becoming too *learned*."[12] Amelia's frosty reception in the best Philadelphia drawing rooms led her to warn her friends "to display no learning, or sentiment, for the moment it is discovered, your reputation is lost forever."[13] Duly apprised of these dangers, novelists attempted to steer a middle course between the sensual and ornamental, on one hand, and the useful and solid, on the other. Unca Winkfield's education was cited as a happy compromise. "I made a great progress in the Greek and Latin languages, and other polite literature," she owned modestly, "whilst my good aunt took care of the female part of my edu-

---

[10] *Kelroy*, p. 238.
[11] Wells, *Constantia Neville*, I, 137.
[12] *Ibid.*, III, 343.
[13] Wood, *Ferdinand and Elmira*, p. 189.

cation with equal success."[14] Although these accomplishments were matched by the attainments of Constantia Dudley in Brown's *Ormond*, a command of the classics was a fairly rare distinction for a heroine. Most of them with small Latin and less Greek resembled the volatile Miss Darlington, who "had never heard of the fall of Ilium, or the ten years' siege which it sustained."[15]

The training of the heroine of *Ferdinand and Elmira* was contrasted favorably with the more fashionable reading of a less solid friend. "The mind of Elmira was enlarged and improved by the study of history, the works of the poets and philosophers," Mrs. Wood noted with approval, while "that of Maria was polished by romances only."[16] It was the pious Hannah More rather than the dangerous Mary Wollstonecraft who was the preferred mentor for the American fair, although Constantia Dudley's ideas smacked suspiciously of "Wollstone-craftism." Brown regretted in *Ormond* that "Women are generally limited to what is sensual and ornamental: music and painting, and the Italian and French languages, are bounds which they seldom pass."[17] His heroine's education was of a different order: "Instead of making her a practical musician or pencilist, he conducted her to the school of Newton and Hartley, unveiled to her the mathematical properties of light and sound. . . ."[18] Such startling knowledge carried her to the dangerous verge of masculinity. Only her susceptibility to swoons saved her from becoming "a new woman."

Less rigorous discipline than a study of "the mathematical properties of light and sound" was sought in the books which comprised the reading of most heroines. Too often, as Dr. Hitchcock lamented, they wasted their time over romantic nonsense which ill-fitted them to become the helpmeet of man. "Shady groves and purling streams," he concluded sadly, "fashions, etiquette, and romantic scenes of love and high life, filled

[14] [Anon.,] *The Female American*, p. 32.
[15] Wells, *Constantia Neville*, I, 109.
[16] Wood, *Ferdinand and Elmira*, p. 189.
[17] C. B. Brown, *Ormond*, p. 38.   [18] *Ibid.*

up the mighty void."[19] Ferdinand was confident that the taste of his beloved Elizabeth was superior to those who wept over such trash as *"Misplaced Confidence, Female Frailties* and *Excessive Sensibility."*[20] The author of *Monima* ridiculed one of these fiction addicts who cried peevishly: "How I do wish I was a novel-character, for what is life? one dull round of sameness; no variety in love affairs; no such delicacy of sentiment in the lover, but all is as vulgar as the *vulgarest* clown in a novel."[21] These giddy readers were mentioned only to point a moral. They had much in common with Dorcasina, the heroine of *Female Quixotism,* whose mind was "filled with the airy delusions and visionary dreams of love and raptures, darts, fire and flames, with which the indiscreet writing of that fascinating kind of books, denominated Novels, fill the heads of artless young girls to their great injury, and sometimes to their utter ruin."[22]

Since the delicate and pensive heroine was intended as a model for emulation, her reading was usually of the most approved kind. Few were as judicious, however, as Margaretta, who eschewed most novels although she found *The Vicar of Wakefield* to be a shining exception, and admitted "there are a few, which in my opinion, might rank among the foremost of literary productions."[23] Among these was *Evelina.* "I have again been weeping over the sufferings of Lady Belmont," Margaretta wrote. "May God protect me from the cruel impositions of base and interested man!"[24] The tender sensibilities of heroines often drew them to volumes in which vice and virtue were too closely blended to please moralists. Mrs. Franks thus swallowed the "subtle poison" of *Eloisa.* "Here, reclining on the soft bosom of the earth," she wrote sympathetically, "I retraced the pathetic epistles of Eloisa, till I became entranced in a gentle slumber."[25] Monima was warned against this seductive novel by her prudent father. "It is the production of a strong

[19] *Memoirs of the Bloomsgrove Family,* II, 81.
[20] Davis, *Ferdinand and Elizabeth,* p. 62.
[21] Read, *Monima,* p. 254.
[22] Tenney, *Female Quixotism,* I, 6.   [23] [Anon.,] *Margaretta,* p. 20.
[24] Murray, *The Gleaner,* II, 95.   [25] Relf, *Infidelity,* p. 60.

judgment rendered pernicious by a weakness of sensibility, that disgraces the soaring genius of its author," he charged. "My daughter, it is a book, that of all others, I desire you to refrain from reading."[26] Constantia did not allow her admiration of Sterne's style to blind her to the danger of his sentiments although she found his letters "superior as epistolary effusions to any she had ever read." Yorick and Eliza, she decided judiciously, "had entered into engagements, which made an indulgence of that ardent attachment improper."[27]

The sentimental heroine was a bulwark of orthodoxy in religion as well as in manners. A luckless suitor in *The Art of Courting* was made to pay dearly for the heresy of urging his betrothed to read Bolingbroke, Hume, and Paine. "I am chagrined and mortified beyond expression," she replied indignantly, "to find the man, whom I have esteemed more than any other, has imbibed sentiments which must separate us forever."[28] Constantia Neville made a merit of her ignorance of Dr. Priestley's writings on Deism. "There are books enow which will inform the mind and tend to purify the heart," she said staunchly, "without having recourse to disquisitions on points of faith."[29] Unca Winkfield was pleased to note that even savages were able to refute the Deists. "These writers labored to prove that christianity was repugnant to plain uncorrupted reason. Yet I found this assertion entirely false," she reported triumphantly, "for, here a people, who had no other guide but their reason, no sooner heard christianity plainly and simply expounded to them, but they soon embraced it."[30] Chesterfield fared no better than the Deists. "His instructing his son in the arts of seduction and adultery," declared the author of *The Hapless Orphan,* "is an error which can never be approved, save by the most licentious and depraved."[31] Mary Wollstonecraft was recognized as another enemy of the

[26] Read, *Monima,* p. 368.
[27] Wells, *Constantia Neville,* I, 319, 321.
[28] Bradford, *The Art of Courting,* p. 188.
[29] Wells, *Constantia Neville,* III, 101.
[30] [Anon.,] *The Female American,* pp. 152-153.
[31] [Anon.,] *The Hapless Orphan,* II, 38.

conventional code cherished by most heroines. Constantia cautioned women that the writings of Miss Wollstonecraft contained "so much of the poison of the new-fangled systems of philosophy, that it requires no common powers of discrimination to select what is excellent from what is execrable."[32]

Sentimental heroines were delighted, of course, with sentimental novels; in them they found mirrored a flattering picture of their own lives. Elizabeth's favorite author was Charlotte Smith in whose pages she found "an inexhaustible source of pleasure and delight."[33] Mary Carter sent her copy of *The Wedding Ring* to the heroine of *Emily Hamilton*. "The character of Miss Sidney . . . is truly amiable," she wrote. "Often have I wept at her sufferings, and admired her exalted mind, too noble to be depressed by them."[34] Sterne's beauties overpowered Sophia who enjoyed reading her favorite passages to her suitor. "It was the pathetic story of Maria, by Sterne," he reported. "As she proceeded her voice became tremulous and disturbed: at length unable to go on, she dropt the book and rushed out of the room in tears."[35] The drama of sentiment also afforded a source of tender pleasure. Steele's *Conscious Lovers* was a universal favorite. Mrs. Wentworth in *The Step-Mother* never missed a performance of John Home's *Douglas*.[36] Fanny Gardiner's swoon at a performance of Richard Cumberland's *The Brothers* first awakened the interest of the heroine of *The Hapless Orphan*. "Her heart was full; the pearly tear glistened in her eyes: she could not articulate . . . ," Caroline observed. "My attachment for her increased."[37] Emily Hamilton, who struggled vainly to fight back her tears at a production of *The Grecian Daughter,* found her example was followed by "a great part of the audience."[38] In *The Champions of Freedom* an entire audience wept at the pathos of a sentimental comedy. "Convulsive sobs could be distinctly heard

[32] Wells, *Constantia Neville*, I, 370.
[33] Davis, *Ferdinand and Elizabeth*, p. 18.
[34] Vicery, *Emily Hamilton*, p. 75.
[35] Watterston, *Glencarn*, II, 159.   [36] Wells, *The Step-Mother*, I, 13.
[37] [Anon.,] *The Hapless Orphan*, II, 98-99.
[38] Vicery, *Emily Hamilton*, p. 182.

in every direction," a witness noted. "The soft contagion ran through every bosom, and appeared in every eye, whether in gallery, pit, or boxes."[39]

The heroines of these novels would have been something less than true daughters of their time had they failed to worship at the shrines of delicacy, propriety, and decorum. The curriculum of Mrs. Foster's boarding school was in harmony with the spirit of the age in its aim "to inspire a due sense of decorum and propriety."[40] Novelists, moreover, clothed feminine punctilio as one of the eighteenth-century graces. "Narrow is the path of propriety," warned Caroline Warren in *The Gamesters,* "and doubly guarded on every side should be the steps of woman."[41] Mrs. Sally Wood approved of Julia's scruples about attending a masquerade ball. "She had an innate and lively sense of female propriety," wrote the author, "and never had she once deviated from it." "She had always thought it highly inconsistent, with the true dignity of a young woman, to appear in a borrowed character. For this reason, she refused any garb, that would disguise herself. . . ."[42] Heroines studied the female proprieties until they were able to discern nice differences between the various shades of behavior; no distinction was too subtle for these zealous metaphysicians. So fantastic was Caroline Wentworth's respect for the difference between her social status and fortune and those of the man she loved that she refused to confess her attachment even though this self-denial was the direct cause of her lover's death. "I could at no period of my life ever bring myself to think, with any degree of composure," she maintained, "on matches where there existed such a disparity in those points."[43] Where outside the pages of sentimental fiction was there so complete a triumph of punctilio over passion?

Respect for feminine decorum informed the action of almost all young ladies in these novels. Not even the most adverse tricks of Fate could be pleaded in extenuation of the

[39] Woodworth, *The Champions of Freedom,* II, 51.
[40] *The Boarding School,* p. 7.   [41] *The Gamesters,* p. 285.
[42] *Julia and the Illuminated Baron,* p. 142.
[43] Wells, *The Step-Mother,* I, 207.

slightest deviation from the narrow path of female rectitude. Unca Winkfield did not permit her plight upon a remote island inhabited by savages to modify her conception of what was proper for a delicate female. She was more alarmed at the prospect of outraging convention than of suffering from the frigid weather. "If I could not come at my clothes," this female Crusoe noted in her journal, "I considered that I should be very uneasy to myself, and started at the thought of going naked. . . ."[44] When an amazing accident tossed upon the island Unca's clerical cousin, her welcome was tempered by a sense of their compromising position. "I could not satisfy myself with the reflection of being much alone with a man, as it hurt my modesty," she confided in her notebook.[45] Unca also shrank from being seen alone with him because she feared that an unchaperoned couple might give "notions" to the savages. Fortunately for her peace of mind, a marriage satisfied her inclinations and her sense of delicacy. Female propriety was also preserved under trying circumstances by the valiant heroine of *The Female Review*. Miss Sampson, whose zeal to serve her country led her to adopt the disguise of a soldier in the Continental Army, not unnaturally found it difficult to preserve in the barracks the chaste atmosphere of her boudoir. "Had this been her customary plight in her kitchen at home, she might not have passed for an agreeable companion: for she was perfectly besmeared with gunpowder," her biographer admitted. Fastidious readers were assured, however, "that this was not the effect of indolence or sluttishness, but . . . of the most endearing attachment to her country. . . ."[46] Modesty under the stress of circumstances beyond her control had no more heroic exemplar than Miss Sampson. Upon one occasion, her boot rapidly filling with blood, she vowed to bleed to death rather than reveal her sex to the surgeon. Throughout her adventures, during which she kept a Pamela-like journal, her constant prayer was "that she might never be lost to all sense of virtue and decorum, as to act a part unworthy of her *being*,

[44] [Anon.,] *The Female American*, p. 50.
[45] *Ibid.*, p. 187. [46] Mann, *The Female Review*, p. 140.

thereby not only bring infamy on herself, but leave a blemish and stigma on the female world."[47]

Delicacy of conduct was frequently accompanied by a diction equally fastidious. Language was tortured to avoid the expressions for such persistent realities as birth, marriage, and death. In fiction which was largely devoted to recitals of attempts to violate the body of the heroine, there is practically no evidence to indicate that the heroine was aware that she possessed a body. Although the effects of physical passion were constantly before the readers of these novels, there is no mention of sexual feeling. The sentimentalist blanched before the facts and resorted to a mask of verbal prudery to hide his blushes. "About this time my Julia introduced a little cherub of innocence into this world . . . ," announced an enraptured father in *The Gamesters*.[48] This unwillingness to call a baby, a baby, was characteristic of novelists who contrived to bring children into the universe *between* chapters. Clemenza's pregnancy was announced in an elegant circumlocution designed to please the most fastidious modesty. "My companion's situation now appeared to be such," remarked Welbeck in *Arthur Mervyn*, "as, if our intercourse had been sanctioned by wedlock, would have been regarded with delight."[49] A more popular formula to describe the condition of a virtuous wife about to become a mother was used by the author of *Constantia Neville*. She "was in that state 'in which women wish to be who love their lords,'" wrote Helena Wells, "and consequently she could not venture to be his companion on the voyage. . . ."[50] Mrs. Noble hit upon a pleasant euphemism to avoid mentioning her second marriage in *The Hapless Orphan*. By a neat

[47] *Ibid.*, pp. 108-109. Heroes were forced to go to extreme lengths to match the decorous conduct of their lovers. Mercutio's heroic self-restraint was made the subject of praise in *Fortune's Foot-ball*. "It is worthy of remark," wrote the author, "that though Mercutio's connection with Isabella, had been sanctioned by a rite of the Church of Rome . . . yet, as a member of the Church of England, he considered it in no other light than as a mere espousal. He had some time previous to their marriage, convinced her of the propriety, and apprized her of his intention of keeping separate beds, until this obstacle could be removed—a line of conduct from which they never deviated" (II, 186).   [48] Warren, *The Gamesters*, p. 74.
[49] C. B. Brown, *Arthur Mervyn*, p. 98.   [50] *Constantia Neville*, I, 31.

sentimental evasion, she assured her friends that she had merely "renewed her first marriage."[51] These writers attained some skill in dismissing unpleasant realities by assuming they did not exist. They also laid the flattering unction to their souls that an elegant synonym was able to dissolve an irritating fact.

The heroine's outlook upon a world which she had been taught to regard as a vale of tears was a melancholy one. To be gay was to offer an affront to the religious precepts which promised death as an escape from the sufferings of innocence. Indulgence in the pensive mood became a habit with many heroines, who, like Maria in *Ferdinand and Elmira,* "almost thought it criminal, or at least, want of delicacy, to be cheerful."[52] Madam de Shong confessed she found a subtle pleasure in grief. "I thought it virtuous to be wretched," she declared. "I indulged my afflictions; I even nursed them. . . ."[53] This fashionable melancholia was accompanied by a love of solitude and a delight in the more somber aspects of nature. It also shared the romanticists' interest in the "graveyard school" of poetry and found frequent expression in the female elegiac verse and mortuary art which embellished early American magazines. Young's *Night Thoughts* was the favorite volume of languishing ladies; every respectable death chamber had one. "When I entered her chamber she was sitting in an easy chair," wrote a visitor to the dying Sophia. "Young's *Night Thoughts,* in which she had been reading, lay in her lap."[54] The fashion produced a gloom so universal that Joseph Dennie felt it necessary to repeat Dr. Beattie's warning "to beware of immoderately indulging in the perusal of such works as the *Night Thoughts* of Young."[55]

"The Lay Preacher" also accused Laurence Sterne of fomenting this interest in genteel decay. "I am sorry," he lamented, "that so shrewd a remarker as Sterne should have asserted that a shattered fortune and a shattered frame are but light afflic-

---

[51] *The Hapless Orphan,* I, 9.   [52] Wood, *Ferdinand and Elmira,* p. 190.
[53] Wood, *Julia and the Illuminated Baron,* p. 233.
[54] Vicery, *Emily Hamilton,* p. 23.   [55] *Port Folio,* III, 226.

tions, if we have the *satisfaction of shattering them ourselves.*"[56] Shenstone was placed near the head of the list of writers responsible for the sober moods of American women by a "sharp visaged matron" in *Kelroy.* "Yes, I will put Shenstone on the list," she added, "a fellow who cut up a handsome estate into a garden, and spent his time in planting flowers, and making rhymes, while he suffered his house to go to ruin over his head, and luckily died just in time to escape jail."[57] John Blair Linn admitted the pleasures of pensive melancholy, but feared the consequences of a too somber cast of feminine imagination. "The female sensibility being naturally more refined than the male," he advised, "they ought for the reason just mentioned, to shun the gloomy Melpomene and seek the gay, the lively, and descriptive muse."[58]

Thoughts of mourning and death were constant companions of these delicate children of adversity. They regarded the world as a sepulchral vestibule to eternity. "But, ma'am, you know that I always was of a serious turn of mind," Polly wrote to Sophia, "and I think I have some love for religion; nor do I confine my ideas of happiness to this world. . . ."[59] Mourning was not only virtuous, it served as a badge of social respectability and had other pleasing compensations. "The house of mourning, my dear Mary, is instructive," Emily confided. "I would not exchange my present melancholy sensations, this sweet pensiveness which is far from being unpleasing, for all the giddy mirth I ever experienced."[60] Constantia shared Emily's love of pleasing sadness. "I had the happiness of being early taught," she wrote, "that it was better to go to the House of Mourning, than to that of Feasting; and I have experienced more calm delight from knowing myself an inmate of the former, than I ever did while a guest of the stately dome where Festivity and Mirth kept their Court."[61] Females who entertained these sentiments were appropriately clothed in customary suits of solemn black. "Her dress was sable, emblematic

[56] *Ibid.*, V, 219.
[58] *Miscellaneous Works*, p. 104.
[60] Vicery, *Emily Hamilton*, p. 30.
[57] Rush, *Kelroy*, p. 43.
[59] [Anon.,] *Fidelity Rewarded*, p. 7.
[61] Wells, *Constantia Neville*, III, 336.

of the gloom of her soul," announced the author in presenting Monima to the readers. "From her cradle she had been the child of adversity."[62]

Young ladies who were taught that the good die young were ever eager-eyed for premonitions of early dissolution. Thus the heroine of *Glencarn* informed her anxious lover, "I think I will not live long: there rushes across my mind, when I am alone and weeping, a presentiment that my heart is breaking. I feel it in every pulse, I feel it in every throb."[63] The task of replying to such announcements bristled with difficulties. Perhaps the most acceptable response was a tactful blending of regrets at the prospective bereavement with congratulations upon unmistakable signs of immortality. The complete sentimentalist could do nothing less than fall into "a sympathetic decline" and assure his lover of the joys of "sweetly languishing into eternity" together. The "decline" became a fashionable attribute of the daughters of sensibility. There was high authority for it in Dr. Gregory's *Father's Legacy*. This widely read manual cautioned females that the possession of even an average share of vitality and animal spirits was something less than fashionable and more than feminine.[64] Heroines with "an attractive pallor" had an unfair advantage with men; the pages of sentimental fiction record few examples of "interesting" healthy females. Gentlemen preferred "declines."

These novels also reveal an unwholesome interest in decay. ". . . and, if she was a less lovely and attractive object, she was certainly a more interesting one," wrote an admirer of the languishing Countess Lapochin in *Ferdinand and Elmira*, "for she now touched the soul, and penetrated the heart. . . ."[65] There is the same morbid interest in the appearance of Maria in *The Step-Mother*. "I thought Maria unusually grave; but never was she more lovely," a friend noted. "An interesting languor overspread her fine features, that made her something more than human."[66] Sophia's "decline" invested her with

[62] Read, *Monima*, pp. 13-14. [63] Watterston, *Glencarn*, II, 202.
[64] *The Father's Legacy* (New York, 1775), p. 21.
[65] Wood, *Ferdinand and Elmira*, p. 125. [66] Wells, *The Step-Mother*, I, 97.

similar charms. "She was pale and wan, her eyes were swoln with weeping, a shade of deep inquietude hung over her countenance," a visitor reported in *Glencarn,* "and she appeared like the spirit of melancholy, mild, pensive and interesting."[67] Even hardy pioneer maidens, inured to life on the frontier, were unable to resist the fashion. Thus Catharine, who could face a catamount without trembling, wasted away during her lover's absence: "Many tardy weeks lingered as they passed, vivacity fled, health gradually declined, and the once blooming Catharine was but a pallid spectre of her former self."[68] Languishing ladies were fully conscious of their powers. Sophia Westyn enjoyed her melancholy posture a bit too complacently. "The nature of my thoughts had modified my features into an expression," she wrote proudly, "which my friends were pleased to consider as a model for those who desired to personify the genius of suffering and resignation."[69] Few sentimentalists made their final exits without due regard for the general effectiveness of the scene.

This fashionable melancholia led inevitably to a morbid preoccupation with the spectacle of death. Sentimental heroines had a partiality for mortuary matters. They were forever watching beside deathbeds, sewing shrouds, and contemplating coffins. "Blush ye that dread to watch the expiring lamp of life, that quit with indecent haste where lie the remains of those whom, when living ye affected to honor," exclaimed Constantia.[70] Most heroines had no need to blush on this account. "O that you could have witnessed Amelia at the death-bed of Harriet Palmer . . . sustaining her head on her bosom, and wiping the clammy dews of death from her sunken cheeks," cried an admiring friend. "O George, it is in such scenes that lovely woman shines. . . ."[71] Nothing less than a midnight visit to a charnel house illuminated by flashes of lightning could sate Julia's morbid curiosity. "Julia looked in with a mixture of fear, awe, and satisfaction," declared Mrs. Wood,

[67] Watterston, *Glencarn,* II, 163.
[68] Woodworth, *The Champions of Freedom,* I, 199.
[69] C. B. Brown, *Ormond,* p. 279.   [70] Wells, *Constantia Neville,* I, 183.
[71] Woodworth, *The Champions of Freedom,* II, 100-101.

"and as she cast her eyes upon a row of coffins that were placed upon a shelf of black marble, heaved one sigh, for what they contained." After opening several coffins, Julia climaxed her orgy with a study of comparative decay. "I thought indeed that laying [sic] twenty years in this damp place, would have destroyed every vestige of a face, and yet every feature remains," she observed with rare objectivity under the circumstances. "Only the tincture of the complexion is changed . . . the crimping is not out of the linen."[72] Scenes of death also provided Margaretta with her favorite topics. "It was an awful scene, as the pall-covered bier of the youthful victim, was moved in slow procession down the gloomy avenue . . . ," she wrote of Louisa's funeral. "Oh! how I love to dwell on such themes! dear Elce, how swiftly the subject flows from my heart to my pen."[73] The revolting imagery of Alonzo's outburst in *The Asylum* shows to what lengths writers were forced to go to gratify the taste of the decadent cult of morbidity. "Must that heavenly frame putrify, moulder, and crumble into dust! Must the loathsome spider nestle on her lily bosom?" he asked deliriously. "The odious reptile riot on her delicate limbs! the worm revel amidst the roses of her cheek, fatten on her temples, and bask in the lustre of her eyes! Great God! what a thought! Alas!"[74] Alas, indeed! These novelists respected only one rule of composition: "Everything too much."

If readers of these sentimental tales failed to conjure up a distinct picture of their lovely heroines, it was not for lack of abundant testimonials to their beauties. It would be something worse than graceless to conclude without a sample of their charms compounded of Eliza's sensibility, Griselda's patience, and Cleopatra's infinite variety. And if the composite at times seemed too good for human nature's daily food, much may be allowed for the nature of the ingredients and the difficulty of the task. Novelists were offered many suggestions by contributors to magazines who vied with each other in presenting patterns of female excellence. "She is meek as him, whose

[72] *Julia and the Illuminated Baron*, pp. 189-191.
[73] *Margaretta*, p. 350.   [74] Mitchell, *The Asylum*, II, 133.

meekness is proverbial: Her bosom is the abode of the purest friendship and benevolence," wrote the author of "A Character," an outline of an ideal heroine. "Her sensibility is of that kind, it can never be questioned. . . . Her bosom never refused a sigh, nor her eye a tear, to the plaintive tale of distress."[75] More specific qualifications were listed by Strephon in *The Art of Courting*. "I should wish she might be above the common size of woman, well proportioned in body and limbs; her skin white and ruddy; her eyes black and sparkling; her hair brown and flowing, and her features well proportioned one with the other," he specified with some exactness. "But what I should prize above all the rest . . . some peculiar qualifications of heart . . . with a soul turned for love."[76] The sketches of Camilla and Flora in the *New York Magazine* reveal a friendly difference of opinion as to the precise degree of ardor which the ideal heroine should inspire. "While Camilla inspires a reverence that keeps you at a respectful yet admiring distance, Flora excites the most ardent, yet most elegant desire," wrote this discriminating student of feminine charms. "Camilla reminds you of the dignity of Diana, Flora of the attractive sensibility of Calisto: Camilla almost elevates you to the sensibility of angels, Flora delights you with the loveliest idea of women."[77] Novelists did not find these qualities irreconcilable; they frequently combined them in the same soft bosom.

These phantoms of delight walked in an atmosphere of moral and intellectual beauty to which the heart rather than the mirror could do full justice. Sensibility proved an adequate compensation for the lack of regular features. "Her face is not regularly pretty," admitted Mrs. Rowson in describing Meriel, "but she has a lovely pair of hazel eyes, through which you may read every emotion of her soul."[78] The authors, however, were not ignorant of the baser elements in man's nature and knew that suitors had eyes as well as hearts. They were fond of endowing their heroines with all the physical graces and then

[75] *Massachusetts Magazine*, II, 31-32.
[76] Bradford, *The Art of Courting*, p. 43.
[77] *New York Magazine*, II (N. S.), 98.   [78] *Trials of the Human Heart*, I, 13.

protesting that beauty was only a secondary consideration. Thus Mrs. Wood provided Amelia with the ravishing charms "of a complete voluptuary," and then, lest sex be too much emphasized, hastened to add lamely, "But she was not a beauty; it was her fine and open countenance, beaming forth with intelligence and sweetness, that threw a charm over every feature. . . ."[79]

The author of *The Gamesters* was also apprehensive that Amelia Stanhope's personal attractions, which certainly should have satisfied any reasonable lover, would overshadow her less earthy appeal. "But when Amelia spoke," declared her champion, "all other beauties were eclipsed in the delicacy of her sentiments, and the purity of her language."[80] Despite their protestations of the unimportance of mere physical beauty, few writers failed to present a specific inventory of them. They were realists enough to know that few men were ready to prostrate themselves before sexless sensibility. "To a complexion dazzlingly fair, was added the brightest glow of the carnation," wrote Mrs. Wood of Elmira. "Her hair was a light auburn; it was curled over a neck, whose extreme whiteness, fine polish, and elegant form, might have vied with the finest statuary; and her mild blue eyes, shone with a soft radiance, the harbingers of virtue, truth and innocence."[81] The catalogue of Adelaide's charms included items which would have delighted a voluptuary. "Her eyes are black, lively, and brilliant; her brown hair falls in ringlets on a neck of dazzling whiteness," described the admiring author. "I never saw finer teeth, nor such vermillion lips; and without being either a lover or a poet, I may say, that the rose humid with the tears of Aurora, has neither the freshness, nor the lustre of her cheeks, her complexion is a blossom, her *tout-ensemble* a grace."[82] Cynics had reason to smile when the fortunate possessor of such transcendent charms boasted that he was first attracted by his wife's delicate and ethereal sensibility.[83]

[79] *Amelia; or, The Influence of Virtue,* pp. 10-11.
[80] Warren, *The Gamesters,* p. 35.   [81] *Ferdinand and Elmira,* p. 21.
[82] *Dangerous Friendship* (Baltimore, 1807), p. 60.
[83] Strong claims, however, were made for the cosmetic powers of sensibility. Mrs.

By almost unanimous consent, the ideal age for a sentimental heroine was "about seventeen." "At that age, sensibility is most acute," stated the author of *Monima*.[84] Ferdinand, who had left his home when Elmira was only fifteen, returned to find that the delectable age had worked an astounding transformation. "A year, too, had wrought a great change in the person of Elmira," observed Mrs. Wood, ". . . a thousand sweet and feminine graces . . . had been surprisingly improved and matured in his absence. . . ."[85] The heroine of *Constantia Neville* came into her charms somewhat earlier, "for though but just turned thirteen, Miss Neville's height and appearance induced all who beheld her to conclude, that she was in her seventeenth year." This departure from the norm was satisfactorily explained by the author, who cited "the well known fact, that in warm climates both mind and body sooner arrive at maturity than in cold ones."[86] Constantia, born in the West Indies, was the exception which proved the rule. Most American heroines were forced to wait a few years before discarding their dolls. Isaac Mitchell was at some pains to point out that Melissa "was now about seventeen years of age" at the beginning of her adventures; this appeared to be the favorite age.[87] It remained for George Watterston, whose own heroine in *Glencarn* "was now in her sixteenth year, with a figure of more than Grecian elegance or Asiatic delicacy," to explain the appropriateness of this age for the ideal heroine. "The soul of a girl, at the age of sixteen, unadulterated by the fashions of the world . . . is the very seat of love," he declared. "Her body swells at the touch of man. Every fibre of her form trembles with extasy. Every pulse beats to pleasure, and her heart dissolves in rapture. She feels, hears, and thinks of nothing but love."[88]

Murray testified that Margaretta had no occasion for rouge because "A sentiment well delivered, has a pleasing effect on her countenance, it gives to her cheek a charming glow, and to her eye it conveys the soul-subduing glitter of benevolence." "A Sentimental Perfumer" in the *New York Weekly Magazine* recommended "Modesty" as "the very best rouge, giving a becoming bloom to the cheek" (II, 7).

[84] Read, *Monima*, p. 218.   [85] Wood, *Ferdinand and Elmira*, pp. 149-150.
[86] Wells, *Constantia Neville*, I, 110, 131-132.
[87] *The Asylum*, I, 37.   [88] *Glencarn*, I, 28, 30.

It was not *romantic* or *passionate,* but *domestic* love which was deemed proper for the sentimental heroine. Charlotte Temple and Eliza Wharton were only the most celebrated of scores of the "deluded fair" who had been ruined by romantic attachments. "Oh my dear girls—for to those only am I writing—listen not to the voice of love, unless sanctioned by parental approbation," counseled Mrs. Rowson in *Charlotte,* "be assured, it is now past the days of romance: no woman can be run away with contrary to her own inclination."[89] Mrs. Foster had the same warning to make against "the indulgence of that romantic passion, which a blind and misguided fancy paints in such alluring colours, to the thoughtless and inexperienced."[90] Passion and romance were able to boast of no pleasures so solidly satisfying as those reported by an enthralled witness of Amelia's happy family: "I have entered an apartment, where Sir William has been a delighted spectator, and partaker of scenes interesting and transporting; while Amelia has been giving nourishment from the purest source of health and life, to her infant, two rosy cherubs hanging at her knee, and Charles seated upon the arm of her chair, just dressed in boy's clothes, and proud of this distinction, first stealing a kiss from his angel mother, caressing the babe, and in turn playing with his kitten. . . . The innocence of the children, the beauty and virtue of the mother, the manly affection of the father, and the dignity and tenderness of the grandmamma, have all conspired to fill my bosom with such sensations, that I have been forced to leave them to conceal or give way to my emotions."[91] Here are all the ingredients of a happy final chapter: a wayward husband reclaimed by his wife's long-suffering patience, a reunited family circle blessed by the prattle of young innocents, and the benediction of serene old age. Readers of Mrs. Wood's artless tale of the influence of virtue will be the last to begrudge Amelia the rewards of her hard-earned triumph.

No such felicity was reserved for the most memorable of all the heroines in these early novels, Eliza Wharton in Hannah

[89] *Charlotte,* I, 36. [90] *The Boarding School,* p. 99.
[91] Wood, *Amelia; or, The Influence of Virtue,* pp. 240-241.

Webster Foster's *The Coquette*. She makes her chief appeal to us across the years as a rebel against the terrific decorums which stifled the individuality of her sex. She alone dared to question the eternal proprieties. Before accepting the inevitable duties of marriage, Eliza demanded the right to live her own life. She chafed at the well-meaning attempts of her friends to provide her with a suitable husband. "Marriage is the tomb of friendship," she protested. "It appears to me a very selfish state."[92] When her friends urged the propriety of an early settlement, Eliza replied spiritedly, "But I despise those contracted ideas which confine virtue to a cell. I have no notion of becoming a recluse."[93] Although she could be "sentimental and sedate" when the occasion demanded, she found the conversation of the Reverend Mr. Boyer a bit cloying. "So sweet a repast, for several hours together, was rather sickening to my taste," she confided to her anxious friend.[94] His epistolary "effusions" were also somewhat too sententious for her taste. "I have just received a letter from Mr. Boyer, in the usual style," she wrote Lucy Freeman. "He expects the superlative happiness of kissing my hand next week. O dear! I believe I must begin to fix my phiz. Let me run to the glass and try if I can make up one that will look *madamish*."[95] A young lady might be volatile, she insisted, and virtuous, too. Eliza was destined to learn that "natural volatility" and independence were not prized as feminine virtues by those who made a modern ideal of the conduct of the patient Griselda. We are allowed a glimpse of her tortured soul in the contrite letter in which she belatedly offered her hand to Boyer. The miserable death which followed her yielding to Sanford probably seemed to many of Mrs. Foster's readers a just retribution. In the feverish world of sentimental fiction, this was the fate of all lovely heretics who refused to worship at the shrines of feminine punctilio, delicacy, and propriety.

[92] *The Coquette*, p. 35.
[94] *Ibid.*, p. 46.
[93] *Ibid.*, p. 18.
[95] *Ibid.*, pp. 88-89.

3.

THE TENDER LANDSCAPE

Since his departure it had been her constant custom to repair to the little temple in the grove, where first her father sanctioned their growing love; there for hours would she sit pensively listening to the bubbling stream . . . an urn sacred to love was erected on a spot, where oft they hailed the tender flame. Her drawings were hung in the Gothic pavilion, and an elegant Mosaic altar, composed of different coloured pebbles, decorated the temple of Hymen; a seat was happily disposed near a natural grotto, by the cascade which was overhung with weeping willows and a thousand aquatic shrubs.

— *New York Weekly Magazine*, 1796.

WHEN THE sentimental heroine ventured out of doors there was rung down upon the stage a backdrop drenched in pale moonlight and painted in the ultraromantic style. Here, if ever, was nature to advantage dressed. The scene to be perceived through the purple mists was embellished with umbrageous arbors and elegant summerhouses. Mazy walks wound their way to delightful grottoes and ornate temples. Distant cascades tinkled softly through the air gently fanned by weeping willows. Over all was the heavy mist of sentiment, and, if a fitful flash of lightning challenged the moon's dominion, it was merely to remind good readers that even the heroine's contemplative retreat was not sacred to the base seducer.

Dr. Enos Hitchcock in his *Memoirs of the Bloomsgrove Family* was careful to explain some of the symbolism of his ideal landscape. "As the principal walk runs in a vermicular direction, and all the others in a similar manner, they do not intersect each other at right angles," he observed with geometric exactness, "but in every direction are cut into segments of circles. This is imitating nature: for she nowhere, in any of her works, exhibits a right angle; and it affords a romantic appearance."[1] Other sentimental gardeners were not merely content with imitating nature, they sought to improve her. Elvira was compelled to admit the truth of her lover's conjec-

[1] *Memoirs of the Bloomsgrove Family*, I, 102.

ture when he saw a common hill "suddenly and unexpectedly changed into an Helicon or Parnassus." "Surely," he cried, "nature never, entirely of herself, formed this spot, but art must also have lent her assistance."[2] Nature certainly did not provide unaided the elegant "white Chinese railing" and "gravel walk" which Margaretta enjoyed showing visitors to her sentimental retreat. "Every day the gardener is employed in cleaning, smoothing and polishing its surface," she boasted.[3]

The landscape which art thus helped to cultivate for genteel females was designed to feed their melancholy and their love of solitary contemplation "in the bosom of nature." Mrs. Rowson's Meriel found much solace in lonely meanderings. "I doat on a gloomy grotto," she declared romantically, "and a moonlight night, with a nightingale under my window, and a streamlet just near enough for its murmurs to be agreeable, fills me with delight."[4] A writer in the *Weekly Magazine* in 1798 pointed the finger of scorn at those who shunned solitude. "This distemper is peculiar to people of vacant minds, and guilty consciences," wrote this critic of "Solo-Phobia." "Such people cannot bear to be alone."[5] The young ladies of our fiction were quick to clear themselves of such charges. "I love to get by myself. Reflection is pleasing," wrote Caroline in *The Hapless Orphan*.[6] The heroine of *Infidelity* told Maria of the sweet privacy of her woodland confessional. "The rooms and balcony in the front are entirely shaded by a row of willows, whose drooping boughs, moved by a gentle breeze, seem to wave in zephyrous music to the victim of solitude and grief. In such a seclusion," she exclaimed, ". . . what a period of divine luxury would be the ensuing summer!"[7] Hostesses who owned pavilions situated in remote parts of their estates naturally expected to see very little of their guests. Margaretta's stay in the country was spent almost entirely in deep seclusion. "I seek the thick embowered temple in her elegant garden," she wrote to a friend, ". . . to respire with freedom, and give full sway to

[2] Linn, *Miscellaneous Works*, p. 179.   [3] Murray, *The Gleaner*, III, 280.
[4] *Trials of the Human Heart*, II, 147-148.
[5] *Weekly Magazine* (Philadelphia, 1798), I, 178.
[6] [Anon.,] *The Hapless Orphan*, I, 85.   [7] Relf, *Infidelity*, p. 15.

the natural bent of my melancholy reflections."[8] The inclination to commune with nature was generally recognized as evidence of superior sensibility. Constantia, who roamed the fields with a copy "of the immortal Thomson" under her arm, was amazed "that the people who lived in the midst of such, to her, romantic scenery, felt none of her enthusiasm; *some* had heard of Thomson's *Seasons,* others had read them *without* emotion. . . ."[9]

The sentimental retreat was a favorite stage property. Almost every eighteenth-century man of feeling boasted of at least one somewhere on his estate and embellished it as a favorite project. Seymour "displayed much taste in his buildings and gardens," wrote Mrs. Murray, "but his elegant fancy has been nowhere so conspicuous as in a beautiful grove, on which he has bestowed every embellishment of art and nature. . . ."[10] The architectural style of these structures was a romantic hybrid of the Classical, Oriental, and Gothic. They ranged in size from Elizabeth's simple "arbour encircled with woodbines and jessamine,"[11] to vast mausoleumlike vaults and stately pleasure domes. St. Herbert built an elaborate edifice for Louisa's daughter. "The roof was supported by eight arches joined at the bottom by a low balustrade, round which some tangled evergreens clung, and the pavement was of white marble," according to the account of an admiring visitor. "An old blue damask sofa rested itself against one side of the building, and opposite to it stood a harpsichord . . . while in one of the arches upon the railing were placed two large jars of porphyry filled with rose bushes."[12] The summerhouse of Meriel was equipped with a full-throated organ. "At the top of a walk at no great distance from the house, but on a little eminence, there is a summer-house greatly admired by all the

---

[8] [Anon.,] *Margaretta*, p. 86.   [9] Wells, *Constantia Neville*, I, 82.

[10] *The Gleaner*, II, 46. The taste was a fashionable one. "Mr. Melworth too, has tried his talents at architecture," Mrs. Murray wrote, "and he has distinguished the paradisaical retirement which he has completed, by the appellation of the Cottage of Amity" (II, 46).

[11] Davis, *Ferdinand and Elizabeth*, p. 30.

[12] *New York Weekly Magazine*, I, 246. The tale of St. Herbert was published in regular installments in this periodical from Feb. 3 to June 22, 1796.

family . . . ," wrote the proud owner. "The moon shone through the windows full upon an organ which was placed there for me to entertain myself with. . . ." Unfortunately, all this elegance failed to restrain the villainous Belger from attempting to seduce the fair tenant while she was seated at the instrument singing a hymn![13] The "temple" of Wieland, in which he died by spontaneous combustion, boasted of a harpsichord and "a bust of Cicero." "Here the performances of our musical and poetic ancestors were rehearsed," Clara wrote. "Here my brother's children received the rudiments of their education; here a thousand conversations, pregnant with delight and improvement, took place; and here the social affections were accustomed to expand, and the tear of delicious sympathy to be shed."[14]

As was true in *Wieland,* these "paradisaical retirements" often were the scenes of dramatic moments in the lives of their occupants. Here it was that Eliza met her betrayer in *The Gamesters.* "Suffice it to say," testified the author delicately, when "the setting sun threw his last rays on the tops of the trees; they shone not on the *virtuous* Eliza."[15] The secluded retreat proved a popular place for courtship as well as for seduction. Ferdinand recalled the lush setting of his delicious hours with Elizabeth. "Umbrageous arbour! Delicious retreat!" he cried. "Never shall I forget the enraptured moments I passed within thy recess."[16] Emily Hamilton reserved her arbor for friendship and music. "Never did the pale moon shine with more radiance than at this hour," she declared, "and Belmont's flute, conspired with the surrounding scenes, to fill the mind with sensations the most pleasing and sublime."[17] That ill-starred, sentimental couple, Amelia and Leander, spent the few happy moments vouchsafed to them in their woodland haven. "Few circumstances in life would admit of a com-

---

[13] Rowson, *Trials of the Human Heart,* III, 106-107.

[14] C. B. Brown, *Wieland,* pp. 24-25. Clara's private temple was less elaborate: "A slight building with seats and lattices . . . the odours of the cedars which embowered it, and of the honey-suckle which clustered among the lattices, rendered this my favorite retreat . . . " (*ibid.,* p. 73).   [15] Warren, *The Gamesters,* p. 268.

[16] Davis, *Ferdinand and Elizabeth,* p. 30.

[17] Vicery, *Emily Hamilton,* p. 143.

parison with their rural excursions," wrote the author, "when, happy as the first created pair in the garden of Eden, they hand in hand sought out the cooling shades, and listened to the plaintive notes of Amelia's guitar, or the livelier strains of Leander's clarionette."[18] The sentimental heroine often selected a sylvan retreat as an appropriate spot in which to plight her troth. Here Melissa agreed to give Alonzo her answer to his suit in a setting in which every detail had been carefully arranged. "Melissa had retired to a little summer-house at the end of the garden," a witness related after the ceremony. "A servant conducted Alonzo thither. She was dressed in a flowing robe of green silk, embroidered with yellow fringe lace. Her hair fell in waving circles; in her hand was a boquette of flowers which she seemed to be critically examining."[19] It is to be hoped that Alonzo kept his appointment promptly, for even the ideal sentimental heroine could not hold a picturesque posture forever. Margaretta characteristically dedicated her pleasure house to humanitarian enterprises, where, despite the "white Chinese railing," "free egress and regress is allowed to every decent villager."[20] This retreat must have been popular, for "During the spring, summer, and autumn months, a servant is stationed in the Mall," wrote the generous proprietress, "who tenders cool lemonade, wine, milk, and a variety of fruits, and other light refreshments. . . ."[21] Margaretta herself on stated occasions appeared at this delightful dispensary to meet those "humble or necessitous friends who have any petition to prefer." Here was a sentimental tableau worthy of the immortality of a steel engraving, for little William, "a sentimentalist from the cradle, tripped by her side" and added his consolations "to the unfortunate stranger . . . in the true spirit of infantile philanthropy."[22]

Next to the retreat in the affections of the sentimental heroine was the grove, sacred to reflection and peace. Primeval groves, however, were rare; few were unimproved by art. How

[18] Warren, The Gamesters, p. 208.
[19] Mitchell, The Asylum, I, 241.   [20] Murray, The Gleaner, III, 280.
[21] Ibid.   [22] Ibid., III, 281-282.

elaborate some of these improvements might be is suggested by Butler in *Fortune's Foot-ball*. "Here, painting, botany, statuary, etc. were carried to the most elevated pinnacle of perfection," he declared. "Endless beauty and variety attracted the sight, and the most exquisite odours pervaded the whole parterre. If there is a place on earth, descriptive of the primeval residence of our first parents, this must be the spot."[23] Monima noted with satisfaction the curvatures so much admired by Dr. Hitchcock. "The rising meadows which lay to the left of the lawn, were verged by the circular direction of the waving woods," she observed, "from whence a stream of water issued that ran in serpentine mazes through the vale of the meadows. . . ."[24] The heroine of *The Hapless Orphan* boasted of a favorite retreat near the Delaware River. "A little to the left," Caroline wrote, "is an enchanting grove of weeping willows, whose romantic shade invites to tread the pleasurable path of retirement, so favorable to reflection."[25] Heroes also had their bowers of bliss. "In a beautiful recess in the Alleghany, I had erected a small bower," boasted Glencarn, who also confessed to a weakness for curves, "which was decorated with aromatic flowers, and ornamented with delicate and winding shrubbery of spring. Here I was accustomed to spend hours in solitary seclusion, and delightful meditation."[26]

The wilder and more somber aspects of nature were often the most congenial to harassed females who found the gloom of night less dark than seducers' hearts. Thus Miss Alfred forsook the serpentine paths and shaven lawns "to ramble, just as the sun dives into the west, among the silent rocks, listening to the mingled noise of the wooing birds, and the echoes which ascend from the adjacent vales."[27] The seduced Matilda in *The Lawyer* sought in nature to match the tempestuous emotions of her own breast. "When the storms raged, the thunder rolled, and the lightning glared with the most terrific corruscations," wrote Watterston, "Matilda would sally forth at the

[23] *Fortune's Foot-ball*, I, 157.
[24] Read, *Monima*, p. 360.
[25] [Anon.,] *The Hapless Orphan*, I, 225.
[26] Watterston, *Glencarn*, I, 23.
[27] Relf, *Infidelity*, p. 16.

dead of night, and wander, exposed to all the violence of the storm, until the bright beams of the sun began to illuminate the earth. . . ."[28] Caroline Franks nursed her woes in a rocky glen where she found tears in running brooks, sympathy in stones, and solace in everything. "Oh," she exclaimed, "when men, and even my fellow fair have denied a tear of commiseration, this breathless, dumb rock has shed showers of pity."[29] Nature invariably inspired reflections which suggest Wordsworth rather than Rousseau. The meanest flower that blows taught Constantia Neville "to look up to the Author of All. . . ."[30] Julia found the same inspiration in natural beauties. "She was never tired of rambling over the pleasure grounds," wrote Mrs. Wood, ". . . they were all surveyed with enthusiasm and delight, and she literally 'looked through nature, up to nature's God.' "[31] Margaretta was forever finding sermons in the skies. "The sweet influence of the beauties of nature pervaded my mind," she wrote to her friend, Elce. "The cloudless sky, the pensive beams of the moon, with the pure air which I inhaled, rapt my soul in adoration to Him who gave it."[32]

This romantic attachment to rural solitude was part of the sentimentalist's disdain of the world to which he believed himself superior. Thus Ferdinand, "sick of the vanity and vexation of the world," whispered to Elizabeth: "Has the thought never occurred to thee, Elizabeth, that we were not made for this deceitful, misanthropic world, but for one another? Didst thou never indulge the romantic but delightful wish that we could find an asylum from the oppression of our fellow creatures in some remote island where human foot-step ne'er yet imprinted the ground?"[33] Julia's lover in *Monima* echoed this desire to escape the contamination of unfeeling man. "How happy I could spend my life, had fate decreed me a villager!" he cried. "Why, Julia, you could have spun, while I would have

[28] G. Watterston, *The Lawyer; or, Man as He Ought Not to Be* (Pittsburgh, 1808), pp. 27-28.
[29] Relf, *Infidelity*, p. 23.   [30] Wells, *Constantia Neville*, I, 219.
[31] *Julia and the Illuminated Baron*, p. 35.
[32] [Anon.,] *Margaretta*, p. 191.
[33] Davis, *Ferdinand and Elizabeth*, p. 90.

ploughed; and in the evening I would have read prayers to the humming of your wheel, and we should have been as happy as monarchs!"[34] Sarah confided to her journal a yearning for the simple life which she shared with many of her sentimental sisters. "A decent competence best suits my disposition," she wrote modestly, "a neat dwelling remote from the noise, hurry, and dissipation of the gay, thoughtless and commercial world. . . . Such a state would be the height of my ambition."[35] The man of feeling regarded the humble rustic as one peculiarly free to follow his generous instincts. "I become more and more sick of the fashionable follies of the town, and more in love with the plain uncorrupted sincerity, and genuine hospitality of the country," protested Belmont in *The Farmer's Friend*.[36]

There is also the romantic conception of the noble savage in the sentimentalist's frequent attribution of his own ideals and motives to "natural man." Walter Kennedy justified his decision to live "in the remotest settlements of the Indians," because "among Indians of the forest," he declared, "I hope to find that tranquility with which I have been unacquainted in the bosom of civilized society."[37] The heroine of Mrs. Bleecker's "Story of Henry and Anne" imagined the redskins to be sentimental philosophers daubed over with bronze paint. "At least, we shall go into a land of simplicity," she predicted confidently, "the artless savages subsist not by rapine and deceit; pride and hypocrisy and avarice are strangers where luxury and titles are unknown."[38] When seen through the mists of sentiment, the America of pre-Revolutionary days seemed to Mrs. Rowson as the home of the Golden Age. The cottage of Dudley and Arabella was given an idealized pastoral setting. "Delightful age of primitive simplicity," hailed the author of *Reuben and Rachel*, "when the mother of a numerous family did not blush (though surrounded by affluence) to set the example of industry to her daughters; when she could preside amongst

[34] Read, *Monima*, p. 112.
[35] *Sarah; or, The Exemplary Wife*, pp. 200-201.
[36] Hitchcock, *The Farmer's Friend*, p. 117.
[37] Davis, *Walter Kennedy*, p. 28.   [38] *Posthumous Works*, p. 101.

them, whilst they were converting the produce of their father's flocks and fields into clothing for the family."[39]

Restraint was almost as rare a quality as humor in these novels. Nowhere outside the covers of their books did sentimentalists find that nature behaved so appropriately. Lovers' meetings, wrote a satirist in the *Port Folio*, "are supplied with a *quantum sufficit* of moonlight, which is an indispensable requisite; it being the etiquette for the moon to be particularly conscious on these occasions."[40] Delicate young ladies clad in thin muslin had no business meandering through damp midnight groves; even sentimental mists might lead to pneumonia, as the deluded Dorcasina Sheldon learned to her discomfort in *Female Quixotism*. "I will not dispute," remarked Brown in 1789, "whether the Novel makes the woman, or the woman makes the Novel. . . ."[41] Confirmed romance-addicts like Dorcasina had a sorry time in attempting to trace the outline of the sentimental landscape in the light of common day. Even the friendly moon failed Dorcasina when she embraced her Negro man-of-all-work snoring unromantically in a summerhouse. This misguided spinster failed to encounter eligible bachelors strolling contemplatively through groves and meadows after sundown. With a sentimentalist directing the performance, however, all things were possible. Rocks gushed tears, thunder promptly punctuated the base proposals of the seducer, and lightning obligingly discriminated between the wicked and the virtuous in its blasts of destruction. Isaac Mitchell, who found room for more thunderstorms in *The Asylum* than Dwight was able to pack into his *Conquest of Canaan*, was not content with ordinary scenic effects. His most masterly achievement, in which he flooded his tender landscape with moonlight and lightning simultaneously, deserves to be remembered: "It was one of those beautiful evenings in the month of June. . . . The moon shone in full lustre . . . while the whippoorwill's sprightly song echoes along the adjacent groves. Far in the eastern horizon hung a pile of brazen clouds,

[39] *Reuben and Rachel*, I, 140-141.   [40] II, 141.
[41] W. H. Brown, *The Power of Sympathy*, I, 67.

which had passed from the north, over which crinkling red lightning momentarily darted, and at times, long peals of thunder were faintly heard." With the sentimentalist, everything was too much, even the weather.

4.

THE HUMANITARIAN IMPULSE

He had visited every prison in Europe, and comforted every son of sorrow, or daughter of affliction, from the burning sands of Lybia to the frozen climate of Russia. The peculiar benevolence of his heart was such, that he was never so happy as when relieving the wretched; and he would have thought that day lost, which was not marked in the calendar of humanity with some deed of kindness and philanthropy.

—S. S. B. K. Wood,
Ferdinand and Elmira, 1804.

THE INDIVIDUAL man of feeling may have been a hard-shell Federalist in politics, but his sensibility was socialistic. Joseph Dennie had protested vainly against the inundation of liberal social ideas from romantic Europe, particularly "the French infidel philosophy" which had threatened to replace the strict, personal Puritan conscience with a mild, general benevolence. The sentimentalists, who had always exalted pity as one of the major virtues, eagerly nurtured this new tender social conscience and widened their embrace to include the whole human species.[1] With the perfectibility of man as a favorite article in their creed, they found generosity in pirates, chivalry in rustics, humanity in Negroes, and nobility in savages, West Indians, and Algerines. They also urged kindness to animals and to servants, and occasionally had a good word to say for such maligned creatures as sailors, soldiers, lawyers, and stepmothers.

[1] "Humanitarianism is just this vague sentimentality of a mind that refuses to distinguish between the golden rule and the precept of Apollo," wrote Paul Elmer More in "Religious Ground of Humanitarianism" in *Shelburne Essays* (New York and London, 1904), p. 251. Dennie, of course, identified the doctrine with Rousseau. In a brilliant critique of humanitarianism, Irving Babbitt admitted that many of Rousseau's ideas about sympathy and pity were anticipated by Hutcheson and Shaftesbury. See Babbitt's "Two Types of Humanitarians: Bacon and Rousseau" in *Literature and the American College* (Boston and New York, 1908), p. 61.

No belief was more highly cherished and more eloquently proclaimed than that of the inherent nobility of the human heart. "The human heart, as it comes from the hand of its Creator, *is* good," declared the author of *Margaretta*. "Its propensities, its qualities, its affections, have their origin in the bountiful munificence of heaven."[2] Benevolence was also hailed as one of the inborn virtues. "The human *heart* is naturally *benevolent;* benevolence is a divine spark of the Deity," wrote a contributor to the *Massachusetts Magazine*. "It humanizes our actions, softens our passions, sweetens our tempers, and points out the various duties we owe our fellow creatures. . . ."[3] The theory of original goodness became a welcome substitute for the doctrine of natural depravity. "Are you ignorant that the soul of Clara was created in a day of jubilee," Eliza asked, "that it escaped perfect from the hands of nature, and that its essence being *goodness,* it can cease to do good, only in ceasing to exist?"[4] No kind of depravity, not even that of the seducer, seemed beyond hope of redemption; goodness was every man's inalienable birthright. The regeneration of the villainous Wiatte was looked for in *Edgar Huntly*. "As an human being, his depravity was never beyond the health-restoring power of repentance," asserted Charles Brockden Brown. "His heart, so long as it beat, was accessible to remorse."[5] Although heroines were of divided opinion about the propriety of attempting to reform a rake, the belief in man's natural goodness made the enterprise peculiarly attractive. Amelia urged Meriel in *Trials of the Human Heart* to help a seducer rediscover his heart. "Mr. Rooksby appears to me a weak young man," she wrote, "but there seems great goodness of heart in him and I think it would be a charitable action to snatch him from ruin."[6]

Sentimentalists shared the romanticist's interest in aborigines. The Indians were cited as spectacular examples of a race of natural nobility unvitiated by corrupt models. De Eresby in

[2] [Anon.,] *Margaretta*, pp. 417-418.   [3] *Massachusetts Magazine*, I, 177.
[4] *Dangerous Friendship*, p. 185.   [5] *Edgar Huntly*, I, 170.
[6] Rowson, *Trials of the Human Heart*, III, 28.

Constantia Neville vowed "that he would sooner take an *Indian Squaw*, from his old friends on the other side of the Atlantic, than seek a wife reared by the *high-born, high-bred* dames of Britain."[7] Another favorite theme was that of the contamination of primeval innocence by the intrusion of civilized races. "The discovery of America by Europeans has introduced many vices among the Indians, but not a single virtue," complained the hero in *Walter Kennedy*. "Before that era, drunkenness was not known among them, and their language had no words to express swearing."[8] Constantia's humanitarianism was outraged at the conduct of wealthy planters in the Barbados, who coerced native women to be their mistresses and compelled their offspring to be "brought up as slaves, and not unfrequently sold on the death of the master of the estate." "We have many Incles and Yaricos in the Leeward Islands," she lamented.[9] Noble savages were made to manifest their sensibility in the most approved style. Thus the generous Ononthio, noticing the tears of a captive taken by his tribe, restored the white man to his family. "I felt that I was a man, that I was an Indian," he told the happy parents in "The Hermit of the Lake." "I begged him of my brethren, and he is now safe."[10]

Nor were the aborigines unused to the melting mood. "He paused, and his untamed spirit swelled even to his eyes," Mrs. Rowson wrote of a red man of feeling, "but he repelled the tokens of his sensibility, that were almost bursting from his glistening orbits. . . ."[11] Sentimental savages also showed a surprising mastery of the diction of sensibility. Eumea, an Indian maiden, would have been a welcome contributor to the most genteel gift-book. "The flowers you had gathered for me the day before you left me," she confessed to Reuben, "I bound upon my breast next my heart . . . they withered and dried, but every day I refresh them with my tears."[12] Unca Winkfield, whose

---

[7] Wells, *Constantia Neville*, III, 49.

[8] Davis, *Walter Kennedy*, p. 145.   [9] Wells, *Constantia Neville*, II, 268.

[10] *New York Weekly Magazine*, I, 347. Contributors to this periodical found the noble savage an attractive theme. The hero of "The History of Mr. Wilfort" won happiness in the wilderness. "I adore your daughter," he told the noble Thaol, "I detest the Europeans, and have fled from their inhumanity."

[11] *Reuben and Rachel*, I, 164.   [12] *Ibid.*, II, 348.

intense evangelical piety foreshadowed the interests of many heroines to appear later in the nineteenth century, was fond of reminding her admirers that she was the daughter of an Indian. The monument she erected over her mother's grave with inscriptions in the Latin, Indian, and English languages, bore witness not only to her pride in her savage ancestry, but to an impeccable mortuary taste and extraordinary linguistic powers. "On the top is an urn, on which an Indian leans, and looks on it in a mournful posture," Unca wrote with pardonable complacency. "The whole is surrounded by iron pallisadoes. This I often visited, and here I drop many a tear."[13] The sentimental and noble savage was a popular subject of "pathetic fragments" in periodicals;[14] occasionally he appeared in full-length novels to remind his civilized brethren of their shortcomings.[15] Familiar with writing of this sort, the hero of Tyler's *Algerine Captive* fully expected to return home with an Algerine Omai to exhibit to his friends. Underhill's experience, however, forced him to admit that sentimental savages were easier to find in fiction than in their native haunts. "It is true," he confessed, "I did not meet, among my fellow slaves, the rich, and the noble, as the dramatist and the novelist had taught me to expect."[16]

Admiration of the noble savage went hand in hand with a detestation of all forms of slavery. "Scratch an ardent Abolitionist and you were likely to find a potential perfectionist," Parrington wrote of the advocates of the antislavery movement in the forties. The humanitarian impulse which flowered in scores of nineteenth-century reforms, particularly in abolition,

[13] [Anon.,] *The Female American*, p. 33.

[14] See "Niko—a Fragment," *New York Weekly Magazine*, I, 239; "Friendship Put to the Test," *New York Magazine*, VI, 393-401; "Azakia: A Canadian Story," *ibid.*, II (N. S.), 31-37; and "The Cacique of Ontario," *Massachusetts Magazine*, VII, 304-306, 343-348, 393-396.

[15] Zelia and Sadi in Mrs. Rowson's *The Inquisitor* belong to the tribe of noble savages. Oosnooqua and Pokahontas play important roles in John Davis's *Walter Kennedy* and in *The First Settlers of Virginia*.

[16] *The Algerine Captive*, II, 27. Their benevolence, however, made up for their lack of nobility: ". . . by dividing the scanty meal, composing my couch of straw, and alleviating my rugged labors, they spake that universal language of benevolence, which needs no linguist to interpret."

is to be found in the pages of many early novels. "I felt my heart glow with feelings of exquisite delight," wrote Harrington in *The Power of Sympathy,* "as I anticipated the happy time when the sighs of the slave shall no longer expire in the air of freedom."[17] Dr. Hitchcock's joy in America's new independence was tempered by his shame at black slavery. "Many, who can defend their own rights with one hand," he noted indignantly, "are extending the other for the purpose of enslaving a part of their own species."[18] Mrs. Rowson appealed to the humanity of slaveowners in *The Inquisitor.* "The man who with unmerciful hand scourges his slave, does he then remember," she asked, "that the person he is chastising is endowed with the same feeling as himself, and is as sensible of pain, hunger, thirst, cold, aye, and all the social blessings of life?"[19] She found the African slave trade a cruel anomaly. "What right has an European to sell an African?" she demanded. "Do they leave their native land, and seek our coast, by arts entice our countrymen away, and make them slaves?"[20] Underhill, the humanitarian hero of *The Algerine Captive,* refused to accept any share of the profit resulting from the slave trade carried on by his ship. "I execrated myself, for even the involuntary part I had borne in this execrable traffic," he confessed with shame. "I thought of my native land and blushed. . . . I would sooner suffer servitude than purchase a slave."[21] The author of *Margaretta* made the generous Vernon express his hatred of the custom which permitted "one half of the human species to enslave the other half." "I abominate it," he declared, "as the most opposed to the sacred injunctions of benevolence. . . ."[22] Prince Nytan, an Oriental humanitarian, conducted his vast philanthropic projects upon a scale which suggests a Federal emergency relief administration. One of these projects was a plan to purchase outright the liberty of all Negroes and to transport them to a kind of Brook Farm Association in Africa. "Yes," Nytan told his amazed friends con-

[17] W. H. Brown, *The Power of Sympathy,* II, 32.
[18] *Memoirs of the Bloomsgrove Family,* II, 232.
[19] *The Inquisitor,* II, 87.   [20] *Ibid.,* II, 88.
[21] Tyler, *The Algerine Captive,* I, 190.   [22] [Anon.,] *Margaretta,* pp. 234-235.

fidently, "the emancipation of the human race from every species of slavery is not far distant. The mists of ignorance are fast dispersing."[23]

Underhill's opinion that the sensibilities of the blacks were fully as exquisite as his own was jeered at by the captain of a "slaver" as "Yankee nonsense about humanity."[24] This callous denial of finer feelings to one's fellow creatures was regarded as rank heresy by the votaries of sensibility who insisted that the capacity for joy and pain was bestowed without respect to creed or color. Upon this capital point, Miss Faugeres dared to enter the lists against the great Jefferson. "Notwithstanding what the learned Mr. Jefferson has said respecting the want of finer feelings in the blacks," she replied, "I cannot help thinking that their sensations, mental and external, are as acute as those of the people whose skin may be of a different colour. . . ."[25] The sentimental heroines eagerly espoused the cause of the Negroes. "The African, the Indian, the Hottentot, are creatures moulded by the hand of Heaven, and supported by the same bountiful munificence which other nations enjoy," observed Margaretta to the ever-assenting Elce.[26] Dorcasina Sheldon, whose immoderate reading of fiction made her ready to enlist under any banner of reform, scouted the slaveowners' argument that blacks were better off in bondage. "Comfortable they may be," she answered spiritedly, "but slavery and happiness are, in my opinion, totally incompatible; 'disguise thyself as thou wilt, still, slavery, thou art a bitter pill.' "[27] Tabitha Tenney burlesqued the zeal of many heroines in Dorcasina's sentimental reverie: "She then indulged herself in the agreeable, humane, but romantic idea, that, being the wife of Lysander, she should become the benefactress of his slaves. She even extended her benevolent reveries beyond the plantation of her future husband, and, wrapt in the glory of enthusiasm, saw his

[23] Sherburne, The Oriental Philanthropist, pp. 163-164.

[24] Tyler, The Algerine Captive, I, 201.

[25] The Posthumous Works of Anne Eliza Bleecker. . . . To which is added a Collection of Essays, Prose and Poetical by Margaretta V. Faugeres (New York, 1793), p. 268.

[26] [Anon.,] Margaretta, p. 155.   [27] Tenney, Female Quixotism, I, 12.

neighbors imitating his example, and others imitating them, till the spirit of justice and humanity should extend to the utmost limits of the United States, and all the blacks be emancipated from bondage, from New Hampshire to Georgia."[28] To Miss Tenney's readers in 1801 this prospect must have seemed an enthusiastic dream of sentimental evangelicalism. Its author, moreover, intended it to be received with amused pity for an incurably diseased imagination. Yet it was a vision not far different, glimpsed in the quiet of the First Parish Church of Brunswick, Maine, which moved Harriet Beecher Stowe to write a novel destined to convulse the nation and to touch with genuine pity the hearts of millions.

The evangelical piety which in the sentimental years[29] established foreign missions, set up asylums for aged, indigent, and respectable females, and inaugurated campaigns to ameliorate the conditions of the unfortunate of every description, is foreshadowed in almost every novel of the preceding generation. "Not distinguishing a particular nation, sect, or party, when man is distressed," exhorted the author of *The Gamesters*, "it becomes our duty to relieve him . . . as a child of the *same common parent*, though he range under the banner of the Cross, or revere a Deity in the laws of the Koran, or wander in the devious mazes of infidelity."[30] Later missionaries might have despaired of attempting to equal the conspicuous success of Unca Winkfield's venture in *The Female American*. Unca saw the opportunity of a long lifetime within her grasp when she accidentally discovered an ingeniously constructed idol which amplified the human voice several hundred times its ordinary volume. "It was nothing less than this," she declared triumphantly, "to ascend the hollow idol, speak to the Indians from thence, and endeavor to convert them from their idolatry. A bold attempt! not rashly to be undertaken."[31] The whole-

---

[28] *Ibid.*, I, 13-14.

[29] The twenty-five year period beginning in 1836 and ending with Lincoln's inauguration in 1860 which Professor E. Douglas Branch has further termed "the first generation of the American middle class" and "the first modern quarter-century of our national life." See his *The Sentimental Years, 1836-1860* (New York, 1934), for an entertaining and interesting social history of this era.

[30] Warren, *The Gamesters*, pp. 48-49.   [31] *The Female American*, p. 92.

sale, immediate conversion of several thousand noble savages set a record which shames the achievements of female evangelists of modern times. Unca's platform technique was as important as her piety. "I stopped at every convenient pause, two or three minutes, that I might not weary their attention," she explained, "and give them opportunity to reflect, as it were step by step, upon what I had said."[32] Although their plans were not crowned with such spectacularly sudden fruition as was Unca's effort, most heroines shared the hope of Mrs. Hayman in *Constantia Neville* that the day "was not far distant, when the glad tidings conveyed through the Gospel, should be spread from pole to pole."[33]

All other philanthropic enterprises pale into insignificance, however, when compared with the achievements of the hero of *The Oriental Philanthropist*. Some of his projects have a strangely contemporary sound, although the dispatch with which they were accomplished has no parallel in modern history. "Now you see before you, the diminutive dwellings of the inhabitants of this island," Nytan ordered one of his agents. "You are this day to provide them with better ones."[34] The colossal proportions of the program of this remarkable reformer may be seen in his creation of a chain of model asylums for lovely "female orphans,"[35] the transportation and resettlement of eighteen thousand unfortunates who were given a fresh start in an ideal island community,[36] the instantaneous and amicable settlement of a grave crisis in the domestic affairs of Persia,[37] and the merciful cessation of a European war for which Nytan made a special flying trip to the Continent.[38] Even his private charities were a bit staggering. He maintained twelve thousand wards "in different parts of Europe" and "settled them on good farms, which he purchased."[39] "He had likewise, built a number of towns and cities, and settled a family in every house," chronicled Sherburne. "So that the

[32] *Ibid.*, p. 129.
[34] Sherburne, *The Oriental Philanthropist*, p. 57.
[35] *Ibid.*, p. 67.
[36] *Ibid.*, pp. 79-80.
[38] *Ibid.*, p. 103.
[33] Wells, *Constantia Neville*, III, 249.
[37] *Ibid.*, p. 93.
[39] *Ibid.*, pp. 106-107.

whole number of citizens, men, women and children . . . were an hundred thousand."[40] The motives, if not the means of this almoner plenipotentiary, were shared by other less opulently endowed humanitarians in our fiction, who also aimed "to kindle the sacred flame of philanthropy in foreign courts, where it appeared . . . to be almost, if not altogether extinguished by vice, luxury, and intemperance."[41]

The domestic scene provided a more convenient sphere for philanthropic activity than foreign courts. "I am become the Lady Bountiful of all our poor tenants and their families," Meriel boasted to Celia. "I walk round every morning or evening, that the weather permits, and administer to the diseases of both body and mind."[42] The benevolence of the Countess de Launa in *Julia* is typical of the ministrations of mercy so frequently described in these novels. "She now lived only for others," declared Mrs. Wood, "to bless a numerous train of dependents; to comfort the afflicted, to' bind up the broken-hearted, to pour the oil and wine of kindness and sympathy into the bosom of the oppressed, was her business, and her pleasure. . . ."[43] The hero of *Reuben and Rachel* devoted his entire fortune to charity. "He liberated the poor debtor, afforded relief to depressed merit," wrote Mrs. Rowson, "and wiped away the tear from the eye of suffering virtue."[44] The philanthropy of Mr. and Mrs. Walgrave in *Moreland Vale* was famous throughout the countryside. "The hungry were fed—the naked were clothed—from having been children of sorrow themselves, they feel for all who come under that denomination," the author stated. "The poor heap blessings on their heads; and their children, ere they can well speak, were taught to lisp the names of Henry and Eliza."[45] Marriage was often welcomed by sentimental heroines as a means of extending the scope of their humanitarian activities. Indeed, the chief occupation of the married woman, when not engaged in

[40] *Ibid.*, p. 111.   [41] *Ibid.*, p. 45.
[42] Rowson, *Trials of the Human Heart*, III, 104.
[43] *Julia and the Illuminated Baron*, p. 28.
[44] *Reuben and Rachel*, II, 364.
[45] [Anon.,] *Moreland Vale; or, The Fair Fugitive* (New York, 1801), p. 184.

educating her own children, was that of teaching and nursing others. "From that auspicious day," remarked the author of *Monima* on the date of the heroine's wedding, "Monima became the soother of the afflicted, the mother to the orphan, the supporter of the oppressed, and the indulgent friend to the sufferer of sensibility."[46] Benevolence as well as sensibility boasted its martyrs, for neither heat nor cold or gloom of night stayed these angels of mercy from the swift completion of their appointed rounds. "Her death may be ascribed to the excess of her benevolence," Dr. Hitchcock diagnosed correctly in *The Farmer's Friend*. "A violent fever, occasioned by her unremitting attention to a sick friend, cut off her parent's hopes in a few days. . . ."[47]

Humanitarians took special delight in recognizing a kindred spark of benevolence in the behavior of those classes of people popularly regarded as calloused to the finer shades of feeling. The long line of nobly disinterested soldiers in these novels was designed to prove that regimentals might adorn the heart of sensibility as well as that of the libertine.[48] There was also an occasional attempt to rehabilitate the character of the sailor by attributing to him good deeds instead of girls in every port. "Tom Tarpaulin's heart beats higher when he's done a benevolent action, than if he *kill'd a shark, or caught a dolphin*," exclaimed the generous tar who rescued Amelia from a would-be seducer.[49] Nor was the heart of Lafitte, the notorious Barratarian pirate, found destitute of chivalry in Woodworth's *The Champions of Freedom* in which he was made to save Catharine from her abductor, and deliver her unharmed to her friends in New Orleans.[50] The lawyer, to be sure, had received unflattering treatment in Watterston's *The Lawyer; or, Man as He Ought Not to Be;* but Helena Wells charitably created a benign barrister, the estimable Mr. Lambton, to defend his

[46] Read, *Monima*, p. 464.   [47] *The Farmer's Friend*, p. 192.
[48] The wicked officer was a stock figure, but his example was offset by such models of propriety and humanity as Colonel R—— in *Glencarn;* Major Willoughby in *The Champions of Freedom;* and Colonel Wentworth in *The Step-Mother.*
[49] Warren, *The Gamesters*, p. 173.
[50] *The Champions of Freedom*, II, 325.

profession in *Constantia Neville*. "Blush, ye who throw indiscriminate censures on every branch of this profession," he complained, "promising that your characters are drawn from the life, and from having actually suffered all the tortures of suspense and delay that legal oppression can invent."[51] The same novelist also attempted the task of vindicating the character of the stepmother from the aspersions of those to whom second marriages seemed blasphemous. "The character of *stepmother* (in general deemed an odious one) I will allow to be the most difficult to fill of any allotted to our sex," admitted Caroline Wentworth.[52] By her devoted care of the children of her husband's first marriage, Mrs. Wentworth's conduct proved that even the dangers of this difficult office might be overcome by tact and sympathy.

The humanitarian, like the patroness in Charles Brockden Brown's "Sky-Walk," "was eagle-eyed after occasions for bestowing a benefit."[53] He followed the example of heroes in popular sentimental drama by vigorously opposing the duel as a means of settling disputes. He urged legislative protection for the unportioned, dependent female; he advocated universal suffrage. Gambling and intemperance were equally repugnant to him. He joined with reformers in their efforts to improve the intolerable conditions existing in the jails, and questioned the justice of imprisonment for debt. His eyes filled with "the rheum of sensibility" at the unhappy lot of policemen, sailors, and soldiers. He protested at the barbarities in the treatment of insane persons, and called public attention to the inadequacies of hospitals and asylums for the poor. He was an ardent champion of racial tolerance. His pity was aroused at cruelty to insects and animals. Black slavery was odious to him. He deplored the evils of child labor and of profiteering employers. These conditions formed the raw stuff out of which novelists fashioned strong scenes and drew sympathetic tears.

[51] *Constantia Neville*, II, 256.

[52] *The Step-Mother*, II, 241. For a typical instance of a treacherous stepmother and an account of her machinations, see *Moreland Vale*.

[53] *Weekly Magazine* (Philadelphia, 1798), I, 228. This novel, completed before the publication of *Wieland* in 1798, appeared only in fragmentary form.

Too often the pity thus aroused became an end in itself, a pleasing variety of emotional self-abuse. It would be rash, however, to assume that these novels failed to develop a public sentiment for reform, or that the humanitarian movement did not draw heavily upon them for support. In the history of reform, the sentimental novel played an important part.

It was temptingly easy to ridicule the victims of "the humane mania." Many humanitarians resembled Edward Montjoy in *Glencarn,* whose "passions were singularly organized; he could not behold the death of a fly without the most violent emotion: he was always in extremes: at one moment laughing in all the distortions of joy, and at the next, weeping in all the agony of sorrow."[54] Their ideas, moreover, often seemed grotesque. "They hold that our nature exists in its utmost purity among savages, and that civilization, and social intercourse are curses," chuckled an unsympathetic reviewer of Kotzebue's plays in the *Port Folio.* He was also amused to find humane readers allured by such inexplicable antitheses as *"Pitiable Adultress, The Noble Lie, Generous Revenge, Honest Thieves, The Guiltless Parricide, Errors of Virtue, Amiable Indiscretions, The Innocent Slanderer, Delicate Anger,* and a thousand other absurdities."[55] The cherished theory of perfectionism seemed especially ludicrous. "And, of late, I suspect my wife has been studying the new doctrine of *perfectibility,"* a contributor wrote in the *New York Magazine* in 1797. "I have little doubt that she looks forward with earnest hope to that happy day when the furniture of a house shall arrive at perfection, when wainscot shall be impregnable to dust, when plate shall shine in perpetual brightness, and the voice of scourers shall be heard no more."[56] Dorcasina Sheldon, who subscribed to all the isms and ologies current in popular fiction, was a staunch perfectionist. When, after falling prey to every adventurer in the neighborhood, she finally confessed that she found more perfidy than perfection in man, her father "more rejoiced

---

[54] Watterston, *Glencarn,* II, 142.   [55] *Port Folio,* II, 191.
[56] *New York Magazine,* II (N. S.), 517.

at this one short sentence, than at any he had ever before heard her utter."[57]

More fundamental was the serious charge that sympathy was merely a cheap and pleasant substitute for action. "I am far from intending to depreciate this humane and exquisitely tender sentiment, which the benevolent author of our nature gave us as a stimulus to remove the distresses of others," wrote a critic in the *Massachusetts Magazine*. "I would only observe, that where it is not strengthened by superior motives, it is a casual and precarious instrument of good . . . Christian charity does not wait to be acted upon by impressions and impulses."[58] Mrs. Foster barbed the point of this criticism with an episode in *The Boarding School*. The exemplary Mrs. Williams discovered Juliana surrounded by her hungry, tattered children in squalid poverty. "Yet she was sitting with a novel in her hand, over which she had apparently been weeping. She expatiated largely on the tale it contained, while her children, who exhibited a picture of real woe, engaged not her attention," the visitor lamented. Juliana was unmoved by rebukes. "I have fortitude sufficient to support my own calamity, but I must sympathize with the heroine of adversity," she replied. "I have not lost my sensibility with my fortune. My only luxury is now imagination!"[59] Such "humane mania" was not to be cured by satire. There was a pleasure in this variety of madness which only humanitarians could understand. One of them shall have the last word. "Strange! that an excess of humanity should often produce those irregularities in behavior and conduct, which constitute madness!" declared a self-styled "lunatic" in the *Weekly Magazine* in 1798. "Persons afflicted with this madness, feel for every species of distress, and seem to pour forth tears upon some occasions from every pore of their bodies. Their souls vibrate in unison with every touch of misery. . . . My constant prayer to the divine fountain of justice and pity— shall be, that I *may never be cured of it.*"[60]

---

[57] Tenney, *Female Quixotism*, I, 242.
[58] *Massachusetts Magazine*, I, 668-669.   [59] *The Boarding School*, pp. 22-23.
[60] *Weekly Magazine* (Philadelphia, 1798), I, 309.

5.

WERTHER-FEVER AND SUICIDE

You ask me when, and how I should like to die. Come to me this
night! my blessed creature! Bring with thee poison! Bring with thee pistols! and when the clock strikes twelve we'll both become immortal!
—John Davis, *The Original Letters
of Ferdinand and Elizabeth*, 1798.

THAT TEARFUL triune of sentimental beauties: Suicide, Seduction, and Sensibility, played an important part in the growing
popularity of American fiction. The high-strung sensibility invoked by Sterne, and the bugaboo of seduction for which Richardson was largely responsible, were now to be supplemented
by suicide, a theme equally rich in emotional possibilities. Our
early novels were destined to suffer the last ravages of that
fever incited by *The Sorrows of Young Werther* which swept
over eighteenth-century Europe like a contagious disease. The
seductive melancholy of Goethe's novel was in such exquisite
harmony with the sentimental mood of the time that the first
American reprint in 1784 was followed by at least seven other
editions in four different translations before the close of the
century. In America, as in England, no other German work
enjoyed the popularity of *Werther* or inspired so many imitations.[1] The conduct of young Werther caused a profound
commotion. Moralists saw in it an insidious apology for suicide. Critics warned readers that Werther's example constituted a graver menace to impulsive youth than that of Lovelace
who threatened to make seduction fashionable. Magazines and
novels were filled with efforts to dispel the false glamour with
which self-murder had been invested, and to provide antidotes
for Werther's subtle poison.[2]

The ease with which the suicide motif was made to fit into
the familiar sentimental formula was aptly set forth by Susanna

[1] O. W. Long, "English Translations of Goethe's Werther," *Journal of English
and Germanic Philology*, XIV, 169-203.

[2] One of these efforts achieved the impressive form of an antisuicide novel, *The
Slave of Passion; or, The Fruits of Werter* [*sic*], reprinted in Philadelphia in 1802
from the original Dublin edition of 1790.

Rowson in her recipe for a popular novel: ". . . remember to mix a sufficient quantity of sighs, tears, swooning hysterics, and all the moving expressions of heart-rending woe. . . . Be sure you contrive a duel; and, if convenient, a suicide might not be amiss. . . ."[3] The author of our first native novel found room for all these precious ingredients, but it was suicide which worked most havoc. Harrington, the earliest of Werther's American cousins, killed himself when he learned that the lovely Harriot, his betrothed, was his half sister. "At midnight the gentleman heard the report of a pistol, and went into the house," testified Worthy. "—he found the unhappy youth weltering in his blood. . . . A letter that he had written for me, laid unsealed upon the table, and *The Sorrows of Werter* [sic] was found lying by its side."[4] Like his famous German prototype, Harrington overlooked few opportunities for sentimental soliloquies; he also kept a friend fully informed of the state of his anguish in a series of feverish letters. "Tomorrow I shall go—," he confided, "But ah! whither?"[5] Almost his last moment of reflection, with his finger on the fatal trigger, was devoted to a self-conscious concern about an appropriate epitaph.[6] The morbidity of the hero was contagious and spread rapidly to other characters. Suicide also claimed the hapless Ophelia, who had the misfortune to be seduced by her brother-in-law. She noted, as the hour of her death approached, that "her sensibility became more exquisite."[7] Henry also joined the popular cult after his beloved Fidelia yielded to the seducing arts of Williams. Although Harrington and Ophelia had demonstrated that pistol and poison were effective enough, Henry varied the means by plunging "into the river—to close his sorrows with his life."[8] The persuasive appeal of the suicide theme was attested to by the *Massachusetts Magazine* which promptly reprinted Harrington's impassioned defense of self-

---

[3] *The Inquisitor*, III, 188.

[4] W. H. Brown, *The Power of Sympathy*, II, 149.

[5] *Ibid.*, II, 145. Letters LVI, LVII, LIX, LX, LXII, and LXIV are devoted to this subject. See *ibid.*, II, 128-130, 130-132, 135-137, 144-146, 150-154.

[6] *Ibid.*, II, 154.

[7] *Ibid.*, I, 101-102.　　　　　　　　　　　[8] *Ibid.*, I, 133.

murder under the admiring caption: "Beauties of *The Power of Sympathy.*"[9]

The sentimentalist whose nerves vibrated agonizingly at every distress, and the votary of sensibility who disdained this world as an abode of baseness were equally susceptible to the temptations of suicide. "Why should we endure life," asked Eumea in *Reuben and Rachel,* "when the nights are passed in anguish, and every day is a day of sorrow?"[10] Bleeding from her contact with the thorns of life, Elizabeth exulted in the easy relief offered by an ounce of poison or a touch of the trigger. "My desiring soul longs to be disencumbered from its terrestrial shackles," she told Ferdinand, "and to wing its way to the bosom of eternal light."[11] Ferdinand's reply was encouraging enough. "Yes, Elizabeth," he responded. "I will not survive thee, but my soul shall bear thine company to that undiscovered Country from whose bourne no traveller returns."[12] Franks, in Relf's *Infidelity,* was ready to debate the ethics of suicide with the most orthodox. "Is it vice," he challenged, "to spurn at the fascinations of earth, and rush into the embraces of deity?"[13] Ashley, whose proud boast was that he never was without a copy of *Werther* in his pocket, saw no merit in bearing the pangs of disprized love. He charged "that mind must be pusillanimous indeed, that could content to drag out a wretched life...."[14] Goethe's hero was his model. "Life, without Fanny, is unsupportable," he declared. "Werter could not exist when Charlotte was beyond his reach."[15] Escape, ever a popular theme of the sentimentalist, was made easy by suicide. "Often have I wished to slide obscurely and quietly into the grave," wrote the hero of *Jane Talbot.* "Never felt I so enamored of that which seems to be the cure-all."[16]

Those disciples of sensibility who toyed with the idea of suicide, but were able to resist the fascinating temptation, were

[9] *Massachusetts Magazine,* I, 52. The other "beauties" were "Seduction" and "Sensibility."   [10] Rowson, *Reuben and Rachel,* II, 349.
[11] Davis, *Ferdinand and Elizabeth,* pp. 124-125.
[12] *Ibid.,* p. 127.   [13] *Infidelity,* p. 158.
[14] [Anon.,] *The Hapless Orphan,* II, 199.
[15] *Ibid.,* II, 194.   [16] C. B. Brown, *Jane Talbot,* p. 288.

proud of their sympathetic understanding of the motives which led to the deed. "The heart of tenderness," wrote the author of "The Felo de Se," "while it abhors the crime, cannot but feel the most real sorrow for that distress which urged him on to the fatal deed."[17] To condemn unfeelingly the victims of suicide was to betray a heart insensible to the finer shades of feeling. "Those whose bosoms have felt no other love but the love of gain," objected John Davis, "are not proper judges of their conduct."[18] Even the robust Captain Farrago in *Modern Chivalry*, an avowed enemy of the cant of sensibility, hesitated to condemn suicide. "It remains only with heaven's chancery to reach the equity of the case, and absolve her from a crime; or at least qualify that which was an excess of virtue."[19]

Whether it was a sin or merely an excess of virtue to rush unbidden into the presence of one's Maker was a question frequently debated. Certainly the contemplation of suicide became a fashionable avocation for the sons and daughters of sensibility. The virtuous Pamela had demonstrated how delicious were the thrills of peering over the brink into the beckoning pool of destruction while remaining dry and comfortable on the bank. Werther-fever was not always malignant; sometimes it assumed an extremely mild form. John Davis described an unharmed victim in his *Travels:* "He delighted in the perusal of *The Sorrows of Werter* [*sic*], perfumed his handkerchief with lavender, brushed his hat of a morning, and went every Sunday to church."[20] Delicate heroines not unnaturally found pistols and poison to be forbidding subjects, even for harmless contemplation. The sensitive Sylvia selected a less revolting method. "A pink silk girdle was the instrument with which she resolved to terminate her misery, and this was lengthened by another made of gold thread," related the author of "The Story of Miss Sylvia S——."[21] To those who were consistent enough to act upon their resolves, sentimentalists bestowed their highest compliments. "Surely thy soul must be

[17] *Massachusetts Magazine*, II, 181.   [18] *Ferdinand and Elizabeth*, p. 141.
[19] Brackenridge, *Modern Chivalry*, II, 67.
[20] *Travels of Four Years and a Half* . . . , p. 137.
[21] *New York Magazine*, V, 436.

possessed of a finer spiritual essence than commonly falls to the share of woman," wrote Elizabeth's admirer upon hearing of her fatal resolve.[22] Although storytellers were rarely at a loss to provide their victims with enough personal woes to drive them to suicide, there were some exquisitely organized beings whose sympathetic sensibilities were alone sufficient to induce self-murder. "I have heard of men," asserted the author of "The Man at Home," "who though free themselves from any uncommon distress, were driven to suicide by reflecting on the miseries of others." It is reassuring to learn that such cases were exceptional. "No doubt," he added, "their minds were constituted after a singular manner."[23]

Of all the causes of suicide in our early fiction, seduction was by far the most powerful.[24] Sensibility, seduction, and suicide had more than an alliterative affinity in these novels. The heroine whose sensibility exceeded her prudence found in suicide a ready escape from the shame, if not the sin, of seduction. "If suicide," proclaimed an apologist for the abandoned Maria, "can meet compassion from an insulted God, surely it must be the seduced female."[25] The editors of the *New York Magazine* printed approvingly "An Instance of Female Heroism," based upon an incident which was alleged to have occurred in the metropolis in 1773. After the hapless lady in the case found too late that men betray, "she retired and shot herself."[26] A similar fate was reserved for the heroine of *Fortune's Foot-ball*. " 'Pardon your wretched daughter—who cannot, will not survive her disgrace!' As she pronounced these words," wrote Butler, "she, to the astonishment of all present, plunged a poniard in her breast, and expired instantly."[27] Charles Brockden Brown, who exploited the suicide theme in *Wieland, Jane Talbot, Ormond,* and *Clara Howard,* also made conven-

[22] Davis, *Ferdinand and Elizabeth*, p. 128.
[23] *Weekly Magazine* (Philadelphia, 1798), I, 320.
[24] For examples of the many "Affecting Historiettes" and "Pathetic Fragments" on this subject in early periodicals, see: *Massachusetts Magazine*, I, 674-677; II, 44-46, 181-182; V, 738-743; VI, 643-645; *New York Magazine*, V, 436; *Universal Asylum and Columbian Magazine*, V, 269.
[25] *New York Magazine*, VII, 14.
[26] *Ibid.*, II, 647.   [27] *Fortune's Foot-ball*, I, 58-59.

tional use of it in *Arthur Mervyn,* where the hero's sister, "escaped from the upbraidings of her parents, from the contumelies of the world . . . in a voluntary death." "She was my sister, my preceptress and friend," cried Arthur, "but she died —her end was violent, untimely, and criminal!"[28] Even Captain Farrago reserved judgment upon the case of a fair victim of seduction and suicide. "Doubtless the Almighty must blame and chide her for this premature and rash step," he said in his new role of sentimental traveler. "Yet, O world, thou dost her wrong in sentencing her to so low a bed."[29] Matilda whose sad fate was the subject of a pathetic interlude in *Emily Hamilton,* made her dramatic exit on a stage appropriately set for the melancholy deed. "Unable to bear her disgrace," Eliza Vicery declared, ". . . she walked to the place where she had been accustomed to meet her seducer, and with a ribband he had given her, suspended herself from the branch of a tree on which he had engraved his name and her own."[30]

The comfortable compromise which so often weakened the position of the sentimentalist is nowhere so clearly exemplified as in his attitude to suicide. It is revealing to note the devices of those novelists who aimed to eat their cake and have it, too; who delighted to bring their characters to the verge of suicide, only to feast fully on the luxury of the situation, and then avert the catastrophe by a sudden show of prudence, or a happy accident. Constantius was saved from self-destruction only by the intervention of good fortune which was so often the dower of sentimental heroes. "In despair he drew his sword and was on the eve of falling upon its point, thereby putting a period to an existence which he no longer could consider a blessing," reported the author of *Constantius and Pulchera,* "but fortune which always favors the virtuous, suggested to his mind a towline . . . which had been left there by accident."[31] Pulchera's starving brother was also saved by a pleasant chance in the same novel. He had taken up "the fatal gun, well loaded, and

[28] *Arthur Mervyn,* pp. 195-196.
[29] Brackenridge, *Modern Chivalry,* II, 68-69.
[30] *Emily Hamilton,* p. 46.
[31] [Anon.,] *Constantius and Pulchera,* pp. 15-16.

had got it to his face, and was just pulling the trigger in order, to lodge its contents in his head," the author recounted, "when he chanced to raise his eyes a little, and discovered a bear wallowing in the snow."[32] It is hardly necessary to add that the bear was dropped in his tracks and provided a savory meal for the famished adventurer. The surprising coincidences which ruled the strange action of this artless narrative did not fail the heroine in her hour of need. Pulchera, however, was saved by a more natural, if no less an unexpected interposition: "Frantic in despair she beat her breast, tore her hair, cursed her fate and prayed for annihilation, and was just about committing her body to the watery grave, when she was prevented therefrom, by her father's taking hold of her arm."[33] Mrs. Rowson employed less melodramatic means to avert Clara's suicide after she had "conceived the impious idea" of ending her existence. "I arose from my seat to put my design into execution," she declared, but changed her mind upon "hearing a rustling on the other side of the hedge. . . ."[34] Sometimes, as befitted the age of prose and reason, rational discussion was effective. The highwayman in *Fortune's Foot-ball* listened "while Mercutio and Charles endeavoured both by moral and philosophical arguments to dissuade him from his desperate purpose—in which they happily succeeded."[35] Horatio's counsel of prudence was delivered not a moment too soon in *Amelia,* for the heroine had already made her "awful appeal to the throne of grace, for the vindication of the act by which she had resolved to terminate her woes."[36]

Narrowly averted suicides proved to be a popular source of thrills. Charles Brockden Brown, who was unusually adept in visiting Gothic chills as well as sentimental fevers upon his luckless characters, had Edgar Huntly consider suicide by means of his trusty "Tom-hawk." "I took it in my hand," he wrote, "moved its edge over my fingers, and reflected on the force that was required to make it reach my heart. I investi-

[32] *Ibid.,* p. 60. [33] *Ibid.,* p. 21.
[34] *Trials of the Human Heart,* III, 99. [35] Butler, *Fortune's Foot-ball,* I, 28.
[36] [Anon.,] *Amelia; or, The Faithless Briton,* p. 21.

gated the spot where it should enter, and strove to fortify myself with resolution to repeat the stroke a second or third time. . . . You will not wonder that I felt some reluctance to employ so fatal though indispensable a remedy. I once more ruminated on the possibility of rescuing myself by other means."[37] Novelists were occasionally hard pressed to account for the close calls of would-be suicides. Caroline Matilda Warren resorted to the suggestion of a supernatural agency to save Leander in *The Gamesters*. "He approached the margin of the stream, and was about to tempt the perilous wave," she wrote of one of his attempts, "when fancy gave him the resemblance of his father, that seemed to cross him in his way."[38] Delia's rescue in "The History of Delia and Lorenzo," is, however, more typical of the desperate expedients to which writers were driven. "She cast herself into the stream of the blushing flood! —Rash deed!" exclaimed the author. "But happy, happy circumstance! At a small distance, her ever faithful Lorenzo was crossing the river in a boat. . . ."[39]

Perceiving that the mood of despair was native to the sentimentalist, and that suicide was his ultimate luxury, moralists were soon in full cry against the threatening evil. A contributor to the *Massachusetts Magazine* employed the graphic arts to combat suicide fever by sending the editor a diagram of "A Moral and Physical Thermometer, said to be the invention of the celebrated Dr. Rush, of Philadelphia." In this ingenious device, suicide is listed as the very lowest of an exceedingly generous assortment of vices; while the printer, sensing the heinous nature of the sin, printed the awful word in black-face.[40] The novelists themselves, although not above the trick of bringing their heroes to the edge of self-destruction, rarely failed to preach a homily against it. Mrs. Rowson's Charlotte Temple resisted the temptation with a strength of character appropriate to so celebrated a heroine. "Never did human be-

[37] *Edgar Huntly*, II, 137.
[38] *The Gamesters*, p. 277. Upon another occasion, just as Leander was about to make what he hoped would be a fatal plunge, "some unseen divinity seemed to arrest his mad career."
[39] *New York Magazine*, II, 620.   [40] *Massachusetts Magazine*, I, 88.

ing wish for death with greater fervency or with juster cause," the author boasted, "yet she had too just a sense of the duties of the Christian religion to attempt to put a period to her own existence."[41] Royall Tyler endowed the hero of his *Algerine Captive* with equal fortitude. Although he suffered all the horrors of life on a "slaver" and spent six years in cruel captivity in Algiers, Underhill stoutly refused to end his sufferings by suicide. "I bless a merciful God that I was preserved from the desperate folly of suicide," he exclaimed thankfully. "I never attempted my life...."[42] Even those who had not been able to resist the blandishments of a Lovelace prided themselves upon spurning the easy release suggested in *Werther*. The drooping spirits of Eliza Wharton in *The Coquette* were revived whenever she recalled that she was innocent of self-slaughter, the darkest sin of all. "God forbid," she cried in gratitude, "my breath is in his hands, let him do what seemeth good in his sight!"[43] Heroines considered it their high duty to warn too impressionable lovers about the rank nature of Werther's deed. Jane Talbot's letters to Colden, who was half in love with easeful death, proclaim her deep abhorrence of the crime. "There is but one calamity greater than my mother's anger," she told her lover. "I cannot mangle my own vitals. I cannot put an impious and violent end to my own life."[44]

The question of the comparative iniquity of seduction and suicide was solemnly debated by moralists. There were those who held with the friend of Constantia Dudley in *Ormond* that suicide was "the obvious, but not the only, or morally speaking, the worst means" of escape from suffering. "Paroxysms of drunkenness," she maintained, "is one method of obtaining the bliss of forgetfulness, in comparison with which suicide is innocent."[45] Suicide also had its champions who regarded infidelity as far more culpable. The infidel "acts without principle, or a view of the hereafter," argued Franks in *Infidelity*, while the suicide "justifies the deed."[46] Sophistry

[41] *Charlotte*, II, 143.
[43] Foster, *The Coquette*, p. 223.
[45] C. B. Brown, *Ormond*, p. 30.
[42] *The Algerine Captive*, II, 201.
[44] C. B. Brown, *Jane Talbot*, p. 264.
[46] Relf, *Infidelity*, p. 158.

of this sort led a critic in the *Weekly Magazine* to deplore Werther's example as far more insidious for susceptible readers than that of Lovelace. "Werter is drawn with a richness," he continued, "that, however pitiable the real character might be, the danger of a mistaken passion or an immoral indulgence of amorous affection, is too great to be safely or prudently intrusted to the consideration of minds not strongly formed."[47] Goethe's novel made its chief appeal, moreover, to minds of this impulsive cast. One of these misguided daughters of sensibility in *Ferdinand and Elizabeth* boasted "with a coquettish air that she slept every night with the *Sorrows of Werther* under her pillow."[48] Dr. Hitchcock recorded his conviction that such conduct was entirely too fashionable. In *Memoirs of the Bloomsgrove Family,* he showed his impatience with "young ladies, who weep away a whole forenoon, over the criminal sorrows of a fictitious Charlotte or Werter [*sic*]. . . ."[49] The mood of sickly despair, thus induced, also alarmed James Butler, who warned his readers that "persons under such circumstances sometimes become lunatic, or raving, and too frequently having recourse to suicide, in order to shun misfortunes which are commonly imaginary."[50]

Suicide was the worst, but not the only, evil for which *The Sorrows of Young Werther* was made responsible. Goethe's hero had also thrown a false glamour over illicit love. "Illustrate to my immature judgment that metaphysical nicety by which love is discriminated from friendship," demanded Alfred, who was hopelessly enamored of a married woman.[51] Courtney, another professed admirer of Werther's conduct, justified the worst fears of the moralists. "It is as impossible," he declared, "to prevent a refined and susceptible heart from admiring an amiable and beautiful woman, either married or single, as it would be to annihilate any natural appetite of the body."[52] Alfred bestowed the name of Charlotte upon his married lover,

[47] *Weekly Magazine* (Philadelphia, 1798), I, 331.
[48] Davis, *Ferdinand and Elizabeth*, p. 63.
[49] *Memoirs of the Bloomsgrove Family*, II, 296.
[50] *Fortune's Foot-ball*, I, 47-48.
[51] Relf, *Infidelity*, p. 99.   [52] *Ibid.*, p. 51.

but he enjoyed the game too keenly to put an end to the delicious excitement by killing himself. "Charlotte I must call her," he declared, "though I should be unwilling to be thought a Werter."[53] It was as a plausible sanction for suicide, however, not as an invitation for the "immoral indulgence of amorous affection," that *The Sorrows of Young Werther* was most feared. "Neither sublimity of composition, an energetic and affecting style, nor the false appearance of argument," wrote the author of *The Hapless Orphan,* "can ever compensate for the injury that vague minds receive, from the perusal of those publications, where suicide is represented as heroism; nor can the writer of the *Sorrows of Werter,* ever make atonement for the injury he has done to society."[54] The same criticism was made by "The Ubiquitarian" in an attempt to dissuade booksellers from handling pernicious novels: "Among these I shall only mention the *Sorrows of Werter,* a book which has proved the bane of more than one family."[55]

With the exception of Clarissa and Lovelace, no character in foreign fiction created a more profound disturbance in our early novels than that of young Werther. The nerves and sensibilities which had been quickened so exquisitely by Sterne, were ready to welcome a new thrill, the more seductive because the more dangerous. Rousseau, with his head dangling over the beetling cliff, enjoying at once the sensation of falling and the comfort of solid safety; Pamela, on the grassy verge of her pond, anticipating with relish the effect of her drowning, but with no desire to venture too close to the water: these examples may also have given the sentimentalists their inspiration. For not the least of the felicities enjoyed by those sensible souls who reached the secure haven of a happy last chapter, was the feverish recollection of a timorous glance at the brink of destruction.

[53] *Ibid.,* p. 76.

[54] [Anon.,] *The Hapless Orphan,* II, 205-206.

[55] *Weekly Magazine* (Philadelphia, 1798), I, 331. Such preachments, it is to be feared, had little practical effect. Caritat puffed *Werther* as "an immortal work" in constant demand; he also recommended an anthology of Werther's letters to Charlotte.

VI

THE SENTIMENTAL FORMULA

I wonder that the novel readers are not tired of reading one story so
many times, with only the variation of its being told in different ways.
—Susanna Haswell Rowson,
The Inquisitor, 1794.
A fig for your plots and unities of design . . . mere formalities; fetters
to pathos and sublimity. . . .   —Isaac Mitchell, *The Asylum*, 1811.

THE READER who seeks in these early American novels for some
discussion of technique or concern with the problems of fiction
is destined to thumb their yellowed pages in vain. There is no
imitator of Henry Fielding to advance genially to the footlights
for one of those chatty asides oh the nature and scope of his
art which delighted Thackeray and George Eliot. Nor is there
evidence that any of the novelists suffered much travail in
bringing their books into the world or that they spent even a
modest fraction of the "some thousands of hours" which were
packed into the writing of *Tom Jones*. To author and critic
alike, fiction appeared to be an unexacting literary form without a scrupulous technique or a dignified tradition. When
critics did occasionally deign to notice novels, they were content to offer a few desultory observations upon poetic justice
and didactic purpose, or to extract several samples to illustrate
the author's sensibility.[1] For their condescending attitude they
could point to the high sanction of Dr. Johnson, who had not
been able to bring himself to finish *Joseph Andrews,* and who
held pontifically that fiction was beneath the serious regard of
cultivated readers. "These books are chiefly to the young, the
ignorant, and the idle," he had declared. "They serve as lectures of conduct, and introductions into life."

[1] This is exactly what happened to *The Power of Sympathy* from which were
culled that triune of "beauties" which struck the tremulous keynote of American
fiction: "Suicide," "Seduction," and "Sensibility." See *Massachusetts Magazine,* I,
50-53.

The foundations of American fiction were laid at a lustre-less period in the history of the British novel. When *The Power of Sympathy* made its apologetic bow in 1789, the four great masters had completed their contributions. Fielding had been dead for more than a generation. Richardson, who survived him seven years, died in 1761. Laurence Sterne lived less than a decade longer; and Smollett, the last of the giants, died in 1771, the year of the publication of *Humphry Clinker*. The high ground which they had occupied in the name of prose fiction was not, however, to be maintained by their imitators who stocked the lending libraries with their flimsy wares.[2] It was of these miserable productions that many moralists were thinking when they fulminated against novels. Between 1770 and 1800 the term *novel* had become a label broad enough to cover almost all varieties and blends of fact and fiction. Subscribers to Caritat's circulating library might have taken home under the guise of fiction, the pseudo-biographies of prostitutes and pirates, actresses and adulteresses; secret memoirs,[3] travels, histories and adventures; and improving sacred and domestic tales "founded on real life." The tenth-rate scribblers who produced them succeeded in copying merely the externalities of the work of the great geniuses of the mid-century. The facility with which they were able to supply the novel market by slight variations of a simple formula seemed to bring the writing of fiction within reach of anyone capable of holding a pen.

The first problem faced by beginners ambitious to write "the great American novel" was the choice of a suitable form for their stories. To this question, Richardson's epistolary novels seemed an easy answer. More than enough has been written earlier in this study to indicate the avidity with which

[2] The last word upon this swarm of camp followers who flocked into the marshlands of fiction has been said with gentle wit and sympathetic understanding by Dr. J. M. S. Tompkins in *The Popular Novel in England, 1770-1800*. The author bravely withstood the temptation to ridicule these faded favorites and has succeeded in renewing something of their once popular appeal.

[3] These "memoirs" were a favorite target for critics. Helena Wells, in *Constantia Neville*, cautioned her readers against the "many courtezans who have of late years obtruded their *memoirs* and *apologies* upon the public. . . ." Their works, she declared, were "little calculated to amend the heart or improve the morals" (II, 217).

our early novelists seized upon the letter form.[4] Women, if we may believe the complaints of neglected husbands and the testimony of the heroines themselves, were forever scribbling.[5] Letters, moreover, seemed easy to write; their formlessness imposed little discipline upon the author; and most important of all, they afforded the sentimentalists a welcome opportunity for minute dissections of the heart. Richardson also offered a comfortable warrant for bulk and discursiveness. "What a great deal of writing does the reciting of half an hour's conversation make, when there are three or four speakers in company; and one attempts to write what each says in the *first person!*" exclaimed Harriot Byron in *Grandison*. "I am amazed at the quantity, on looking back. But it *will* be so in narrative writing." And, indeed, so it *was* in American epistolary fiction. A two-volume novel was the rule rather than the exception; there were occasional three-deckers, while Susanna Rowson's *Trials of the Human Heart* attained the dignity of four. John Davis decided that his first novel had not been long enough and accordingly resolved to undertake another which he promised "to make more voluminous." "Americans," he observed, "expect quantity in a book not less eagerly than in other merchandise. . . ."[6] Digressiveness and garrulity were accepted by readers and critics as conventional attributes of the epistolary way of writing. The very faults of ordinary composition became virtues when enclosed in an envelope. That it seemed beguilingly simple was the result of the imitator's failure to recognize and achieve the uses to which Richardson had put the letter form. His true greatness, like that of Laurence Sterne, eluded those who tried clumsily to separate form and content, treatment and subject matter. Fielding's regard for the architectonics of *Tom Jones* made that book too exacting a

---

[4] See Chapter III, "The Elegant Epistolarians," pp. 52-73. The climax of the vogue of letter fiction in England coincided almost exactly with the appearance of *The Power of Sympathy*.

[5] So universal was the passion for scribbling that an expressed distaste for letter writing by Miss Hartley in *The Step-Mother* was immediately taken as evidence of her want of virtue as well as of a lack of refinement! (II, 37). Many heroines resembled Jane Talbot, who "seemed never at ease but with a pen in her fingers."

[6] *Travels* . . . , I, 165.

model to encourage imitation. Of all the patterns in fiction bequeathed by the eighteenth-century English novelists, none proved so popular as the letter form.[7]

The formula, in which the letter was such an important factor, was usually made to serve a didactic purpose. Although critics were generally silent upon matters of technique, they were fond of affirming that the primary function of the novelist was to teach. Mrs. Rowson found little difference between her former office as a governess and her later position as a novelist. The task of "cultivating the minds and expanding the ideas of the female part of the rising generation," which as a teacher, had been "inexpressibly delightful," as a novelist, "Became now indispensable duty."[8] The prefaces to many novels were filled with disarming declarations of a desire to inculcate morality by precept and example. "The value of such works," remarked a critic in the *Weekly Magazine* in 1798, "lies without a doubt in their moral tendency."[9] With this tenet as a cherished article in their creed, few reviewers arose to protest at the welter of irrelevant material frequently interpolated to point a moral. Mrs. Rowson's attitude was a typical one. "I confess I have rambled strangely from my story: but what of that?" she demanded in *Charlotte*. "If I have been so lucky as to find the road to happiness why should I be such a niggard as to omit an opportunity of pointing out the way to others?"[10] Such digressions were welcomed by critics as fulfilling the aim of novel writing. Essays and "fragments" were a popular feature of periodicals, and no one seemed to find them out of place when they variegated the pages of a novel, provided, of

[7] Although Richardson provided the model usually followed, the epistolary scheme of George Watterston's *The L—— Family at Washington; or, A Winter in the Metropolis* (Washington, 1822), was derived from *Humphry Clinker*. The letter form was not, by any means, the only mould in which American novelists cast their stories. *The Female American* was based upon *Robinson Crusoe*. Defoe's straightforward narrative method, however, was not sustained by the anonymous author, who yielded to the popular taste for melodrama and sentiment. Hugh Henry Brackenridge acknowledged his debt to Fielding in *Modern Chivalry*, which is a vigorous example of the loosely constructed picaresque tale of adventure. *The Algerine Captive* and *Fortune's Foot-ball* represent types of adventure fiction popular in England between 1770 and 1800.   [8] *Reuben and Rachel*, I, iii.

[9] *Weekly Magazine* (Philadelphia, 1798), I, 202.

[10] *Charlotte*, I, 45-46.

course, that they were properly "affecting." Novels were also larded with solid chunks of information designed to give ballast to a form commonly considered flimsy enough. Readers were thus duly apprised of the benefits of early rising and retiring, the proper conduct of a family during the wife's pregnancy, the dangers of low temperatures, and of sensible precautions to be taken during severe thunderstorms. This extra freight, which at times taxed even the generous capacity of a "three-decker," did not always receive from readers the ready approbation with which it was greeted by critics. As Amelia Parr protested in *The Boarding School,* an American novel, with its interminable moralizing, was frequently enough to give one the vapors. Helena Wells had such volatile souls in mind in *Constantia Neville.* " 'And this is called a novel?' says one of my youthful readers at the conclusion of the last Chapter. . . . 'I shall send the remaining Volume back to the library.' "[11]

It would be without profit to exhibit in detail all the threadbare devices by which the popular theme of persecuted innocence was worked out in these novels. Mrs. Rowson spoke with peculiar authority when she exclaimed in *The Inquisitor* that the same old story was told again and again with only slight variations of the sentimental formula. From Richardson came not only the epistolary form, but the familiar figures of the persecuted or seduced female, the glittering rake, the avaricious parent, and the faithful confidante. The gallery of rogues was increased by such stock characters as the designing governess, preferably French; the hardhearted landlady, the cruel stepmother, the inhuman creditor, the flinty jailer, the vile procuress, and the mercenary wet nurse. Upon the side of the angels were to be found, with wearisome monotony, the noble soldier dispensing good cheer out of a meager pension, with a gesture or two borrowed from my Uncle Toby; and the generous sailor endowed with some of the more genial characteristics of Smollett's seamen. The sentimentalists' conten-

[11] *Constantia Neville,* I, 171.

tion that sympathy is the mainspring of human nature was exemplified in numerous instances of the good apprentice, the philanthropic merchant, the chivalrous rustic, the noble savage, the highborn benefactress, and the long-suffering wife. To turn the pages of these novels is to find with Tabitha Tenney, "numerous instances of persecuted lovers, cruel parents, and tyrannical guardians."[12] With these counters to move about, the novelists set promptly to work to achieve an orgy of "strong scenes." Indeed, it was this very lack of depth or individualization in their characters, which drove writers to fall back upon the shock of violent external incidents for their effects. Although sensational situations are hardly peculiar to sentimental fiction, sensationalism and sentimentality are parallel tendencies. As William Allan Neilson has pointed out, both are defective forms of art planned to thrill at all costs, both are ready to sacrifice "truth and sincerity for the sake of emotional dissipation. . . ."[13]

Nothing less than emotional dissipation followed this constant striving to keep the reader's chords of sympathy in perpetual vibration. Victims were jostled through one harrowing experience into another. Fenimore Cooper's favorite contrivance of pursuit and escape was anticipated by these authors whose heroines were forever jumping out of the frying pan into the fire. "I had been followed by a train of misfortunes, so progressive, so rapid, that my faculties were almost benumbed and my mind enervated by their repetition," declared the hero of *Glencarn*.[14] Against such shameless bids for his sympathy, the reader is forced to adopt an attitude of stony indifference. Mrs. Rowson was compelled to admit that Heaven alone could suitably reward the protracted suffering of Meriel. "Generous, noble spirited girl, it is only for such hearts as yours to be tried in the ordeal of affliction," she wrote in *Trials of the Human Heart*, "but surely heaven has some future reward in store, that will amply compensate the sufferings you

[12] *Female Quixotism,* I, 130.
[13] *Essentials of Poetry* (Boston, 1912), pp. 240-241.
[14] Watterston, *Glencarn,* II, 242-243.

are ordained to endure."[15] Sentimental novelists loved explosive panics and emotional crises. They were not given to writing leisurely opening chapters, set in the low, but confident key of "the great still books," but plunged pell-mell into their narratives with a few hasty strokes to invoke the mood. The opening lines of *Monima* serve as an ominous prelude to the incredible suffering which follows hard upon: " 'This is a bleak morning,' said Monima's father, as he was covering his silver locks with his white cap; 'how excessively the storm rages. Are you entirely out of work, Nima?' "[16] Impatient to disclose the variety of their stock of thrills as soon as possible, authors occasionally treated their readers to a preview of the excitement in store for them. The Preface to *The Asylum* should have persuaded any hesitating purchaser that he was looking at a bargain: "In the ardent prospects raised in youthful bosoms, the almost consummation of their wishes, their sudden and unexpected disappointment, the sorrows of separation, the joyous and unlooked for meeting—in the poignant feelings of Alonzo, when at the grave of Melissa, he poured the feelings of his anguished soul over her miniature by 'the moon's pale

[15] *Trials of the Human Heart*, II, 121. Meriel needed this comfort, for she faced the prospect of two volumes of agony before release was granted her.

[16] Read, *Monima*, p. 1. Although the plot of this novel is not exceptionally lurid, it affords a fair sample of the soul-wringing sufferings to which uncomplaining virtue was often subjected. Monima's aged father, the noble Fontanbleu, had been banished from France, and his estate confiscated by the criminal machinations of Pierre de Noix, who had also killed Fontanbleu's favorite son, Ferdinant. In St. Domingo, where the sorely beset family took refuge, an insurrection cost the lives of two other sons, and wiped out the little that remained of their fortune. This misfortune was barely over when a visitation of yellow fever proved fatal to Fontanbleu's wife and three more of his children. These tragedies, however, were a mere curtain raiser for the trials in store for the broken father and his surviving daughter when they reached New York. By a neat dramatic economy, the base Pierre was awaiting their arrival to attempt the seduction of Monima, who now supported her father by begging. His persecutions were competently abetted by his mistress, Madam Sontine, who vented her own motiveless malignity on the hapless Monima. There followed in breathless succession, a series of abductions, imprisonments, falsely trumped up charges of debt and murder, and an outrageous conspiracy to commit Monima to an asylum for the insane. Fontanbleu was further afflicted by disease and temporary blindness, and Monima by an all but fatal attack of the plague, before father and daughter were jostled into the last chapter where a sadly delayed poetic justice began its grinding.

ray' . . . these will not fail to interest the refined sensibilities of the reader."[17]

The almost consummation of their wishes! One character after another was subjected to this excruciating device until their careers became a seemingly endless series of frustrations, a pitiless succession of exquisite "might-have-beens." After months of fruitless searching, the friend of Monima arrived a moment too late to save her from falling into Pierre's trap.[18] Lucinda's "decline" in *Fortune's Foot-ball* ended in death on the eve of the date set for her marriage to Mercutio.[19] Lady Mary was seized with a fatal stroke of apoplexy just as she was about to reach for a pen to change her will which would have made Rebecca independent and saved her from countless indignities.[20] Amelia's father arrived in London only to see his daughter go insane, and to throw the last handful of earth over the coffin of his granddaughter.[21] At this popular game of playing hide-and-seek with the sensibility of readers, Mrs. Rowson acknowledged few equals. Part of the amazing appeal which has induced readers to exhaust more than two hundred editions of *Charlotte Temple* is to be found in the deft manipulation of the might-have-beens. The heroine was dangled over the edge of destruction only to be hauled back again so many times that there is little cause for surprise when she swooned at the critical moment. Charlotte's important message which would have revoked her fatal appointment with Montraville was intercepted by a ruse of a trusted governess. Her meeting with the villain was consented to for the express purpose of announcing her refusal to accompany him to America. Her crucial hesitation was caused entirely by her excessive humanity and sensibility. The pathetic note Charlotte wrote to her parents, which would have prevented the embarkation had it reached its destination, was destroyed by the seducer. Mrs. Beauchamp, the heroine's benefactress, left for Rhode Island

[17] Mitchell, *The Asylum*, p. ii.
[18] Read, *Monima*, p. 369.　　　　[19] Butler, *Fortune's Foot-ball*, I, 31.
[20] Rowson, *The Fille de Chambre*, p. 58.
[21] [Anon.,] *Amelia; or, The Faithless Briton*, p. 22.

at the very instant her presence was most needed. Montraville's ample provision for his victim was withheld by Belcour. Every one of Charlotte's letters to her parents was lost in the mails. Colonel Crayton, who could have averted much of the suffering, was away from home when Charlotte appealed to him for succor. Montraville's repentant return was unaccountably delayed until his only greeting was the death knell of the girl he ruined, "a solemn toll that seemed to say, some poor mortal was going to their last mansion."

The translator of *Alexis; or, The Cottage in the Woods,* had defined a plot as "a concatenation of events which taken separately will be worthy of belief." There is little or no evidence, however, that novelists gave much thought to the structure of their plots. Although Mrs. Rowson was an actress and a playwright, and William Hill Brown, Mrs. Murray, Hugh Brackenridge, Royall Tyler, and Samuel Woodworth were dramatists, their fiction reveals little dramatic economy of character or incident. Almost every minor character seemed to feel the need of rehearsing the story of his life, with the result that books frequently spilled over with enough surplus material to furnish forth a new novel. The epistolary form, moreover, invited a loose stringing together of letters with scant regard for unity. The easygoing picaresque fashion also sanctioned a breadth of scope and a lavishness of incident. There was, too, the high authority of Sterne to support almost any breach of proportion or coherence. "A century when past is but a moment," announced Mrs. Rowson, who swept majestically through three hundred years of adventures and intrigues in *Reuben and Rachel.* Plots moved in mysterious ways their wonders to perform in a universe where accident and coincidence operated as immutably as the laws of gravity. No coincidence seemed too preposterous. If the hero chanced to rescue a lady from a runaway horse and carriage, she was sure to be his long-lost mother.[22] Should a distressed female wandering "from the desarts of Siberia" to England in quest of her husband happen to lose her way in the forests of Poland, a

[22] Watterston, *Glencarn,* II, 224-245.

friendly light in the clearing was likely to be shining from the house of her brother.[23] If the villain found it necessary to seek shelter in a miserable hovel during a storm, he was certain to be confronted by the corpse of the innocent fair he had previously seduced and harried to death.[24] A learned article is yet to be written upon the variety of birthmarks with which heroes and heroines were tattooed in the interest of that last chapter "recognition" which was burlesqued in *Joseph Andrews,* and beloved by romancers of every age. In the novels under consideration, "the ripe mulberry" seemed to enjoy a slight lead over "the strawberry," but a more scientific count might reverse this precedence.[25]

Even the authors betrayed some slight uneasiness at their shameless trickery. The "resurrection" of Melissa, which provided an unlooked-for sensation at Alonzo's wedding in *The Asylum,* naturally demanded a special explanation.[26] Mitchell assured his readers that he had not taken any unfair advantage in thus sporting with their feelings, and reminded them that there had been no "unmeaning and inexplicable incidents." "When anxieties have been excited by involved and doubtful events," he boasted in his Preface, "they are afterwards elucidated by the consequences."[27] The concatenation of preposterous incidents which often made up the plots drew exclamations of wonder from the characters themselves. Glencarn was forced to admit that his foe's villainy was unusual even for

---

[23] Wood, *Ferdinand and Elmira,* pp. 100-102.

[24] Watterston, *The Lawyer,* p. 41.

[25] For typical instances of this device, see *The Fille de Chambre* in which Oakly, a noble foundling, was identified by "the mark of the mulberry." Mrs. Hayman's son, De Eresby, was similarly recognized in *Constantia Neville:* " 'If I am your son, you will know me by this mark:' opening his collar De Eresby displayed, to the longing eyes of Mrs. Hayman, a spot on the left side of his throat, which resembled a ripe mulberry; a token so strongly imprinted on her remembrance, that on perceiving it she no longer attempted to restrain her feelings" (III, 329-330).

[26] Mitchell, *The Asylum,* II, 217-249. The hero was certainly justified in believing Melissa to be dead. He had read her obituary in a newspaper, and was informed of the sad circumstances by the girl's own brother and sister who were dressed in deep mourning. The repentant Beauman also confirmed the report upon his deathbed, and this testimony was further corroborated by the wife of the sexton who showed Alonzo the grave and tombstone! See *ibid.,* II, 217-219.

[27] *Ibid.,* p. i.

fiction. "History has no parallel and poetry could scarcely feign a monster so debasing to humanity," he declared.[28] So adroitly contrived were the events making for general happiness in the final chapter of *Fortune's Foot-ball* that Mercutio's father was moved to cry, "The events of yesterday evening were unaccountable; but those of this day are absolutely astonishing." As additional wonders continued to be brought about, his amazement knew no bounds. "Miracles! miracles all!" he exulted, "all bounteous Providence! unsearchable are thy ways, gracious God!"[29]

The sentimental formula was a simple equation resting upon a belief in the spontaneous goodness and benevolence of man's original instincts. It could point to what passed for philosophical justification in the admired writings of Shaftesbury, Hutcheson, and Adam Smith. It was informed throughout with a moral purpose to which all its other elements were subordinated. Into its capacious framework were poured the stock characters and situations dear to popular storytellers of every generation. The final solution was neatly reserved for the last chapter where the punishment was made to fit the crime, and the reward to equal the virtue. To achieve it, authors subjected the long arm of coincidence to the rack of expediency where it was stretched and fractured to suit every need of the plot. The reader, meanwhile, was made to cry— and to wait. As a "true-feeler," he was expected to match pang for pang, and sigh for sigh with the persecuted victim; he was mercilessly roasted over the slow fires of suspense. This recipe, moreover, was employed to add sentimental fevers to the Gothic chills in such novels as Charles Brockden Brown's *Wieland*. It was also used to soften the bugle notes and war cries in historical romances like John Davis's *The First Settlers of Virginia* and Samuel Woodworth's *The Champions of Freedom*. It was ready at hand, too, for Harriet Beecher Stowe. By enlisting the same old formula in the service of humanity, she appealed in a universal language to the hearts of Christians everywhere.

[28] Watterston, *Glencarn*, II, 241.   [29] Butler, *Fortune's Foot-ball*, II, 182-184.

Serviceable as the sentimental pattern proved to be for our early novelists, and popular as it was with most readers, there were some sounds of dissent. "A sentimental novel will hardly pay you for time and paper," bewailed Mrs. Rowson. "A story full of intrigue, wrote with levity, and tending to convey loose ideas, would sell very well."[30] The author of *Monima* complained that the newfangled taste for Gothic romances made sentimental tales seem old-fashioned. Patrons of the circulating libraries were demanding goose flesh and shivers, as well as tears and sentimental fevers in their fiction. "It must be something out of the common course of nature," Monima heard a bookseller declare regretfully. "Sprights, Hobgoblins, and Sorceresses! Blue blazes! Subterranean abodes for banished queens, and offending servants! Rusted daggers and mouldering skeletons with apparitions, to warn young ladies of approaching dissolution."[31] The author of *Charlotte* showed her self to have been aware of the growing impatience with the formula upon which she had relied so successfully to gratify the popular taste. "Bless my heart!" she made a jaded reader exclaim rebelliously. "I shall never have patience to get through these volumes, there are so many *ahs!* and *ohs!* so much fainting, tears, and distress, I am sick to death of the subject."[32]

It is only just that this playful indictment of the overused sentimental pattern should have come from the pen of Susanna Haswell Rowson. She was not only the most prolific of the female novelists whose names have appeared on these pages, but also the most popular. Her *Charlotte Temple* still commands tears in what Carl Van Doren has aptly called "an increasingly naïve underworld of fiction readers." No one will deny her the right to come forward for a final bow. Nor will anyone be disposed to question the appropriateness or the truth of her epilogue: "It is called *Annabella; or, Suffering Innocence*—my heroine is beautiful, accomplished, and rich; an only child and surrounded by admirers—she contracts an

[30] *The Inquisitor*, I, 53.
[31] Read, *Monima*, p. 258.   [32] *Charlotte*, II, 138.

attachment for a man, her inferior in point of birth and fortune; but honourable, handsome, &c.—She has a female friend,
to whom she relates all that passes in her breast—her hopes,
fears, meetings, partings, &c.—She is treated hardly by her
friends—combats innumerable difficulties in the sentimental
way, but at last overcomes them all, and is made the bride of
the man of her heart.

"Pshaw, said I, that is stale; there are at this present day,
about two thousand novels in existence, which begin and end
exactly in the same way."

BOOK TWO

The Sentimental Years
1820-1860

America is now wholly given over to a d——d mob of scribbling women, and I should have no chance of success while the public taste is occupied with their trash—and should be ashamed of myself if I did succeed. What is the mystery of these innumerable editions of the "Lamplighter," and other books neither better nor worse?—worse they could not be, and better they need not be, when they sell by the 100,000. . . .

—Letter of Nathaniel Hawthorne
to William Ticknor, 1855.

I

POPULAR ISMS AND OLOGIES

The supreme folly of the hour is to imagine that perfection will come before its stated time.

—James Fenimore Cooper,
The Crater, 1847.

THE EBULLIENT prophets of the sentimental generation were confident that the millennium was just around the corner. Dreamers were busy flying their Utopian kites gaily bedecked with long tails of isms. "In the history of the world," Emerson wrote in 1841, "the doctrine of Reform had never such scope as at the present hour." The pot of national Uplift, heated with what one novelist was pleased to call "moral electricity," frothed with a heady brew of Mesmerism, Mormonism, Bloomerism, Animal Magnetism, Transcendentalism, Spiritualism, Perfectionism, Teetotalism, and Abolitionism. Skeptics, distrustful of pleasant panaceas, derided New England as a western Holy Land with Boston as its New Jerusalem, "the very centre and source of all the isms of the day."

Into the generous mould of popular fiction was poured this effervescent stream of new ideas. "If there be any excuse for the publication of works of fiction," declared Brisbane in his Utopian novel, *Ralphton,* "it is to be found in the desire to introduce new propositions to the consideration of the reflective world. . . ."[1] Novelists, moreover, were quick to recognize the dramatic possibilities of these strange and wonderful "sciences." Even the authors of historical romances were compelled to pander to the popular taste for "imaginary wonders." Since "the apotheosis of phrenology and animal magnetism," complained James Kirke Paulding, readers were demanding that sober history be spiced with the "concentrated soup of

---

[1] A. H. Brisbane, *Ralphton* (Charleston, S. C., 1848), p. v.

depravity."[2] Fenimore Cooper, whose stout common sense could admit of no mystical short cuts to the perfectibility of the human race, scoffed at "These improvements upon improvements" which "very often come out at the precise spot from which they started."[3] The doctrine of Christian perfectionism had been cherished by sentimentalists for too long a time to be easily shaken by ridicule. Sylvester Judd, author of the transcendental *Margaret,* voiced the more popular attitude in his confident prediction that the people of New England "might lead the August Procession of the race to Human Perfectibility; that here might be revealed the Coming of the Day of the Lord, wherein the old Heavens of sin and error should be dissolved, and a New Heavens and New Earth be established, wherein dwelleth righteousness."[4]

Sentimental novelists were naturally interested in the moral overtones of the new isms. Phrenology was hailed as providing an infallible method "to expound and improve humanity." By means of animal magnetism, gifted souls were to be enabled to instill ideal aspirations into dull clods. Spiritualism was welcomed as offering scientific proof of the immortality of the soul. "Brothers in Uplift" were to be empowered to identify each other by the blessed arts of physiognomy. "Moral hygiene" and "moral homeopathy" seemed to bring new aids to those who labored for the perfectibility of man. Wishful thinkers were not slow to accept the claims of what passed in many respectable quarters as "pure Science." Reading men, as Emerson had observed, carried the drafts of ideal communities in their waistcoat pockets; spiritualists went so far as to boast that they possessed "spectral blueprints" of Utopian commonwealths. Despite Nathaniel Hawthorne's bitter warning in "The Celestial Railroad," optimistic pilgrims continued to book their passage for a speedy and comfortable ride to the City of Salvation.

The sentimental heroine's education was not considered to

[2] *The Puritan and His Daughter* (New York, 1850), II, 10-11. [First edition, 1849]
[3] *The Redskins,* (New York, 1846), I, 231.
[4] *Margaret* (Boston, 1845), p. 268.

have been complete without some instruction in at least the rudiments of the new isms. Italian and embroidery, which had sufficed genteel females of an earlier generation, were not enough for the modern woman. "This girl, now, that I've educated," boasted a progressive teacher in *The Old Homestead,* is "taught everything, music, painting, all the *ologies* and other sciences. . . ."[5] The young idea was also taught to shoot high; heroines were invariably perfectionists; their favorite occupation was "stepping heavenward." When anxious friends cautioned them of the strain of attempting to live without sin, they usually replied as did Gazella in *The North and South,* "that Jesus took upon himself the form and the infirmity of the flesh, and yet he was without spot and blameless." "In a word," explained the author, "she had taken the Saviour of Mankind as an example, and her life from day to day was a constant aim to be like him."[6] A life of such intensity often induced a fatal "decline" which exacted a fearful toll of ethereal victims. Insanity, too, was an imminent danger. Thus Henry Hamilton, the hero's uncle in *Henry Russell,* was "too much of a perfectionist," for he "became intensely fixed upon the attainment within himself of a perfect character. . . . His insanity in the meantime consisted in the idea which had taken possession of him that he was Christ. . . ."[7] Ever present, also, was the threat of a relapse. "The most sanguine believer in perfectibility is in danger of forgetting the capacities of man," warned Miss Sedgwick in *Clarence,* "and giving up his creed altogether when he looks upon the actual interests and pursuits that occupy him."[8] For those who found the path to perfection beset with perils, Mrs. E. D. E. N. Southworth suggested the remedial properties of "moral hygiene," which she carefully explained was "a moral pharmacopœia, dispensed with perfect skill only by the great Physician of souls."[9] The efficacy of "moral homeopathy" was also praised, but the author of *Elinor*

[5] A. S. Stephens, *The Old Homestead* (Philadelphia, 1855), p. 387.
[6] C. Rush, *The North and South* (Philadelphia, 1852), p. 314.
[7] [Anon.,] *Henry Russell* (New York, 1846), pp. 22-23.
[8] C. M. Sedgwick, *Clarence* (Philadelphia, 1830), II, 72.
[9] E. D. E. N. Southworth, *Virginia and Magdalene* (Philadelphia, 1852), p. 129.

Wyllys was somewhat vague about its virtues.[10] Presumably it was intended for those heroines who were cursed with what Mrs. Hentz called "an extra set of nerves." Since the patients were highly susceptible to deliriums, it was fortunate that Miss Sedgwick was able to announce in *The Poor Rich Man* that "No disease is so completely under the control of moral treatment as hysterics."[11]

The theory of animal magnetism was prized chiefly as a "scientific" basis for the communion of kindred souls and as a source of their power to transfigure the lives of the unregenerate. That the phenomenon had met with some hostility was admitted by Maria McIntosh. ". . . yet who doubts the thing itself?" she challenged confidently in *The Lofty and the Lowly.* "Who doubts that there resides in some a wonderful power of attraction, by which they win to themselves the sympathies of all hearts, and move the minds of men hither and thither at their will?"[12] James Hall in *The Soldier's Bride* also testified to his belief that "There are certain affinities in human bosoms, certain influences which seem to operate imperceptibly by attraction, as the magnet impels the metal, and draws kindred spirits into contact and communion."[13] Although the author of *Resignation* was not prepared to accept the entire theory of animal magnetism, she recognized its effects clearly enough. "What is that mysterious power of sympathy, with an instantaneous and electric touch of feeling," she asked when confronted with the evidence, "conveying from heart to kindred heart, the sentiment of joy or of sorrow!"[14] Mrs. Mowatt appealed to the experiences of her readers for support of her cherished conviction: "That we are encircled by a spiritual sphere, through the medium of which we affect others." She found further encouragement in "the belief of many wise and

[10] S. F. Cooper, *Elinor Wyllys* (Philadelphia, 1846), II, 81. [First edition, 1845]
[11] *The Poor Rich Man and the Rich Poor Man* (New York, 1843), p. 130. [First edition, 1836]
[12] M. J. McIntosh, *The Lofty and the Lowly* (New York, 1853), I, 121.
[13] J. Hall, *The Soldier's Bride* . . . (Philadelphia, 1833), p. 49.
[14] S. A. Evans, *Resignation* (Boston, 1825), I, 279.

great men" of all eras of history.[15] "Who doubts animal magnetism?" boldly asked the author of *Charms and Counter-charms.* "Let him who does, recall the thrill that ran through his frame at receiving the cordial grasp with which a friend welcomed him back, after long wanderings, to his native land."[16] Unfortunately, this "electrical attraction," which Mrs. Southworth described as a "meeting of the eyes, in a sort of mutual recognition," could be exceedingly dangerous to susceptible ladies. The seducer's charms had proved potent enough without the aid of science. Novelists found it necessary to remind their feminine readers that "magnetism" served only to make an affair the more inflammable, and that illicit passion by any other name would inevitably lead to the same sorry conclusion. Thus Metta Fuller in *Mormon Wives* dealt severely with elegant ambiguities such as "Free Love and Psychological Twinships, Passional Attractions, etc. etc." which sophisticated rakes glibly bent to their base uses. They are "not seldom invested with the glory and fascination of genius," she declared.[17]

Even those writers like Timothy Flint, who held that the doctrine of animal magnetism was "exploded," retained their faith "in the invisible communication between minds, of something like animal magnetism and repulsion."[18] This mysterious power was made to work many miracles. After all hope had been abandoned for the "declining" Amelia in Mrs. Hentz's *Eoline,* the resourceful heroine charged her smiles with magnetism: "Amelia gave back an answering smile to the sweet smile of Eoline. An electric spark had struck the palsied mass, and life was slowly stealing through it."[19] Novelists also found it a godsend with which to unravel plot complications. Thus "Fanny Fern's" desolate heroine was about to give up her bootless search for her husband, when she suddenly felt herself

[15] A. C. Mowatt, *The Fortune Hunter* (Philadelphia, 1854), p. 49. [First edition, 1844]
[16] M. J. McIntosh, *Charms and Counter-charms* (New York, 1864), pp. 252-253. [First edition, 1848]
[17] M. V. Fuller, *Mormon Wives* (New York, 1856), p. 139.
[18] T. Flint, *Francis Berrian* (Boston, 1826), I, 5.
[19] C. L. Hentz, *Eoline* (Philadelphia, 1869), p. 214. [First edition, 1852]

being drawn mysteriously to New Orleans. "Had you asked," the author wrote innocently, "she could have given no reason for the magnetism which had drawn her thither."[20] Mrs. Hentz also employed this handy device to dignify the old trick of coincidence. "It was not chance that brought us together at the fountain's side," the hero cried ecstatically. "It was the impulse of the soul seeking its kindred soul, the heart reaching after the mutual heart."[21]

Some of the most startling of the wonders wrought by animal magnetism were achieved by dreamers in fashioning their ideal commonwealths. Not the least of these was the rehabilitation of the stultified laborers in Robert Grahame's factory village. The hero discovered that his employees were suffering from the effects of machine production, but his strong "magnetic powers" were fully equal to the situation. Within an incredibly short time the workers found themselves singing at their jobs. The author was careful to explain that the transformation was effected by the "infusion" of "intelligent souls" into the "untutored clods," and the direction of their aspirations "Heavenward."[22] This contribution to the solution of one of the most persistent problems of the machine age was child's play when compared with the international scope of the operations described in *Henry Russell*. Happily, the hero possessed "to a very unusual degree the power of animal magnetism, or mesmerism, as it was then called."[23] Nothing less than this potency was required for his world-wide program designed to usher in the millennium. The Herculean task of influencing the Congress of the United States to outlaw war was only one of Russell's projects. This accomplished, he moved swiftly to end white and black slavery, to cure the evils of intemperance, to provide for an equal distribution of the world's goods, and to establish a chain of ideal communities.[24] The novel ends

[20] S. P. W. Parton, *Rose Clark* (New York, 1856), p. 203. The author, Sara Payson Willis Parton, was widely known as "Fanny Fern." Her *Fern Leaves from Fanny's Port-folio* (1853) sold seventy thousand copies, and established her as a favorite in the feminine fifties.
[21] C. L. Hentz, *Marcus Warland* (Philadelphia, 1852), p. 131.
[22] McIntosh, *The Lofty and the Lowly*, I, 154.
[23] [Anon.,] *Henry Russell*, p. 71.   [24] *Ibid.*, pp. 70-78.

appropriately with Russell's address to ten thousand peace delegates delivered in "a noble language" which had been "constructed from the spoils of the ancient languages, and from the best of those spoken in modern times. . . ."[25]

Mrs. Southworth championed animal magnetism as "one of the greatest ministers of health, happiness, and life," and claimed that it was "divinely prefigured" in the religious ordinance of "the laying on of Hands."[26] Magnetic influence was often referred to as the source of the amazing powers possessed by evangelical heroines. Certainly they needed all the supernatural assistance their authors could provide for them. That "moral sunbeam," the heroine of *Dora Deane,* who "improved" every person with whom she spent five minutes, was endowed with mesmeric powers. She used them harmlessly enough, however, to quiet crying babies, and to revive the drooping spirits of her friends.[27] Similar magnetic ministrations were also the delight of Gertrude in *Rose Clark.* When the heroine was about to lose her reason, "Gertrude passed her soft hand magnetizingly over Rose's closed lids and temples; gradually the bright flush left her cheek, and she sank quietly to sleep."[28] Gabriella, the extremely sensitive heroine of Mrs. Hentz's *Ernest Linwood,* was so powerfully "charged" with "the magic fluid" that upon at least one occasion she hypnotized herself simply by brushing her hair! "I brushed out the damp tresses," she explained to her astounded friends, "till, self-mesmerized, a soft haziness stole over my senses, and though I did not sleep, I was on the borders of the land of dreams."[29] Claude Vellemonte, "the galvanic hero" of Mrs. Southworth's *Shannondale,* enjoyed an enviable record of mesmeric mercies which included the recovery of the heroine's precarious health,

[25] *Ibid.,* pp. 102-103. The nature of the language to be spoken in the millennium was a matter of concern to several novelists. The idealistic Dr. Hopkins in Mrs. Stowe's *The Minister's Wooing* told Aaron Burr, "That will probably be decided by an amicable conference. . . . Brother Stiles thinks it will be Hebrew. I am not clear on that point."

[26] E. D. E. N. Southworth, *Shannondale* (New York, 1851), p. 160. Mrs. Southworth found a similar divine sanction for Hydropathy in the rite of Baptism!

[27] M. J. Holmes, *Dora Deane* (New York, 1870), p. 73. [First edition, 1858]

[28] Parton, *Rose Clark,* p. 350.

[29] C. L. Hentz, *Ernest Linwood* (Philadelphia, n.d.), p. 330. [First edition, 1856]

the restoration of a friend's sanity, and the regeneration of a villain, who had hitherto been quite impervious to the efforts of reformers. When pressed for an explanation of his powers, Vellemonte showed a becoming modesty: "I prayed for it— believed in it; and sought with my strong electric life to galvanize yours into a new vigor; that is all."[30] He was a master of several isms and ologies, as Imogene was to learn when she inquired about his unusual power. "Now, my power—which power, Imogene, I have several," the wizard replied.[31]

Mesmeric influence was not possessed exclusively by the good and the pure; it was as commonly exerted by the villains as by the heroes and heroines. Timothy Shay Arthur, who assigned mesmerism to "a disorderly, and, therefore, evil origin," noted ominously that "A woman may be made to believe that any person is her . . . husband, and she will act accordingly; and afterwards she will have no recollection of it, excepting such as the operator pleases."[32] Such a convenient weapon could not fail to commend itself to adroit seducers, who promptly abandoned Lovelace's methods and "potions" as hopelessly outmoded. Withers, the evil minister in *The Deserted Wife,* demonstrated how effectively it might be used by compelling the fawnlike Sophy to submit to his will. "Oh, *what* is this? What is this closing around me like irresistible destiny?" she cried helplessly. "Why cannot I awake, arouse from this? I know I'm free; *why* can't I use my freedom? What a spell, what a mystery, what a horror! Oh! my Heavenly Father!"[33] Lenora, a malignant female in *The Homestead on the Hillside,* employed the same power. "She reminds me of the serpent, who decoyed Eve into eating that apple," Maggie told her mother, "and I always feel an attack of the nightmare whenever I know that her big, black eyes are fastened upon me."[34]

[30] Southworth, *Shannondale,* p. 98.   [31] *Ibid.*

[32] *Agnes; or, The Possessed* (Philadelphia, 1848), p. 4. The author quoted a "professor of the art and mystery," who asserted that "one person in twenty is susceptible to this peculiar influence." Arthur concluded his story with a sharp warning: "To all, the writer would say, Beware of mesmerism" (p. 103).

[33] E. D. E. N. Southworth, *The Deserted Wife* (Philadelphia, 1855), p. 94.

[34] M. J. Holmes, *The Homestead on the Hillside* (New York, n.d.), p. 9. [First edition, 1856]

Novelists who reserved their private judgment about the moral value of mesmerism showed no hesitancy in employing it to provide surprises and thrills for their readers. It performed sturdy service for Mrs. Hentz in *Ernest Linwood;* Augusta Evans used it dexterously in the plot of *Beulah;* while Mrs. Holmes's hero in *Meadowbrook,* drew Rosa to her salvation, with "the Mesmeric touch of two large, warm hands."[35] It remained for the popular Mrs. Ann Stephens to make what was, perhaps, the most spectacular use of mesmerism in one of her intricate plots. Even this author, who was the fertile mistress of so many tricks of plotting, would have been at a loss for the solution of her difficulties in *The Heiress of Greenhurst* without the blessed aid of mesmerism. The heroine, Zana, whom Mrs. Stephens had neglected to provide with a birthmark, seemed unable to establish her identity as the daughter of Lady Clare until she was put into a trance by the gypsy who had formerly been jilted by the girl's mother. "As I looked him in the face quick gleams of lightning shot around us," Zana declared later, "my soul grew fierce and strong beneath the lurid flashes of his eyes; my own scintillated as with sparks of fire."[36] Amid this display of pyrotechnics, all mysteries were satisfactorily resolved and every plot wrinkle was ironed out neatly. In view of the service it performed for them, there is little wonder that sentimental novelists found mesmerism to be "divinely inspired," and, when used properly, to reveal "great Hygeian virtues."

A number of mesmeric heroes, like Delafield in *Meadowbrook,* also enjoyed "physiognomic powers."[37] Although physiognomy was less spectacular in its immediate effects than mesmerism, it afforded wide scope for practice; for most readers, it was assumed, had a sufficient smattering of the "science" to enable them to recognize a villain when they were introduced to one. As Maria Cummins remarked in *The Lamplighter,* the world was full of "tell-tale faces, that speak the truth and

[35] M. J. Holmes, *Meadowbrook* (New York, 1857), p. 132.
[36] A. S. Stephens, *The Heiress of Greenhurst* (New York, 1857), p. 311.
[37] Holmes, *Meadowbrook,* p. 275.

proclaim the sentiment within. . . ."[38] Novelists strove to draw the faces of their men and women with the hope that, as in *The Children of Light,* "To the student of expression, the characteristic, the individuality of each of these persons, might easily be discovered from a glance at their countenances."[39] Fleda in *Queechy* was only one of many heroines who were "of Lavater's mind, that everything has a physiognomy." "I think he was perfectly right," she told Carleton, ". . . but the expression is so subtle that only very nice sensibilities, with fine training can hope to catch it; therefore to the mass of the world Lavater would talk nonsense."[40] Plain girls were frequently given the dubious compensation of "physiognomic charms." At a casual glance, Beulah may have seemed "rather homely, nay, decidedly ugly," admitted Augusta Evans, but she was quick to add that "to the curious physiognomist, this face presented greater attractions than either of the others."[41] It is not surprising, however, that ordinary young men preferred less science and more dimples. When Dick Martin defended Beulah's features as constituting what "the lecturer on physiognomy, would call 'a striking face,'" he was given a blunt answer. "Yes, strikingly ugly. . . . Her forehead juts over like the eaves of the kitchen. . . ."[42]

Heroes soon learned how to read the faces of their female friends to determine their fitness for domestic life. They were instructed to look for the "strikingly intellectual, large black eye, inclosed in a proportionally-ample socket," which the author of *The Black Gauntlet* held to be "a rare perfection," indicative of the "inner graces of adhesive perfection."[43] An appearance of "absolute repose" was also highly prized, for instead of denoting a lethargic spirit, "to the practiced Physiognomist, it expressed the perfect peace of mind and heart; completely harmonious."[44] Lovers were especially warned to be on

[38] *The Lamplighter* (Boston, 1854), p. 165.
[39] C. Chesebro', *The Children of Light* (New York, 1853), p. 44.
[40] S. Warner, *Queechy* (New York, 1852), II, 213.
[41] A. J. Evans, *Beulah* (New York, 1899), p. 8. [First edition, 1859]
[42] *Ibid.,* p. 34.
[43] [Mrs.] M. H. Schoolcraft, *The Black Gauntlet* (Philadelphia, 1860), p. 20.
[44] Evans, *Beulah,* p. 300.

their guard against "a dreamy languid expression," because it was an infallible sign of the lack of that "inner chamber where dwell the graces which make a woman what she ought to be."[45] Mrs. Southworth's "physiognomic hero" in *The Curse of Clifton* had been taught to eschew the merely "beautiful or classical" and to insist upon "a higher order of physiognomy." His discriminating self-sacrifice was suitably rewarded when he discovered that his beloved Kate possessed "a Maria Theresa face without the wickedness."[46] Choice was simplified for the practicing male physiognomist because the ideal heroine could invariably be depended upon to betray her inmost thoughts in her countenance. As Sylvester Judd explained in *Margaret,* material substances are transmuted into "moral emotions." Thus the nerves of his heroine's face were "sympathetic throughout, a beautiful flower for example, borne in on the optic nerve, would come out an irradiation of joy generously spread over the whole countenance."[47] Wife-hunting heroes were given further help by the convention which decreed that authors present their women in pairs. Contrasting sisters and cousins abound in these novels. Blonde and brunette, sunshine and tempest, seraph and sensualist, sense and sensibility, demure fairy and tricksy sprite, the divinely plain face and the showy, flashy face—these were sketched in seemingly endless numbers for the scrutiny of man. Fortunate indeed was that lover blessed with sufficient physiognomic penetration to choose wisely and well.

Easily the most popular of all the isms and ologies of the middle years of the century was phrenology. The more conservative minds had viewed mesmerism and spiritualism as emanating from the powers of darkness, but even Henry Ward Beecher found it possible to endorse the subject of "Phrenological Physiology." When the arts of physiognomy failed, as many trusting heroines too often found they did, the disciples of Spurzheim boasted that "bumps" never lied.

Novelists who were a bit cautious about accepting all the

[45] M. J. Holmes, *Cousin Maude* (New York, n.d.), p. 80. [First edition, 1860]
[46] E. D. E. N. Southworth, *The Curse of Clifton* (Philadelphia, 1852), pp. 39-40.
[47] *Margaret,* p. 223.

claims made by professors of the interesting science of "bump fingering" had no scruples about using the jargon of phrenology; they rarely neglected, moreover, to provide their characters with appropriate cranial topographies. Even those historical personages who were born too early to know the advantages of a phrenological examination were usually given "bumps" to fit their peculiar eminence. Thus Mrs. Stephens described "the great and good Washington" as possessing the "breadth of forehead . . . which marks a well-regulated character."[48] The author of *Blonde and Brunette* used praiseworthy caution in introducing Donald McAboy, who "had an immense volume of brain gloriously housed; while over the orbits of his penetrating eyes, the perceptive faculties (using the language of phrenology, without meaning to say, if I think it true or false) had built their most imposing, low-browed arch."[49] There is the same kind of credulous circumspection in the description of an atheist in *Confessions of a Reformed Inebriate.* "I know not whether phrenology be true or false," wrote the author, "but I remember being forcibly struck, the first time I met this man, with the close resemblance of his head to that of Robert Dale Owen . . . and it is certain that his character was such as to sustain the inference which a phrenologist would draw from this fact."[50]

Mrs. Southworth, who was hospitable to all isms, welcomed phrenology with her usual ardor and often introduced her characters with a hint about the nature of their "bumps." "Education, perhaps, never will be fully understood and perfected," she declared in *Virginia and Magdalene,* "until phrenology, the youngest of the sciences, be elevated to an equal rank with its sisters."[51] She asserted it as her profound conviction that in "Craniology," the "character is written as plainly, as clearly, and as truly, for those who can read the language, as the letter-press of a printed volume."[52] For compelling reasons

---

[48] A. S. Stephens, *Mary Derwent* (Philadelphia, 1858), p. 280.
[49] C. Burdett, *Blonde and Brunette* (New York, 1858), p. 114.
[50] [Anon.,] *Confessions of a Reformed Inebriate* (New York, 1844), pp. 80-81.
[51] E. D. E. N. Southworth, *Virginia and Magdalene,* p. 39.
[52] *Ibid.,* p. 48.

such as those cited by Mrs. Southworth, many heroines were subjected to phrenological examinations almost before they were able to walk. Up-to-the-minute boarding schools were well equipped with "Phrenological Charts" and pupils were taught to explore the topography of the head as well as that of the "globes." Miss Manly, preceptress of Magnolia Vale in *Eoline*, regarded this subject as her "favorite science," and took her young charges "to hear a celebrated lecturer on Phrenology."[53] It is reassuring to learn that Miss Manly's own "bumps" confirmed her skill as a teacher, for an expert diagnosis had revealed that "her organs of Self-Esteem and Firmness, were, indeed, most wonderfully developed."[54] The later career of Ruth Hall confirmed fully the accuracy of Professor Finiman's "phrenological examination." "Your physiology indicates a predominance of the nervous temperament," he told the girl. "Few suffer or enjoy with such intensity as you do. . . . You are religiously disposed. You are also characterized by a strong belief in Divine influences, providences, and special interpositions from on high."[55]

Model suitors cursed with serious cranial limitations felt that the only decent thing to do was to disclose them before it was too late. "A celebrated German phrenologist examined my head," Ernest Linwood manfully confessed to his beloved Gabriella, "and pronounced it decidedly deficient in the swelling organ of self-appreciation."[56] The heroine verified the awful truth by an independent examination. "He took my hand and placed it on his head, amid his soft, luxuriant hair," she reported, "and it certainly met no elevation." Gabriella loyally gave her lover full benefit of the doubt. "I was not skilled in the science of phrenology," she admitted, "and there might be a defect in the formation of the head. . . ."[57] Readers were frequently given full specifications upon which to base their phrenological conclusions. "Both had sweet low foreheads," noted Burdett impartially in presenting his twin heroines, "but

---

[53] Hentz, *Eoline*, p. 137.   [54] *Ibid.*
[55] S. P. W. Parton, *Ruth Hall* (New York, 1855), pp. 319-320.
[56] Hentz, *Ernest Linwood*, pp. 268-269.
[57] *Ibid.*

Melaine's was higher than Xanthine's by measurement, though not broader." "Xanthine's lovely hair waved in broad masses over a soft antique fulness in the region of ideality."[58] Descriptions invariably began at the top and worked downward. "There was in this gentleman's high and broad forehead . . . the indisputable stamp of power," the author of *Two Lives* remarked significantly. "His closely curling brown hair grew up in points at the temples, leaving that part of his forehead with its full spiral veins, quite exposed to view."[59] When phrenological defects were hidden from view, authors were sometimes sporting enough to give fair warning to their readers. "As she reclines there," wrote "Fanny Fern" of a cruel matron in a charity school, "we will venture to take a look at her: not a phrenological glance, for she has a cap on her head. . . ."[60] Quite appropriately, this same dame was later wooed and wed by a shortsighted bachelor "with a small fortune, and a large bump of credulity."[61] Mrs. Mowatt followed the familiar formula in commending her hero to readers of *The Fortune Hunter:* "His head was a study for a painter; and to have examined its developments, would have been a delight to Spurzheim. Nature's own hand clustered the dark curls around his broad high forehead."[62] The cranium, not the clothes, made the man in these novels. When Richard Edney's rustic coat prejudiced an employment agent against him, the author exclaimed indignantly: "Could not the three thick volumes of Lavater outweigh the short jacket? Why had not Neson been appointed Head Phrenological Custom-House Inspector,—and he might have determined in a trice that Richard contained no fraud in his composition."[63]

Since the popular mind was more than half disposed to accept the theory that character traits were revealed by cranial "bumps," novelists often justified the behavior of their favorites by pointing to the appropriate organ of the brain. To account

[58] *Blonde and Brunette*, p. 25.
[59] M. J. McIntosh, *Two Lives* (New York, 1846), p. 68.
[60] *Rose Clark*, p. 17.
[61] *Ibid.*, p. 27.   [62] *The Fortune Hunter*, p. 23.
[63] S. Judd, *Richard Edney* (Boston, 1850), p. 126.

for Imogene's profound obedience to her parents, Mrs. Southworth neatly referred to this heroine's "one eminently distinguishing trait of character." "So elevated above every other
trait was this, that a phrenologist must have been struck with
it at once in the high, pale forehead, towering to its highest
point—*veneration*."[64] In *The Deserted Wife,* the same facile
author found this organ a convenient one by which to account
for the ancestral pride of Southern families. "Truly the organ
of veneration must be largely developed," she explained.[65]
Mrs. Southworth also made use of a "bump" to lend plausibil-
ity to one of her cherished scenes of "recognition" and reunion.
"Miss Joe had to rub her organ of eventuality," she wrote in
The Discarded Daughter, "before she could recognize in the
writer a cousin. . . ."[66] The extent to which the jargon had
become part of the popular consciousness may be seen in some
of Mrs. Stowe's novels. Her presentation of the character of
Dr. Hopkins in *The Minister's Wooing* reveals an effort to
draw his portrait in accord with phrenological principles.
"Whoever looked on the forehead of the good doctor," she remarked, "must have seen the squareness of ideality giving
marked effect to its outline."[67]

Even the spawn of minor characters often were equipped
with "bumps" to fit their habits. Thus a careless servant was
provided with a "bump of destructiveness,"[68] a merchant with
his "bump of caution,"[69] a jolly youngster with her "bump of
mirthfulness,"[70] and a speculator with his "bump of acquisitiveness."[71] Novelists must have been delighted with the elaborate
"Symbolical Phrenological Chart" which presented graphically
a wide variety of "propensities" and "sentiments" with their
corresponding "organs." Upon it, the domestic novelists could
find a pictorial representation of their beloved hearth-side virtues: amativeness, philoprogenitiveness, adhesiveness, and in-

[64] E. D. E. N. Southworth, *Shannondale*, p. 88.
[65] *The Deserted Wife*, p. 295.
[66] *The Discarded Daughter* (Philadelphia, 1852), I, 136.
[67] H. B. Stowe, *The Minister's Wooing* (New York, 1886), p. 92. [First edition, 1859]
[68] Parton, *Ruth Hall*, p. 75.   [69] *Ibid.*, p. 144.
[70] Parton, *Rose Clark*, p. 325.   [71] S. F. Cooper, *Elinor Wyllys*, I, 106.

habitiveness. Religious novelists were able to point to cranial authority for man's natural benevolence, veneration, hope, spirituality, sublimity, and ideality. The authors of temperance fiction wisely made the most of the organ of bibation, but it served equally well for the champions of hydropathy because it signified a propensity for baths as well as for beer.

The favorable popular attitude to the subject may further be seen in the novelists' confident assumption that the general principles of phrenology would be understood readily by ordinary readers. That there might be "something in it" was the opinion of many writers who hesitated to record their unqualified endorsement. Only occasionally does one encounter a hint of burlesque, and then it was usually directed at the vanity of those who were unduly proud of their "bumps," rather than at the "science" itself. Thus the affectation of Dr. Julius Cake, who was arrogant about the size of his "organ of language," proved fair bait for the satirist. "For phrenological reasons— to prove at once his capacity and the science—," wrote Thomas in *East and West*, "he wore his hair very short, but cultivated the growth of an enormous pair of whiskers. . . ."[72] The same brand of affectation, along with that of ultrarefined sensibility, was a source of ridicule in *The Match Girl*. Certainly, "a literary evening," in which the chief attraction was a bevy of "the poetesses of America," provided ample material for raillery: "Ringlets streamed over the face of one—inflated bands extended like wings beyond the ears of others—whilst from the broad forehead of a third, the hair was literally torn from the roots, to display the intellectual brow on which genius and thought were supposed to sit."[73] Fun of this sort at the expense of foolish "bump fanciers" hardly indicates a distrust of the general principles of phrenology any more than burlesque of false delicacy proves that sensibility was no longer a prized attribute of the ideal heroine.

The widespread belief in isms and ologies was only one manifestation of a larger faith in the ever-coming millennium

[72] F. W. Thomas, *East and West* (Philadelphia, 1836), I, 212.
[73] [Anon.,] *The Match Girl* (Philadelphia, 1855), p. 279.

toward which Christian perfectionism had been pointing. The pages of fiction were filled with Utopias and rumors of Utopias. A spirit of jaunty optimism, engendered by the country's seemingly inexhaustible natural resources, made all things appear to be possible. As Mrs. Stowe had observed, New England was "the only example of a successful commonwealth founded on a theory, as a distinct experiment in the problem of society." "It was for this reason," she declared, "that the minds of its greatest thinkers dwelt so much on the final solution of that problem in this world."[74] Men's minds were dazzled by the prospect of planning for perfection. "Not one-fourth of the United States territory is now even occupied by civilized man," exulted the author of *Ralphton*. "Hundreds of millions of human beings are to become the tillers of this interminable tract of country. Organize your occupants . . . and allow to each family one hundred acres of land."[75]

Less ambitious dreamers began their planning on a smaller scale. Many daughters of slaveowners, like little Eva in *Uncle Tom's Cabin,* cherished plans for communities of emancipated blacks in Canada and in Liberia.[76] Benevolent capitalists, shocked at slum conditions, projected private vest-pocket Utopias of their own. "I will buy a large farm, eight or ten miles from the city," promised a reformer in *The Mysteries and Miseries of New York*. "There shall be no drinking, no dissolute conduct. The women shall have a separate department. . . . I will have prizes for those who behave well—I will kindly reason with those who do not."[77] The hero of *The Lofty and the Lowly* devoted his energies to the creation of a model industrial community. Spurning the bequest of a lordly estate in Great Britain, he turned patriotically to rural Connecticut where he "pictured to himself the change when a village should arise, in each smiling home of which his name should be dear; when a library should send forth streams of useful

---

[74] *The Minister's Wooing*, p. 136.   [75] Brisbane, *Ralphton*, p. 225.

[76] For examples of this well-meaning, but futile, method to resolve the problem of slavery, see Chapter III, "Uncle Tom's and Other Cabins," pp. 267-270, 276-280.

[77] E. Z. C. Judson, *The Mysteries and Miseries of New York* (New York, 1848), II, 35.

knowledge, and a church should shed the light of Heaven over all."[78] The conspicuous success which crowned Margaret's efforts should have been a spur to other Utopia builders. Within a short time, the consumption of liquor "diminished from six or eight thousand gallons to a few scores," the author announced proudly. Nor was this all. The unsightly village jail, which was tenantless under the new regime, was converted into an attractive civic center; relief rolls were reduced seventy-five per cent; domestic bickering ceased with the result that divorces were unknown in the community; five distilleries were dismantled; the militia corps suddenly lost its "bump of combativeness" and voted unanimously to disband; public school buildings increased in number from two to six; and the town tavern, now strictly a temperance house, changed its name to "The Cross and Crown."[79] As if these transformations were not in themselves sufficiently impressive, visitors were called upon to testify that although they visited "a hundred houses, at all hours of the day, they have not heard a woman speak scandal, or scold her children."[80] All that seemed necessary to usher in the millennium was to multiply such villages throughout the country.

A permanent world peace was to be the natural result of conditions which could support such ideal communities. "I cannot believe that the general spread of human interests, which is now uniting all nations into one great family," stated Brisbane, "will allow of the political intrigue of any particular people to avert so grand a consummation."[81] Some slight disagreement was to be expected in fixing the precise date of the advent of the millennium. Warned, perhaps, by the discomfitures suffered by the Millerites when their predictions were confounded in 1843 by an obstinate world which refused to come to an end, the perfectionists were more wary. The end of the twentieth century seemed a likely date to the author of *Henry Russell,* who prophesied a race of supermen and a society at "the very summit of physical and social well-being."[82]

[78] McIntosh, *The Lofty and the Lowly,* II, 47.
[79] Judd, *Margaret,* pp. 403-405, 427-430.   [80] *Ibid.,* p. 429.
[81] *Ralphton,* p. 191.   [82] [Anon.,] *Henry Russell,* pp. 9-10.

The year 2135 A.D. was appointed as the date for the realization of the Utopian conditions described in *Camperdown*. The author, Mrs. Griffith, had only compassion for the benighted souls of the nineteenth century who read impure literature, smoked and chewed tobacco, drank spirits, and tolerated slavery and warfare. Viewed from the vantage point of 2135 A.D., the conduct of the author's own contemporaries seemed full of anomalies. "Why drag the poor sailors and soldiers to be butchered like cattle to gratify the fine feelings of a few morbidly constructed minds?" asked the enlightened citizens of the Golden Age.[83] They voiced their surprise upon reading in social histories of the nineteenth century "that well educated men could keep a pungent and bitter mass of leaves in their mouths for the pleasure of seeing a stream of yellow water running out of it."[84] Personal habits of this sort, of course, were only subjects for amused speculation by antiquarians in the society "three hundred years hence" about which Mrs. Griffith wrote in 1836. Gone, too, was the need of all private charitable agencies; dueling had long been outlawed; crime was treated understandingly as a disease; and the taste for liquor, which in the days of Andrew Jackson had created a national problem, was, by the year 2135, almost extinct. National prohibition, the author predicted with not too conspicuous accuracy, had been functioning flawlessly since 1935!

Although the sentimental generation was dazzled by the prospect of a short cut to perfection, there were those who criticized the folly of attempting to rush the advent of the millennium. Fenimore Cooper preferred improving his acres in New York State to the setting up of whole principalities in Utopia. "Thrice happy the nations," he wrote in *The Oak Openings*, "which can be made to understand, that the surest progress is that which is made on the clearest principles, and with the greatest caution!"[85] Cooper had little faith in the sudden improvement of human nature: "The notion of setting up anything new in morals, is as fallacious in theory as it will

[83] M. Griffith, *Camperdown* (Philadelphia, 1836), p. 67.
[84] *Ibid.*
[85] *The Oak Openings* (New York, 1848), II, 80.

be found to be dangerous in practice."[86] "If the political economists, and reformers, and revolutionists of the age," he advised in the same novel, "would turn from their speculations to those familiar precepts which all are taught and so few obey, they would find rules for every emergency. . . ."[87] Even on "those remote and sweet islands," described in *The Crater*, where the Craterinoes planned their ideal community, the evils of sectarianism proved the bane of the colony.[88] Other voices objected that while the millennium seemed attractive enough, it was everlastingly slow in arriving. "It is small comfort to anticipate a time of blessedness for future generations," complained Beulah, who was tired of waiting for the coming harmony. "What benefit is steam or telegraph to the mouldering mummies in the catacombs? I want to know what good the millennium will do you and me, when our dust is mingled with mother earth, in some silent necropolis?"[89]

These protesting notes were drowned in the overwhelming chorus of sentimental optimism. "It is wonderful what a disposition there is among men to run into octaves in everything they do," Cooper observed in 1850 in *The Ways of the Hour*. "There is as much of the *falsetto* nowadays in philanthropy as in music."[90] The same robust critic in *The Oak Openings* lamented that "The *ignis fatuus* of human happiness employs all minds, all pens, and all theories, just at this particular moment."[91] The sentimentalist, however, turned a deaf ear to these warnings. His heart was quickened by the shrill and the false, not the natural notes. Phrenology and mesmerism seemed to him to offer more hope to mankind than geology and anesthetics. His "bump of eventuality" had been enlarged by too much wishful thinking for sentimental quackery to effect a cure. There was hope, of course, in the bracing, "Hygeian virtues" which are derived from a sense of fact and reality. But for the sentimentalist, this medicine was too bitter. He preferred pleasanter prescriptions.

[86] *Ibid.*   [87] *Ibid.*, II, 21.
[88] J. F. Cooper, *The Crater* (New York, 1847), II, 198-199, 207-208.
[89] Evans, *Beulah*, p. 338.
[90] *The Ways of the Hour* (New York, 1850), p. 80.
[91] *The Oak Openings*, II, 20.

II

TEN THOUSAND AND ONE NIGHTS
IN A BARROOM

The wildest dreams of fiction would prove tame in comparison. Tragedies more fearfully startling than Avon's bard ever traced, had often occurred. Scenes which would mock to scorn the artist's pencil, were of daily occurrence.

— Thurlow Weed Brown's Introduction to
J. K. Cornyn's *Dick Wilson*, 1855.

THE CAPTAINS of the antirum army found themselves in friendly disagreement upon the nice point of whether the temperance reform was the work of Jehovah or of Uncle Sam. The Reverend Lebbeus Armstrong, a devoted historian of the cold-water movement, believed that in origin, at least, it "was evidently the work of Jehovah."[1] Other authorities, such as the patriotic Cyrus Mann, author of *The Clinton Family*, held it to have been purely "an American invention," and therefore a convenient way of discharging "our obligations for European, and especially English literature."[2] There was no difference of opinion, however, about the thoroughly native character of the second annual convention of the American Temperance Union at Saratoga on the fourth day of August, 1836. Uncompromisingly American were the embattled reformers, four hundred delegates from nineteen states and territories, who met to renew their attack upon ardent spirits and to extend their hostility to include all intoxicating beverages. Scarcely less epochmaking was their formal vote endorsing prose fiction and the "products of the fancy" as weapons in the crusade against Prince Alcohol. Thus was the novel, that wayward daughter of letters, baptized in Saratoga's crystal founts, and officially

[1] *The Temperance Reformation* (New York, 1853), p. 26.
[2] *The Clinton Family* (Boston, 1833), p. 191.

welcomed as a useful handmaiden in the "one great temperance family."

Walt Whitman, who confessed privately that he had written *Franklin Evans,* his temperance novel, "with the help of a bottle of port or what not," claimed even higher sanction than the resolution of the Saratoga convention. "Without being presumptuous," he submitted in his apology to the reader in 1842, "I would remind those who believe in the wholesome doctrines of abstinence, how the earlier teachers of piety used parables and fables, as the fit instruments whereby they might convey to men the beauty of the system they professed. In the resemblance, how reasonable it is to suppose that you can impress a lesson upon him whom you would influence to sobriety, in no better way than letting him read such a story as this."[3] Even those who still regarded novels with misgiving were convinced that temperance stories were more exciting than dull arguments and dry statistics. "The didactic and abstract, much as he might prefer them," admitted Pharcellus Church, "are not the weapons for a steam and lightning movement."[4] The approval thus given to fiction was not without grave reservations. The author of *The Senator's Son* carefully qualified her sanction. "But it is only when some effort at human improvement is robed in its captivating garb that fiction should be tolerated," she declared at the outset of her long story.[5]

Most reformers were ready to grant that the novel had come to stay and that they had better make the most of it. "This form of literature meets an instinctive want," conceded Church. "Instead of carping against light literature, it were better to charge it with truths and influences purifying, profound and enduring, and send it abroad on a mission of love to mankind."[6] The marked increase in the number of temper-

[3] *Franklin Evans* (New York, 1929), p. 5. [First edition, 1842] Whitman's apologia was repeated in many later volumes. "The method of conveying important truths, exposing error, and urging duty by means of Fables," observed the editor of *Temperance Fables* (New York, 1850), "is one of the oldest and most successful ever practiced" (p. iii).

[4] P. Church, *Mapleton* (Boston, 1853), p. iii.

[5] M. V. Fuller, *The Senator's Son* (Cleveland, 1853), p. vi.

[6] *Mapleton,* p. iii.

ance novels in the fifties indicates that this had become the popular view. Maria Buckley testified in 1853 that "Many able and talented pens have preceded hers in portraying the evils of the greatest scourge with which the world was ever infested."[7] By 1854, the author of *The Unjust Judge* could declare that temperance was "a subject which already has employed the pens of the most gifted authors of the age. . . ."[8] No longer did temperance writers feel the need of apologizing for their use of fiction. "There was a time in the history of the Temperance reformation," admitted John Cornyn in 1855, "when it would have been necessary, in presenting a work upon this subject to the public, to have fortified it well with apologies."[9] That day was over by the middle of the decade: "The literature of our reform is assuming a more refined and elevated character, and clothing great truths in purer and more attractive garb; and never was there a wider field for the exercise of intellectual effort."[10]

Although fiction rapidly became the favorite form of temperance propaganda, its readers were never permitted to forget for a split second that its basis was sober-suited truth. "And I would ask your belief when I assert that what you are going to read is not a work of fiction, as the term is used," Walt Whitman wrote piously in *Franklin Evans*. "I narrate occurrences that have had a far more substantial existence, than in my fancy."[11] Thurlow Brown, who declared that he wrote *Minnie Hermon* "with a throbbing nib" and baptized it "with a scalding tear," made the same claim of authenticity. "You will bear in mind that every chapter in the book is *drawn from life,* with the necessary change of names and dates," he asserted, "the only difficulty having been in selecting from the mass of materials collected during an active participation in the Temperance Reform."[12] Timothy Shay Arthur, the teetotalers' prose laureate whose *Ten Nights in a Bar-Room* in 1854 was

[7] M. L. Buckley, *Edith Moreton* (New York, 1853), p. 4.
[8] [Anon.,] *The Unjust Judge* (Mansfield, Ohio, 1854), p. 5.
[9] J. K. Cornyn, *Dick Wilson* (New York, 1855), p. iii.
[10] *Ibid.*, p. xxi.   [11] *Franklin Evans*, p. 4.
[12] T. W. Brown, *Minnie Hermon* (New York, 1857), p. [v].

destined to become the household classic of the movement, stated that the success of his earlier work "resulted entirely from the fact, that, in nearly every one of the stories presented, there has been, as its groundwork, a basis of real incidents. . . ."[13]

These novels, we are continually being assured, are tame copies of the actual facts upon which they were founded. "The caricature is not here, but in real life," Church insisted in *Mapleton.* "Had the author's sketches reached the extreme limit of history, they would have lacked the essential requisite of an air of credibility."[14] So frightful were the results of the liquor habit, according to De Witt, that her chief task was to subdue nature, not to heighten it. "The history of the Stanley family is strictly true," she maintained, "with this exception: instead of four, there were *five* sons, *all* of whom died, in the most fearful manner, in consequence of intemperance."[15] It would have been a serious tactical error to admit that the horrors of the rum evil were even remotely capable of exaggeration. Not content with the usual claim of factual support, the publishers of *The Beacon!* advertised that "the leading facts and circumstances, embodied in it, are, the most of them *literally true,* and none of them are exaggerated. Names, places, and dates only, are fictitious."[16] Nature, moreover, seemed ready to satisfy the most exacting demands of poetic justice. The horrible ends neatly reserved for every offender against sobriety in Joel Wakeman's *The Mysterious Parchment* were defended as having been taken from actual life. "Indeed, some of the most horrible and shocking which are mentioned are true, with little or no variation," he added with considerable mortuary evidence, "such as the death of Howland by falling from the bridge—Philip Hopkins, who froze to death—Philip Saxbury, who fell in the fire and was burned to death—Davidson's son,

---

[13] T. S. Arthur, *Temperance Tales; or, Six Nights with the Washingtonians* (Philadelphia, 1848), I, iii. The first edition, published in 1842, is entitled *Six Nights with the Washingtonians.*   [14] *Mapleton,* p. iii.

[15] J. D. De Witt, *The Sting of the Adder* (Philadelphia, 1853), p. 3.

[16] *The Beacon!* (Providence, 1839), p. [iv]. Other authors professed their fear that the originals of the characters would be recognized. "Many a citizen of New York will recognize, under assumed names, the different characters we have feebly endeavoured to portray," wrote Buckley in *Edith Moreton.*

who was killed by drinking too much whiskey—Mrs. Sturde-
vant, who was knocked down, her flesh and limbs hacked with
a sharp knife, by her drunken husband . . . and many others
mentioned in this work are true, and are given without embellishment or color."[17] Generous as this assortment of catastrophes is, it was more than matched by many others, including
a spectacular death by combustion compared with which Wieland's fate seems almost natural. "Let not any of our readers
say this is fiction," pleaded the author of *Edith Moreton*. "It is
true—true as that the wine-cup intoxicates. . . ."[18] Novelists in
the preceding century had advanced timidly with their stories
"founded on truth" as a means of escaping the stigma attached
to works of fiction. Temperance writers made the same claim,
but only after solemnly insisting that fiction's most lurid scenes
paled before the reality of an ordinary case of delirium tremens.

A favorite tenet maintained by temperance novelists was
that the evils of alcohol formed the lowest rung in the ladder
of vice. "Talk of other vices," protested Wakeman, "these all
follow rumselling and tippling as legitimately as one link follows another in a chain."[19] Prince Alcohol topped all the
legions in horrid hell with his frightful devastation. "I have
done more towards peopling these regions of fire than any ten
Devils within these walls," boasted the rum demon in *An Account of the Marvelous Doings of Prince Alcohol*.[20] Intemperance was represented as the parent stock from which all
other sins sprouted. Twelve years of experience as a reporter
in New York moved Charles Burdett to express his "solemn
conviction, that nine-tenths of all the vice, the wickedness, the
crime, and the poverty, which meet us at every step in life, may
be traced to the indulgence in habits of intoxication."[21] John
Marsh proclaimed drunkenness to be "a sin of deepest dye in
the sight of God, and the parent of other sins." "And its guilt
is charged," he continued mercilessly, "not only upon each successive act, but also back upon that moderate drinking and

[17] J. Wakeman, *The Mysterious Parchment* (New York, 1857), pp. 4-5.
[18] Buckley, *Edith Moreton*, p. 17.   [19] *The Mysterious Parchment*, p. 134.
[20] *An Account of the Marvelous Doings of Prince Alcohol* (n. p., 1847), p. 7.
[21] C. Burdett, *Mary Grover* (New York, 1855), p. vii.

those early habits which induced it."[22] The number of deaths recorded in temperance fiction alone would amply justify Tator's execration in *Brother Jonathan's Cottage*. "Rum! Rum!" cried a bereaved father whose child had been killed by a drunken stage-driver, "if the names of all thy victims were written one beneath another, the record of thy butcheries must fill a scroll that would belt the globe!"[23] Intemperance was viewed as the greatest foe of religion and as "the sum and substance, the root and branch, of all the outward developments of crime and degradation." "It blots out the image of divinity more effectually, and changes the human into the beastly more rapidly," charged Mrs. Southworth, "than all the other powers of darkness combined."[24] No scene was more frequently sketched than that of the rum-ridden village with its flourishing tavern and decaying church. Uncle Benedict in *Fountain Rock* led his friends to a dilapidated meeting- and schoolhouse to point his moral. "That shows," he concluded sadly, "that it is just as easy to build a pyramid of snow before a furnace seven times heated, as to build up the church and school before the rum furnace."[25]

A lecture hall full of teetotalers, the conservatives were fond of saying, was also likely to be a room full of abolitionists; but to your thoroughgoing cold-water man, slavery was the lesser of the two evils. Did not rum and brandy enslave the soul as well as the body? "Talk about the abolition of slavery! let us abolish liquors first," counseled Lynn in *Durham Village*. "We northerners have enough to do to 'take the beam out of our own eye,' before we *look* at the mote in our brother's eye."[26] That there were benevolent plantation owners, even antislavery novelists were willing to concede, but to the temperance writer, every bartender was a Simon Legree in a white apron. "Sir, if my child is to be enslaved at all," argued Cyrus Mann, "I say,

---

[22] J. Marsh, *Hannah Hawkins* (New York, 1849), p. 52.
[23] H. H. Tator, *Brother Jonathan's Cottage* (New York, 1854), p. 48.
[24] S. A. Southworth, *Lawrence Monroe* (Boston, 1856), p. 98.
[25] H. Meeks, *Stories of the Fountain Rock* (Philadelphia, 1846), p. 46.
[26] C. Lynn, *Durham Village* (Boston, 1854), p. 73. This novel was issued in Glasgow in 1856 under the more descriptive title, *Fast Life; or, The City and the Farm*.

let it be the slave-dealer, and not the rum-dealer, that shall catch him." Slaves might enjoy the blessings of God, he continued, "But if it is the rum-tyrant that enchains him . . . he is *lost*—lost to the hopes of the Gospel—*lost—forever*."[27] The scourge of the distillery was the most cutting of all. "It stings sharper, deeper, than the driver's whip," asserted the hero of *Dick Wilson,* "for it strikes both the body and the mind, and with maddened fury drives them together into the cheerless vortex of desolation!"[28] In their anxiety to return a telling indictment against alcohol, these novelists claimed everything and conceded nothing. The grim carnage of famine, pestilence, and war was a mere bagatelle compared with the blight of intemperance. "The other spectres may boast of having slain and carried terror and dismay to the hearts of thousands," exulted John Barleycorn to Uncle Sam, "but I have slain my *tens of thousands*."[29] Maria Buckley found these statistics too modest to indicate the magnitude of the toll of rum. "War has slain her millions," she admitted in *Edith Moreton,* "but intemperance has slain her hundreds of millions—we might almost say billions."[30] The brewers' big horses, which were defied so ecstatically in a favorite temperance hymn, seem to have been driven by the four grim spectres of the Apocalypse.

Temperance writers were not entirely comfortable until they traced to alcohol all the delusions from which this world has suffered. "The voluptuous habits of Mahomet made him a visionary," charged Pharcellus Church, "and gave birth to his sensual heaven."[31] With the origin of Mohammedanism thus ascribed to a bottle, this same ingenious author turned his attention to Mormonism, an evil nearer home. It appears to have arisen from its founder's inability to distinguish properly between a spiritual and a spiritous dream. "Joe Smith was indebted to the bottle for his early inspirations," Church wrote curtly.[32] Our narrow escapes from disaster during the Revolution were similarly accounted for. "All remember the defeat

[27] Mann, *The Clinton Family,* p. 257.   [28] Cornyn, *Dick Wilson,* p. 361.
[29] E. Wellmont, *Uncle Sam's Palace* (Boston, 1853), p. 307.
[30] *Edith Moreton,* p. 33.
[31] *Mapleton,* p. 92.   [32] *Ibid.*

at Monmouth," wrote Thomas Hunt in *It Will Never Injure Me*. "Lee was skilful and brave, yet . . . he had never insulted the father of his country as he did, had his lips never received the drunkard's drink. Lee was never sober after." Benedict Arnold's treachery might have been avoided under a national prohibition law, continued Hunt. "For rum he betrayed his country."[33] Temperance novelists whose work appeared after the Civil War had sufficient tact to leave undiscussed the personal habits of General Ulysses S. Grant.

The seducer, whose glittering wiles blasted so many tender buds and fragile blossoms in eighteenth-century fiction, finally was forced to yield his bad eminence to a new disturber of domestic tranquility, the confirmed sot. "If there was one thing on earth she detested and despised it was a drunkard," wrote an author in presenting his heroine. "If there was one vice or frailty for which she felt no sympathy it was intemperance."[34] The seducer, moreover, was forced by the nature of things to limit the range of his intrigues, but no one was either too old or too young to be scorched by the flames of alcohol. The history of many a bloated corpse went back to the cradle where a fond but mistaken mother had prescribed a sip of rum to cure "the colic." Alcohol had an honored place in every medicine cabinet. "It was a catholicon," bewailed Hunt, "a panacea for every ill."[35] Mrs. Stone's fatal practice in *Benjamin, the Temperance Boy* is a melancholy instance of contemporary medical misinformation. "I don't hold to well folks drinking much spirit," she remarked judiciously, "but we have to keep a little for sickness. I used a whole gallon of gin in one week, when the twins had the measles." Little Benny, a survivor, added the inevitable epitaph. "And what good did it do?" he asked his mother bitterly. "Oh, mother! they were such dear little girls,—and both to die in one day."[36] There is the same protest from John Hall. "I have known respectable females to give their children punch or toddy to make them

[33] T. P. Hunt, *It Will Never Injure Me* (Philadelphia, 1845), pp. 22-23.
[34] [Anon.,] *The Price of a Glass of Brandy* (Baltimore, 1841), p. 12.
[35] T. P. Hunt, *Jesse Johnston and His Times* (Philadelphia, 1845), p. 49.
[36] C. C. Dean, *Benjamin, the Temperance Boy* (Boston, 1853), pp. 21-22.

sleep," he lamented in *Harvey Boys,* "and many of the medicines which are given to infants to stop their cries, derive all their virtue from alcohol."[37] The shadow of the bottle seemed to darken every doorway. "From fifteen to thirty years ago, the practice of drinking had become nearly universal," noted the bottle-scarred hero of *Confessions of a Reformed Inebriate* in 1844, ". . . fathers provided it for their families, and mothers, with injudicious kindness, sweetened and made it palatable for their children."[38]

Safely past the dangers of maternal ministrations of love and liquor at the cradle, unwary children found the pathway to adolescence beset with countless snares. Too many prattlers had fathers who resembled the genial Talbot in *Harvey Boys,* who "would sometimes allow them to sip a little out of his tumbler as a great favour; and in this manner Robert began really to love the taste of liquor."[39] The fearsome fate of "the beautiful female child" in *Hannah Hawkins,* "who was early taught to drink the health of her papa and mama at her father's table," had many parallels. "At length," chronicled the author, "her vacant eye, and bloated face, and silly speech, and feeble gait, were nature's signals of distress." Unheeded, alas, for we are told she died "years after, in a hospital, of the drunkard's mania."[40] Patriotism rather than discretion led Senator Madison in Mrs. Fuller's novel, *The Senator's Son,* to permit his boy to emulate an old Congressional custom on Washington's Birthday. "The child of four years stepped forward and seized the glass," according to an awed witness. "Holding it as he had seen his father do, he spoke out boldly,—in his clear, baby voice,—'To the memory of George Washington, the Father of his Country.' "[41] The author found three hundred pages all too brief a compass in which to portray the consequences of that juvenile pledge. If the patriotic toast or the sparkling glass failed to ensnare guileless youth, mince pie and plum pudding were innocent, but potent, substitutes. Not many chil-

[37] J. Hall, *Harvey Boys* (Philadelphia, 1834), p. 121.
[38] [Anon.,] *Confessions of a Reformed Inebriate,* pp. 13-14.
[39] Hall, *Harvey Boys,* p. 32.
[40] Marsh, *Hannah Hawkins,* pp. 53-55.   [41] *The Senator's Son,* p. 4.

dren, it is to be feared, were endowed with the superior discernment of little Alice, heroine of *The Drunkard's Daughter,* who spurned mince pie at a boarding-school Christmas dinner. "I think it wrong to drink spirits," she declared to her dumbfounded classmates. "I think it equally so to eat it."[42] The sequel was planned to satisfy the stern necessities of the plot rather than the appetites of the hungry girls, for they heroically renounced the steaming pastry and seemed to find a liberal portion of temperance statistics quite as nourishing. "The lady talks of intemperance, as it is, the most degrading of vices," Alice said in an ungrateful allusion to the donor of the pie, ". . . but she must have brandy and wine for her mince pies."[43] Of such hardy stuff were the mothers of the Woman's Christian Temperance Union!

In view of the ubiquitous temptations hourly encountered by characters in these novels, Mrs. Bradshaw's estimate in *Uncle Sam's Farm Fence* "that two-thirds of Christendom have been in some way, directly or indirectly, sacrificed by alcohol," seems a mild understatement.[44] Before the reformation had really begun to make headway, John Marsh conjectured that the country contained "not less than three hundred thousand common drunkards."[45] Statements such as these were promptly challenged by the rum advocates whose tests for sobriety were not always acceptable to cold-water men. They count a man to be sober, scoffed the author of *The Unjust Judge,* "until he cannot sit, stand, nor lie in a ten acre field, nor distinguish between his mouth and a hole in the ground."[46] Whatever criteria were finally accepted as a fair test, most men agreed that whiskey flowed freely enough. "It was the fashion among the inhabitants of the town of Harwood to have and to use whiskey as plenty as milk," recorded Wakeman. "It was their custom

[42] J. Thayer, *The Drunkard's Daughter* (Boston, 1842), p. 77.
[43] *Ibid.,* p. 80.
[44] A. D. Milne, *Uncle Sam's Farm Fence* (New York, 1854), p. 202.
[45] *Hannah Hawkins,* p. 11. Temperance statistics, of course, were somewhat elastic. Charles Giles estimated in 1835 that "500,000 drunkards are now living in our blessed America, all moving onward to the dreadful verge." The rate of progress must have been comforting, for Giles put the annual loss of life from acute alcoholism at fifty-six thousand souls.   [46] *The Unjust Judge,* p. 93.

to use it three times a day," he continued, "excepting in haying, harvesting, loggings, and raisings, on which occasions they took license to use it as freely as water."[47] Even the most wholesome occupations were made dangerous by the presence of the coiled serpent. Walt Whitman devoted several pages of *Franklin Evans* to warn farmers against the "lamentable habit" of serving "liquor in the fields during the hot farm-work of the summer." It was upon such an occasion that the hitherto exemplary schoolteacher, Fanning, tasted his first drop. "Before the end of the summer," Whitman reported, "he could drink his two or three glasses with great satisfaction, and even became an habitual visitor at the bar-room."[48]

The farmer in his fields might naturally be expected to face a certain amount of peril, but it would be a mistake to assume that the patient in the quiet of his sickroom enjoyed any greater protection. "For colds, for fever, for inflammatory, for chronic, for almost all sorts and kinds of suffering," wrote the author of *Jesse Johnston,* "liquor was the remedy. A gallon of fourth-proof spirits was sometimes administered in four and twenty hours!"[49] Much less liberal was the prescription which sent Monroe to his doom. "It was but a little thing at first," wrote Mrs. S. A. Southworth ominously. "His physician recommended brandy as a protection against cholera. . . . Sad, fatal mistake! for who would not rather see cholera, malignant and fatal as it is . . . than to see a monster not less fearful in its results. . . ."[50] The popular family doctor was as vulnerable to the ever-lurking temptation as were his patients. While making his rounds in sub-zero weather, the amiable Dr. Spencer found it difficult to decline pressing invitations of refreshments. The author of *The Beacon!* described the aftermath: "The man, the gentleman, the Doctor, the husband, the father, the esteemed

[47] *The Mysterious Parchment*, p. 9.

[48] *Franklin Evans*, p. 125. Farmers may have been cheered by the result of an experiment in *Harvey Boys* which proved that four men who drank only cold water could harvest more grain than six laborers who permitted themselves an occasional bracer! The author admitted, however, that in the very hottest weather he sweetened the water with molasses.

[49] Hunt, *Jesse Johnston and His Times*, p. 48.

[50] *Lawrence Monroe*, p. 65.

and popular Spencer . . . became such a brute, that his wife fled from him, his children were dispersed, and he became a vagabond!" The final indignity was reserved for the end: "Upon his wife's hair sofa, the rum-seller's wife now sat."[51] T. S. Arthur included an account of the degradation of Dr. Harper in *Six Nights with the Washingtonians.* "At each house he drank as a matter of course," Arthur wrote. "First, because liquor was placed before him, and he was expected to drink it; and second, because he felt inclined to drink, and believed that it would do him good."[52]

Temperance novelists belabored the point that in total abstinence was the only safety. Touch not, taste not, handle not —this was the burden of their constant refrain. Even the most innocent departures from this rule were certain to lead to ruin. Thus the exemplary Edward Grover, surrounded by his rejoicing family, proposed "to drink the health of his employers on the occasion of their having voluntarily increased his salary."[53] Within a few weeks, this once promising young merchant was a confirmed tippler. Equally affecting was the sad fate of John Ray in *The Drunkard's Daughter.* All went well with this industrious mechanic, who passed the village tavern daily with firm steps on his way to work, until the birth of his first child. A "harmless glass" in honor of the new arrival, however, led to a fatal taste for spirits which made the young father become a brutal husband and an untrustworthy idler.[54] "What indeed could seem further removed from evil than a friendly call upon one's minister of the Gospel? Yet it was in the parsonage," declared Brown in *Minnie Hermon,* that Whitney's appetite for alcohol was aroused. A few hours later, his horribly mangled corpse was found beneath a mill wheel![55] Even the fumes of this poison might prove fatal to one, like John Murray, who had the misfortune to live near a brewery. Such close proximity to the fiery liquid "has a surprising effect on the system,"

[51] [Anon.,] *The Beacon!* p. 28.
[52] *Six Nights with the Washingtonians,* II, 7.
[53] Burdett, *Mary Grover,* p. 23.
[54] Thayer, *The Drunkard's Daughter,* pp. 6-7.
[55] *Minnie Hermon,* pp. 230-234.

averred the author of *The Distillery,* "and has been known to be so powerful as to intoxicate, without *a drop passing the lips.* . . ."[56]

Few occupations seemed to offer a refuge from the temptation. The most industrious apprentice was forced constantly to be on his guard. "At one time there were twelve of us as apprentices," recalled a reformed toper in *Hannah Hawkins,* "eight of the twelve have died drunkards; one is now in the almshouse in Cincinnati, one is now in the almshouse in Baltimore, one is keeping a tavern in Baltimore, and here am I."[57] The law proved to be a convivial as well as a jealous mistress. A member of the bar of Ohio deemed conditions so intolerable that he penned a formidable novel, *The Unjust Judge,* to reveal the extent of the corruption. "There are many exceptions," he admitted, "but I regret the truth compels me to admit that a very large majority of the members of the bar, everywhere, are in the habit of tippling."[58] If the legal profession was full of snares, politics was a veritable mantrap. The hard cider campaign, according to the hero of the *Confessions,* was regarded "by many, as giving a tacit sanction to the free use of intoxicating liquors, in any and every form."[59] Candidates were fully as susceptible as voters. Thus Alfred Lennox, the chief sufferer in T. S. Arthur's "The Widow's Son," was intoxicated for six weeks following the election. The author was moved to assert that "An electioneering campaign resembled, in some respects, the Bacchanalian orgies of old, rather than a general rational movement of the people, preparatory to an expression of their honest sentiments at the polls."[60]

Nor did the sorely beset husband find his family hearth a safe haven from the temptations of the larger world outside. Hard pressed by tippling friends during business hours, Mr.

[56] [Anon.,] *The Distillery* (Boston, 1842), p. 19.
[57] Marsh, *Hannah Hawkins,* p. 15.   [58] [Anon.,] *The Unjust Judge,* p. 17.
[59] [Anon.,] *Confessions of a Reformed Inebriate,* p. 156. The confessor's testimony indicates the use to which rum was put by politicians: "For weeks together, I was drunk every night; and generally without expense to myself" (p. 157).
[60] *Six Nights with the Washingtonians,* II, 82.

Stanley begged his wife to banish wine from the house. "But his arguments were of no avail," related the author of *The Sting of the Adder.* "Mrs. Stanley would as readily have received visitors in the kitchen, as have had her table prepared without wine, so she carried her point, and had it all to her own fancy."[61] The fashionable custom of "boarding out" only served to make matters worse. Mrs. Sarah Hale wrote a novel to show its dangers, and traced the declining fortunes of the once contented Barclay family with the admonition that "oyster suppers never added to the value of a man's credit when they were washed away with the exhilarating glass!"[62] Fenimore Cooper, who was not a friend of prohibition, admitted that at the beginning of the century "every dinner-table, that had the smallest pretensions to be above that of the mere laboring man, had at least one of these liquors [i.e., rum or brandy] on it."[63] The laborer, of course, found his solace elsewhere. "The poor husband has been working hard all day; comes home at night to a filthy, dark, cold room—his wife cross, or half sick and dumpish, and crying children," wrote Miss Sedgwick sympathetically, "—no wonder he goes out to the corner grocery, that looks so light and cheerful!"[64] Frederick Stanley told his wife that women had much to answer for. "There is not one lady in ten upon whom I call, who would not coax me into taking a glass of wine," he protested, "if I did not set my face like flint against it."[65] Flinty qualities, unfortunately, were not usually at the command of the male when presented with a sparkling glass by a beautiful woman. "It is seldom that a man not distinguished for his social qualities falls into the sin of drunkenness," remarked the author of *The Unjust Judge.*[66] That it was almost always the genial and gifted who succumbed was attested to on every hand. "The dull, phlegmatic, the cold, the calculating miserly man, whose greatest

---

[61] DeWitt, *The Sting of the Adder,* p. 9.
[62] S. Hale, *Boarding Out* (New York, 1846), pp. 120-121.
[63] *The Crater,* I, 36.
[64] Sedgwick, *The Poor Rich Man and the Rich Poor Man,* p. 176.
[65] DeWitt, *The Sting of the Adder,* p. 6.
[66] [Anon.,] *The Unjust Judge,* p. 99.

stimulant is selfishness, takes a long time to become a drunkard; nay, may escape entirely . . . ," observed T. P. Hunt. "But
not so with him of generous mood."[67] This truth was sensed
readily enough by the novelists who provided a monotonous
round of betrothals, quiltings, weddings, sociables, barn
dances, husking bees, sleighing parties, harvest suppers, raisings, christenings, and housewarmings as congenial settings for
the fatal first glass or the equally perilous relapse. Nor was the
funeral neglected. These writers even attained some skill in
describing the sickening odor of fresh varnish, sweetish flowers, black gloves, and gin which seemed to have been as
inevitable an accompaniment of these occasions as the corpse
itself.

These more or less natural temptations did not satisfy the
imperious demands of cold-water fiction. As in the old moral-
ities, man's soul had to be assailed by the vices with a resourcefulness and vigor which rivaled the zeal of the good angels.
Every toper acted as though he were under the stern necessity
of drawing others with him to destruction. Bartenders coaxed
and cajoled; they were forever "standing treat." "He poured
out his rum like water to all who would drink, either with or
without paying for it," wrote Edwards of a tavernkeeper in
My Sister Margaret.[68] The man whose principles of abstinence were well known was the object of the most intensive
attacks. Thus young Parke in *The Senator's Son* was lured
into a dive by means of a sham call for help, kidnapped by
his former cronies, and forced to break his pledge under a
threat of violence.[69] Strong-arm methods of the same kind
were used to ruin Dr. Howard in *Minnie Hermon*. As the
temperate physician passed an inn he was attacked by the
profligate Colonel Weston, who "sprung upon Howard with
all the reckless, frenzied strength of partial intoxication,
crowding the glass against his lips and teeth until the blood
mingled with the stains of the brandy from the corners of his

[67] *Jesse Johnston and His Times*, pp. 26-27.
[68] C. M. Edwards, *My Sister Margaret* (New York, 1859), p. 262.
[69] *The Senator's Son*, pp. 110-111.

mouth."[70]   A favorite pastime of "the gay b'hoys" was the placing of a wager that a total abstainer might be induced to violate his oath. Such unholy alliances against sobriety were sometimes formed for high stakes. The activity of the conspirators in *Ashmore* was increased by a bet of five thousand dollars that the hero could be prevailed upon to drink two glasses of champagne.[71]

Once implanted, even by artificial methods, the taste for alcohol swept all before it. The most horrible examples seemed to be without power to deter the victim. The cronies of the late Peter Cumstock suffered no diminution of appetite as they watched his frozen body being chopped from a cake of ice on the morning after their revels. "I remember, that among those, who helped to take the body out of the brook," wrote a witness, "were some of his drunken companions, who fain would have drank the contents of the bottle, found in Peter's pocket; had not the coroner interfered and dashed it on the ice!"[72] Members of a coroner's jury, however, might lack even this last vestige of decency as the hard case of Leonard Bascomb proved. The corpse, with "the jug clenched firmly in the stiffened fingers . . . was carried to a deserted cabin," Brown reported in *Minnie Hermon,* "where the jury of inquest drinked from the dead man's jug before any testimony was taken!"[73] Countless cases of suicide for which John Barleycorn, not young Werther, was the inspiration, served no more successfully as object lessons. "Yet there are many who know all this," asserted the author of *It Will Never Injure Me,* "and, while the blood of the drunken suicide is spattering on the floor, with cup in hand, will finish the narrative of the tragic scene, by drinking and saying, 'Poor fellow, drink ruined him; but it will never injure *me*!' "[74]

Temperance logicians were fond of tracing the causal relationship which zigzagged its pathway from the first glass to

[70] T. W. Brown, *Minnie Hermon*, p. 88.
[71] G. Laughlin, *Ashmore* (Boston, 1858), p. 7.
[72] [Anon.,] *The Beacon!* p. 12.
[73] T. W. Brown, *Minnie Hermon*, p. 204.
[74] Hunt, *It Will Never Injure Me*, pp. 4-5.

the grave. Not even the crystal goblet of cold water to which they paid such frequent homage was clearer than the fact that every drunkard once took his first sip. "Alas! when will our young men learn," asked Harry Spofford in *The Mysteries of Worcester,* "that to *taste* the poison, is but to take the first step toward the *drunkard's grave?*"[75] Drunkards never wearied of ascribing their woes to the first taste. "If I had not taken that first brandy sling," bemoaned Mortimer, "I should never have been what I now am."[76] Upon this subject of the first glass, novelists lavished their most arresting imagery and their most eloquent prose. "You have seen accounts of those sliding glaciers, and dashing snow slides of the Alps and Pyrenees," wrote John Cornyn, "with the havoc they have made, as they leaped from crag to crag, overtaking the swift-footed chamois in their descending fury." "There was a time, sir, when that mighty avalanche was but a snow-flake. . . ."[77] The alcoholic snowflake, however, often assumed most appealing forms. Frequently it was a lovely lady who tendered the cup to one whose chivalry exceeded his prudence. "O woman, woman! when wilt thou cease to be mediator between man and his arch enemy?" implored Edwards. "Heaven forgive thee the wrongs thou hast committed."[78] The highly fashionable custom of "giving a sentiment" made it difficult for young gentlemen to refuse gracefully. "They had never reflected that it was to please them, that young men often took the first glass," charged Hunt, "and that the strongest reason that restrained many from adopting the principle of total abstinence, was the fear of being compelled to refuse a lady, when invited by her to drink a sentiment."[79] The lovely Ellen Fleetwood thus became the unwitting cause of the doom of her betrothed. Pledged never to taste liquor, Edward successfully repulsed the invitations of a bevy of ravishing maidens only to yield to the taunts of his lover: " 'Some boyish whim. Fie! you afraid of one glass of wine!' she leaned close to him and he felt the

[75] H. Spofford, *The Mysteries of Worcester* (Worcester, 1846), p. 20.
[76] Wakeman, *The Mysterious Parchment*, p. 228.
[77] *Dick Wilson*, p. 220.   [78] *My Sister Margaret*, p. 92.
[79] *Jesse Johnston and His Times*, pp. 20-21.

warm words. . . ." And when he drank, the author related melodramatically, it was "so fiercely that the ring upon his finger snapped in two pieces and fell into the river."[80] The ring, as practiced readers of temperance fiction will instantly surmise, was the parting gift of a sainted mother, whose last moments were made serene by her son's promise to touch not, taste not, handle not!

This chain of cause and effect, which novelists had deftly forged between the first sip and the everlasting bonfire, was not without its spurious links. Wisely left unexplained was the curious paradox by which men persisted in swallowing what was invariably described as a foul, noxious, nauseating emetic. "No one tasted of alcohol for the first time in life, without disgust," declared Frink in *Alow and Aloft*.[81] Disgusting as the first sip may have been, its effect was to demand a second and a third. "By the time I had taken another glass it seemed to improve," admitted the hero of *Walter Woolfe,* who discovered that the first taste was the hardest, "and every succeeding sip mellowed its taste, and aided to overcome that repugnance so natural to man."[82] The problem of explaining why this ingrained repugnance usually manifested itself by inspiring an insatiable craving for more of "Hell's own broth," taxed the heaviest intellects of the temperance forces. T. S. Arthur applied himself manfully and produced a somewhat desperate analogy. "You know the power of habit in the case of the tobacco-chewer," he wrote in "The Moderate Drinker." "At first the weed is nauseous to his taste, but after a few attempts to chew it, its effects upon the nervous system become so pleasant, and his desire for it so strong, that he cannot do without it. So it is with stimulating drinks. . . ."[83]

Various as were the methods of attack upon the rum evil, novelists were generally agreed that the most effective warnings were to be found in detailed pictures of the awful effects of alcohol on the human race. Temperance storytellers com-

---

[80] T. W. Brown, *Edward Carlton* (Auburn, 1854), pp. 98-99.
[81] H. C. Frink, *Alow and Aloft* (Rochester, 1842), p. 148.
[82] T. D. English, *Walter Woolfe* (New York, 1847), p. 7.
[83] *Six Nights with the Washingtonians,* II, 111.

peted with each other in serving up horrible *exempla of* bloated corpses whose staring eyes "no one heeded to close." In this gruesome business, novelists were aided by the artists whose steel engravings frequently flanked the title pages to give a sample of the chamber of horrors into which the reader was about to be ushered. Indeed, a great majority of the novels were illustrated in a manner which fell somewhere between the grotesque realism of Hogarth's drawings and the vividness of the Currier and Ives lithographs. Timothy Shay Arthur, who had been praised for his "sharply drawn sketches of a Daguerrean vividness" in *Ten Nights in a Bar-Room,* prefaced his earlier work, *Six Nights with the Washingtonians,* with six engravings crowded with painful details. He would have undoubtedly approved of the recent motion-picture version of his famous book which made full use of its rich possibilities for melodrama and sentiment. The stage version by Pratt belongs with that of Aiken's production of *Uncle Tom's Cabin* in a cherished corner of our folk history.

Nothing is quite so typical of temperance fiction as the lurid waxworks realism with which they appealed to the morbidity of their readers. The author of *Mapleton* confessed that he found it "extremely graphic and powerful" to recount "The effect of alcohol upon the vital organs, in changing them from scarlet to crimson, and from crimson to purple, and from purple to blue, and from blue to the black of gangrene and putrefaction. . . ."[84] When not engaged in ringing color changes of this sort, novelists busied themselves with gruesome tableaux which rival the horrors of contemporary photographic journalism. "At the foot of the bed was a spectacle to freeze the blood," wrote Brown in *Minnie Hermon.* "Stretched at full length was Mrs. Ricks, and upon the floor, mats of hair, its whitish blue ends indicating its violent wrenching from the living head. It had been wrenched from *her* head, and the bloody scalp lay bare in hideous spots. Above the ear the blade of the iron fire-shovel had cleft the skull, driving the hair into the brain, and splitting the ear through the rim. The blood

[84] Church, *Mapleton,* p. 216.

had oozed out and ran down into the eye, where it was now frozen, the other glaring wildly in death and covered with frost."[85] Judge Albans, whose tipsy charges to none too sober juries had caused many miscarriages of justice, met an end which should have satisfied his most vindictive enemy. The judge, staggering home from "a scene of midnight debauchery," stumbled into a ravine, a bystander testified, and "falling headlong he burst asunder in the midst, and all his bowels gushed out."[86]

The strange death of the "refined" Mrs. Arnold, who had never been seen in the village tavern, provided an unexpected thrill for the readers of *The Drunkard's Daughter*. All mystery disappeared, however, when the daughter told the coroner that her mother for three years had been "in the habit of drinking *Cologne Water*."[87] The results of Mrs. Arnold's post mortem were mere commonplaces when compared with the findings in the deaths of Dobson and his wife in *Mapleton*. As a close friend "approached the house, a horrible odor assailed him, such as he had never before encountered," the author wrote without undue exaggeration. A subtle fume "exuding from the chimney and crevices" did not deter him from forcing the door, "When, lo! out rushed a volley of fetid air . . . and, horrible to tell! there lay the charred and blackened remains of Dobson, manifestly dead by spontaneous combustion!" "The room, and all its furniture," Church described further, "were covered with a thick yellow substance, filthy and fetid, to shock every delicate sensibility. In another part of the room his wife also lay dead, as it appeared partly from suffocation from inhaling the fumes of her burning husband,

[85] *Minnie Hermon*, p. 110.

[86] [Anon.,] *The Unjust Judge*, p. 280. One of the requirements for writing a temperance novel was a total lack of humor. The rare occasions upon which authors tried to raise a ghastly grin do not inspire regret that they occur infrequently. A sample of mortuary mirth from this novel will be sufficient: "The horse finally drew the vehicle off him, but his spirit was departed. The spirits in the barrel had also departed. The head of the cask as well as Sykes, had been driven in, and his lifeless body was swimming in alcohol" (*ibid.*, pp. 252-253). Death under the wheels of a brewer's wagon appealed to the sense of justice of these novelists and they used it unsparingly. For an excruciating instance, see *My Sister Margaret*, p. 208.

[87] Thayer, *The Drunkard's Daughter*, p. 51.

and partly from her own excessive drunkenness."[88] No less eminent authorities than the president of Union College and the professor of chemistry at Yale might have been cited in support of the author's explanation of the cause of the tragedy.[89] "Dobson probably drank more than his share of the liquor," he wrote judiciously, "and, his constitution was already rendered combustible by previous drinking, this deep potation set it on fire; and it went off in a blue flame and exhaling fluid, extinguishing both his own life and that of his wife."[90] Violent deaths were so frequently suffered by the victims of alcohol that novelists were enabled to reserve their peaceful deathbed scenes almost exclusively for the innocent. Even here, however, the calm atmosphere was rudely disturbed. Mary Morgan's death in *Ten Nights in a Bar-Room* was hastened by the wild cries of her father who was suffering from delirium tremens in an adjoining room. Horrible, too, were the last moments of the innocent daughter of John Monroe in *The Distillery* who died while "stretched between the bloated, mangled body of the expiring father, and the more insensible and attenuated form of the faithful mother."[91]

Anything short of an elaborate table of vital statistics would fail to do justice to the variety of deaths resulting from alcohol in these novels. Authors occasionally disposed of their dramatis personae by wholesale methods as in *Brother Jonathan's Cottage* and *The Unjust Judge* in which tipsy trainmen were

[88] *Mapleton*, pp. 306-307.

[89] The "Scientific Department" of the *Journal* of the American Temperance Union admitted that such cases might seem incredible, but added that since 1837 they "have multiplied so much, and been so well attested, that few are disposed to call them in question." The editor cited a diagnosis by Professor Silliman of Yale which held: "The entire body having become saturated with alcohol absorbed into all its tissues, becomes highly inflammable, as indicated by the vapour which reeks from the breath and lungs of the drunkard; this vapour, doubtless highly alcoholic, may take fire, and then the body slowly consumes" (I, 40). President Nott told his students at Union in 1838 that deaths "by internal fires" had become too numerous to admit of any doubt of their existence. The *New York Times* for Jan. 9, 1836, described an experiment conducted to show that a drunkard's blood constituted a fire-hazard. A medico in Berwick, Maine, ignited a bowl of blood drawn from a sot and "a conflagration ensued, burning with a blue flame for a space of twenty-five or thirty minutes."

[90] Church, *Mapleton*, p. 307.   [91] [Anon.,] *The Distillery*, p. 54.

responsible for wrecks costing hundreds of lives. More common, but scarcely less frightful, was the extinction of an entire domestic establishment as depicted in *The Sting of the Adder* where the once happy Stanley family of six persons was destroyed by liquor. Equally complete and even more dramatic was the fate of Charles Durham's ménage in *Mapleton*. The husband had stopped at a tavern to fortify himself against the sub-zero weather only to drink more than was good for him. "But, O, horror! horror! God have mercy on the drunkard's family!" exclaimed Church in describing the scene which greeted the errant Durham upon his return following a spree of a fortnight. "There lay Mrs. Durham on her bed, cold and stiff, with a new-born infant, naked, at her side, also dead and frozen! Behind the mother, and pressed close against her person, was dear little Charles, with his icy arms enfolding her, and every drop of blood congealed in his veins. They then hastened to the little girls' room, and found them in their bed, emaciated to mere skeletons, but not so long dead as to be completely frozen."[92]   After this catastrophe, Durham could do no less than hang himself with reasonable confidence that hell had no torture to exceed his present suffering. "Dear, dear ones," he cried as he adjusted the noose, "I follow you to the spirit-land!"[93]   Although Joel Wakeman estimated that there were two thousand suicides annually resulting from alcohol— and the temperance novels included many of them—writers found a more effective object lesson in delirium tremens which they exploited to the last soul-piercing shriek. "Imagine before you an enormous anaconda, rendered fierce by excessive hunger, holding in his slimy jaws a brother of yours, whom no earthly power can rescue!" wrote Tator in a characteristic passage. "Imagine his bloody eyes ready to burst from their sockets, looking up imploringly to you for help. . . . The poisonous viper still continues his coils with increased fury, and bones still continue to crack beneath the mighty pressure. Blood is now oozing from his mouth and ears; nay, literally bursting from every part of his body." The author imme-

[92] Church, *Mapleton,* p. 116.   [93] *Ibid.,* p. 118.

diately felt constrained to apologize for his account as merely, "a feeble outline, a faint sketch, of the living reality."[94]

The inevitable learned monograph on "Deaths Resulting from Acute Alcoholism in American Fiction from the Beginnings to the Present Day" will undoubtedly be given us in the fulness of time. In it, deaths by freezing will have prominent place, for temperance novelists seem to have been fascinated by scenes in which the body, "stiff as buckram," was chopped from the ice with a jug clutched firmly in the dead man's hand.[95] Deaths by cremation will also bulk large. How easy for a reeling mother to drop her babe in an open fireplace, or, as did Mrs. Wild in *The Little Cider Merchant,* fall into the flames herself and be burned, as Porter described it, "almost to a cinder."[96] The incineration differed only in degree in *The Mysterious Parchment,* where the author preferred to have his victim done "to a crisp."[97] The variety of the catastrophes is almost as amazing as their number. Drunken captains ran their heavily freighted barks upon the rocks to prove that lemonade was more wholesome than grog for sailors; intoxicated stagecoach drivers cascaded their passengers over steep embankments; bad bartenders heaved beermugs at the skulls of tiny tots who entered the swinging doors in quest of errant papas;[98] while insane alcoholics used crowbars, knives, poison, guns, and pitchforks to work their fatal mischief. The curious reader who is not sated by deaths caused by "internal fires" or by excessive draughts of *eau-de-Cologne,* may find more to his taste the fate of ex-Congressman Hargrave, who awoke from a stupor to find himself more than half devoured by a big, bad and very hungry wolf;[99] or the unfortunate error of Messrs.

[94] *Brother Jonathan's Cottage,* p. 84.

[95] Lynn, *Durham Village,* pp. 164-165.

[96] A. E. Porter, *The Little Cider Merchant* (Boston, 1856), p. 185.

[97] Wakeman, *The Mysterious Parchment,* p. 283.

[98] T. S. Arthur, *Ten Nights in a Bar-Room, and What I Saw There,* p. 51. Simon Slade, who threw the now notorious mug, met a death calculated to satisfy the most rigorous demands of poetic justice. His drunken son, Frank, broke a bottle "into a hundred pieces" over his father's head.

[99] Meeks, *Stories of the Fountain Rock,* p. 67. This catastrophe climaxed one of the "many delightful memoirs or memoranda of individuals, with which he [the didactic Uncle Benedict] would entertain visitors."

Robbins and Simmons, who drained to the last drop a bottle of what they fondly believed to be rum, but proved instead to be a concoction not untruthfully advertised as "Dead Shot for Bed-Bugs."[100] A complete catalogue of horrible examples must await a more scientific study. The present writer can do no better than to heed the admonition of the author of *Fountain Rock*. "We are sorry that we cannot give these to our reader now," he lamented under somewhat similar circumstances, "but we are admonished that we are making our book too large (considering the value of the matter) for the price at which we shall be able to print it."[101]

There remains to be told something of the means by which temperance novelists sought to remedy the evils they painted so luridly. Their first objective was to demolish the respectable position enjoyed by the moderate drinker. In *The Sea Lions,* Fenimore Cooper had praised the decent tippling of Parson Whittle and Deacon Pratt. They took "their rum and water; but it was in moderation, as all the gifts of God should be used," he wrote approvingly. "As for the intemperate cry which makes it a sin to partake of any liquor, however prudently, it was then [1819] never heard in the land."[102] Against this plausible sentiment, the advocates of total abstinence trained their heaviest guns. "The greatest obstacle, in fact, in the way of the temperance reformation," warned Cyrus Mann, "is, moderate drinkers."[103] T. P. Hunt decried the damage done by these "temperate men." "Nothing has done more to make this a drunken world," he announced sorrowfully, "than the influence exerted in favour of the moderate use of liquor by men of respectable standing in church and state."[104] This

---

[100] Porter, *The Little Cider Merchant*, p. 140.

[101] Meeks, *Stories of the Fountain Rock*, p. 70.

[102] *The Sea Lions* (New York, 1849), I. 57. Cooper went to some pains to record his hearty dislike of temperance reformers. He has the rascally Steadfast Dodge try to organize a total abstinence society among the steerage passengers in *Homeward Bound*. Holmes, a despicable "moral lecturer" in *The Redskins*, is made to champion total abstinence as well as antirentism. In *The Crater*, Cooper permitted wine to be made in his ideal commonwealth; in fact, the life of the hero was preserved by his use of wine during a critical illness.

[103] *The Clinton Family*, p. 35.

[104] *Jesse Johnston and His Times*, p. 59.

fact was clearly recognized by the rum interests. Prince Alcohol boasted that his favorite regiment was composed of moderate drinkers. "It was, in many respects, the very basis of all his military operations," noted an observer from the cold-water army, "since all his advanced companies received their recruits, either directly or indirectly from this division."[105] The chief of the wet forces feared above all others "those who remained inflexible in the Touch-not ranks, under the command of that brave and inestimable commander, Total Abstinence."[106]

Total abstinence, however, seemed a radical step to many temperate men who could not bring themselves to support the teetotalers. "No; they are the temperance new lights," protested Jewett in *A Christmas Box*. "I only renounce distilled liquors."[107] This was the conservative position maintained by many good men. "Even some of the ministers and deacons," objected A. E. Porter, "thought the temperance men were going too far, and advised moderation and caution."[108] Moderation, unfortunately, proved to be a term elastic enough to fit any thirst. H. C. Frink in *Alow and Aloft* wrote that he "had known men drink a quart of whiskey before breakfast, just to steady their nerves by a moderate dram"; while in London, he found "seven English pints are quite a common allowance; and not unfrequently twice that quantity is taken."[109] T. S. Arthur, who never neglected an opportunity to demonstrate the fallacy of the moderation theory, told about a "temperate" drinker whose efforts at self-control suggest Mark Twain's achievement in limiting himself to one cigar at a time. "He restricted his number of glasses a day to ten," the author declared, "an amount that he could have borne very well, if it had not happened that he filled them nearer to the brim than before." This self-denial induced a serious relapse, for we are told later that his allowance was increased to "six glasses an hour."[110] Toleration of moderate drinking was shown to have

---

[105] [Anon.,] *An Account of the Marvelous Doings of Prince Alcohol*, p. 17.
[106] *Ibid.*
[107] T. S. Arthur, *A Christmas Box* . . . (Philadelphia, 1847), p. 32.
[108] *The Little Cider Merchant*, p. 27.   [109] *Alow and Aloft*, pp. 141, 146.
[110] *Six Nights with the Washingtonians*, II, 117, 140.

been the weakness of the earlier temperance organizations such as the Massachusetts Society formed in 1813. "They did not go to the root of the evil," complained the author of *Harvey Boys,* "for they did not oppose *moderate* drinking, which is the very source of drunkenness."[111] These novelists had too wholesome a respect for the seductiveness of wine when it was red, to put much faith in principles of moderation, no matter how sincere. "Talk of moderation to the unloosened wind! There is no moderation in wine drinking!" wrote T. D. English in *Walter Woolfe.* "A word—a song—and before you know it; you are precipitated into the abyss of drunkenness."[112]

Closely allied with those who supported the principle of moderation were the advocates of "moral suasion" as the most effective method of restraining intemperance. All cold-water men were grateful for the pioneer efforts of the champions of "sweet reasonableness." These formed "the seed of the great *temperance reformation,*" according to Armstrong, who returned thanks for the progress "brought to pass, solely through the blessings of Almighty God on the various divinely appointed instrumentalities of *moral suasion.*"[113] In 1808, even mild remonstrance was thought incurably radical, but it soon became apparent that prayer and admonition were not enough. "I am no longer in favor of moral suasion for the restraint of intemperance," concluded the author of *The Unjust Judge.* "Its mission and purpose have been fulfilled. It has spent its force. . . ."[114] Thurlow Brown came to the same melancholy opinion. "God never designed that a wicked world should be governed by moral suasion," he noted in *Minnie Hermon.*[115] Eloquent testimony on the impotence of moral suasion unfortified by law is to be found in the suspiciously warm championing it received from the liquor interests. "Let temperance societies be formed all over the country," urged a "wet" candidate for office in *Uncle Sam's Farm Fence,* "and let ministers preach more against drunkenness; and I think before many

---

[111] Hall, *Harvey Boys,* p. 117. [112] *Walter Woolfe,* p. 8.
[113] *The Temperance Reformation,* p. 29.
[114] [Anon.,] *The Unjust Judge,* p. 177. [115] *Minnie Hermon,* p. 192.

years, the business will die of itself."[116] Squire Dunton in *Hemlock Ridge* took the same comfortable view. "I don't think this pledging people never to taste it, is the right way to go to work," he argued. "I believe in moral suasion, and wouldn't give much for those folks that cannot abstain from strong drink, without being pledged."[117] The ulterior motives of many of these oily advocates of persuasion moved Brown to resort to the grand style. *"Moral suasion!"* he replied scornfully. "Let the stricken mother go pray upon the slippery deck of the pirate when blood leaps smoking from the scuppers, and beg the life of her boy! Send childhood with a tear on its cheek, into the den of the famished tigress, and with a silvery voice beseech the life of a parent, writhing in her remorseless fangs!"[118]

The intermediate step between the moral suasion of the temperance pioneers and the legal prohibition advocated by those who urged a nationwide acceptance of the Maine Law, was the pledge. Although it was a compromise measure limited at first to include only distilled spirits, it seemed radical enough. "For in those days," wrote Jennie De Witt, "men would as soon have thought of pledging themselves never to taste sugar, as never to taste wine."[119] The power of the pledge soon became a popular theme of rhapsody. "O the *magic* of that pledge!" sang a reformed drunkard in his autobiography. "How many it has saved from destruction! How many it has exalted from the very filth and mire of drunkenness to posts of respectability and usefulness!"[120] Re-united family circles inspired many sentimental pictures. "They may now be seen, as the curtains of evening are drawn around them," wrote John Marsh of the happy Hawkins family, "father, mother, and children, happily seated around a common table, reading useful books, enjoying each other's society, and grateful, too, it is believed, for the mysterious change which has come over them

[116] Milne, *Uncle Sam's Farm Fence*, p. 46.
[117] C. E. Babb, *Hemlock Ridge* (Boston, 1858), p. 63.
[118] *Minnie Hermon*, pp. 194-195.   [119] *The Sting of the Adder*, p. 28.
[120] [Anon.,] *Autobiography of a Reformed Drunkard* (Philadelphia, 1845), p. 145.

by means of the pledge. Sweet scene!—one that the angels might rest upon with unmingled delight."[121] The contagion of the pledge often proved irresistible. "He signed his name, his wife followed, then the eldest son, and so on, until all the members of the family had their names enrolled," Joel Wakeman reported of the Scribner household. "A neat little black frame was procured, in which this rare document was placed, covered by a glass, and hung directly over the fire-place."[122] There it perhaps formed a companion-piece to an illuminated copy of the wedding certificate, a double guarantee of domestic bliss. There were backsliders of course, but as Walt Whitman remarked in *Franklin Evans,* "it is twenty to one but the improvement will be effectual at last." "A good resolution, once formed, may be broken it is true," he wrote comfortably, "but the very process of reflection which leads to the forming of the resolution, is favorable to improvement."[123]

The weakness of the early form of the pledge was soon revealed, because it permitted the use of distilled spirits when prescribed by a physician and it made an exception of wine when imbibed at public dinners. "The wine drinker might reel from the midnight revel, or drool in the saloon," objected Brown, "and yet be all that the old pledge demanded."[124] The new pledge of total abstinence, given strong impetus by the Washingtonians at Baltimore in 1840, seemed to promise the dawn of a Utopia of sober men. "The Washingtonian movement has reformed many drunkards. Death is rapidly removing the rest," optimistically predicted T. P. Hunt. "And were it not for the moderate drinker, that great army of drunkards, which once mustered four hundred thousand strong, and of which forty thousand died annually, would soon be extinct."[125] The author of *Hannah Hawkins* detected portents of the millennium at a convention of Washingtonians. "Go to Baltimore and see our now happy wives and families. Only look at the

---

[121] *Hannah Hawkins,* pp. 59-60.   [122] *The Mysterious Parchment,* p. 14.
[123] *Franklin Evans,* p. 127. The hero later was forced to admit that "the old pledge" was too easy, for it "allowed people to get as much fuddled as they chose upon wines and beer and so on."   [124] *Minnie Hermon,* p. 217.
[125] *Jesse Johnston and His Times,* p. 74.

procession . . . ," he shouted in a cold-water delirium. "Two thousand men, nearly half of them reformed within a year, followed by two thousand boys of all ages, to give assurance to the world that the next generation shall be all sober. But where were our wives on that occasion? at home, shut up with hungry children in rags as a year ago? No, no! but in carriages riding round the streets to see their sober husbands!"[126] Armstrong saw this new crusade as "a preparation for the divinely foretold blessings of millennial purity," while Timothy Shay Arthur proclaimed proudly, albeit prematurely, that "The era of intemperance, as a national curse, is past."[127] Sobriety seemed to be just around the corner.

Reformers were fond of describing the "one great temperance family." Over its charmed circle presided a lovely woman whose eyes "beamed benevolence and purity of heart," caroled Walt Whitman, and "in her hand she held a goblet of clear water."[128] Clustered about her were children, who might be heard as well as seen, if their theme was temperance. "Young people, even boys and girls, are inoculated with the fervor, and are heard about the streets, singing the temperance songs," Whitman continued, "and conversing upon the principles of the doctrine, by which their fathers or brothers have been regenerated and made happy."[129] Both sides recognized the importance of enlisting these persuasive soldiers under their banners. Prince Alcohol made a special appeal to them. "Children, youths, dear little creatures, how my tender heart loves you!" he warbled to the youngsters. "Ladies, charming ladies, ye lilies of the earth, the pride, the boast, and ornament of creation; come into my ranks, I have a place for you."[130] Lydia Sigourney, the sweet singer of temperance as well as of Hartford, put the case for the side of virtue. "What then is the aid that woman can most fitly lend to the noble science of being 'temperate in all things'?" she asked. "Not the assumption of masculine energies, not the applause of popular assemblies; but

[126] Marsh, *Hannah Hawkins*, p. 33.
[127] *Six Nights with the Washingtonians*, I, 44.
[128] *Franklin Evans*, p. 219.   [129] *Ibid.*, p. 247.
[130] [Anon.,] *An Account of the Marvelous Doings of Prince Alcohol*, p. 11.

the still, small voice singing at the cradle-side,—the prayerful sigh, that cries where seraphs veil their faces."[131] As for the child: "This is the first thing that she has to learn," counseled John Marsh, "that she has influence, and that she is exerting it over her little companions every day and every hour . . . and if it can be an influence to save a beloved brother or a kind father from ruin, what will be its value?"[132]

The cult of the temperance child had its martyred saint in little Mary Morgan, the heroine of *Ten Nights in a Bar-Room,* who was the innocent victim of a beermug thrown at her none too steady father. His conversion, which dated from the last breath of the daughter, is the only bright spot in the lurid gloom of this notorious landmark of temperance fiction. Mary's deathbed, of which the reader is given generous glimpses for more than sixty pages, has earned a place with those of Uncle Tom and little Eva among the lachrymose favorites of the generation. "I am not going to get well. So, you see, mother, he'll never go again—never—never—never," she whispered to the accompaniment of dropping tears, or, in the stage version, to the tremulous notes of the violin. "Oh dear! how my head pains. Mr. Slade threw it so hard. But it didn't strike father; and I'm so glad. How it would have hurt him—poor father! But he'll never go there any more; and that will be good, won't it, mother?"[133] Children learned that when loving fathers drank to folly, the only way to make them keep the pledge was to die. The last moment, too, proved an auspicious time to distribute temperance tracts. Walt Whitman skimmed all the keys of sentiment in his scene depicting the death of little Jane in *Franklin Evans:* "The dying child held the young man's hand in one of hers; with the other, she slowly lifted the trifling memorial [a temperance tract!] she had assigned especially for him, aloft in the air. Her arm shook— her eyes, now becoming glassy with the death-damps, were cast toward her brother's face. She smiled pleasantly, and as an

[131] *Water Drops* (New York, 1850), p. v.
[132] *Hannah Hawkins,* p. 49.
[133] Arthur, *Ten Nights in a Bar-Room,* p. 72.

indistinct gurgle came from her throat, the uplifted hand fell suddenly into the open palm of her brother's, depositing the tiny volume there. Little Jane was dead."[134] Temperance children did not, of course, confine their activities to their death-beds. They had at their fingers' ends the latest statistics on inebriety and discoursed learnedly upon the physiological aspects of the problem. Charlie Plimpton, the hero of *The Little Cider Merchant,* had a winning way of smothering his opponents under an avalanche of apposite data upon subjects animal, mineral, and vegetable. He was always ready to discuss the virtues of water, that "universal fluid" which "irritates no nerve of sensation." "It is thus fitted to penetrate unfelt into the subtlest tissues," he informed a playmate, "and without causing the slightest jar, to flow along the finest, most sensitive and most hair-like vessels."[135] Little Benjamin's qualities were no less remarkable, although they were of another kind. His restraint at a wedding where he was permitted to kiss the bride deserves honorable mention. "I had my wish," he confided to his Aunt Prudence, "but just as I was standing on tiptoe to reach her, I smelt that rummy smell, and thought of poor Brown's corpse; I went out the room like a shot."[136]

Children marching in the temperance army were often accompanied by their mothers, who also had an honored place in the regiment of Home Influences. "What blessed things these wives are!" exclaimed Leblond, who owed his salvation to the Griselda-like conduct of his wife.[137] "In a world," corroborated T. P. Hunt in *Wedding Days of Former Times,* "from the cradle to the tomb, there is nothing like woman, in the relation that a kind Providence seems to have rendered necessary for man in the several stages of life through which he has to pass."[138] It was in the most important relation of all, that of marriage, in which women were urged to strike a vital

---

[134] *Franklin Evans,* p. 165.

[135] Porter, *The Little Cider Merchant,* p. 86. Charles's resourcefulness seemed to be equal to any emergency. When he learned that a juvenile friend had swallowed the poison of *Tom Jones,* he hastily prescribed *My Mother's Gold Ring* as an antidote.

[136] Dean, *Benjamin, the Temperance Boy,* pp. 19-20.

[137] [Anon.,] *The Unjust Judge,* p. 295.

[138] *The Wedding Days of Former Times* (Philadelphia, 1845), p. 4.

blow for temperance. The Ladies' Union in *Fountain Rock* led the way by resolving "solemnly and deliberately" to "bloom in perpetual and happy celibacy" unless their swains agreed to support the principles of total abstinence. Such a drastic interdiction bore immediate fruit, "and we will not say," boasted the author of the plan, "how many tippling swains, and toping lovers were made to walk straight to the Ballot Box and vote against the enemy."[139] Miss Chatterwell, in *Uncle Sam's Palace*, wished to extend the ban to include all persons engaged in the liquor traffic: "I wish I could add a few more to the list, such as, *'Thou shalt not marry an importer of liquors, nor a distiller, nor a wholesale vender, nor a petty retailer in the same traffic.'*"[140] Tactics of this kind naturally made grave demands upon woman's resourcefulness. "But what are women made with so much tact and power of charming for, if it is not to do these very things . . .?" challenged Harriet Beecher Stowe. "It is a delicate matter—true; and has not Heaven given you a fine touch and a nice eye for just such delicate matters?"[141] Female temperance activity was a source of great pain to the unregenerate. "Everything is temperance now-a-days; temperance stores, temperance houses, temperance doctors, and temperance funerals," complained Witham in *My Sister Margaret*. "I wish the old women would have temperance rheumatics."[142]

Female influence sometimes was manifested in unusual ways. "My wife, is one of the greatest temperance women you ever saw," declared Farmer Tracy, "she won't give the baby Bateman's drops, because she feels sure there is spirit in them."[143] Others, such as Alice Ray, renounced the use of perfume and toilet water. "So long as ladies will use perfumery, it will be made," she replied to her quizzical friends, "and as long as it is made, there will be those . . . who will not be satisfied with merely putting it upon their handkerchiefs."[144] Ellen and Hannah, those lovely enthusiasts in

[139] Meeks, *Stories of the Fountain Rock*, pp. 75-76.
[140] Wellmont, *Uncle Sam's Palace*, p. 225.
[141] *The Coral Ring* (Glasgow, 1853), p. 9.
[142] Edwards, *My Sister Margaret*, p. 18.
[143] Milne, *Uncle Sam's Farm Fence*, pp. 92-93.
[144] Thayer, *The Drunkard's Daughter*, p. 53.

Fountain Rock, felt that temperance workers had neglected to appeal persuasively to the voter's esthetic sense. They set about to remedy the situation by preparing hand-painted ballots fashioned to melt all opposition at the polls. The finished product, which resembled an expensive valentine, was striking, if not legal. "At the top was a beautiful representation of the matrimonial altar, and Cupid laboring to rekindle the flames of love, nearly extinguished by rum," described the admiring author, "and Temperance snatching the goblet away with one hand, and pointing with the other to a fountain of water bubbling from a rock; beneath were the names of the regularly nominated candidates in blue, and then in gold the important words, 'No License.' "[145] It is unnecessary to report that the rum interests were hushed by this artistic display and that temperance triumphed. When all the blandishments of delicacy and tact failed, women were enjoined to take a sterner course. "I say, Slay yourselves, rather than give your right hand to wine-bibbers in the bonds of wedlock," demanded the author of *Brother Jonathan's Cottage,* "pluck out the very heart from your bosom, sooner than bestow your love on those who use strong drink."[146] Some of the fascination of these faded novels still derives from the amazing behavior of their heroines. Any inconsistencies or shortcomings in their conduct may be attributed to their readiness at a moment's notice to play the dissimilar roles of Griselda, Joan of Arc, and Carrie Nation.

With imploring children, sweetly entreating wives, and dying mothers gently waving temperance banners to remind men of their pledge, the cause seemed virtually won. Temperance statistics, moreover, could be marshaled to prove it. Were not those four hundred thousand drunkards, popularly supposed to be extant in the United States, dying off at the rapid rate of forty thousand each year? By a sure process of rotting at the top and pure replacements at the bottom, ten years would surely see the glorious work accomplished. "Besides," added Tator encouragingly, "an increasing intelligence, and a longing

---

[145] Meeks, *Stories of the Fountain Rock,* pp. 78-79.
[146] Tator, *Brother Jonathan's Cottage,* p. 23.

for purity and perfection of life, are leading the rising generation to eschew it; and that same benign influence will shame
out the habit in those who are advanced in years."[147] The great
American water wagon appeared to be rolling triumphantly
toward a teetotalers' Utopia.

But, alas, there was many a slip, even when the cup was
filled with pure water and the lip was that of sobriety. Fenimore Cooper's inimitable "Commodore of the Lake" in *Home
as Found* proposed an awkward question. "If liquor is not
made to be drunk, for what is it made?" he asked merrily.
"Any one may see that this Lake was made for skiffs and fishing; it has a length, breadth, and depth, suited to such purposes. Now, here is liquor distilled, bottled, and corked, and I
ask if all does not show that it was made to be drunk; I dare
say your temperance men are ingenious, but let them answer
that if they can."[148] The genial Captain Truck, the Commodore's companion, replied with a can-emptying, soul-filling
draught—and the fishing went serenely on.

And so in America. The four hundred thousand drunkards
were doubtless gathered to their fathers in the fulness of time
and temperance recruits very likely signed the pledge with the
very best intentions in the world; but "liquor was distilled,
bottled, and corked," and men found a natural way to dispose
of it. Was not the body of Edgar Allan Poe found "somewhat
the worse for wear" in the gutters of Baltimore? And had he
not just become a Son of Temperance? When hopes seemed
darkest, a new light appeared in the East. "A sovereign State
had flung out a new banner, and given a new battle-cry to the
retrograding hosts of the reform," jubilantly cried Thurlow
Brown at the passage of the Maine Law in 1851. "At one
stroke the traffic had been annihilated in that State. . . . The
heart of a Christian people throbbed responsive to the shout
from Maine, and to the peal of one common war-cry, rallied
in solid phalanx."[149] Others also hailed the star of hope shining against the morning sky. "A light looms up in the east,

[147] *Ibid.*, p. 59.
[148] J. F. Cooper, *Home as Found* (Philadelphia, 1838), II, 79.
[149] *Minnie Hermon*, p. 411.

full of hope and cheer to the friends of humanity!" announced Cornyn. "By it you may read the *mene, mene, tekel, upharsin* —the rum-seller's doom! *The Maine Law is enacted!* Already have its benignant influences pervaded the border State, and have swept, with electric rapidity, over every State in the Union. On this, Humanity fixes her hope. . . ."[150] Walt Whitman added his garland of praise for what he called "the wondrous doings of Temperance in Maine." "I consider it a sight," he continued, "which we may properly call on the whole world to admire."[151] To the cries of "unconstitutionality," A. D. Milne answered reverently, "It is the law of fraternity and equality, of love and brotherly kindness, the law of Heaven *Americanized*."[152] Drunkards were made to urge the national adoption of Maine's legislation as a measure of self-protection. "Friends! if that law had been passed twenty years ago, I should have been the richest man in this State," declared the profligate Gus Elliot in *The Senator's Son*. "All that I can say is, that I wish it had been passed before I was born. . . ."[153] Even the spirit of the dead was invoked to urge its passage. The grief-stricken Parke believed that he saw "his mother leaning out of Heaven with the banner in her hand, waving it gently to and fro."[154]

The legislative control of the liquor traffic as embodied in the provisions of the Maine Law became the ideal of reformers. "I should regard the universal reign of the Maine Law, or a prohibitory law, similar in its features, in every State of this Union," asserted Barber in *The Unjust Judge*, "as an indication that God, in the plenitude of his mercy, was smiling upon our highly favored Republic."[155] None of these temperance novelists was permitted to see that blessed day arrive. They were also spared one of the minor ironies of the temperance reformation in the United States; for, when in 1933, after more than a decade of "the law of Heaven *Americanized*," three-fourths of the states voted to repeal this indication of God's mercy, the State of Maine rather lamely followed suit.

[150] *Dick Wilson*, p. 55.
[151] *Franklin Evans*, p. 248.
[152] *Uncle Sam's Farm Fence*, p. 94.
[153] Fuller, *The Senator's Son*, p. 266.
[154] *Ibid.*, p. 279.
[155] [Anon.,] *The Unjust Judge*, p. 46.

The star which had blazed in the East for eighty-three years, and for a time shone alone in her glory, finally sputtered, flickered, and ignominiously went out!

In his highly diverting volume *Queer Books*, Edmund Pearson has given the place of honor to a brief but pleasant chat about temperance novels. Queer they certainly are, judged by any standards; and least of all does the reader who has staggered his way through this chapter, need to be reminded of their shortcomings as works of art. Any list of the world's worst fiction would probably contain them all. If the modern reader's sense of humor fails him, surely his sense of justice should demand that he treat charitably novels which were so humbly and abjectly and earnestly offered for the public weal. Thus Walt Whitman claimed exemption from critical scrutiny for *Franklin Evans*. ". . . my book is not written for the critics," he apologized meekly, "but for *the people*."[156] Most authors professed a complete ignorance of the elements of their craft. "Nothing but the hope of being useful," wrote the author of *Confessions of a Reformed Inebriate*, ". . . could have led me to an undertaking so entirely without the sphere of all my former pursuits."[157] Others, such as Frink in *Alow and Aloft*, claimed only the credit of editing the story told him by a rehabilitated sot. "Properly arranging the facts thus collected, and recording them in language appropriately brief and expressive," he wrote modestly, "is the only share claimed by its author in the preparation of this work."[158] Other writers disarmed unfavorable critics by pleading that all receipts from the sale of their books, as in the instance of *The Price of a Glass of Brandy*, were *"to be applied exclusively to the aid and promotion of the cause of Temperance."*[159] Cyrus Mann expected his novel to be used as a campaign manual. He included a special

---

[156] *Franklin Evans*, p. 5. Whitman's further plea that he was moved to write "not altogether by views of the profit to come from it," ill accords with his later confession to Traubel that he had perpetrated "the rot" for one hundred and twenty-five dollars. See Emory Holloway's introduction to the Merrymount Press edition (New York, 1929), pp. v-vi.

[157] [Anon.,] *Confessions of a Reformed Inebriate*, p. 10.

[158] *Alow and Aloft*, p. 27.

[159] *The Price of a Glass of Brandy*, p. 4.

note in *The Clinton Family* for any young person who might read the volume: "To such let me say, commit some part of a speech or an address, and use it in declaiming before your companions."[160] The extremely loose, episodic structure of many temperance novels may be attributed to the method of composition by which Brown produced *Minnie Hermon.* The novel "was commenced two years ago in the *American Temperance Magazine,* but abandoned in consequence of more pressing duties," he explained. "Detached chapters, however, have appeared in *The Chief* from time to time . . . it has been completed under unfavorable circumstances; the most of it having been written in the night-time . . . and at almost as many points as there are chapters."[161] The didactic purpose of these books appeared to sanction the inclusion of temperance history, biography, statistics, and anecdotes until the narrative often was lost in the maze of argument. "But the story of Jesse Johnston has almost passed out of mind in this digression," admitted Thomas Hunt after a long sketch of the early history of the reform. Sometimes he was forced to ask rhetorically: "But where was left the thread of our story?"[162] Upon several of these occasions, one reader, at least, was unable to answer.

The most popular pattern followed was that made famous in the Currier and Ives lithograph "The Drunkard's Progress." Here was depicted in well-defined steps a series of episodes leading from the first glass to the grave. All that remained for the writer was the addition of an appropriate commentary at each step. This was the method employed by Burdett in *Mary Grover.* "These pictures, in themselves a perfect history of the drunkard's progress," he wrote, "again awakened in the author an earnest desire to write a Temperance Story in illustration of them. . . ."[163] Such a scheme lent itself readily to the picaresque "confessions" of which *Franklin Evans* is an example. *Ten Nights in a Bar-Room* was also planned as a succession of "steps." The Preface promised "a series of sharply drawn sketches of scenes, some of them touching in the extreme, and

---

[160] *The Clinton Family,* p. vi.   [161] *Minnie Hermon,* p. [v].
[162] *Jesse Johnston and His Times,* pp. 66-67.
[163] *Mary Grover,* p. vii.

some dark and terrible."[164] Scenario writers should have encountered little difficulty in adapting it to the screen. Not only has this tearful classic a beginning, middle, and end; but each episode is conveniently numbered so that the veriest child can follow it.

That such a stereotyped procedure might result in a deadly sameness, the novelists were the first to admit. "A history of intemperance, in one town, is a pretty correct history of the evil in most other towns . . . ," conceded the author of *The Beacon!*[165] As early as 1842, Walt Whitman was bothered with the same problem. "To expatiate upon the ruins and curses which follow the habitual use of strong drink," he wrote, "were at this time almost a stale homily."[166] Edwards's attitude in *My Sister Margaret* was one of hopeless resignation. "I have felt that it was quite too much worn to be presented in any new form of argument or narrative," she apologized.[167] Irksome as these difficulties were, the redeeming purpose of temperance fiction atoned for all blemishes. The author of *Waverley* seemed an idle storyteller compared with the immortal Lucius Sargent. "Mr. Sargent has no small portion of the genius of Sir Walter Scott," a critic remarked in the *Journal* of the American Temperance Union, "but while the latter devoted his great powers to unwarrantable caricatures of good men of other times, the former is engaged in the noble and blessed work of emancipating the world from an evil which has filled unnumbered families with grief and desolation."[168]

Temperance novelists tried to gratify the prevailing taste for sentimental love stories by allowing a stream of romance to trickle through their thickets of statistics and arid stretches of argument. "Now fiction appeals chiefly to the heart," Meeks observed wisely in *Fountain Rock*. "What sort of world would that be from which the glorious sunlight of woman's smiles

<hr/>

[164] *Ten Nights in a Bar-Room*, p. 3. There is the same general plan in *The History of the Bottle, Brother Jonathan's Cottage, Autobiography of a Reformed Drunkard, Edward Carlton*, and *Confessions of a Reformed Inebriate*. The author of the last-named volume described the formula as the presentation of "the successive stages of the downward process."

[165] *The Beacon!* p. 18.

[166] *Franklin Evans*, p. 244.

[167] *My Sister Margaret*, p. 5.

[168] *Journal* (Philadelphia, 1837), I, 7.

should be excluded? 'Tis horrible to think of!"[169] Pharcellus Church justified the inclusion of a love plot in *Mapleton* on much the same plea. Although Mrs. S. A. Southworth ruthlessly subordinated the romantic element in *Lawrence Monroe* to more weighty matters, she confessed that her appeal was directed chiefly at the heart. "Well, what better part of you is there to appeal to?" challenged Mary Browning in *The Senator's Son*. "Reason, of which you men are so boastful, forever and forever runs away with itself unless restrained and directed by the heart."[170] The publishers of T. S. Arthur's collected tales guaranteed them "to touch the feelings with electric quickness." "No one can read them without feeling intensely, for the characters stand out in bold relief," declared the laudatory introduction, "while the very pulsations of their hearts are seen."[171] The material at hand should have satisfied the most ardent sentimentalist. At his beck and call were scenes to wring every heart. The Preface to *Dick Wilson* served fair notice of what was to follow in this and countless other novels: "The desolate home, with its heart-broken wife and mother, with her pale cheek channelled with tears of unutterable woe . . . the child-group shivering in the blast, or clinging to that mother, as they moan for bread; the orphan turned out, with no friend but God, into the wide world; youth wrecked and palsied with premature age; manhood reeling amid the ruins of mind and moral beauty, . . . genius drivelling in idiocy and crumbling into ruin; . . . these and ten thousand other combinations of warp and woof, are woven into tales of wondrous intensity and power."[172] Compared with these choice ingredients, the materials of the earlier tales of seduction must have seemed tame indeed.

Of such stuff is the concoction of weak tears and strong drink known as temperance fiction. Not unlike the goblets of cold water they so often invoked, they are, in all truth, sobering enough to the modern taste. Clear, they are, too; but, alas, without the gladsome sparkle and the generous warmth, which

---

[169] *Stories of the Fountain Rock*, pp. 13-14.
[170] Fuller, *The Senator's Son*, p. 273.   [171] *Temperance Tales*, p. 9.
[172] Cornyn, *Dick Wilson*, pp. xxii-xxiii.

in fiction at least may be enjoyed without fear of the morning after. Hydropathy may be overdone in art as well as in medicine; and certainly delirium tremens is a more exciting malady than unimaginative dropsy. But the temperance novel is dead; and, unlike John Barleycorn, whose demise they so confidently anticipated, these doubly dry pages are quite without that lusty gentleman's surprising power of resurrection.

III

UNCLE TOM'S AND OTHER CABINS

The inadequacy of southern thought was identical with that of north-
ern; blinded by sectional economic interests, they saw only half the truth.
They beheld the mote in a brother's eye, but considered not the beam that
was in their own.
—Vernon Louis Parrington,
The Romantic Revolution in America, 1927.

THE MISDEEDS of Prince Alcohol were gradually eclipsed by the
lengthening shadow ominously cast athwart the mid-century
years by King Cotton. Into the vortex of the irrepressible conflict were drawn most of the lesser reforms of the time. Crusaders like Frances Willard, moreover, had declared that
although everything was not in the temperance movement, the
temperance movement should be in everything. Mrs. Stowe
was only the most prominent of many novelists whose pens
served both causes. Scratch a cold-water man and you were
likely to find an abolitionist. Enemies of innovation, therefore,
were easily persuaded to regard antislavery reformers and teetotalers as children of the same bothersome breed. Thus a
demagogue in *Mapleton* had no difficulty convincing Southerners that "as soon as this giant innovation had emptied the
contents of the groggeries into the gutter, it would continue its
desolating march over all the sunny South, breaking every
chain, putting knives into the hands of the slaves . . . and de-
luging the land in blood."[1] Apologists of slavery made merry
over the teeming spawn of isms begat under the transcendental
skies north of Mason and Dixon's line. "The fact is, you
northern people are full of your *isms,*" scoffed the author of
Aunt Phillis's Cabin, "you must start a new one every year."[2]
Mormonism, mesmerism, socialism, and the manufacture of

[1] Church, *Mapleton,* p. 330.
[2] M. Eastman, *Aunt Phillis's Cabin* (Philadelphia, 1852), p. 77.

wooden nutmegs and hams: "All these," charged E. W. Warren in *Nellie Norton*, "are to be the mature fruits from the tree of abolitionism. . . ."[3] "Northern society is a partial failure," concluded George Fitzhugh, "but only because it generates *isms* which threaten it with overthrow and impede its progress."[4]

These attempts to dismiss abolition along with free love and table rapping were dictated by an ingenious strategy, but they were not sufficient to cope with the most important American manifestation of the widespread progress and accomplishment of the humanitarian movement.[5] This spirit of humanitarianism was, of course, not confined to the North. Before technological advances in the cotton industry and the invention of the cotton gin had revolutionized Southern agricultural methods, slavery seemed to many Southerners to be in a fair way to natural and gradual extinction. Planters like Frank Meriwether in *Swallow Barn* viewed their peculiar institution as a necessary evil and indulged in vague, but sincere, hopes that Providence would find a happy solution for it. As early, however as 1832, when Kennedy published his idyl of the Old Dominion, the extension of cotton growing had made slavery an indispensable basis of the South's economic structure. In the North, moreover, reformers like Garrison were abandoning the older methods of mild sermonizing and resorting to imperious demands for the immediate social and political equality of the blacks. Faced with the rapidly mounting economic value of slavery below the line of demarcation, and irked by the prying interference with their institution from above it, the South shifted its attitude from that of mild apology to militant defense. Leadership changed, as Parrington has shown, from the idealistic humanitarians of Virginia to the fire-eating economic realists of South Carolina. Observers on both sides were beginning to foresee a house hopelessly divided against itself.

[3] E. W. Warren, *Nellie Norton* (Macon, 1864), pp. 91-92.
[4] G. Fitzhugh, *Cannibals All!* (Richmond, 1857), p. xx.
[5] For an excellent discussion of the international relations of the movement, see Michael Kraus, "Slavery Reform in the Eighteenth Century: An Aspect of Transatlantic Coöperation," *Pennsylvania Magazine of History and Biography*, LX, 53-66.

Although many of the temperance reformers and their methods of promotion were usurped by the antislavery cause, the two movements contrasted sharply. No apologist for alcohol had come forward in fiction to answer *Ten Nights in a Bar-Room,* while at least fourteen proslavery novels followed hard upon the publication of *Uncle Tom's Cabin.*[6] Every village had its grocery or tavern and temperance writers needed only to observe the habits of the less steady of their neighbors to make notations on the evils of rum. The abolitionists, on the other hand, came from a region where the wrongs of black slavery were virtually nonexistent; they saw their "darkies" on the minstrel stage, not the plantation. The peculiarly sectional nature of the problem, moreover, led those who were attacked to resent outside interference as meddlesome and ungentlemanly. Critics of slavery were all too prone to ignore the complexity of an institution which few of their number had opportunity fully to understand. They yielded to the demands imposed by propaganda and painted every overseer as a Simon Legree and every slave mart as a shambles. The defenders of the slave economy responded by representing the North as saddled with white slavery and groaning under the ills of an unlovely, exploitative industrialism. Seen through the golden haze of sentiment, the South became a modern Garden of Eden, perfumed by magnolia blossoms, in which an ignorant and childlike people were being benevolently taught the arts of Christian civilization. Both sides contented themselves with half truths and constantly needed nothing so much as to be reminded that charity begins at home.

The plantation setting which formed the background for these attacks and apologies had been a favorite one with domestic sentimentalists for some time before the rise of the abolition movement had sharpened sectional antipathies.[7] In the new excitement, the old pattern became heavily charged with drama. Mrs. Stowe was keenly aware of the richness of

[6] See Jennette Tandy's interesting article, "Pro-Slavery Propaganda in American Fiction in the Fifties," *South Atlantic Quarterly,* XXI, 41-51, 170-178.

[7] For an admirable account of the plantation tradition in American literature, see Francis Pendleton Gaines, *The Southern Plantation* (New York, 1924).

the materials in the Southern scene. "First, in a merely artistic point of view, there is no ground, ancient or modern, whose vivid lights, gloomy shadows, and grotesque groupings, afford to the novelist so wide a scope for the exercise of his powers," she wrote in *Dred*. "Two nations, the types of two exactly opposite styles of existence, are here struggling; and from the intermingling of these two a third race has arisen, and the three are interlocked in wild and singular relations, that evolve every possible combination of romance."[8] The author of *Uncle Tom's Cabin* was, however, too stern a daughter of Puritanism to write solely from what she disparagingly called "a merely artistic point of view." The daughter, sister, wife, and mother of ministers, she rarely wrote without a moral purpose. "It is the moral bearings of the subject involved," she declared, "which have had the chief influence in its selection."[9]

Mrs. Stowe's frank acceptance of the didactic mission of popular fiction was echoed by novelists on both sides. "We have but one great object in view," wrote the author of *Our World*, "that of showing a large number of persons in the south, now held as slaves, who are by the laws of the land, as well as the laws of nature, entitled to their freedom."[10] Although the propaganda was frequently softened by the inclusion of a love story, readers were seldom permitted to lose sight of the chief purpose of the book. "Mine are no silken sorrows, nor sentimental sufferings," disclaimed Archy Moore, hero of *The Slave*.[11] Proslavery writers readily conceded the value of presenting their cause "under the allurements of fiction." "Let me write the *fictions* for a people, and I care not who makes the *speeches*," boasted Lucien Chase in 1854, when hundreds of thousands were weeping over the death of the saintly Uncle Tom.[12] "Fine, profitable speculation may be made from negro fiction," Caroline Rush charged in 1852. "Wrought up into

[8] H. B. Stowe, *Dred* (Boston, 1856), I, iii.
[9] *Ibid.*
[10] F. C. Adams, *Our World* (New York, 1855), p. 376.
[11] R. Hildreth, *The Slave* (Boston, 1848), p. 5. [First edition, 1836]
[12] L. B. Chase, *English Serfdom and American Slavery* (New York, 1854), title page.

touching pictures, they may, under the spell of genius, look like truth and have the semblance of reality. . . ."[13] The author of *Nellie Norton* chafed at the amount of preaching against slavery under the guise of fiction as though it were the only sin "to which humanity is heir." "A Sabbath School book cannot be written in a style acceptable to the Northern mind," he protested, "unless it condemns it in some part."[14]

Now that the feverish emotions excited by the conflict have subsided, these novels, with few exceptions, are read only as embodiments of the opposing philosophies in that struggle. Their value derives from their interpretations of the Northern and Southern points of view and doctrines, rather than of life itself. Despite their limitations, however, they reveal a fertile ingenuity in the contrivance of incidents designed to illustrate their arguments and to substantiate their charges. Their pages also yield convincing evidence of the conspicuous failure of the sentimental philosophy to solve the most troublesome and inflammable problem of the generation. Fuzzy benevolence and well-meaning compromise served only to prolong the bitter agony.

The novelists of both camps fought under the banner of truth. Frequently they followed Mrs. Stowe's lead by fortifying their volumes with appendices or by buttressing their pages with footnotes. Readers of Tower's *Slavery Unmasked* were assured that they had not been "indulging in fictions; but in facts, in realities, in history, written out in *blood* and stereotyped with *tears and groans*."[15] Abolition novelists resembled the temperance crusaders in their repeated insistence upon the impossibility of exaggerating the pathetic and sensational nature of their materials. One of their chief problems, they complained, was to soften the horrors of the life they described to fit the tender sensibilities of the average reader. "Indeed, had the author introduced scenes depicting some of the actual events," declared Victor in *The Unionist's Daughter*, ". . . the pages of the novel would have assumed the character of a

---

[13] Rush, *The North and South*, p. 23.   [14] Warren, *Nellie Norton*, pp. 46-47.
[15] P. Tower, *Slavery Unmasked* (Rochester, 1856), p. xiv.

romance of Robespierre and Danton's reign—would have repelled the reader by its truly horrible element."[16]   Similar
restraint was exercised by J. R. Gilmore in *Among the Pines*.
"If the whole were related—if the Southern system, in all its
naked ugliness, were fully exposed—the truth would read like
fiction, and the baldest relation of fact like the wildest dreams
of romance."[17]   The autobiographical form was freely used to
win the confidence of readers.   Thus the heroine of the *Autobiography of a Female Slave* appealed to the public: "This
book is not a wild romance to beguile your tears and cheat your
fancy.   No; it is a truthful autobiography of one who has suffered long, long, the pains and trials of slavery."[18]   The "editor"
of *Fifty Years in Chains* asserted that his hero's life would be
put into jeopardy were his identity known.   "The story which
follows is *true* in every particular," he testified.   "The subject of
the story *is still a slave* by the laws of the country, and it would
not be wise to reveal his name."[19]

Proslavery novelists tried to offset these claims to authenticity by bringing to bear upon their subject a wide variety of
narrative devices.   By far the most popular method was to send
an ardent abolitionist to the South for a visit with a college
friend or a favorite cousin.   Once across the line, Northern
prejudices were made to melt like snow beneath Dixie's sun.
Harriet Freeman, the heroine of *The Sable Cloud,* who had
been taught that every black man was a Toussaint in chains,
underwent immediate conversion.   " 'Uncle,' said she, 'what I
have seen here in fifteen minutes shows me that at least one
half of that which I have learned at the North about the slave
is false.   Our novels and newspapers are all the time misleading
us.' "[20]   Mark Littleton's sojourn in the Old Dominion was

[16] M. Victor, *The Unionist's Daughter* (New York, 1862), p. 217.

[17] *Among the Pines* (New York, 1862), pp. 303-304. Gilmore had been inspired
to write by Mrs. Kirkland's stern injunction after the fall of Fort Sumter: "If you
cannot shoulder a musket, you can blow a bugle." In *My Southern Friends* he admitted that although, "his blasts are not as musical as they might be . . . they have,
at least, *the ring of truth.*"

[18] M. Griffiths, *Autobiography of a Female Slave* (New York, 1857), p. 86.

[19] [Anon.,] *Fifty Years in Chains* (New York, 1859), p. i.

[20] N. Adams, *The Sable Cloud* (Boston, 1861), p. 61.

equally convincing. "I came here a stranger, in great degree, to the negro character . . . and somewhat disposed, indeed, from prepossessions, to look upon them as severely dealt with, and expecting to have my sympathies excited towards them as objects of commiseration," he told his host. "I have had, therefore, rather a special interest in observing them. The contrast between my preconceptions of their condition and the reality which I have witnessed, has brought me a most agreeable surprise."[21] The time-tried epistolary device was pressed into service to enable visitors to give their Northern friends an intimate account of actual conditions in the South. Kate Conyngham had scarcely been ushered to her room before she dashed off a letter of retraction. "I am already getting reconciled to slavery," she scribbled to an abolitionist back home, "since I find that it does not, in reality, exhibit the revolting horrors I was taught in the north. . . . I am almost ready to acknowledge that the African is happier in bondage than free!"[22] Accustomed to think of slave quarters as vermin-infested hovels, Melville, another converted visitor, was moved to admiration at his first glimpse of "the neatness of the out-buildings and the rural appearance of the white-washed cabins. . . . They were surrounded by flowers and creeping plants, and in a little garden attached to each were vegetables and herbs."[23] Nellie Norton was ecstatic in her praise of the Southern way of life. "This must be an approximation to the beautiful and delightful home of our first parents," she wrote rapturously, "before it was polluted by the appearance of the tempter."[24] Nor was she disappointed in slaveowners. "I find them to be men of highly refined sensibilities and tender sympathies," she reported, "—patterns of unselfishness."[25]

[21] J. P. Kennedy, *Swallow Barn*. This quotation is from the revised edition published in New York in 1852. The first edition, which was issued in two volumes in Philadelphia in 1832, has been used for subsequent citations from the work. Although Kennedy enlarged and revised his treatment of the slave quarters in Chapter XLVI, he did not change his attitude to the general subject of slavery.

[22] J. H. Ingraham, *The Sunny South* (Philadelphia, 1860), p. 59.

[23] R. Criswell, *"Uncle Tom's Cabin" Contrasted with Buckingham Hall, the Planter's Home* (New York, 1852), p. 55. Cited hereinafter as *Buckingham Hall*.

[24] Warren, *Nellie Norton*, p. 96. [25] *Ibid.*, p. 70.

Dr. Nehemiah Adams, a Boston clergyman who wrote two able proslavery novels, made much of the quick conversion of Northern visitors to the Southern point of view. His *Southside View of Slavery* and *The Sable Cloud* became conspicuous targets for attack by abolitionists. After describing the barbarity of a slave-hunt, Philo Tower waxed scornful of tourists who "wore the green specs of slavery." "That Rev. gentleman way up in Boston, in his three months tour through the South, never saw this sight, I conclude, besides a thousand and one other horrifying illustrations of the institution, that a murderous Arab of Sahara could but notice, were he here only half of three months."[26] Reformers were equally unimpressed by the invitation of planters to question the slaves themselves about their condition and their desire for freedom. Guests in the South filled their letters with exclamations of surprise at the complacency with which the blacks gloried in their bondage. "Ask *them*!" hooted the author of *Ida May*. "That would be equal to the farce of taking Daniel Webster to a certain plantation, where everything had been prepared beforehand, and telling him he might ask any questions he pleased, and find out for himself just how the negroes were treated."[27]

Antislavery writers did not underestimate the genuine charms of plantation life. The white mansion with its graceful columns and white verandas, the faithful darkies whose wool had grown white in their master's service, the crinolined beauty of Southern belles, the savory dinners of ham and chicken, the sentimental strains of a banjo from the "quarters" in the magnolia-scented air of early spring—these attractions were more or less reluctantly conceded by abolitionists. "What wonder that he should narcotize his moral sense with the aroma of these social fascinations!" exclaimed Epes Sargent in *Peculiar*. "Even at the North, where the glamour they cast ought not to distort the sight, and where men ought healthfully to look the abstract abomination full in the face, and testify to its deformity,—how many consciences were drugged, and how many

[26] *Slavery Unmasked*, p. 153.
[27] M. H. G. Pike, *Ida May* (Boston, 1854), p. 140.

hearts shut to justice and to mercy!"[28] Dr. Adams relished this discomfiture of the reformers. "Whoever goes to the South, or has anything to do with slave-holders, is apt to lose his integrity," he remarked with mock gravity, "there is a Circean influence there for Northern people; thousands of once good anti-slavery men now lie dead and buried as to their reputations here at the North, in consequence of having to do with the seductive slave-power. . . ."[29] If stalwart reformers felt their zeal shrink under the compelling graces of plantation life, the more susceptible Northern misses succumbed almost without a struggle. Prepared to give their hearts to the cause of the slaves, they more frequently lost them to the sons of wealthy planters. "Oh, I would be so happy!" purred Nellie Norton, whose abolition prejudices were forgotten in her love for Mortimer, an attractive slaveholder. "I intend to study his beautiful and exalted character—I think the study will be quite as fascinating to me as was that of Botany, especially if I come in as frequent contact with him as I did with the flowers."[30] There is plenty of evidence for Ingraham's caustic observation, "that ninety-nine out of every hundred of the governesses, tutors, professional men, and others, who flock to the South . . . remain, (the young ladies, if they can obtain 'Southern husbands,') and identify themselves fully with Southern institutions."[31] Temperance, as well as slave reformers, must have noted with misgiving the cooling effects of mint julep on abolition ardor!

In their attempts to picture the happiness of the slaves and the humanity of the planters, defenders of the peculiar institution made full use of the plantation setting and its narcotic effects. They could rely on a tradition well established by Kennedy in *Swallow Barn* and by Caruthers in *The Cavaliers of Virginia*. Here was a wealth of material, as Professor Gaines has well shown, which was suggestive of many sentimental moods and which might be made to provide welcome relief

[28] E. Sargent, *Peculiar* (New York, 1864), pp. 264-265.
[29] *The Sable Cloud*, p. 17.
[30] Warren, *Nellie Norton*, p. 74.   [31] *The Sunny South*, p. 5.

from the dull burden of argument and statistics which pro-slavery novels were forced to carry. Mark Littleton's capitulation to the charms of Southern life set a popular fashion. "I begin to grow moderate in my desires," he soliloquized half-humorously, "that is, I only want a thousand acres of good land, an old manor-house, on a pleasant site, a hundred ne-groes, a large library, a host of friends . . . with some few et ceteras not worthy mentioning."[32] Readers apparently never tired of being regaled with a jocund succession of Negro wed-dings, christenings, and holiday festivals. Mary Bradley prom-ised readers of *Douglass Farm* they would find "these very scenes—the old Hall, the lawn, the avenue, the chubby little negro children who ran to open the carriage gate in our drives, the 'Aunties' and 'Uncles' of the large kitchen department,— the bountiful Christmas cheer. . . ."[33]

Ample justice was done to the mansion house, although few could compete with the palace owned by the Heyward family which "contained twenty-one rooms, each thirty feet square," and was situated picturesquely in an amazing grove of palmetto, olive, pomegranate, mimosa, popynack, orange, lemon, and citron. The author was probably correct in her observation that the odor "is too strongly aromatic to be wholesome."[34] A fair specimen of the lengths to which a mas-ter in this cult of the picturesque could go to cater to the pop-ular conception of the plantation setting is offered by that ex-perienced purveyor of domestic sentiment, Mrs. Caroline Lee Hentz. Her heroine, Julia, found Southern scenery had been underrated even in fiction: "She walked through avenues of orange-trees, whose rich, vivid green leaves quivered above her head with a soft, joyous rustle, half covering and half revealing innumerable balls of vegetable gold; through rows of fragrant lemons, whose fruit melted into a paler gold; and then she seemed lost in a labyrinth of verdure, through which the glow-ing scarlet of the pomegranate flashed like the wing of the

[32] *Swallow Barn*, II, 60.
[33] M. E. Bradley, *Douglass Farm* (New York, 1858), p. 5.
[34] Mrs. M. H. Schoolcraft, *The Black Gauntlet*, p. 165.

flamingo, and the sweet-scented jessamine sent the white gleam of its virgin blossoms; and, high above all, stately pillars of this beautiful colonnade, the superb magnolias rose in verdant majesty, and every large, lustrous leaf seemed as a mirror to the sun."[35] After exposure to this floral set piece, Julia could do nothing less than remark of her new home, "A second edition of the garden of Eden, only revised and improved."[36] So much for the Southern *flora*. Antislavery novelists were pleased to complete the landscape by providing the *fauna*. Their additions usually included a liberal number of crocodiles and lizards, but their specialty was a canine breed popularly known as the bloodhound; although he had a preternatural relish for scents, they were not those which emanated from the blooming jessamine.

No matter how often Southern novelists praised the spacious life behind the white façades of the mansions of the planters or how reluctant they were to rise from tables laden with fried Maryland chicken and baked Virginia ham, their primary concern was to portray the unconfined merriment of the joyous Negroes. Northern guests were made to remark upon it as soon as they had exchanged greetings with their hosts. "Nellie had never seen such merry servants," declared E. W. Warren. "Not one seemed borne down with that mighty incubus of care and oppression she had expected; but decked out in bright colors, and new shoes, and flaming 'head handkerchers,' they followed her as entirely free from care and liberty-longing as school children upon any academy lawn."[37] What, after all, did the blessings of liberty amount to when compared with a slave jamboree? "No race, either in civilized or uncivilized lands, appears to enjoy a holiday with the zest of the Southern negroes," asserted Randolph in *The Cabin and the Parlor*. "They enter into it with an unctuousness that our elder and more correct Anglo-Saxon blood cannot comprehend. At all times they are a happier people than we are."[38]

[35] C. L. Hentz, *Robert Graham* (Philadelphia, 1855), pp. 107-108.
[36] *Ibid.*, p. 109.   [37] *Nellie Norton*, pp. 15-16.
[38] J. T. Randolph, *The Cabin and the Parlor* (Philadelphia, 1852), p. 78.

Pickaninnies at play were an engaging sight. "They are a strange pack of antic and careless animals," wrote Kennedy, "and furnish the liveliest picture that is to be found in nature, of that race of swart fairies which, in the old time, were supposed to play their pranks in the forest at moonlight."[39]

Presiding benignly over this round of barbecues and hunting parties was the planter, tempering his pleasure with thoughts of his sober responsibility as master of the lives of so many human beings. When an English Quaker asked Buck why he chose to remain a slave after his master had offered him freedom, the black was nonplused. "Me slave, massa?" he replied scratching his wool. "I sprise at my massa! He know belly well, he been work heself 'most to def at home for he nigger. . . . He de slave—me de gemmon what keeps care of him. Dat trute, massa."[40] The complete loyalty of the slaves to the families of their masters was a constantly recurring theme in proslavery fiction. "None but those who live under our peculiar institutions can imagine the strong bond existing between faithful servants and the families with whom they are connected," wrote Caroline Gilman in *Recollections of a Southern Matron*. "They watch our cradles; they are the companions of our sports; it is they who aid our bridal decorations, and they wrap us in our shrouds."[41] Slaveowners were frequently represented as undergoing a rigid apprenticeship before they assumed their positions as masters. Thus the proprietor of Roseland "attended medical and surgical lectures, that he might supply with advice the accidental wants of his people," and interested himself in mechanics, as a means of saving labor on his plantation.[42] The characteristics of the planter were those which are today popularly suggested by the term "a Southern gentleman." When Peyton, a model plantation-owner, traveled in Canada he was looked upon with nostalgia by fugitive slaves shivering under a social ostracism almost as cold as the Northern blasts. "It was easy for the gazers to dis-

---

[39] *Swallow Barn*, II, 58.
[40] W. T. Thompson, *The Slaveholder Abroad* (Philadelphia, 1860), p. 18.
[41] C. Gilman, *Recollections of a Southern Matron* (New York, 1838), p. 94
[42] *Ibid.*, p. 202.

cover that he was a Southern planter," Mrs. Hale wrote. "Many of them knew the little signs and tokens which gave so distinct a character to that class, too well to be mistaken. The carelessly-fitting, yet scrupulously neat dress, with its abundance of spotless linen, the slow and dignified movement, the air at once commanding and benign. . . ."[43] These reminders of their former days of pleasant dependence induced many freed slaves to yearn to be taken back to the South. "Ah, ef I could only jest see the ole North State onct more," sighed Johnson, a North Carolina black who had been given his liberty, "an git some raal Macklenburg baked hominy, fried with midlin, an hear a good corn song, an go to camp-meetin, 'pears like I could die more happier."[44]

To the charges of abolitionists that every Negro's lacerated back was an unanswerable antislavery document, apologists countered by citing instances of barbarous cruelty to Northern "hired help." The occasional whippings made necessary by the nature of the slave economy they held to be exceptions in which the overseer invariably suffered more than his victim. Asked whether he knew of any cases of brutal punishment on the Courtenay plantation, Dr. Worthington was indignant. "Of course not," he replied. "We read of such things in novels sometimes. But I have yet to see it in real life, except in rare cases, or where the slave has been guilty of some misdemeanor, or crime, for which, in the North, he would have been imprisoned, perhaps for life."[45] Kate Conyngham had the same answer for conditions on her host's plantation in Louisiana. "You will be interested to know that I have not heard a blow struck on this estate," she informed her astonished Northern friends, "and the colonel says he has not punished one of his slaves in seven years."[46] The college mates of Arthur Weston were equally surprised to hear him declare, "I have never seen a slave woman struck in my life. . . ."[47] His friends, however,

[43] S. J. Hale, *Liberia* (New York, 1853), p. 123.
[44] Thompson, *The Slaveholder Abroad*, p. 99.
[45] Randolph, *The Cabin and the Parlor*, pp. 39-40.
[46] Ingraham, *The Sunny South*, p. 143.
[47] Eastman, *Aunt Phillis's Cabin*, p. 74.

were unable to give so pleasant an account of conduct in the North. Abel Johnson confessed that he had witnessed much maltreatment of the "white slaves" in department stores. "They're nothing but white niggers, after all, these Irish," he reported having heard an employer declare as he beat an underpaid orphan "until blood spouted."[48] Nor did the hired men on New England farms fare any better. Henry Harley told his mother how he had been stripped, tied to a tree, and beaten to insensibility by his employer, Timothy Hardgripe. "He turned me over on my side, with a malicious leer on his face," the juvenile victim continued, and "he squeezed the [lemon] juice into the open cuts on my back. Oh! God, oh! my mother, can you imagine the torture he inflicted upon me?"[49] Pro-slavery novelists had not forgotten that Simon Legree was born in New England. They enjoyed reminding Mrs. Stowe that the North was full of his breed.

Slavery propagandists often made the slaves testify to the joys of their blessed bondage. "An ef you could jest see how fast our little niggers increase, Marster," Buck told an English abolitionist, "an how many on 'um grows up, and how many gits to be powerful old, you wouldn't bleeve that any on 'um, old or young, was 'bused or bad treated much."[50] The author of *The Black Gauntlet* insisted that the planter's neighbors "would publicly prosecute him, if he overworked or was cruel to his slaves." That this was unlikely to occur, however, she was comfortably confident, for she added pleasantly that "all experience in the South proves that you cannot overwork a negro."[51] Lucien Chase found the lot of the average British wage-earner far less happy than that of the Southern black. "His childhood is devoted to recreation; in manhood his powers are not over-taxed; and in old age he is provided with a home."[52] Little wonder, in light of these advantages, that the return of the owner after even the shortest absence, was a signal

[48] *Ibid.*, pp. 72-73.
[49] Rush, *The North and South*, pp. 253-254.
[50] Thompson, *The Slaveholder Abroad*, pp. 354-355.
[51] Mrs. M. H. Schoolcraft, *The Black Gauntlet*, p. 49.
[52] *English Serfdom and American Slavery*, p. 209.

for wild demonstrations of affection from the servants. The simplehearted Mr. Frank, a Northern guest at the Manley estate, not unnaturally mistook such a frenzied reception for a dreaded insurrection. He was alarmed "by a crowd of negroes of both sexes, and all ages and sizes; who were dancing, singing, shouting, and hallooing. . . . His first impression was that they were a marauding band of slaves, who were about to attack the carriage," wrote the amused author. "It was truly a gratifying sight, to see the feelings of pure attachment which they manifested to their young master."[53]

It was this familiar relationship of affection between proprietor and servant which appealed to James Kirke Paulding. In *The Dutchman's Fireside* he wrote that "there was something in the connexion of mutual services, mutual good will, and mutual protection, thus established, that made the relation of master and slave, in those simple, honest times, one of the most endearing and respectable of all those which subsist between man and man."[54] The days which Paulding recalled with fondness were not essentially different from those which Kennedy had chronicled with so much grace in *Swallow Barn,* and which George Tucker had described in *The Valley of Shenandoah,* where he found every slave happily contented as "a member of a sort of patriarchal family."[55] Paulding resembled his master, Fenimore Cooper, in his distrust of reform by legislative methods and felt that the slaves "were far more happy, virtuous and useful both to themselves and society, than the wretched victims of a rash and miscalculating philanthropy we see every day at the police and quarter-sessions."[56] The Dutch were the kindest of slaveowners, and Cooper's regret at the changing status of the black was genuine. "Alas! alas!" he lamented in *Afloat and Ashore,* "—Among the improvements of this age, we have entirely lost the breed of the careless, good-natured, affectionate, faithful, hard-working, and yet happy blacks of

[53] Vidi [pseud.], *The Underground Mail Agent* (Philadelphia, 1853), pp. 157, 159.
[54] *The Dutchman's Fireside* (New York, 1837), I, 72. [First edition, 1831]
[55] *The Valley of Shenandoah* (New York, 1824), II, 207.
[56] *The Dutchman's Fireside,* I, 72-73.

whom more or less were to be found in every respectable and long-established family of the State, forty years ago."[57] Of too uncompromising an intellectual honesty to attempt to justify slavery on moral or ethical grounds, and yet apprehensive of the efforts of the reformers to tinker with perfection, Cooper's attitude was somewhat equivocal. He reserved for his scamps like Deacon Pratt in *The Sea Lions,* or Timms in *The Ways of the Hour,* attempts to find a moral basis for slavery. Some of the most engaging passages in *Satanstoe* and the other novels of the Littlepage trilogy have to do with the affectionate gratitude shown by Corny's faithful slave, who spurned with indignation his master's offer of freedom and survived to the end of the series as an honored friend of the family. Cooper's father had purchased slaves to fill vacancies in his household staff, but as Susan Cooper has remarked, their freedom was always granted immediately and they were paid wages along with the other servants. In some such way, perhaps, did the author envisage a gradual emancipation of the Negroes. He believed to the end that somehow or other good might come out of evil. "How often, in turning over the pages of history," he wrote in *The Oak Openings,* "do we find civilization, the arts, moral improvement, nay, Christianity itself, following the bloody train left by the conqueror's car, and good pouring in upon a nation by avenues that at first were teeming only with the approaches of seeming evils! In this way, there is now reason to hope that America is about to pay the debt that she owes to Africa. . . ."[58] Had he lived beyond 1851 into the bitter years which immediately preceded the Civil War, Cooper would have heard much the same hope voiced by many lesser men who had neither his high disinterestedness nor his sturdy integrity. These apologists never hesitated to hide their selfish economic motives beneath a cloak of sentiment.

In their portrayal of slavery's blight upon Southern life, abolition novelists placed a chief reliance upon scenes of dramatic contrast. Seldom has the raw material of fiction been so

---

[57] *Afloat and Ashore* (Philadelphia, 1844), II, 241.
[58] *The Oak Openings,* II, 221.

prodigal of its riches, so infinite in its variety of lights and shadows. Ready at hand were the sharply divergent ideals and economies of North and South, the presence of a subjugated race in a land of chivalry and freedom. Here, too, were the seemingly boundless possibilities for drama and pathos to be found in the peculiar relationship between the planter's wife and his mulatto mistress, between the arrogant heir to the estate and his dusky half brother, between the master and his slaves. Pathetic episodes were inherent in a social order which permitted families to be separated and domestic ties to be violated at the will of a master. All these and more might be enacted against a background which changed swiftly from parlor to cabin, and from Southern plantation to New England farm. In her mastery of this welter of material and in her zeal to bring its lessons home to the business and the bosoms of her fellows, the author of *Uncle Tom's Cabin* had no peer. Trained in the rigid school of a New England household where every child "was the absolute bond slave of the *ought*," and profoundly sympathetic with the spiritual heritage of her Puritan ancestors, she was unusually sensitive to the evils of the hateful institution which every passing hour made more of an anachronism. Nor was she a "parlor abolitionist" who derived her knowledge of the black race from the "darkies" in Christy's Ethiopian Minstrels. She lived for a time in the electric atmosphere of Cincinnati and had heard there the ugly shouts of mob violence, she had participated in the excitements of a family which had helped to speed fugitives on their way to Canada, and she had visited the South with eyes that were far from blind to many of the mitigating circumstances and the genial aspects of domestic servitude.

Underlying all her writing and informing almost every attitude to the problem was this deeply bred New England Puritanism. "But you ought to see the *northern* working people," exclaimed Nina, who had been educated in the North and was shocked at the indolence she found on her plantation. "Why the governors of the States there are farmers, sometimes, and work with their own men. The brain and the hand go together, the work is *done* up there differently from what's done here!"[59] She was intensely aware of the contrast between the poor whites and the ambitious Yankees. "This is so strange, and so different from what it is in the northern states!" she declared in *Dred*. "Why all the children go to school there— the very poorest people's children! Why a great many of the first men, there, were poor children!"[60] Not unlike the character of Ophelia in *Uncle Tom's Cabin*, Mrs. Stowe groaned over the spoiled offspring of the planters. Their conduct revealed to her the lack of that old-fashioned New England "principling" which "could be comprised in very few words: to teach them to mind when they were spoken to; to teach them the catechism, sewing, and reading; and to whip them if they told lies."[61] She also realized the complexity of the problems implied in the contrast between little Eva and Topsy. "They stood the representatives of their races," she wrote earnestly. "The Saxon, born of ages of cultivation, command, education, physical and moral eminence; the Afric, born of ages of oppression, submission, ignorance, toil, and vice!"[62] The author tellingly gave to a humane planter the task of answering those who believed that it was the abuse, not the system of slavery itself which was at fault. "Talk of the *abuses* of slavery! Humbug!" cried St. Claire. "The *thing itself* is the essence of all abuse! And the only reason why the land don't sink under it, like the Sodom and Gomorrah, is because it is *used* in a way infinitely better than it is!"[63]

Mrs. Stowe's sensitivity to the lights and shadows of her theme resulted in a series of brilliant sketches in *Uncle Tom's Cabin* and in *Dred*. Few readers of these novels have been able to forget the characters of Harry and Tom Gordon, as closely related by blood as they were separated by humanity; the St. Claire brothers, one a frugal farmer in Vermont, the other an opulent Louisiana planter; the pleasant plantation of the Shelbys and the horrible shambles ruled by the lash of Simon Legree; Uncle Tom leading his fellow slaves in prayer while

[59] Stowe, *Dred*, I, 267.
[60] *Ibid.*, I, 129.   [61] *Uncle Tom's Cabin*, II, 38.
[62] *Ibid.*, II, 43.   [63] *Ibid.*, II, 11.

his master was negotiating his sale down the river; Harry reading the Declaration of Independence to fugitives lurking in the Dismal Swamp; the *La Belle Rivière* with its unhappy freight of black "purchases" separated by a thin partition from care-free whites where "everything was going on quite easy and comfortable." These and countless other scenes were drawn with varying power, but with a pathos which recognized no bounds. Beloved by the sentimentalists were those tearful set pieces which Aiken's stage version helped to fix more vividly in the national imagination, the deaths of little Eva and of Uncle Tom. Surer in its restraint and more unmistakable in its genius, was the matter-of-fact reporting of the death of old Prue: "I hearn 'em saying that the *flies had got to her,—*and *she's dead!*"[64] No other American novel of the century made so wide an appeal to the common conscience and humanity of readers everywhere. Long after the tense moral excitement which produced it has died, the book still retains, in its high moments of profound and authentic passion, the power to stir the hearts of men.

Mrs. Stowe's compelling weapons were, of course, used less skilfully by other abolition writers, and were eagerly seized by a small host of proslavery novelists who sought to turn them upon her own position in a counterattack. The titles of some of these efforts indicate their themes: Robert Criswell's *"Uncle Tom's Cabin" Contrasted with Buckingham Hall, the Planter's Home;* Mary Eastman's *Aunt Phillis's Cabin; or, Southern Life as It Is;* J. W. Page's *Uncle Robin in his Cabin in Virginia and Tom without One in Boston;* S. H. Elliott's *New England Chattels;* L. B. Chase's *English Serfdom and American Slavery;* and J. T. Randolph's *The Cabin and the Parlor.* These and other novelists who arose to the defense of their institution applied every variety of ingenuity to the task of refuting Mrs. Stowe. They measured skeptically the length of some of Eliza's more breath-taking leaps over the ice; they gleefully commented upon Simon Legree's New England babyhood. Most of the defenders pretended to be quite unable to compete with

[64] *Ibid.,* II, 6.

"our daring, dashing, witty romancer, Mrs. Stowe," and her ideal "millennial world; where all are born equal, where one man is not a dribbling idiot, and another a genius like Napoleon, Calhoun, or Webster."[65] Others disavowed "in advance, the idea of having written . . . for mercenary considerations . . . to steal a part of a lady's hard-earned reputation."[66] Mrs. Eastman professed dismay at the activities of meddling females. "Ah! Washington Irving, well mayst thou sigh and look back at the ladies of the Golden Age," she wrote in *Aunt Phillis's Cabin.* " 'Those were the honest days, in which every woman stayed at home, read the Bible, and wore pockets.' These days are for ever gone. . . . Alas! we neither stay at home, nor read our Bible. We form societies to reform the world, and we write books on slavery!"[67]

In their grudging testimony to the popularity of Mrs. Stowe's work, her detractors assumed the garb of humility. "I do not for a moment imagine that anything I can write can equal in style, logic or depth, that far-famed work of Mrs. Stowe, which has aroused a nation's sympathy," wrote Caroline Rush. *"Uncle Tom's Cabin* is a highly wrought fiction, abounding in touching incidents, and clothed with that dangerous sophistry, that indeed looks so much like truth, that it is often mistaken for it."[68] Robert Criswell also professed a modest reluctance to take up his pen "to allay the great agitation" which "that talented authoress, Mrs. Stowe," had increased.[69] Aroused by its exaggerations, Dr. Nehemiah Adams classed *Uncle Tom's Cabin* with the incendiary publications of agitators who represented the South as "a Golgotha, a valley of Hinnom," and who charged that "compacts with it are covenants with hell."[70] So neatly did the material presented in *The Sunny South* serve as a rebuttal to Mrs. Stowe's indictments that Ingraham hastened to deny that he wrote his novel as "an answer," but merely as "a simple representation of southern life as viewed by an intelligent Northerner." "As

---

[65] Mrs. M. H. Schoolcraft, *The Black Gauntlet,* p. 6.
[66] Randolph, *The Cabin and the Parlor,* p. 6.
[67] *Aunt Phillis's Cabin,* p. 275.   [68] *The North and South,* p. 9.
[69] *Buckingham Hall,* p. 7.   [70] *The Sable Cloud,* p. 7.

these Letters were commenced, and many of them published before Mrs. Stowe's Uncle Tom was written," he protested a bit too eagerly for complete conviction, "its pictures of Southwestern life have no reference to that work nor were influenced by it."[71] Whatever their attitude to the truth of Mrs. Stowe's narratives, writers on both sides agreed that the heart of the nation had been profoundly stirred. W. T. Thompson reported that everybody talked about Uncle Tom in England. "It was soon in the hands, heads, and mouths of all classes . . . ."[72] Caroline Rush also complained of the way in which the English "look upon our poor 'Uncle Tom and his Cabin' with ravenous sympathy," and, as she added bitterly, forget that charity begins at home.[73] Philo Tower, an antislavery writer, observed it was snatched up eagerly in the South by everybody "from sire to chick" and that slaveholders were seen looking at it furtively in Charleston hotel lobbies.[74] The author of *The Sable Cloud* was rebuked when he asked an acquaintance whether he had read *Uncle Tom's Cabin*. Such an inquiry seemed equivalent to a challenge of one's literacy. "Ask me if I know how to read," was the prompt reply. "Every lover of liberty and hater of oppression has read 'Uncle Tom.' "[75]

Apologists tried desperately to use Mrs. Stowe's most effective characters and incidents as boomerangs. They dismissed Simon Legree as a creation of purple melodrama. "We planters well know that no such monsters exist as that Legree," retorted Criswell, ". . . although some of our planters are hard masters, they do not beat their slaves to death, or *burn them alive,* or *murder* them, as Legree is represented to have done."[76] Others, such as Dr. Adams, assumed for the sake of argument that Legrees might exist, but insisted that slavery did not produce them. "There are as many Legrees at the North as at the South," he maintained in *The Sable Cloud*. "Legree would be Legree in Wall Street, or Fifth Avenue; Uncle Tom would not be Uncle Tom in the wilds of Africa."[77] Mrs. Eastman,

[71] *The Sunny South,* p. 5.
[72] *The Slaveholder Abroad,* p. 19.
[73] *The North and South,* p. 18.
[74] *Slavery Unmasked,* p. 156.
[75] Adams, *The Sable Cloud,* p. 135.
[76] *Buckingham Hall,* pp. 140-141.
[77] *The Sable Cloud,* pp. 135-136.

with the instinct of a trained debater, pounced upon Legree's New England upbringing as an insult to American motherhood and declared that "The saddest part of this book would be, (if they were just,) the inferences to be drawn from the history of this wretch, Legree."[78] The author then proceeded to quote one of Mrs. Stowe's choicest bits: "Mrs. Stowe says, 'He was rocked on the bosom of a mother, cradled with prayer and pious hymns, his now seared brow bedewed with the waters of baptism. In early childhood, a fair-haired woman had led him, at the sound of Sabbath bells, to worship and to pray. Far in New England that mother had trained her only son with long unwearied love and patient prayers.' " This opportunity to pose as a champion of New England nurture was too tempting to be done casually and Mrs. Eastman made the most of it. "Believe it not, Christian mother, North or South!" she cried. "Thou hast the promises of Scripture to the contrary. Rock thy babe upon thy bosom—sing to him sweet hymns—carry him to the baptismal font—be unwearied in love—patient in prayers; he will never be such a one. He may wander, but he will come back. . . ."[79] Even the doctrine of perfectionism, which for obvious reasons was not popular in the South, was called upon to prove the absurdity of Simon Legree.

The death of little Eva, which in the stage versions had done so much to impress youthful imaginations with the scenic wonders of heaven, was not allowed to go unchallenged. "I too have known my little Evas," claimed Caroline Rush, thinking of children in Northern slums, ". . . but I have seen likewise the cheek grow paler, and the eye more dim; I have seen the soft curls hang damp and matted around the pure spirit-like brow, and have watched Death as she bore away the slight fragile forms, so slight, so very fragile, because they had suffered for bread . . . so often withheld from the worthy and industrious poor."[80] Nor did Eva's loving conduct with Uncle Tom escape censure. "Eva is a sweet, angelic creature," admitted Criswell, "yet she is made by the authoress, the companion of a slave,

---

[78] *Aunt Phillis's Cabin*, p. 269.
[79] *Ibid.*, pp. 269-270.   [80] *The North and South*, p. 10.

sitting in his lap and embracing him, as if he were a *brother*. . . . Kindness without familiarity is sufficient. . . ."[81] Eliza's perilous flight over the floating ice, a more exciting if not quite so gaudy an episode as Eva's ascension with the doves, was frequently ridiculed. "[All] would have been very well," hooted the author of *Buckingham Hall*, "if we could believe that she leaped *ten feet* across the current in the Ohio river and scampered over broken ice like a cat, and all the while with a child in her arms."[82] Mrs. Stowe's question: "Is *man* ever a creature to be trusted with wholly irresponsible power?" was made to apply to matrimony and regarded as proving altogether too much. "Although she is here speaking of slavery *politically*, can you not apply it to matrimony in this miserable country of ours?" chuckled Mrs. Eastman. "This is the era of mental and bodily emancipation. Take advantage of it, wives and negroes! But, alas for the former! There is no society formed for *their benefit* . . . they must wear their chains."[83]

The saintly Uncle Tom, that archangel in ebony, was shown as little mercy by proslavery enthusiasts as he was by Simon Legree. Critics attempted to ridicule him as the epitome of the abolitionists' tendency to create slaves in their own image with a liberal daub of burnt cork. Mrs. Stowe had, indeed, credited Tom with an amazing number of good works including the reform of his master's taste for mint juleps.[84] "No matter how low, how ignorant, how depraved, the very sight of Tom turned them into advanced, intelligent Christians," observed Mrs. Eastman with some show of truth. "The poor fellow dies at last—converting two awful wretches with his expiring breath."[85] "He is the most perfect specimen of Christianity that I ever heard of," declared an admirer in *The Sable Cloud*.[86] Certain it is that this noble black captured the popular imagination which pictured him with his Bible on his

[81] *Buckingham Hall*, p. 140.
[82] *Ibid.*, p. 139.   [83] *Aunt Phillis's Cabin*, p. 111.
[84] *Uncle Tom's Cabin*, I, 294. St. Claire signed the temperance pledge after Tom reminded him that "The good Book says, 'It biteth like a serpent and stingeth like an adder!' "
[85] *Aunt Phillis's Cabin*, p. 269.   [86] Adams, *The Sable Cloud*, p. 135.

knee "threading his slow way from word to word," and cherished his heroic resolve to remain with his mistress in her time of need, his reverent attitude to little Eva, his tender solicitude for other unfortunates, his humble attempt to justify his master's decision to separate him from his family, his dogged refusal to escape by violating his pledge, and his Christian resignation which endured to the end. "I don't believe that such a being ever existed, save in the realms of fancy," wrote Caroline Rush, who reluctantly conceded that "a nation's sympathy has been awakened. . . ."[87] Mrs. Eastman suggested facetiously that his master neglected only one opportunity of exploitation. "One would have thought that his master . . . would have kept him until he died, and then have sold him bone after bone to the Roman Catholics," she remarked. "Why every tooth in his head would have brought its price. Saint Paul was nothing but a common man compared with him, for Saint Paul had been wicked once. . . ."[88] Even Mrs. Stowe recognized that she had created something of a paragon, "a moral miracle." It remained, however, for Dr. Adams to give the coup de grâce. "What made him the model Christian?" he asked rhetorically. "You do not reply, and I will tell you. SLAVERY MADE UNCLE TOM. Had it not been for slavery, he would have been a savage in Africa, a brutish slave to his fetishes, living in a jungle, perhaps; and had you stumbled upon him he would very likely have roasted you and pickled your bones. A system which makes Uncle Toms out of African savages is not an unmixed evil."[89]

Dr. Adams's neat application of the sentimental formula to the troublesome question by which Uncle Tom became an exhibit of the glories of human slavery was characteristic of much of the wishful thinking of the time. The sentimentalists welcomed private benevolence, but were uncomfortable when it led to drastic action. "Kindness, most certainly, we should feel towards every one," counseled Mrs. Steele in *The Mustee*, "but to think of radically changing the condition of a whole race of

[87] *The North and South*, pp. 127-128.
[88] *Aunt Phillis's Cabin*, p. 266.   [89] *The Sable Cloud*, p. 135.

men, and that too by the stroke of the pen, seems to be a most delusive dream!"[90] Edward Clayton found that his plans for the education and emancipation of his slaves were tolerated amiably as long as he merely talked about them. "They will have great patience with you—they will even have sympathy with you," predicted Edward's father in *Dred*, "so long as you confine yourself to the expression of feeling; but the moment your efforts produce the slightest movement in the community, then, my son, you will see human nature in a new aspect. . . ."[91] General benevolence without any of the accompanying embarrassments of charity was a popular creed. When Grace appealed to Mrs. Herbert to relieve the distress of two runaway slaves, she received the usual equivocation: "I do particularly wish to avoid involving myself in this inconvenient subject of slavery. No one disapproves of slavery in the abstract more than I do. . . . But you know I stand on delicate ground."[92] Comfort and convenience were persuasive bribes for the maintenance of moral compromise. "The comforts and luxuries of life, its roast-beef and plum-pudding, are the oil that keeps the machinery of society in operation," Miss Sedgwick pointed out accurately. "The arguments of the southern cotton-planter and the northern manufacturer may be reduced to this element."[93]

The sentimental generation could not pretend successfully to ignore slavery, but it preferred to handle it with velvet gloves. "There are but two means by which moral revolutions can be effected. One is the all-convincing power of Truth and Love; the other is the irresistible argument of Physical Force," asserted the author of *The Underground Mail-Agent*. "In the present enlightened era of the world, the latter is very justly excluded from the field of moral reforms. . . ."[94] Caroline Rush attempted to reconcile the irreconcilables by urging her readers "to regret the necessary evils of the Slavery of the South, without bitter feelings, animosities or dissensions to-

---

[90] B. F. Presbury, *The Mustee* (Boston, 1859), p. 140.
[91] Stowe, *Dred*, II, 152.
[92] C. M. Sedgwick, *Married or Single?* (New York, 1857), II, 17.
[93] *Ibid.*, I, 246.
[94] [Anon.,] *The Underground Mail-Agent*, p. 227.

wards those who are born and reared amid the peculiar rights and duties of the slave-holder."[95] Sympathy stopped short of action. Epes Sargent protested at the contemporary middle-class morality which was becalmed in a futile compromise. He derided the churchgoer who "thinks it an impertinence to mix up morality with religion," and showed little patience with the attitude of "the distinguished American divine, who the other Sunday began his sermon with these words, 'Brethren, I am not here to teach you morality, but to save your souls.' As if a saving faith could exist allied to a corrupt morality!"[96] Comfortable, too, was the easy plea to allow time to cure the ills of slavery. "It would be far better for the Southern slaves, if our institution, as regards them, were left to gradual mitigation and decay, which time *may* bring about," advised Mrs. Eastman. "The course of the abolitionists, while it does nothing to destroy this institution, greatly adds to its hardships."[97] Consoling to the slave must have been the compensations which this same facile author discovered that Providence had provided. "Yet has the Creator, who placed him in this state, mercifully provided for it," she wrote soothingly. "The slave has not the hopes of his master, but he is without many of his cares. . . . His eye can see the beauties of nature; his ear drinks in her harmonies; his soul contents itself with what is passing in the limited world around him."[98] Less unselfish, but equally unanswerable, was the argument Joseph Holt Ingraham urged for the perpetuation of slavery. It was a convenient solution, he declared, for that perennial source of vexation—the servant problem! "How necessary to the happiness and comfort of the beautiful daughter or aristocratic lady of the planter, is the constant presence of an Africaness, black, thick-lipped, and speaking broken English—a black daughter of Kedar—whose grandmother may have danced the Fetish by the fires of human bones. . . . Yet these descendants of barbarians . . . possess every quality that should constitute a good servant. No race of the earth makes such excellent domestics.

[95] *The North and South*, pp. vi-vii. [96] *Peculiar*, p. 30.
[97] *Aunt Phillis's Cabin*, p. 135. [98] *Ibid.*, pp. 123-124.

It is not in training! They seem born to it!"[99] Even Mrs. Stowe had failed to anticipate this adroit defense! Ingraham returned to this argument again and again. "They love to look up to someone who 'takes the responsibility,'" he wrote with rare logic, "and for this responsibility they are ready to give in return their labor and life-service. Certainly *free* negroes are the worst public servants...."[100]

Apologists were happier in taking refuge behind a higher motive, for what more noble vocation was there than the Christianizing of a heathen race delivered to one's own doorstep by God's own providence? "I am so satisfied that slavery is the school God has established for the conversion of barbarous nations," declared the author of *The Black Gauntlet*, "that were I an absolute Queen of these United States, my first missionary enterprize would be to send to Africa, to bring its heathen as *slaves* to this Christian land, and keep them in bondage until *compulsory* labor had tamed their beastliness, and civilization and Christianity had prepared them to return as missionaries of progress to their benighted black brethren."[101] Seldom have principles and profits been yoked so deftly. Dr. Adams lent the dignity of the cloth to a similar hope. "I like to cherish the idea...," he wrote in *The Sable Cloud*, "that we have an embryo nation in the midst of us, whom God has been educating for a great enterprise ... and when, like California and Australia, the voice of the Lord shall shake the wilderness of Africa and open its doors, it may appear that American slavery has been the school in which God has been preparing a people to take it into their possession."[102] This pleasant contingency was sufficiently remote to cause little discomfort to those who were enjoying the profits of slavery. When Adams was asked how long an apprenticeship was to be served by the blacks, he answered significantly, "God only knows."[103]

The scheme to colonize Africa with Christian Negroes after they had completed their somewhat extended course of compulsory education in the cotton and rice fields, had peculiar

[99] *The Sunny South*, p. 118.   [100] *Ibid.*, p. 473.
[101] Mrs. M. H. Schoolcraft, *The Black Gauntlet*, p. vii.
[102] *The Sable Cloud*, p. 185.   [103] *Ibid.*

charms for the sentimental mind because it united the favorite projects of emancipation and foreign missions. "And who can doubt that, in thus providing a home of refuge for 'the stranger within her gates,'" exclaimed Mrs. Hale, "our beloved Union was nobly, though silently, justifying herself from the aspersions of oppression and wrong so often thrown out against her?"[104] Mrs. Stowe was also attracted by the plan of transporting the Negroes to Liberia. She deemed it a proper haven for the persecuted George Harris and his family in *Uncle Tom's Cabin.* "I go to *Liberia,* not as to an Elysium of romance," the fugitive declared bravely, "but as to *a field of work.*"[105] In *Northwood* as well as in *Liberia,* Mrs. Sarah Hale anticipated and answered objections to colonization with the beguiling glibness of a realtor. Was the climate wholesome? "But yet our thermometer has never risen above ninety degrees, and it is often much warmer than that in Virginia," a colonist replied.[106] Were the fields fertile enough for farming? "They just scratch the ground and throw the seed in," declared another propagandist, who knew how to appeal to certain tendencies in the habits of the Negroes.[107] Were the first emigrants homesick? "Never for one minute," testified a leader of the first expedition to the colony. "The first moment I stepped my foot on Liberia, I felt like a different man; and if I had known that I should have died in the first six months I would not have regretted my coming."[108] As a clinching argument, Mrs. Hale noted that Liberia had fewer poisonous snakes than Virginia![109] Colonization plans were gratefully slow and thus popular with those who wished to enjoy the thrills of humanitarianism without doing very much about it. They also enabled slaveowners to preach the beauties of Christian resignation while the great work of orientation matured. "We are, for your own good and ours, obliged to keep you in bondage for the present," Walter Tucker reasoned with a recalcitrant black, "and we are justified by the laws of God and man. I've no doubt that some day our people will do the best they can for

---

[104] Hale, *Liberia,* p. iv.
[106] *Liberia,* p. 207.
[108] *Ibid.,* p. 219.
[105] *Uncle Tom's Cabin,* II, 303.
[107] *Ibid.*
[109] *Ibid.,* p. 216.

the negroes. . . ."[110] Until that distant day arrived, it was the duty of the planters to inculcate the comforts offered by religion. "If he has been religiously instructed—as most of the slaves are in this State," wrote the author of *Northwood*, "he goes forth a priest bearing the Ark of God's Covenant of mercy to Ethiopia: Millions on millions of his black brethren will bless his name."[111] Ingraham pointed with pride to the efforts of the slaveholder to provide a suitable place of worship for his blacks. "The body of the chapel is reserved for them," he wrote unctuously in *The Sunny South*.[112] The lesson most frequently heard in such edifices was that of obedience. Mrs. Stowe laid bare the real motives often cloaked by this pious concern for the souls of the slaves. "I can tell you, that, in a business, practical view,—for I am used to investments," boasted Jekyl, a slave dealer in *Dred*, "that since the publishing of those catechisms, and the missionaries' work among the niggers, the value of that kind of property has risen ten per cent. They are better contented. They don't run away, as they used to."[113]

The benevolent dreams of the advocates of colonization unfortunately had no appreciable effect on the astonishing birth rate of the Negroes. Buck had truth on his side when he cried proudly, "An ef you could jest see how fast our little niggers increase . . . an how many on 'um grows up. . . ." Criswell saw the futility of efforts to solve the problem by transplanting it. "We might as well attempt to clear one of our large forests by cutting down a tree every year," he exclaimed despondently, "for while we are making the removal, thousands are growing up instead."[114] The Negroes, too, quite properly had their own objections to transportation. "I ain't gwine to Africa, 'cause I'se bred and bornd here; I ain't gwine to Africa, ef I'se as free as a frog," protested Cleopatra warmly. "I ain't gwine. If all my forefaders done staid dare, den I shouldn't know any-

[110] C. H. Wiley, *Adventures of Old Dan Tucker* . . . (London, 1851), p. 111. Appeared in 1849 as *Roanoke; or Where Is Utopia?*
[111] S. J. Hale, *Northwood* (New York, 1852), p. 408. [First edition, 1827]
[112] *The Sunny South*, p. 66.
[113] *Dred*, I, 193.   [114] *Buckingham Hall*, p. 48.

ting 'bout dis sher country, an' I doesn't prefar to know any-
ting 'bout dat."[115] John Peterkin spoke for many slaves when
he charged, "They wish to send the poor negro away to the
unknown land from whence his ancestors were stolen. We
virtually say to the Africans, now you have cultivated and
made beautiful our continent, we have no further use for
you."[116]

The amalgamationists, those "noodles" as one writer called
them, who believed in the elevation of the black race by the
process of absorption or amalgamation, felt that colonization
was merely an evasion of the duty to treat the Negroes as social
equals. They respected the justice of Violet's criticism of the
inconsistent conduct of abolitionists. "Nebber heerd of a white
man north bein' more willin' to marry a black gal dan a white
man here," she complained in *The Cabin and the Parlor*. "Dat
don't look like bein' a brodder."[117] Instead of transporting the
blacks to Liberia, the amalgamationists wished to rush the
millennium by substituting intermarriage between the two
races. These "ultras" occupied a precarious position upon the
outermost edge of the lunatic fringe of the isms and were, of
course, vulnerable to attack from both sides. Proslavery writers
cited amalgamation as the *reductio ad absurdum* of the abolitionists' whole case, while even the extremists touched this
delicate subject rather gingerly. Epes Sargent was courageous
enough to declare that the matter was a problem for physiol-
ogists and charged pointedly that "Many of these men who cry
out the loudest against amalgamation keep colored mistresses
and practically confute their own protests. To marriage, but
not to concubinage they object."[118] The author of *Our Nig*
dared to treat with sympathetic understanding the marriage of
Jim, a black, to a white woman who had been seduced and deserted. "You can philosophize, gentle reader, upon the impropriety of such unions, and preach dozens of sermons on the
evils of amalgamation," he asserted. "Want is a more powerful

[115] E. C. Pearson, *Ruth's Sacrifice* (Boston, 1863), p. 171. Published in 1853 as
Cousin Franck's Household.
[116] [Anon.,] *Autobiography of a Female Slave*, p. 198.
[117] Randolph, *The Cabin and the Parlor*, p. 48.
[118] *Peculiar*, p. 149.

philosopher and preacher."[119] The amalgamationists, however, made little headway against popular prejudice. Sympathizing with Negroes was one thing, living with them, quite
another. There was much truth in St. Claire's remark that
Northern reformers preferred to do their uplift by proxy. "You
would not have them abused; but you don't want to have anything to do with them yourselves," he told Ophelia. "You
would send them to Africa, out of your sight and smell, and
then send a missionary or two to do up all the self-denial. .... .
Isn't that it?"[120] The general attitude to amalgamation was
voiced by Mrs. Schoolcraft, wife of the historian of the Indians,
when she declared, "I believe a refined Anglo-Saxon lady
would sooner be burnt at the stake, than married to one of
these black descendants of Ham."[121]

The possibilities of satire in the conception of marriage between loutish blacks and delicate lady abolitionists were too
palpable to be neglected. In Mrs. Flanders's *The Ebony Idol,*
a greasy rascal posing as a fugitive slave so worked upon the
sympathies of Deacon Hobbs that he vowed to curry favor
with the amalgamationists by forcing his daughter to wed the
black. Mary was "so fragile, so pure-hearted, so ethereal in
person and spirit," wrote the author, "that she might have
sprung from the bosom of sleeping flowers, wooed by the passionate starlight."[122] So fragile a female could, of course, be
nothing less than horrified at the proposal. When news of the
"advanced" plans of the deacon reached his neighbors, they
punished him with a coat of tar and feathers, while the bridegroom elect skulked away to try his fortune as an abolition lecturer in another state.[123] More fantastic was the Swiftian satire
*A Sojourn in the City of Amalgamation in the Year of Our
Lord 19—* in which the reader is introduced to a community of
amalgamationists who were "commingled into a *hodge-podge*
of black flesh and white flesh, and *yellow flesh* . . . of all kinds
of flesh the most disgusting, because it is a compound and has

[119] H. E. Wilson, *Our Nig* (Boston, 1859), p. 13.
[120] Stowe, *Uncle Tom's Cabin*, I, 257.   [121] *The Black Gauntlet*, p. vii.
[122] G. M. Flanders, *The Ebony Idol* (New York, 1860), p. 42.
[123] *Ibid.*, pp. 215-216.

no purity in it. . . ."[124] The inhabitants had prepared themselves for their emancipated notions by "whipping their olfactory nerves into the astonishing belief that manure is ambrosial, and not foul and disgustful, as their diabolical prejudices led them to imagine."[125] The members of this cult, we are solemnly informed, "do nocturnally slumber with a platter of this excrement smoking before their noses. . . ."[126] Even this rigorous discipline had to be supplemented by an ingenious mechanical device before intermarriage could be made completely free of annoyance. The contrivance bore some resemblance to that invented by Greene in his *A Yankee Among the Nullifiers* which he appropriately called *"The Anti-African-Odor-Gas-Generator."*[127] Visitors to the City of Amalgamation inspected the machine with interest. "It seemed composed of fans and little vials, ingeniously intermingled," explained the author, ". . . its object being to protect the husband from those disagreeable evaporations exhaling from the odoriferous spouse, which it did by fanning off the offensive air, and at the same time dispensing, by means of the vials, a delightful perfume."[128] The greatest attraction in the city, however, was Boge Bogun, "a man half black, half white; the lower half being black, the upper half white; the line dividing the two colours being clear and distinct."[129] Boge described his marvelous make-up in his popular "Memoirs": "When dawn broke upon the intestinal regions, a motley scene was exposed to view."[130] The love story which does not entirely succeed in sweetening the atmosphere of this novel, reached its climax when Albert, the hero, disguised as a Negro, married Julia, the daughter of an ardent amalgamationist, who had designed her for a repulsive black, Cosho.[131]

Burlesque of amalgamation was one way to obscure the issue of slavery. Another, even more popular, was to suggest that abolitionists confine their humanitarian activities to the

[124] O. Bolokitten [pseud.], *A Sojourn in the City of Amalgamation* . . . (New York, 1835), p. 11.   [125] *Ibid.*, p. 141.   [126] *Ibid.*
[127] A. Greene, *A Yankee Among the Nullifiers* (New York, 1833), p. 92.
[128] *A Sojourn in the City of Amalgamation* . . . , p. 17.
[129] *Ibid.*, p. 69.   [130] *Ibid.*, p. 74.   [131] *Ibid.*, p. 190.

slums of their own cities. "Who ever heard of them making any continued and systematic effort to ameliorate the condition of the over-worked and starving seamstresses in the North, or to secure to the unfortunate bond-children, apprentices, and operatives in our factories, the rights and blessings to which they are entitled?" asked the author of *The Underground Mail-Agent*.[132] Epes Sargent was guilty of the fallacy committed by most of the antislavery novelists in his belief that the Southern slave trader was the only exploiter of labor. "Take away slavery, and he would perish of inanition," he wrote in *Peculiar*. "He would be, like the plesiosaur, a fossil monster, representative of an extinct genus."[133] Mrs. Stowe, however, was too tolerant and too well informed to believe that economic exploitation was confined to the South. "The slaveowner can whip his refractory slave to death,—the capitalist can starve him to death," she wrote in *Uncle Tom's Cabin*. "As to family security, it is hard to say which is the worst,—to have one's children sold, or see them starve to death at home."[134] It was not enough merely to deny, as did J. T. Trowbridge in *Cudjo's Cave*, that white slavery was unknown in the North because "Education alone makes free men."[135] Educational advantages were not usually enjoyed by Northern child laborers. "If you doubt it, go to one of the northern cities," advised J. T. Randolph, "and look at the sharp, prematurely thoughtful faces of the news-boys, of many of the errand-boys, and indeed, of all who, at an age they should be at school, are compelled to earn their living. . . . Pale, patient faces!"[136] Northerners were also urged to go behind the glittering front of a mercantile palace and to reflect "what an army of pale, consumptive women it had taken to build it; how their hearts' blood had been drained away, drop by drop; how the flesh had been worn down from their marrowless bones, the sight from their eyes and slumber from their eyelids, that Mr. Smith might build a handsome store, do a flourishing business,

---

[132] [Anon.,] *The Underground Mail-Agent*, p. 130.
[133] *Peculiar*, p. 256.   [134] *Uncle Tom's Cabin*, II, 21.
[135] *Cudjo's Cave* (Boston, 1864), p. 29.
[136] *The Cabin and the Parlor*, p. 91.

and become in a few years, a millionaire."[137] In their defense of black slavery by their shrewd attack on wage slavery, apologists of the Southern economy frankly admitted the element of exploitation in both systems, but insisted that the plantation ideal was more humane than industrial slavery. "It is far more cruel than the black slave trade, because it exacts more, when we say, that the *profits* made from free labor are greater than those from slave labor."[138] Jefferson Davis had envisioned a civilization based upon slavery: "But the new Confederacy must be a Missionary to the Nations, to teach the ruling classes throughout the world, that slavery is the normal status for the mechanic and the laborer."[139] Abolitionists were shocked at such pronouncements, for in their indictment of the slave economy they had closed their eyes to their own ruthless, exploitative industrialism.

Southern spokesmen followed up their attack with much shrewd analysis. "There *must* be two classes in every society," declared Colonel Vance in *Ida May.* "The learned, the cultivated, the wealthy, must be the *patricians;* and the laboring class must be the plebeians, and it makes little difference whether they are black or white."[140] Lucien Chase's study of England's boasted democracy convinced him that it was based upon white slavery. A genuine white democracy, he declared, can exist only with black slavery; let America emancipate her slaves only if she is prepared to force into serfdom a large portion of her white population. "At an age when little American Negroes are sporting on their playgrounds," Chase told a group of London abolitionists, your "little white serfs drop into the grave with broken constitutions, at seven years of age."[141] "I saw some of your redeemed, regenerated, disenthralled people," a Virginia planter remarked to an English guest in *Aunt Phillis's Cabin.* "I saw such features on women's faces that haunted me afterwards in my dreams. I saw children with shrivelled, attenuated limbs, and countenances that were

[137] C. Rush, *The North and South*, p. 136.
[138] Fitzhugh, *Cannibals All!* p. 25.
[139] E. Sargent, *Peculiar*, p. 396.   [140] Pike, *Ida May*, p. 194.
[141] *English Serfdom and American Slavery*, p. 87.

old in misery and vice—such men, women, and children as Dickens and Charlotte Elizabeth tell about."[142] The wave of immigration which reached its crest of four hundred thousand in 1854, seemed to bear out Southern claims that "slave America" for all its inhumanity, was more wholesome for the common man than "free England." "Not only are we yearly deriving large accessions to our numbers from England and Scotland," Chase stated with a wealth of statistical evidence, "but the stampede from Ireland is so great, that it threatens to depopulate that portion of the British Empire."[143] To tamper with black slavery, he concluded boldly, would be "at the imminent risk of subverting the most glorious system evoked by the wisdom of the human race!"[144]

To the charges of the industrial North that the slave economy was an anachronism, the plantation South countered with its ideal of a Greek democracy. The slave states served notice that they would struggle "until the hope of the philanthropist and the dream of the wise is fulfilled, until the glorious days of Greece are restored, and her institutions and her children, her arts and her literature, shall people these western wilds."[145] In their anxiety to ridicule this ideal, abolitionists forgot the ugly aspects of industrial feudalism in the North. They derided the concept of a Greek democracy in the South as a scheme of "hyper-aristocratic vagueness, coupled with an arbitrary determination to perpetuate its follies for the guidance of the whole Union." "And the effect of this becomes still more dangerous," Adams further charged in *Our World,* "when it is attempted to carry it out under the name of democracy,—American democracy!"[146] Aroused at this counterattack by Southern thinkers, Sargent rallied all men to oppose "the theories of the shallow *dilettanti* of the South, who, claiming to be great political thinkers and philosophers, maintain that capital ought to own labor, and that there must be a

---

[142] Eastman, *Aunt Phillis's Cabin,* p. 95.
[143] *English Serfdom and American Slavery,* p. 207.
[144] *Ibid.,* p. 86.
[145] Wiley, *Adventures of Old Dan Tucker . . . ,* p. 176.
[146] F. C. Adams, *Our World* (New York, 1855), p. 43.

hereditary servile race. . . . As if God's world-process were kept
up in order that a few Epicurean gentlemen may have a good
time of it. . . . "[147] That this might have also included millowners in Lawrence and Lowell did not seem to have occurred
to him. It was one of the sources of Mrs. Stowe's power that
she was not blind to the grim exactions of industry, and yet at
the same time recognized the beauty of the plantation ideal.
The author of *Uncle Tom's Cabin,* however, knew that the
wage-earner enjoyed a full measure of political freedom which
was denied to the slave by the laws of the land. Even under
ideal conditions, slaves trembled at the prospect of the death of
a kind master and at the uncertainty of their status. "Whoever
visits some estates there," she wrote of Kentucky, which she had
seen at first hand, "and witnesses the good-humored indulgence
of some masters and mistresses, and the affectionate loyalty of
some slaves, might be tempted to dream the oft-fabled legend
of a patriarchal institution, and all that; but over and above
the scene there broods a portentous shadow—the shadow of the
law."[148]

The inadequacy of the sentimental philosophy to resolve
the slavery problem into a simple equation is strikingly shown
in the futile, but well-intentioned, plans advanced by the novelists for its solution. Mrs. Stowe's suggestion of gradual emancipation was not much different from that intimated by Kennedy in *Swallow Barn* published twenty years earlier. Her
noble ideal of Christian pacifism, her high hopes of a Christian
civilization of blacks in Liberia and in model plantations such
as Edward Clayton had established for his former slaves in
Canada, only serve to indicate how irrepressible the conflict
had become. It was comfortable, no doubt, to assume with
Nathaniel Hawthorne in his campaign biography of Franklin
Pierce, that slavery was an evil which God alone could remove.
"The true way for all is to wait till the clouds clear," counseled
Randolph. "We are now in Egyptian darkness as it were. All
we know is that God leads our country by an especial Provi-
dence, and that the pillar of fire will appear in due time."[149]

<hr/>

[147] *Peculiar,* p. 356.   [148] *Uncle Tom's Cabin,* I, 23-24.
[149] *The Cabin and the Parlor,* p. 260.

While scanning the skies for this sign, Northerners were advised to keep their hands off the peculiar institution and Southerners were urged to treat their slaves kindly. "If they were to let us alone," Criswell begged, "there is no doubt that, in the course of years, not a slave State would be in existence. . . ."[150] Gradual emancipation was the panacea recommended by many. "Slavery is decreasing throughout the world," announced Mrs. Eastman with more optimism than the facts warranted, ". . . and our planters are setting a number of theirs free, and sending them to Africa. I know a gentleman in Georgia who liberated a number, and gave them the means to start in Liberia as free agents and men."[151] Dr. Adams asked all men to adopt an attitude of Christian resignation by which he meant a policy of doing nothing piously. ". . . but anything like impatience and passion at the existence of slavery, I hold to be a sin against God," he declared. "I pity those good men whose minds are so inflamed by the consideration of individual cases of suffering as not to perceive the great and steadfast march of the divine administration."[152] As for abolition? "This may be delayed for centuries to come," he wrote not very long before the inauguration of Abraham Lincoln.[153]

This somewhat indeterminate period of preparation and waiting was to be sweetened for the slaves by the ministrations of the benevolent female. Her lot in temperance fiction had been a busy, if not a happy, one; she was given an even more arduous part to play in slavery fiction. "Let me here take occasion to remark," stated Caroline Rush, "that as a general thing, the greatest slave on a plantation is the mistress. She is like the mother of an immense family, of some fifty up to five or six hundred children."[154] Unable to take an active stand against the institution which supported them, the wives and daughters of planters found scope for their benevolence in going the rounds from cabin to cabin with baskets filled with tidbits from their own tables. Many resembled Mrs. Preston, who "knew nothing—thought nothing—about the right or

[150] *Buckingham Hall*, p. 58.
[151] *Aunt Phillis's Cabin*, p. 77.   [152] *The Sable Cloud*, p. 138.
[153] *Ibid.*, p. 140.   [154] *The North and South*, p. 226.

wrong of slavery; but cheerfully and prayerfully . . . went on in the round of duties allotted to her, leaning on the arm of the Good All-Father, and looking steadfastly to Him for guidance and support."[155] The planter, meanwhile, laid the flattering unction to his soul "that his wife had piety and benevolence enough for two," and as Mrs. Stowe observed, indulged in "a shadowy expectation of getting into heaven through her superabundance of qualities to which he made no particular pretension."[156] "It's a monster work," admitted an active mistress of a model plantation, "but monster evils can be removed if females will give their hearts and hands to the task."[157]

Sentimental heroines, however, were not content to limit their activities to bathing pickaninnies and visiting sick mammies; they entertained more ambitious plans. Had not their sisters in the cold-water crusade vowed never to give their hands to topers? Slavery would soon disappear, they reasoned, if all Southern belles refused to encourage the attentions of slaveholding suitors. This device was fully exploited by novelists who embroidered the theme with much sentimental languishing and despair. Thus the heroine of *Ruth's Sacrifice* rejected the man she loved rather than become the wife of a slaveowner: ". . . and although the struggle between conscience and affection well nigh rent soul and body asunder, her convictions of duty were triumphant," wrote Mrs. Pearson. "With a breaking heart, she told him that they must part forever!"[158] Julia Tennyson insisted that her suitor free his blacks before she announced their engagement. "If you will prove your love and devotion for my daughter by emancipating your slaves," her father told the lover, "I will not refuse to grant my sanction to your mutual wishes—but, not until then."[159]

Every plantation contained an ethereal daughter, a grown-up little Eva, whose health wasted away at being compelled to live close to so much suffering of the slaves. Such a sensitive plant was nineteen-year-old Georgiana Wilson, who died of

[155] J. R. Gilmore, *My Southern Friends* (New York, 1863), p. 125.
[156] *Uncle Tom's Cabin*, I, 26.   [157] F. C. Adams, *Our World*, p. 129.
[158] Pearson, *Ruth's Sacrifice*, p. 253.
[159] Criswell, *Buckingham Hall*, pp. 80-81.

grief induced by the cruel punishment of a favorite slave.[160] More hardy were those heroines like Eleanor Beaufort in *The Unionist's Daughter,* who spurned her lover's advances as long as he advocated secession. "Not one kiss, as lover or wife, Sinclair Le Vert," she demanded staunchly, "till I give it under the shadow of the dear old national flag!"[161] Although Mrs. Sarah Hale approved heartily of these female efforts to remedy the evil, she proposed a practicable one of her own. It was nothing less than an annual Thanksgiving Day offering to be taken in each of America's forty thousand churches. "If the sum averages but *five dollars* per congregation, the aggregate would be *two hundred thousand dollars!"* she computed enthusiastically. This sum was to be augmented by various philanthropic agencies, she declared with mounting fervor, "till finally, every obstacle to the *real freedom* of America would be melted away before the gushing streams of sympathy and charity, as the ice of the polar seas yields to the warm rains of summer."[162] In the same sentimental tradition, and, alas, of the same futility, was little Eva's fond wish to sell her diamond necklace and to "buy a place in the free states, and take all our people there, and hire teachers, to teach them to read and write."[163]

Simple, plausible, and well meaning enough were almost all these emanations of the sentimental mind—a mind, as Mrs. Stowe neatly put it, "that might not be unaptly represented by a bale of cotton,—downy, soft, benevolently fuzzy, and confused." Many problems less complex and less far-reaching in their implications than slavery might have yielded. But the humanitarian impulse which could attract donations for asylums for aged, indigent, and respectable females; that was successful in engineering church suppers and in dispatching missionary barrels to the remote corners of the earth; and could keep the village pastor in warm mufflers and woolen socks, was not able to encompass the stubbornly diverse elements of the irrepressible conflict. Slavery proved to be a malignant growth

[160] W. W. Brown, *Clotelle* (Boston, 1867), p. 72.

[161] *The Unionist's Daughter,* p. 38.

[162] *Northwood,* p. 408.   [163] Stowe, *Uncle Tom's Cabin,* II, 69.

and the salve of sentiment was not destined to be the sovereign remedy. As a recent historian of the generation which had found comfort so frequently in the healing properties of that popular emollient, has well said: "The attenuated fabric of middle-class idealism could not stretch quite far enough to conceal the ugly protuberance—although it tried hard enough. When, in the Eighteen Sixties, the national body got rid of the tumor by cutting it out, the fabric was cut too."[164]

[164] E. D. Branch, *The Sentimental Years, 1836-1860*, p. 404.

IV

HOME, SWEET HOME

These American novels unconsciously reveal all the little household secrets; we see the meals as they are put on the table, we learn the dresses which those who sit down to them wear . . . we hear their kindly family discourses, we enter into their home struggles, and we rejoice when they gain the victory.

—Mrs. Gaskell's Preface to the Tauchnitz Edition of Maria Cummins's *Mabel Vaughan*, 1858.

"Home, Sweet Home" was written by an American in Paris, set to a Sicilian air by an English composer, and first sung in an operatic drama on an Italian theme in London in 1823. To the sentimental generation in the United States which cherished it as a favorite song, the words seemed more important than the music. Dearest of all were the domestic joys and virtues which it evoked in a mood of pleasant melancholy. "How strange to think of the millions who have sung, and listened to that song," remarked Caroline Chesebro', a domestic sentimentalist. "Soft voices have sung it, and many tears have fallen in joy, or hope, or pure determination."[1] It was not strange, however, that the household gods should be worshiped in a society controlled by women. As Mrs. Stowe had declared in *The Minister's Wooing*, the Christian home was the "appointed shrine for woman, more holy than cloister, more saintly and pure than church or altar. . . . Priestess, wife, and mother, there she ministers daily in holy works of household peace. . . ."[2] To this feminine world with home as its all-engrossing center, the domestic novelists made their chief appeal. Mobilized to defend and to extol the household virtues, battalions of women novelists advanced, and gained such numbers and influence

[1] C. Chesebro', *The Children of Light* (New York, 1853), p. 205.
[2] *The Minister's Wooing*, pp. 567-568.

that by the middle of the century they completely dominated the field.

The domestic novels in which these writers sought to glorify the American home were as limited in scope as the narrow sphere of interests of the women readers for whom they were designed. "It is seldom that her wishes cross the limits of the domestic circle which to her is earth itself, and all that it contains which is most desirable," Fenimore Cooper noted of the American wife. "Her husband and children compose her little world, and beyond them and their sympathies, it is rare indeed that her truant affections ever wish to stray."[3] Domestic fiction records few instances of discontent with this circumscribed life. The "new woman" who entertained ambitions outside the family circle was regarded as "the moral horror of the time." "We do not therefore counsel our young friends to nourish a spirit of enterprise," advised Miss Sedgwick, "nor of necessity, even to enlarge the plain and natural circle of their duties."[4] That these duties were narrow enough is made clear in *The Linwoods*. "I often say," the author declared, "all a woman need know is how to take good care of her family and of the sick."[5] To the "feeling wife" such a career was full of compensations. "My life, for many years, has been a life purely of the affections," confessed Mrs. Montrose in *The Lofty and the Lowly*. "I have read little, thought little, and felt—oh how much!"[6] Home was viewed not only as a place in which to prepare for Heaven, but as a foretaste of Paradise itself. "What place this side Heaven, besides *home*," asked the author of *The Sunny South*, "a home of love and confidence, resembles Paradise above?"[7]

Nothing is quite so characteristic of these domestic novels as the numerous pictures which they present of the joys of family life. So great was the authors' zeal to provide these hearth-side tableaux that they sometimes lost track of their

[3] *The Crater*, II, 89.
[4] C. M. Sedgwick, *Married or Single?* I, vii.
[5] C. M. Sedgwick, *The Linwoods* (New York, 1835), II, 19.
[6] McIntosh, *The Lofty and the Lowly*, I, 24.
[7] Ingraham, *The Sunny South*, p. 433.

stories. "The book is rather a series of domestic pictures than a sustained narrative," admitted T. S. Arthur in *The Mother*. "This latter character could not have been given it without a sacrifice of much that the author wished to present."[8] The same apologia might have prefaced many of these novels with their sketches of family christenings, weddings, funerals, reunions, and quiet evenings at home. All shades and tints were employed by the novelists to heighten the attractions of such family gatherings. Mrs. Hentz owned to a partiality for "a soft rich mezzotinto" by which she gave her domestic vignettes "a subdued tint." It is through this gentle medium that we are allowed to glimpse the household of Robert and Julia in which "The hearth-light has softened into harmony with the moonlight lustre of the lamps."[9] More popular were canvases crowded with details after the fashion of Dutch paintings. "I shall never forget the pretty group collected about the little room," wrote Mrs. Seba Smith in *Riches Without Wings*. "Mr. Cleveland was seated by his wife's work-table, entirely absorbed in a book he was reading. Mrs. Cleveland was engaged at her needle, and apparently listening and responding to the conversation of her father-in-law, a venerable looking gentleman, who would instantly suggest an image of one of the patriarchs of old. George and Mary were engaged in a suppressed frolic with little Edward. . . ." Of such scenes the author might well exclaim, "All was order and rational happiness."[10] Even the frolic of the children was decorously suppressed.

The old homestead, aching with sentimental memories of lost sweetness, became a popular subject for panegyrics in domestic fiction. Its familiar pattern was destined to become a cherished part of the folk imagination. There it stood in novel after novel: its broad barns bursting with yellow grain, its wide chimneys suggesting friendly hearthstones and long winter evenings. Cool parlors, clean dairies, cosy kitchens, graceful

[8] *The Mother*, p. iii. Published as the third part of *The Three Eras in a Woman's Life* (Philadelphia, 1848). [9] *Robert Graham*, p. 173.
[10] Elizabeth Oakes Smith, *Riches Without Wings* (Boston, 1838), p. 18.

well-sweeps, sunny meadows, pleasant orchards—all these were heavily freighted with memories kept alive by widely scattered sons and daughters who were forced to live in dusty cities. Well defined, too, were such familiar figures as the venerable patriarch conducting family worship or presiding proudly at family dinner, the stalwart sons and buxom wives, their rosy children, and the faithful hired man. Little wonder that they were able to weave a spell strong enough to perform domestic miracles.

The power of the simple, homestead virtues to transform the lives of those members of the family who had been hardened by contact with the world is the theme of more than one novel. In Cornelius Mathews's *Chanticleer*, the Peabody home became a veritable moral sanatorium for the cure of its wayward sons and daughters. To its hospitable roof for a Thanksgiving reunion came the city-wise William, coldly selfish and arrogant; the stiff-necked daughter, Mrs. Carrack, who brought two liveried servants to wait upon her; a prodigal son who had wasted his substance; and a foppish son-in-law. Less promising subjects for reform would be difficult to imagine, but under the benign influence of homespun honesty and home-cooked food, pride vanished almost as quickly as the Thanksgiving turkey. William, awed by the happiness of his parents, vowed to treat his wife more kindly and burned a mortgage which had "so often disquieted his visits to the old homestead." Mrs. Carrack's "Beacon Hill look" thawed before home fires until she consented to establish the contrite prodigal in a respectable business. Even the dandyish Tiffany Carrack lost some of his airs and condescension. Credit for this wholesale regeneration was shared by "blind Sorrel," the old family horse, whose cries of death agony drew the newly transfigured family to the stable where they were "bound still closer together by so simple a bond as a common sympathy in the death of the poor old blind family horse. . . ."[11] Although not all families stood in so dire need of its curative properties, the virtues of the old homestead were sung in countless novels. "Thanksgiving!"

[11] C. Mathews, *Chanticleer* (New York, 1856), p. 127. [First edition, 1850]

exclaimed the author of *Meadowbrook*. "How many reminis-
cences of the olden time does that word call up, when sons
and daughters, they who had wandered far and wide, whose
locks, once brown and shining with the sunlight of youth, now
give token that the autumnal frosts of life are falling slowly upon
them, return once more to the old hearthstone, and, for a brief
space, grow young again amid the festive scenes of Thanksgiving Day."[12] In face of feelings as strong as these, great was the
storm of protest at attempts by new owners to alter or raze the
old property. "Tear it down! . . . Tear the old homestead
down! don't do it!—don't do it, friend," cried Jacob in *Fashion
and Famine*, after a long absence from his boyhood home.
"There are people in the world who would give a piece of
gold for every shingle on the roof rather than see a beam
loosened."[13]

The priest and priestess in these temples of domestic affections were the husband and wife. A neatly framed marriage
certificate was an *objet d'art* within the means of the poorest
mechanic. "Marriage is the most sacred tie on earth," proclaimed that champion of domestic morality, Mrs. E. D. E. N.
Southworth. "The peace of families, the social welfare of the
whole community, depend upon its being held so."[14] "Did
not Adam *ask* for Eve? and is isolation anything but the sin
of incapacity?" challenged the author of *Victoria*.[15] The
answering chorus of affirmation left no room for doubt. "It is
never wise to run counter to the institutions of Providence,"
counseled Miss Sedgwick. "Marriage is the first and greatest
of these, the central point, whence all the relations of life ra-
diate, the source of all political and social virtue."[16] T. S.
Arthur found it difficult to restrain his indignation at a comfortable bachelor who hesitated to marry. "Does not your heart
become chilled at the soul-revolting idea," he demanded in

[12] Holmes, *Meadowbrook*, p. 22.
[13] A. S. Stephens, *Fashion and Famine* (Philadelphia, n.d.), p. 102. [First edition, 1854]
[14] *The Mother-in-Law* (New York, 1851), p. 167.
[15] C. Chesebro', *Victoria* (New York, 1856), p. 184.
[16] *Married or Single?* II, 81.

Married and Single, "that all the noble deeds and good influences of a Washington would have been lost to this nation and to the world, if his father had acted the strange, unnatural, criminal part you propose to yourself?"[17] If happiness outside the bonds of wedlock was criminal for man, it was the unpardonable sin for woman. "Old maidhood is a wretched, pitiable condition, to which the most unhappy marriage would be vastly preferable, as life, though wretched, is better than annihilation,"[18] asserted Burdett in *Blonde and Brunette.* "Fanny Fern" had little patience with those who objected to woman's loss of independence in marriage. "What is this modern clamor about 'obedience' in the marriage relation?" she asked in *Rose Clark.* "How easy to 'obey' when the heart can not yield enough to the loved one! Ah, the chain can not fret when it hangs lightly!"[19] The heroine of Timothy Flint's sentimental romance, *Francis Berrian,* had the same message. "Foolish girls, this talk is all stuff," she told those who believed in single blessedness. "Be married to worthy men as soon as possible. I have experienced more enjoyment in a day since marriage, than in a year before."[20] Mrs. Hale found the formula for happiness to be simple. "The marriage ceremony is the most interesting spectacle social life exhibits," she wrote in *Northwood.* "Be constant, man; be confiding, woman, and what can earth offer so pure as your friendship, so dear as your affection!"[21] Amid the rapidly shifting standards of American life, the institution of marriage alone seemed steadfast. "Blessed be God!" cried Maria McIntosh thankfully in *Charms and Counter-charms,* "that there are some human ties into which His blessings has infused a Divine principle of life."[22] Even those who had been momentarily misled by the Mormon practice of polygamy were made to repent their folly. "Always, always, my voice shall rise in defense of one love, constant through life, and faithful in death," vowed the penitent Sarah

---

[17] T. S. Arthur, *Married and Single* (New York, 1854), p. 13. [First edition 1843]

[18] *Blonde and Brunette,* p. 179.   [19] Parton, *Rose Clark,* p. 230.

[20] *Francis Berrian,* II, 257.   [21] *Northwood,* p. 105.

[22] M. J. McIntosh, *Charms and Counter-charms,* p. 297.

in *Mormon Wives,* "one home—one father and mother for the children—one joy on earth—one hope in heaven."[23] T. S. Arthur, that arch foe of the celibate as well as the inebriate, produced the most compelling argument for the married state. "If I refuse, from mere ends of personal ease, to enter into this orderly state," he warned, "I cannot be happy, and, of course, cannot enter heaven."[24]

Marriage was the most important, but only the first of many duties urged upon women in domestic fiction. Once led across the threshold of her home, she was expected to stay there. "You ought not only to love home, but you ought to be the abiding corner-stone of home," the author of *Letters to the Joneses* exhorted all American wives. "Your husband's house is not home without your presence and your presidency."[25] Sentimental bachelors musing before their comfortable hearths had the same advice. "I know it is the fashion now-a-days with many, to look for a woman's excellencies, and influence,—away from her home," wrote Donald Grant Mitchell in *Dream Life,* "but I know too, that a vast many eager, and hopeful hearts, still cherish the belief that her virtues will range highest, and live longest within those sacred walls."[26] Fenimore Cooper warned that activity outside of the family circle invariably led to "a sacrifice of womanly character and womanly grace." "The person who would draw the sex from the quiet scenes that they so much embellish," he cautioned in *The Ways of the Hour,* "to mingle in the strifes of the world; who would place them in stations that nature has obviously intended men should occupy, is not their real friend."[27] Susan Warner's domestic classic *Queechy,* which was frequently mentioned for the coveted honor of being "the great American novel," inculcated sound principles upon this much discussed topic. "One woman will learn more wisdom from the child on her breast than another will learn from ten

[23] M. V. Fuller, *Mormon Wives* (New York, 1856), p. 316.
[24] *Married and Single,* p. 12.
[25] J. G. Holland, *Letters to the Joneses* (New York, 1864), p. 265.
[26] *Dream Life* (New York, 1851), pp. 181-182.
[27] *The Ways of the Hour,* p. 406.

thousand volumes," the author declared. "A woman's true sphere is in her family—in her home duties, which furnish the best and most appropriate training for her faculties—pointed out by nature herself."[28] Few would have denied the order of importance given to woman's duties by Mrs. Hentz in *Ernest Linwood*. The glory of God, the happiness of her husband, and the comfort of her home—these she proclaimed as the aims of true womanhood.[29]

Domestic novelists sought to exalt the dignity of the housewife's position. "Every married woman in good health should keep her own house," counseled Mrs. Hale. "It is a sacred office from which she has no right to shrink; it is a part of her married covenant—it gives dignity to her character."[30] Housekeepers were urged to emulate the heroine of *Rena* who found poetry in pans, sermons in suds, and good in everything. "Rena was very fond of the poetry of the kitchen," wrote Mrs. Hentz, "such as the beating the whites of eggs, till they foamed like the cascade of Sunny Dell."[31] Miss Sedgwick invoked the great heroines of world literature to dignify the housewife's lot. "If our young ladies want the examples of heroines to redeem domestic offices from their vulgarity, to *idealize* the housewife," she suggested in *Live and Let Live,* "let them remember Andromache, and Desdemona, and sundry others."[32] The more elegant "female accomplishments" suited to the parlor were held to be mere frippery unless accompanied by dexterity in the kitchen. "She is a beautiful butterfly in society, sipping the honeyed nothings of existence," scoffed Cora Mayfield in *Elmwood,* "but place her in a quiet home with the sober truths of life whispered in her ear, how soon the dust would be removed from her beautiful wings, bereaving her of her all."[33] The helpless bride, who was given to dabbling in poetry rather than pastry, became a frequent object lesson. "I felt at that moment as if I would have given up all my French, German, and every

---

[28] *Queechy,* II, 72.   [29] *Ernest Linwood,* p. 225.
[30] *Keeping House and Housekeeping* (New York, 1845), p. 39.
[31] *Rena* (Philadelphia, 1851), p. 199.
[32] *Live and Let Live* (New York, 1837), p. 92.
[33] C. Mayfield [pseud.], *Elmwood* (Boston, 1856), p. 50.

accomplishment," confessed the mortified Mrs. Lawrence in
Recollections of a Housekeeper, "in exchange for the knowledge which would make me a good housekeeper."[34]

The qualities demanded of the model housewife were little
short of appalling. Accordingly, the novelists endowed their
heroines with the attributes of a Saint Theresa and a Mrs.
Poyser, but even this rare union of faculties was barely adequate for the duties imposed upon many of them. By what
miracle of endurance the heroine of *Queechy* survived her daily
routine is still something of a mystery to readers of that tearful
book. By the most conservative estimate, Fleda performed the
parts of three hired men, cook, dairy manager, nurse, and
teacher. Up before dawn to do the chores and to care for the
livestock, she found time before breakfast to study the latest
agricultural methods by which she turned a run-down farm
into the show place of the county. The produce from her truck
garden commanded the highest prices at market and her new
method of haying resulted in the banner crop of the year. In
addition to the cares involved in these enterprises, she blacked
the boots of her numerous guests, revived the drooping health
of an ailing family, and improved her mind by reading and
study. Her leisure moments, which were necessarily limited,
were spent in dodging the persistent efforts of the villainous
Thorn, who devoted his full time to plotting her seduction!
Domestic paragons of Fleda's stamp abound in the novels of
Susan Warner. Ellen, the heroine of *The Wide, Wide World,*
faced a daily ordeal hardly less arduous than Fleda's. "She had
made her old grandmother comfortable; she kept the peace
with Nancy; she had pleased Mr. Van Brunt; she had faithfully served her aunt."[35] Nor were all these tasks accomplished
at the expense of other pursuits. "Mamma, she beats me entirely in speaking French," conceded a less versatile associate,
"and she knows all about English history; and arithmetic!—
and did you ever hear her sing, mamma?"[36] The phenomenal

[34] C. Packard [pseud.], *Recollections of a Housekeeper* (New York, 1834), p.
115.
[35] S. Warner, *The Wide, Wide World* (New York, 1852), II, 92.
[36] *Ibid.*, II, 152.

success of *The Lamplighter,* which on one occasion moved Hawthorne to profane comment, was due in part to the appeal of Gerty. Her capacity for work seemed without limit. The feeble Uncle True, the blind Emily, the crazed Mr. Cooper, the ailing Mrs. Sullivan, and the brutal Nan Grant, all received regular ministrations of mercy from the heroine and blessed her with their last breaths. Equally expert at saving souls and scouring kitchens, Gerty persuaded the giddy Miss Graham to abandon her dissipated life, and made comfortable the last moments of the villain who had turned her out into a blizzard when she was a child.[37] Mrs. Stowe found the explanation of such superhuman endeavors in *faculty,* a virtue indigenous to New England homesteads. "To her who has *faculty* nothing shall be impossible," she wrote in *The Minister's Wooing.* "She shall scrub floors, wash, wring, bake, brew, and yet her hands shall be small and white; she shall have no perceptible income, yet always be handsomely dressed; she shall have not a servant in her house,—with a dairy to manage, hired men to feed, a boarder or two to care for, unheard of pickling and preserving to do,—and yet you commonly see her every afternoon sitting at her shady parlor-window behind the lilacs, cool and easy, hemming muslin cap-strings, or reading the last new book."[38]

Even when blessed with *faculty,* most wives found their lot a difficult and frequently an unhappy one. Submissive endurance was constantly preached as the highest feminine ideal. Griselda and Penelope, not Cleopatra and Clytemnestra, were held up as models of wifely conduct. "Of course! It's their lot," admitted Mrs. Evelyn in *Queechy.* "Affection always leads a true woman to merge her separate judgment, on anything, in the judgment of the beloved object."[39] Gabriella's uncomplaining conduct under the most unreasonable treatment from her husband was lauded by Mrs. Hentz as a model for all suffering wives to follow. "You dare not murmur," she wrote sympathetically, "you will be the forbearing, gentle wife, who promised to *endure all.* . . ."[40] Miss Sedgwick added her

---

[37] Cummins, *The Lamplighter,* pp. 209-210.
[38] *The Minister's Wooing,* pp. 2-3.
[39] Warner, *Queechy,* II, 134.   [40] *Ernest Linwood,* p. 327.

garland of praise for the meek submission of Mrs. Harrison to her husband's arrogance: ". . . if the maidenly reserve that 'never tells a love,' is the poet's eloquent theme," she wrote in *Redwood*, "the matronly virtue that conceals the want of it, is certainly far more deserving of the moralist's praise."[41] This doctrine of passivity required the bravest of fortitude. "Such is the heroism often demanded of woman—," declared Maria McIntosh, "the heroism of the martyr not the soldier."[42] "Fanny Fern" insisted that the number of these mute, but glorious, martyrs, whose silent suffering bulks so large in the pages of fiction, was small compared to those to be found in actual life. "Ah! could we lay bare the secret of many a wife's heart," she lamented in *Ruth Hall*, "what martyrs would be found over whose uncomplaining lips the grave sets its unbroken seal of silence."[43] Young wives were urged to resort to a bit of casuistry when their principles were at variance with those of their lords. "Oh, young and lovely bride," Mrs. Gilman exclaimed, "watch well the first moments when your will conflicts with his to whom God and society have given the control. Reverence his *wishes* even when you do not his *opinions*."[44]

Sweet wifely submission was an ideal of conduct nurtured by those who taught that woman's charm lay in her winning helplessness. "Woman winds herself about the heart of man by her tenderness, nay, by her very dependence," observed Cooper in *The Heidenmauer*, "in a manner to effect that which his pride would refuse to a power more evident."[45] This was indeed what every woman knew long before J. M. Barrie reminded her of it. The ideal woman was nobly planned to obey, not to command. "She is woman, perfect woman—," wrote John Neal in *Keep Cool*, "helpless, lovely, and shrinking as a sensitive plant, at a breath—that is, she is what woman *should* be."[46] Cooper's heroines were given to flattering the

---

[41] C. M. Sedgwick, *Redwood* (New York, 1824), I, 153.
[42] *The Lofty and the Lowly*, I, 71.   [43] Parton, *Ruth Hall*, p. 36.
[44] C. Gilman, *Recollections of a New England Bride and of a Southern Matron* (Philadelphia, 1852), p. 384.
[45] *The Heidenmauer* (Philadelphia, 1832), II, 40.
[46] *Keep Cool* (Baltimore, 1817), I, 66.

superior strength of their men. "I should almost despise the man," Anna Updyke told Dunscomb in *The Ways of the Hour,* "who could consent to live with me on any terms but those in which nature, the church, and reason, unite in telling us he ought to be the superior." The male response was typical enough. "Well, Anna, this is good, old-fashioned, womanly sentiment," he replied, "and I will confess it delights me to hear it from *you.*"[47] Fenimore Cooper frequently reminded his "female" readers where the source of their true strength resided. "If women thoroughly understood how much of their real power and influence with men arises from their seeming dependence," he noted in *The Sea Lions,* "there would be very little tolerance in their own circles for those among them who are for proclaiming their independence and their right to equality in all things."[48]

This seeming dependence was an incense peculiarly grateful to man's sense of superior strength. Feminine novelists knew full well that many husbands shared Angelo's ambition in *The Children of Light.* "I would be the sun of my domestic world —nothing less," he decreed complacently. "My wife, to use a poet's comparison, should be the moon, whose light must reflect from me."[49] Miss Sedgwick was able to classify every heroine either as "a lean-to" or as "a go-ahead."[50] The former group was by far the larger; it was compounded, she wrote, "of amiability, docility, and imbecility," and invariably captured the best prizes in matrimony. In marriage, these domestic novelists recognized only one law, the survival of the unfittest. Man was viewed as "a noble structure," woman as a lovely "vine." "He must be a pillar of strength on which I can lean and cling round in the storms of life," confided Eoline. "Round this marble pillar of strength the wild-vine of sensibility must twine, the eagle must bear the myrtle in its talons, and the dove carry the laurel to its downy nest."[51] Mrs. Hentz was careful to provide her heroines with suitable pillars in all

[47] *The Ways of the Hour,* pp. 204-205.
[48] *The Sea Lions* (New York, 1849), I, 214.
[49] Chesebro', *The Children of Light,* p. 238.
[50] *Married or Single?* II, 121.   [51] Hentz, *Eoline,* p. 74.

of her novels. The happiness of Julia in *Robert Graham* was held up as a model: "So modest and unobtrusive, so delicate and sensitive, so childlike and yet so womanly, she twined herself round the rougher frame of his character, like the slender tendrils of the vine, whose fibres, at first so frail and light as to be agitated by a breath, become strong and inflexible as oak."[52] The need for "leaning" or "clinging" was explained by Mrs. Stephens as an inborn trait of the feminine nature. "Women were born to look upward with their hearts and cling to others for their support," she wrote in *The Old Homestead*. "Men were made to give this support. You cannot change places and be happy!"[53] The heroine of *The Match Girl* told her faithless lover that woman's existence from the cradle to the grave was one of dependence: "When lying on her mother's breast, she gazes so trustingly on the first face she learns to know, the holy love of a mother guides her; till comes the love of her life, her destiny, her lover, and far holier still than her lover, her honored husband."[54] Few women felt this dependence to be galling; on the contrary, it was represented as affording one of the chief delights of married life. "O, then, of course, we should yield to the sterner sex," concluded the sentimental Julia in *Here and Hereafter*. "It is delightful to feel a sweet dependence upon stronger natures, so like the vine and the oak, you know. The vine is never self-asserting."[55] So thoroughly admired was this "clinging-vine" theory of feminine conduct that some novelists found it praiseworthy for their heroines to cling to anything, even though the pillar were shoddy or the oak rotten at the core. "And though he had become like an oak, defective even to the heart," wrote the author of *Alow and Aloft*, "yet her feelings, like a vine, still twined themselves around him, seeking to hide each blemish, and unwilling to relinquish their grasp. . . ."[56] Mrs. E. D. E. N. Southworth employed a different image, but her approval of Alice Garnet's deportment was complete. "I often compared her to the dove,"

---

[52] Hentz, *Robert Graham*, p. 70. [53] *The Old Homestead*, pp. 413-414.
[54] [Anon.,] *The Match Girl*, p. 392.
[55] F. W. Pike, *Here and Hereafter* (Boston, 1858), p. 49.
[56] Frink, *Alow and Aloft*, p. 20.

she remarked in *The Discarded Daughter,* "folding her wing over her mortal wound, to hide it from all eyes."[57]

Although the ideal of clinging helplessness continued to receive the admiration of most authors, there were those who were bold enough to point out its dangers. In *Charms and Counter-charms,* Maria McIntosh described it as "a self-indulgent passiveness" which played havoc with Evelyn Beresford, whose fate was to cling not wisely, but too well.[58] The chameleonlike conduct of the heroine of *Two Lives* cost her dearly, for she sacrificed her individuality by assuming the mood of everybody with whom she associated: "She was, in consequence, what the objects of her affection—we had almost said, what the associates of the hour—made her . . . full of all sweet domestic affections when nestling at her uncle's side; she was with Mrs. Elliot, the gayest flutterer in her morning drive or evening assembly."[59] Inevitable, too, were many trials for those whose lives had a small portion of independent happiness. "She has woven the tendrils of her soul around many props," declared Mrs. Sigourney of Jane Harwood. "Each revolving year renders their support more necessary. They cannot waver, or warp, or break, but she must tremble and bleed."[60] Novelists exhausted their store of similes in attempting to symbolize the relationship between husband and wife. Sun and moon, oak and vine, eagle and dove, lion and lamb—these were repeated with wearisome monotony until even those who shuddered at the mention of woman's rights began to resent the reiteration of the weakness and helplessness of their sex. Women had become little more than attractive, but plastic clay in most of these domestic tales. "She is in your hands; make of her what you will," a mother in *The Heiress of Greenhurst* told her prospective son-in-law, "a gazelle or a tiger, the thing you call an angel, or the thing you fear as a fiend. That which you make her she will be, a blessing or a curse, which will cling to you for ever and ever."[61] Caroline Chesebro' was

[57] *The Discarded Daughter,* II, 20.
[58] *Charms and Counter-charms,* p. 121.   [59] McIntosh, *Two Lives,* pp. 47-48.
[60] *The Intemperate and the Reformed* (Boston, 1843), p. 15. [First edition, 1833]
[61] Stephens, *The Heiress of Greenhurst,* p. 107.

indignant at the implications of such an attitude to woman. " 'Flower-crowned victims to be offered up to the human lords of creation.' The idea!" she scoffed. "They have a way of smoothing over that fact; but, as the writer means to say, this is the bare truth."[62] A similar protest was lodged by Miss Sedgwick. "I would have every woman, in her own place, maintain her dignity," she declared warmly, "and not submit to those little domestic wrongs and tyrannies of 'your very good men,' which are vestiges of the dark ages."[63] The heroine of Augusta Evans's *Beulah* repudiated angrily the "clinging-vine" ideal as an affront to her sex. "Don't talk to me about woman's clinging, dependent nature. You are opening your lips to repeat that senseless simile of oaks and vines; I don't want to hear it; there are no creeping tendencies about me," she protested. "You can wind, and lean, and hang on somebody else if you like; but I feel more like one of those old pine trees yonder. I can stand up. . . . I feel humbled when I hear a woman bemoaning the weakness of her sex, instead of showing that she has a soul and mind of her own, inferior to none."[64]

Whatever difference of opinion existed about the propriety and dignity of clinging to a stronger nature for support, there was little doubt that it was woman's destiny to sacrifice herself freely for the happiness of others. Mrs. Stowe's heroine in *The Minister's Wooing* had been taught "that there was no feeling so strong but that it might be immediately repressed at the call of duty. . . ." "Self-denial and self-sacrifice had been the daily bread of her life," she wrote of Mary Scudder. "Every prayer, hymn, and sermon, from her childhood, had warned her to distrust her inclinations, and regard her feelings as traitors."[65] The same lesson was an important element in the education of most domestic heroines. "The self-sacrificing spirit is always strong," affirmed Mrs. Hentz in *Eoline*. "There is a sustaining power given to those who are willing to sit in darkness that others may have light—to walk on thorns—that others may tread a path of roses."[66] This theme of self-abnegation was re-

[62] *The Children of Light*, p. 33.
[63] *Married or Single?* I, 153.　　　　[64] *Beulah*, pp. 136-137.
[65] *The Minister's Wooing*, p. 511.　　[66] *Eoline*, p. 196.

ceived with relish by readers of fiction in all periods. In *The Rise of Silas Lapham,* Howells had Bellingham marvel at its popularity: "I suppose you can't put a more popular thing than self-sacrifice into a novel. We do like to see people suffering sublimely."

A favorite motif was the anguished withdrawal of a lover in favor of a less worthy rival. "I will hold no possession too valuable, no feeling too powerful, no hope too dear to be relinquished," asserted Isabella, whose love for Falconer upset Grace's plans, "if her happiness demand the sacrifice."[67] Novelists were unable to resist the temptation to extract every drop of sentimental suffering from so fertile a source. Thus in *Cousin Maude,* the author not only visited upon her heroine a stroke of total blindness, but demanded that she give up her betrothed to a more fortunate sister. "I know you are beautiful, my sister," Maude cried at the approach of the bridal hour, "and if a blind girl's blessing can be of any avail, you have it most cordially."[68] Mrs. Southworth showed her customary adroitness in devising methods to torture her self-sacrificing heroines. In *The Mother-in-Law,* Susan Somerville was not content with resigning the man she loved to her best friend; she also insisted upon serving as bridesmaid at the wedding: "She went, but who could compute the trials of that young heart, when, to save her friend from the mere possibility of uneasiness, she declined to avail herself of the chance of escape, and resolutely determined to be present at the marriage of Louis, the funeral of her own hopes."[69] Even greater capacity for self-punishment was shown by Kate in *The Curse of Clifton,* who rushed in to nurse her dangerous rival who was stricken with "the confluent small-pox."[70] This penchant for self-effacement was by no means confined to Mrs. Southworth's female characters. Theodore Harvey, hopelessly in love with the heroine of *Virginia and Magdalene,* derived a melancholy satisfaction in officiating at her wedding to his successful rival. His appetite for martyrdom whetted by this agonizing ordeal,

[67] McIntosh, *Two Lives*, p. 96.   [68] Holmes, *Cousin Maude,* p. 205.
[69] E. D. E. N. Southworth, *The Mother-in-Law,* p. 71.
[70] E. D. E. N. Southworth, *The Curse of Clifton,* pp. 184-185.

he promptly made possible the marriage of a friend by taking his place in a perilous missionary expedition to the depths of India.[71]

The lack of restraint to be found in all these sentimental novels is nowhere so apparent as in the refinements of torture undergone by the willing victims of self-sacrifice. Richard Delafield, the disappointed suitor in *Meadowbrook,* found it necessary to add to his pangs by presenting his beloved Rosa with the bridal gown in which she was to become the wife of his rival "as a token of the *esteem* he should ever feel for her!"[72] When the rivals were both generous there frequently ensued such an engrossing contest to determine which of the two should sacrifice himself that the lady herself was in grave danger of being forgotten. Thus Duncan and Howard Leslie, the noble brothers in love with Annie, "each resolved, out of regard to the other, to endeavor to conquer his attachment." "Between these two determined self-sacrificers," observed the author of *Here and Hereafter,* "the prospect was of some suffering to Annie, provided she was interested in either."[73] As if her feelings of disappointed affection were not sufficiently poignant, the heroine of *Tempest and Sunshine* asked for the dubious privilege of decorating the rooms for her sister's wedding to the man of whose love she had been cheated. "The hangings and drapery . . . were as white and pure as was she who so patiently worked on," wrote Mrs. Holmes, "while each fresh beauty added to the room pierced her heart with a deeper anguish, as she thought what and whom it was for."[74] Novelists never wearied of embroidering the theme of self-sacrifice with exquisite variations. A favorite method of inducing an extra twinge of gratuitous suffering was to have the luckless suitor hasten his rival's marriage by paying his debts. Robert Grahame felt a sad pleasure in sending forty thousand dollars to his competitor who was more successful in love than in business.[75] James De Vere, in *Cousin Maude,* varied the formula

[71] E. D. E. N. Southworth, *Virginia and Magdalene*, p. 153.
[72] Holmes, *Meadowbrook*, p. 296.   [73] Pike, *Here and Hereafter*, p. 241.
[74] M. J. Holmes, *Tempest and Sunshine* (New York, 1855), p. 291. [1854]
[75] McIntosh, *The Lofty and the Lowly*, II, 145.

by paying the expenses of the wedding and establishing the happy pair in business.[76] Sentimental heroines were equally generous, although few were able to match the gift of twenty thousand pounds which Catharine bestowed upon her rival in *Mary Derwent*. "The pang with which I received the invitation to that wedding was keener than any pain death will bring," she confessed bravely, "but I will give no tokens of the anguish that consumed me. It was strange, but I felt a kind of gladiator's pleasure in goading my heart on to madness—a stern, unrelenting love of self-torture. I resolved to be present at the marriage."[77] Fenimore Cooper's common sense prevented him from allowing Mabel Dunham to sacrifice herself and the happiness of her lover because of an earlier promise to her father to marry Natty in *The Pathfinder*. He followed the conventional formula, however, in *Afloat and Ashore* and in *Miles Wallingford*. In these novels the author exhausted every possibility of sentimental appeal while the broken-hearted Grace died of a lingering decline. Her bequest of twenty thousand dollars to the unprincipled lover who had betrayed her affections is in the well-established tradition of sentimental romance.[78]

This genius for self-sacrifice sometimes led to sensational scenes. Of this sort was the decision of Lady Granby to give herself to a savage Indian rather than see Murray's family perish at the stake. "It was a sublime sacrifice, which every true man must regard with homage," declared Mrs. Holmes, "—an act of chivalric humanity of which few women, and scarcely a man on earth, would have been capable."[79] No less fortitude was demanded of Sophy in *The Deserted Wife*, who learned on her wedding night that she had been united to a lunatic whose former wife had drowned herself in despair. Her friends' advice to have the marriage annulled was spurned indignantly. "The Lord has given me something to do for His sake," she replied truthfully, "and endowed me with strength

---

[76] Holmes, *Cousin Maude*, p. 161.   [77] Stephens, *Mary Derwent*, p. 109.
[78] This theme becalms the action in both novels. See *Afloat and Ashore*, II, chaps. xii-xv; and *Miles Wallingford*, chaps. i-x.
[79] Stephens, *Mary Derwent*, p. 211.

to do it."[80] Little Gertie, whose apparently limitless capacity
for work made her a favorite of thousands of readers of *The
Lamplighter,* also had a marked predilection for martyrdom.
Trapped on a burning steamboat, she first attended to the
rescue of her blind companion and then offered what she believed to be the last chance of escape to the selfish Bella, her
unscrupulous rival for Willie's affections.[81] Few characters
were immune from the contagion. Hobomok, the noble savage
in Mrs. Child's romance of Salem Colony, gloried in his role of
a copper-colored Enoch Arden when he discovered that his
wife's betrothed lover, who was believed dead, had returned.
In the debate in which both men generously volunteered to
leave the scene, it was Hobomok who triumphed. "You have
seen the first and last tears that Hobomok will ever shed," he
declaimed as he bestowed Mary upon his English rival. "Hobomok will go far off among some of the red men of the west.
They will dig him a grave, and Mary may sing the marriage
song in the wigwam of the Englishman."[82]

The impulses which prompted self-abnegation were rarely
free from the taint of exhibitionism and of a selfish indulgence
in the feelings. As Mrs. Stephens remarked in *Mary Derwent,*
self-immolation was often compounded of tender sweetness and
mournful pleasure, a subtle blend always attractive to the sentimentalist. The unwholesome scene in *Richard Edney* in
which the dying Junia "relinquished" Richard to her successful
rival, Melicent, was an emotional orgy dignified by the author
under the name of sublime self-sacrifice. "I love his happiness;
and his happiness is your love . . . I am his bride, but through
you," she told Melicent. "My love for him I give to you." As
the ecstatic girl awaited the approach of death, she attired herself in the bridal gown and veil which she had prepared for

[80] E. D. E. N. Southworth, *The Deserted Wife,* pp. 128-129.

[81] Cummins, *The Lamplighter,* p. 411.

[82] L. M. Child, *Hobomok* (Boston, 1824), pp. 174-175. Mrs. Child's heroines
were especially gifted at the popular game of throwing themselves away for others.
Lucretia's tribute to the heroine of *The Rebels* (Boston, 1825) is a fair sample: "I
never saw one who had such power to curb and endure. If she doubted the firmness
of a man's principles, or feared her father's disapprobation, she could tear an image
from her heart, if every fibre bled at the parting."

her wedding with Richard. This unusual shroud, she explained to Melicent, was worn "for marriage with the ideal vision which your union with him is to my mind." After all of this, Melicent could only inquire, naturally enough under the circumstances, "Art thou a mortal?"[83] Not every heroine, of course, was capable of the subtle metaphysical refinement which accompanied Junia's martyrdom. Most domestic novelists, however, seemed to find a peculiar glory in the sacrifice of two lives for one. William Dean Howells devised an appropriate label for this popular absurdity. He called it "Slop, Silly Slop."

Popular, too, was the cult of the child. The sentimental faith in natural virtue and in virtuous simplicity gave a new significance to childhood. Children were not only to be seen in the pages of domestic fiction, they were also to be heard with the prayerful attention befitting messengers from Heaven. Little Eva and Mary Morgan were the captains of a large host of infant martyrs and evangelists who pointed the way to reform on earth and happiness beyond the grave. Their lot was an arduous one. Novelists pressed them into service to rescue families from divorce, to cheer the poor and to nurse the sick, to soften flinty hearts, and to convert strong men from atheism to the true faith. More often than not, their sole reward was an early, if not a painful death, for a cherished article in the sentimental creed is that the good die young.

In view of this always strenuous and often fatal part assigned to children, it is hardly surprising that large families were depicted with admiration and delight. "A mother, encircled by healthful sporting children, is always a beautiful spectacle," announced Miss Sedgwick in Hope Leslie.[84] Novelists were fond of describing broods of youngsters "all so near alike in age and size, that one might liken them to a flight of steps."[85] Cradles were endlessly rocking. "The parlor, that home room of the house," as Mrs. Pearson called it, was invariably teeming with children. Every household in these

[83] Judd, Richard Edney, p. 428.
[84] Hope Leslie (New York, 1827), I, 103.
[85] Rush, The North and South, p. 30.

novels seemed to be either in a state of excited preparation for an addition to the family or in a condition of exhaustion as the result of it. "The Barclays had now been married fourteen years," wrote the author of *Home,* "and their seventh child was six weeks old . . . of course there was always a baby in the family."[86] This family, however, was not notably prolific. John Phealan's attitude to the size of the ideal family was that of most fathers. "We leave that with the Lord," he remarked comfortably, "if they come they'll find a welcome."[87]

Parents, moreover, were taught to regard their offspring as angel visitants. "Into every household angels may enter," declared T. S. Arthur. "They come in through the gate of infancy, and bring with them celestial influences. Are there angels in your household? If so, cherish the heavenly visitants."[88] The belief that it was the child rather than the parent who was best fitted to impart instruction was echoed in many novels. "Children are God's messengers," wrote the author of *Married or Single?* "Woe to the mother whom they do not persuade to rectitude!"[89] "Fanny Fern" devoted some of her most lyric passages to praise these infant philosophers. "Blessed childhood!" she caroled in *Ruth Hall.* "The pupil and yet the teacher, half infant, half sage, and whole angel! what a desert were earth without thee!"[90] Sentimental logicians were always ready to point out the blessings of children to those poverty-stricken families unblessed by other riches. "What would the poor and lowly do, without children?" asked Mrs. Stowe. "This is one of the roses of Eden that the Lord has dropped down expressly for the poor and lowly, who get few enough of any other kind."[91]

The sentimental belief that the child was purer and more virtuous than the adult was widely accepted. Mrs. Hentz hailed every infant as an ambassador from Heaven: "The incarnation of innocence, sweetness, and grace; fresh from the

[86] C. M. Sedgwick, *Home* (Boston, 1837), p. 50 [First edition, 1835]
[87] *Ibid.,* p. 68.
[88] *The Angel of the Household* (Philadelphia, 1854), p. 5.
[89] Sedgwick, *Married or Single?* II, 77.
[90] Parton, *Ruth Hall,* p. 92.   [91] *Uncle Tom's Cabin,* I, 257-258.

hands of its Creator, before temptation has obscured, or sin marred or passion darkened the image of the Deity; it comes before the world-weary eye, a flower sparkling with the dews of Paradise, and breathing the fragrance of Heaven."[92] George William Curtis, in *Prue and I,* lamented the speed with which the child's early intimations of immortality were lost. "Maturity is the gate of Paradise, which shuts behind us," he observed sadly, "and our memories are gradually weaned from the glories in which our nativity was cradled."[93] Even the unlettered hero of *The Newsboy* was well versed in the popular doctrine. He cheered a band of street urchins by reassuring them that they were surrounded by heavenly influences. "Children are nearest heaven, you may be sure of that," he stated. "Bad men and women, whose crimes make them afraid in the night time, have no fears if they can have an innocent child to sleep with them, for the angels come wherever the child is. . . ."[94] Many adults, harassed by the cares of the world, found a welcome escape in pleasant dreams of regression into childhood. "O! happy, innocent days of childhood!" exclaimed William Lundley in *Durham Village,* who was only one of many who "willingly would have stept back into its purity, and been once again a child."[95]

The child, trailing clouds of glory, was hailed as Heaven's most persuasive minister to man. Lydia Maria Child, whose Greek romance *Philothea* contained much sound New England moral doctrine, had Artaphernes tell Eudora "that children are a bridge joining this earth to a heavenly paradise, filled with fresh springs and blooming gardens."[96] Cynics like Flavel in Catharine Sedgwick's *Clarence,* who was distrustful of all religious teachers, had "nothing to resist in the ministry of children." "He would yield himself to their simplicity and truth, and feel their accordance with the elements of Christian instruction."[97] The numerous conversions wrought by the in-

[92] *Rena,* p. 40.
[93] G. W. Curtis, *Prue and I* (New York, 1899), pp. 202-203. [First edition, 1856]
[94] Elizabeth Oakes Smith, *The Newsboy* (New York, 1854), p. 163.
[95] Lynn, *Durham Village,* p. 5.
[96] *Philothea* (Boston, 1836), p. 251.   [97] *Clarence,* I, 44.

tervention of children in these domestic novels gave point to the conclusion reached by the author of *Here and Hereafter*. "Verily, I believe we draw nearer to our Father," she wrote, "when we give ourselves up to the holy influences of innocent childhood."[98]

Novelists were shameless in their enlistment of children to bring about the happy endings which crown most domestic tales. When selfishness threatened to destroy the peace of the Linwood family, it was little Rosalie who appeared on the scene to avert the catastrophe. "That little child had opened a channel in which our purified affections flow together towards the fountain of all love and joy," announced the happy mother. "Its fairy fingers are leading us gently on in the paths of domestic harmony and peace."[99] Elise, accurately described by the author as "a guardian angel, lent to keep sacred the marriage vow," performed the same service in *Married or Single?* "For the sake of our child," pleaded the errant wife, "let us maintain friendly relations, and live decently in the world's eye."[100] Infant intervention cooled the fever of revenge aroused in a wronged husband in *Robert Graham*. "Like the delicate steel web that surrounds the flame of a safety-lamp, imprisoning with its slender fibres the fire-sparks whose escape may be death," wrote Mrs. Hentz, "the holy charm of infant innocency wove a spell too pure, too strong for one ray of passion to penetrate."[101] When not engaged in preventing duels and divorces, these paragons of pygmy size assumed a heavy burden of household cares. Thus when Rossitur failed in business, the heroine of *Queechy* became "a very Euphrosyne; light, bright, cheerful, of eye and foot and hand; a shield between her aunt and every annoyance that *she* could take instead; a good little fairy, that sent her sunbeam wand, quick as a flash, where any eye rested gloomily."[102] These juvenile wonder-workers performed their miracles in so many households that there is little wonder that Mrs. Stowe could write: "It is as if heaven had an

[98] F. W. Pike, *Here and Hereafter*, p. 217.
[99] Hentz, *Ernest Linwood*, p. 467.
[100] Sedgwick, *Married or Single?* I, 231.
[101] *Robert Graham*, p. 96.   [102] Warner, *Queechy*, I, 241.

especial band of angels, whose office it was to sojourn for a season here, and endear to them the wayward human heart, that they might bear it upward with them in their homeward flight."[103]

Little Eva was certainly made to resemble an unearthly creature with a form "such as one might dream of for some mythic and allegorical being." She possessed other ethereal attributes. Her hair "floated like a cloud" and her "violet blue eyes" shone with "deep spiritual gravity." She walked "with an undulating and cloud-like tread," the author continued. "Always dressed in white, she seemed to move like a shadow through all sorts of places, without contracting spot or stain . . . ."[104] Few of the little ones in domestic fiction were without at least one supernatural power. Many of them were dowered with magic attractions produced by animal magnetism. Mrs. Southworth boasted that Virginia at the tender age of ten showed signs of unusual promise, for she was able "to bring the bright rays of her golden-fringed eyes into an intensely brilliant focus. . . ." This precocious charmer was not unaware of her potent appeal. "Oh! I'm a galvanic battery to those I love!" she lisped proudly.[105] As physiognomists they rivaled the experienced professors of that popular art. "Children are the keenest physiognomists—," asserted the author of *Clarence,* "never at fault in their *first loves.*"[106] There was hypnotic power even in the most casual infant caresses. In *Charms and Counter-charms* it proved strong enough to reclaim a cynical atheist. "That clinging baby-touch, that soft baby-voice, had exercised a magic power over the heart of Euston Hastings," reported Maria McIntosh, "awakening the first pure, unselfish love he had ever known."[107]

These beautiful and effectual angels raised a disturbing question in the ranks of the orthodox. If children shared the purity of Eve before the Fall, it was clear that they stood in little need of baptism. The problem was made acute by the

[103] *Uncle Tom's Cabin,* II, 65.   [104] *Ibid.,* I, 211-212.
[105] E. D. E. N. Southworth, *Virginia and Magdalene,* p. 50.
[106] Sedgwick, *Clarence,* I, 138.
[107] *Charms and Counter-charms,* p. 395.

fact that an appalling number of them died in infancy. "It has been stated," declared Dr. Nehemiah Adams in *The Baptized Child*, "that one-half of all that are born, die within three years."[108] If the good die young, as most sentimentalists believed, then these infant paragons were unmistakably doomed. Mrs. Stowe described the symptoms pointing to early dissolution. "When you see that deep, spiritual light in the eye,— when the little soul reveals itself in words sweeter and wiser than the ordinary words of children—," she wrote ominously, "hope not to retain that child; for the seal of heaven is on it, and the light of immortality looks out from its eyes."[109] These infallible signs of fatal goodness were all too common among children in domestic fiction. The champions of the doctrine of Original Sin were in full cry. Dr. Adams gravely warned all parents that the need of infant baptism was not precluded even by the striking evidences of religious forwardness such as Mrs. Stowe had described. He was ready with an answer to every objection. Will the baby embarrass his parents by squawking in church? "The cry of a child under such circumstances in the house of God," he replied pleasantly, "should never be thought of, either by parents or spectators, but with the same kind of feeling with which we may suppose its Maker hears its voice in His temple."[110] Sylvester Judd insisted that the newborn child presented a problem with far-flung implications which lifted it above all considerations of theological creed or dogma. "Who is it? whose is it? what is it? where is it?" he asked humbly. "It is in the centre of fantastic light, and only a dimly revealed form appears. It may be Queen Victoria's or Sally Twig's. It is God's own child, as all children are . . . it will aspire to the Infinite, whether that Infinite be expressed in Bengalee or Arabic, English or Chinese. . . ."[111]

Whatever shades of opinion existed about the need of regeneration and baptism for children, all agreed that it was the duty of parents to give their offspring proper "principling."

---

[108] *The Baptized Child* (Boston, 1842), p. 29. [First edition, 1836]
[109] *Uncle Tom's Cabin*, II, 65.
[110] *The Baptized Child*, p. 42.   [111] *Margaret*, pp. 3-4.

Even the much admired domestic affections were insufficient security against moral disaster unless they were disciplined by what Miss Sedgwick called "the control and regulation of principle." Sensibility, Fancy, Imagination, Impulse, and Enthusiasm—these were dangerous in the extreme without "principles." It is clear that "principling" was another name for the inculcation of sober-suited reason and prudence. "Helen is, I am sorry to say, wanting in principle," lamented the author of *Elmwood,* "that is, she is not actuated by any ruling motive of right in her conduct. She acts entirely from impulse."[112] Your proper heroine, on the other hand, was especially adroit in steering a prudential course between her feelings and her judgment. She was urged to follow the example of Emma in the same novel, who knew to a nicety just when to permit "a little burst of enthusiasm" to penetrate "the thick lattice work of her rationality."[113] Thus in *Resignation,* when Eliza found herself not unnaturally becoming interested in a romantic stranger who had saved her from plunging to death over the side of a bridge, "She checked the increasing tenderness, with a determined effort," the author wrote in admiration, "for she had learned that *principle,* not *feeling,* should govern the Christian. . . ."[114] Cooper's terrifically decorous heroines derived their perfection from firm "principling." In *Precaution* there are repeated admonitions from Mrs. Wilson that sentiments, no matter how generous, can never effect "what can only be the result of good principles."[115] Cooper also warned against the perils in store for females whose Fancy was stronger than their Principles. "Jane Moseley had a heart to love, and to love strongly," he admitted in his first novel. "Her danger existed in her imagination; it was brilliant, unchastened by her judgment, we had almost said unfettered by her principles."[116] Most important of all were religious principles. They prevented Mary Pratt, the heroine of *The Sea Lions,* from giving her hand to the man she loved until he was ready to acknowl-

[112] Mayfield, *Elmwood,* p. 136.
[113] *Ibid.,* p. 134.   [114] Evans, *Resignation,* I, 71.
[115] *Precaution* (New York, 1820), II, 115.
[116] *Ibid.,* II, 83.

edge the existence of her God. "Most females would have lost
the sense of duty which sustained our heroine in this severe
trial, and, in accepting the man of their heart, would have
trusted to time, and her own influence, and the mercy of
Divine Providence, to bring about the change she desired," the
author noted proudly, "but Mary Pratt could not blind herself
to her own high obligations."[117]

Once these principles were implanted and nurtured properly at home, a world of temptations was powerless to undermine them. "It is difficult to spoil a human being entirely,"
prophesied Mrs. Stephens, "who has spent the first ten years of
life under pure domestic influences."[118] The trials which beset
most heroines were calculated to put to a severe test even the
strongest principles. Julia's sound upbringing in *Fashion and
Famine* stood her in good stead later so "that neither the close
neighborhood of sin nor the gripe of absolute want had power
to stain the sweet bloom of a nature that seemed to fling off evil
impressions as the swan casts off waterdrops from its snowy
bosom, though its whole form is bathed in them."[119] It is not
surprising that suitors first made sure of the principles of their
young ladies before proposing marriage. Captain Stuart comforted his mother in *Two Lives* by declaring that he regarded
Grace "With the tenderest interest, . . . —an interest which wants
only confidence in her principles to become the most trusting
love."[120] "Alas for Grace!" exclaimed Maria McIntosh, for her
waltzing violated "feminine gentleness." "Her soul," she continued, "drew its life not from the great Source of Being, but
from human sources, from the impure fountains of earth."[121]
Woe betide the girl who could confess with Brighty in *The
Mother-in-Law*, "A bundle of fine sentiments have I, instead of
good principles."[122] This everlasting concern with rules of
conduct resulted in an unattractive prudishness in many heroines. The modern reader finds himself in hearty sympathy
with Mrs. Layton in *Clarence*. "I always shudder when a girl,

[117] Cooper, *The Sea Lions*, I, 144.   [118] *The Old Homestead*, p. 282.
[119] Stephens, *Fashion and Famine*, p. 283.
[120] McIntosh, *Two Lives*, p. 130.   [121] *Ibid.*, p. 84.
[122] E. D. E. N. Southworth, *The Mother-in-Law*, p. 45.

minus twenty, begins to talk of principles," she complained.
"Spare me! spare me the virtue, that is weighed in the balance,
and squared by the rule."[123]

The domestic novelists were educationalists; when they
were not teaching their own children, they taught those of
other people. Fiction was welcomed as providing a sweetened
form of tuition. "His object has been to present leading principles," explained T. S. Arthur in *The Mother*, "partially
brought out into life to give them a force beyond a mere
didactic enunciation—from which every thoughtful mother
may deduce rules for specific application in her own family."[124]
The first of these principles was that women in general and
mothers in particular were the best teachers. "The Bible, history, experience, all show the mighty influence of the mother's
teachings," Mrs. Hale proclaimed in *Northwood*. "The religion of the household and of society is mainly woman's."[125]
Hardly less important was the repeated insistence upon the
value of example rather than precept. "Home was the school
in which they were to be taught," counseled Miss Sedgwick in
The Poor Rich Man, ". . . and their parents were *to set them
the copies* which they were to follow."[126] Most novelists urged
that the course of instruction be planned to combine the useful
and the ornamental. "Our young ladies are taught French,
Italian, drawing, music, etc., and let them be; these are the
ornaments and luxuries of education," wrote the same author
in *Live and Let Live*, "but let not the *necessaries* be omitted—
the staff of domestic life sacrificed."[127]

These novels bristled with pedagogical hints. Parents were
advised to allow no opportunity to pass without using it to
further the education of their young. Mr. Harvey's example
was held up for imitation. This father never took his children
for a walk without visiting a jail, a tavern, an almshouse or a
cemetery. "In this way," wrote the author of *Harvey Boys*,
"Mr. Harvey explained every thing to his children, and scarcely
ever cut up a dish at table, without having something to show

[123] Sedgwick, *Clarence*, II, 119.   [124] *The Mother*, p. iii.
[125] *Northwood*, p. 402.   [126] *The Poor Rich Man* . . . , p. 96.
[127] Sedgwick, *Live and Let Live*, p. iii.

them of the joints or bones or muscles of the animals."[128]
Guests at the Butler household often found conversation somewhat difficult under the educational system in vogue there.
"You must excuse the interruption," Mrs. Butler apologized.
"We have taught our children, whenever any place is named,
to which anything important is attached, to resort to their
maps, to learn its geographical situation."[129] The hero of *Say
and Seal* was an ardent advocate of such methods and enjoyed
dropping nuggets of information in everybody's lap. He welcomed a long period of convalescence as a chance to give his
youthful nurse an orientation course in general science. He began with "a very particular account of the whole process of
circulation," reported the authors, "thence diverging right and
left . . . passing from the bright crystal points of chymistry to
the blue mould on a piece of bread, and then explaining to her
the peculiar mechanism of a fly's eye."[130] The lecturer's skill
and erudition were suitably rewarded by marriage to his fair
pupil whose education continued to be a joy to all concerned.
Little orphan Ellen, the heroine of *The Wide, Wide World*,
achieved her remarkable temperament by being subjected to
the exhortations of a self-appointed faculty of her friends.
Thus she learned the truths of religion from the Reverend John
Humphreys, manners and diction from Miss Alice, domestic
economy from Aunt Fortune, and tolerant good humor from
Van Trump. Susan Warner was not guilty of overstatement
when she remarked that "Ellen's sweetness of temper was not
entirely born with her; it was one of the blessed fruits of religion and discipline."[131]

The use of the rod in training the young provoked an expression of all shades of opinion. Mrs. Gilman admitted there
was much to be said on both sides, but went on record as
favoring "a rational, well-managed rod."[132] Miss Sedgwick, on
the other hand, was an antiflagellationist. Her model teacher

[128] Hall, *Harvey Boys*, p. 8.   [129] *The Beacon!* p. 9.
[130] Susan and A. B. Warner, *Say and Seal* (Philadelphia, 1860), I, 279.
[131] Warner, *The Wide, Wide World*, II, 153.
[132] *Recollections of a New England Bride and of a Southern Matron*, p. 358.

in *Home* believed "whipping, and all such summary modes of punishment, on a par with such nostrums in medicine as peppermint and lavender, which suspend the manifestation of the disease, without conducting to its cure."[133] "Fanny Fern" demanded that whipping be outlawed in all public schools. "Let every parent satisfy himself or herself, by *personal inspection,* with regard to these things," she urged. "Many a grave now filled with moldering dust would have been tenantless, had parents, not trusting to showy circulars, satisfied themselves on these points. . . ."[134] "Do not parents, by their own pride and ignorance, often prick their children, and then whip them for crying?" asked Sylvester Judd in *Margaret.* This transcendental novelist's solution of the problem of discipline was impressive even though it may not have been immediately practicable for the schoolroom. "We would encompass our children by the influence of the Good and the Beautiful, which is all they can, primordially, understand of God," he suggested. "Let their characters have an imperceptible development, like rose buds."[135]

The follies of a too fashionable education proved an attractive text for preachments in domestic fiction. Novelists seemed never to tire of contrasting the effects of genteel boarding-school training with the more solid fare provided in common schools. "Thus while Carrie and Anna were going through the daily routine of a fashionable boarding-school," wrote Mrs. Holmes in *'Lena Rivers,* "Lena was storing her mind with useful knowledge, and though her accomplishments were not quite so showy as those of her cousins, they had in them the ring of the pure metal."[136] Sentimental heroines found themselves ill at ease in the company of their superficial friends. "How do you expect to pass current in society," Gabriella was asked in *Ernest Linwood,* "without being able to hang on the instrument as I do, or creep over it with mouselike fingers as most young ladies do?"[137] Graduates of the finishing schools

---

[133] *Home,* p. 26.
[134] Parton, *Rose Clark,* pp. 50-51.   [135] *Margaret,* pp. 441-442.
[136] M. J. Holmes, *'Lena Rivers* (New York, n.d.), p. 108. [First edition, 1856]
[137] Hentz, *Ernest Linwood,* p. 160.

were usually represented as a languishing lot. "Rosabelle Wimpole was a tall willowy-looking girl, who seemed all a-droop," described the author of *Henrietta Harrison*. "Immensely long ringlets, intermixed with downward flowers, dangled down her cheeks and over the front of her neck. . . . Her eyes were half closed in a perpetual languish, and her lips half open as if to exhale a perpetual sigh."[138] Such accomplishments were for the parlor, not the pantry. Mrs. Sarah Hale found them to be a blight upon good housekeeping. Mrs. Harley's graces, which had appeared to be so captivating during the courtship, proved to be of little comfort after marriage. "She painted in water colours, and played upon the piano; she could imitate a mezzo-tint engraving exceedingly well, and make a wax japonica far more superb than a real one . . . ," Mrs. Hale conceded in *Keeping House and Housekeeping,* but added bitterly that she was "so exquisitely sensitive, that plain house-hold affairs could not be discussed in her presence."[139] Wise suitors looked for qualities of a more durable kind. Eudora thus found herself an old maid because "Her whole time, when the most valuable and lasting impressions may be made upon the character, had been spent in *acquiring*." As a result, the author of *The Contrast* concluded sadly, "At eighteen, she came out, a prodigy of accomplishments; at twenty-four, an automaton."[140] Against the claims of the more fashionable boarding schools, D. P. Thompson urged the advantages offered by the public schools. These, at least, he argued, were not conducted by broken-down dancing masters and second-rate elocutionists who too often posed as professors of elegant literature. "Even those ultra-genteel families who had only patronized the select or private school system," he observed in *Locke Amsden,* "now sent in their children, and began to open their eyes to the solid advantages to be obtained from the common schools, under well qualified instructors."[141]

[138] E. Leslie, *Henrietta Harrison* (Philadelphia, 1838), pp. 215-216. Published with *Althea Vernon.*

[139] S. J. Hale, *Keeping House and Housekeeping,* pp. 20-21.

[140] H. F. Lee, *The Contrast* (Boston, 1837), p. 27.

[141] D. P. Thompson, *Locke Amsden* (Boston, 1847), p. 203.

Domestic novelists were not permitted to rest content with offering up paeans of praise to the hearth-side virtues. The Christian home, built upon the solid rock of matrimony and defended by the household sentiments, was a castle perilous threatened on every side with dangerous foes. The city was their spawning ground. In the metropolis the young bride was tempted to forsake the simple duties of home for the cowardly conveniences of a tawdry boardinghouse. Seducers lurked behind every lamppost. The saloon and gambler's den beckoned to the husband by night; French dressmakers and gossip-mongers made overtures to his spouse by day. Wet nurses and charge accounts might be had for the asking. Bills accumulated and men decayed. "No doubt, that with hearts warm and true, we may have a *fireside* in town," admitted the author of *Elinor Wyllys,* "but *home* with its thousand pleasant accessories—*home,* in its fullest meaning, belongs especially to the country."[142] There was no dissenting voice at Ingraham's pronouncement that man was not made for towns. "Adam and Eve were created and placed in a garden," he submitted. "Cities are the results of the fall."[143] All right-thinking men knew that cities were death on the sentiments, on household virtues, and on family life. Even street urchins were made to observe in the habits of insects a striking symbol of the way nature abhorred town life. "I saw how the dragonfly loves the city, but the butterfly avoids it," noted a newsboy to his companions of the gutter, "and I could see a reason why it should be so."[144]

The country village was pictured as the one sure abode of pure, marriageable girls. In a sentimental interlude in Mitchell's *Dream Life,* the successful hero, surfeited with worldly pleasures, returned to marry his boyhood village sweetheart and spend the rest of his days in the country. The city was allowed no attractions not to be found on the farm. "The excitements of the country are under-rated," asserted Miss Sedgwick. "The changes of the seasons, the rising and setting of the sun, droughts and floods, a good crop, a blight,—frosts

[142] S. F. Cooper, *Elinor Wyllys,* I, 44.
[143] *The Sunny South,* p. 434.   [144] Smith, *The Newsboy,* pp. 7-8.

and showers, are all excitements."[145] Even funerals were ordered somewhat better beyond the city's limits. "I love to see the general sympathy manifested, when one is carried to his last home," wrote Mrs. Smith in *Riches Without Wings.* "Every green lane, every dell, and every hillside sends forth its inhabitants to the sad ceremony."[146] Country ways were better, too. Rose Lee's family in *Meadowbrook* were not pleased with their city aunt who "breakfasted in her own room at ten, dined at three, made or received calls until six o'clock, went to parties, soirees, or the theatre in the evening, and seldom got to bed until two o'clock in the morning; a mode of living which was pronounced little better than heathenish by grandma, who had long been anxious for an opportunity of 'giving Charlotte Ann a piece of her mind.'"[147] Country visitors were not impressed with the urban pleasures so highly praised by their city cousins. Magdalene confessed that she was nauseated by her "winter in town, which *smells* so of lamp oil and musk, which they call light and perfume, as if it were sunshine and violets! and *tastes* so of rancid cream and stale eggs, disguised with essences, which they call 'ices!' and *looks* so like Vanity Fair!"[148] City folk, on the other hand, were immediately moved to rapture when they breathed the tonic air of the rural districts. Mr. Bleecker, dissipated and bankrupt by urban luxuries, found blessings in barnyards, sermons in silos, and good in everything. His discouraged wife also turned over a new leaf, while her regenerated husband "took the kindly teaching of the woods and fields, seed-time and harvest, to his heart."[149] City children were commonly viewed with commiseration and alarm. "Oh, it is a blessed thing to live in the country . . . ," cried the author of *The Belle of Washington.* "But in the city, from infancy, children are taught that the great end and aim of life is to attract admiration; consequently, they become selfish."[150] Mrs. Ellison in *Resignation* spurned a fabulously

[145] *Home,* p. 117.
[146] *Riches Without Wings,* p. 64.   [147] Holmes, *Meadowbrook,* p. 24.
[148] E. D. E. N. Southworth, *Virginia and Magdalene,* p. 80.
[149] A. E. B. N. Haven, *Out of Debt, Out of Danger* (New York, 1864), p. 244. [First edition, 1855]
[150] N. P. Lasselle, *The Belle of Washington* (Philadelphia, 1858), p. 166.

large city fortune for the privilege of bringing up her daughter in the country. "She wished to educate her children at a distance from the thoughtless multitude," the author wrote approvingly, "in that tranquil shade where the buds of virtue, sheltered from the scorching sun of earthly splendour, and the blighting frosts of fashionable apathy, expand and bloom for the genial clime of heaven."[151]

Slothful wives doubtlessly existed in farmhouses, but they were not tempted by the advertisements of genteel apartments in which to surrender their domestic duties. "They had not far to look for a boarding-house," a friend of a recently married couple complained, "for signs denoting such are almost as thick here as lawyers' shingles are in Philadelphia."[152] "There is a wretched and unhappy custom in vogue, for young married couples to go to a hotel or boarding-house!" deplored Ingraham. "It is a miserable life, garish, hollow, artificial, love-killing, heart-withering life, this boarding for young couples! . . . Keep house—if only in one room!"[153] "Fanny Fern's" description of the establishment in which her impoverished heroine was forced to live was paralleled in scores of novels: "In a dark, narrow street, in one of those heterogeneous boarding-houses abounding in the city, where clerks, market-boys, apprentices, and sewing girls, bolt their meals with railroad velocity; where the maid-of-all-work, with red arms, frowzy head, and leathern lungs, screams in the entry . . . where one plate suffices for fish, flesh, fowl, and dessert; where soiled table-cloths, sticky crockery, oily cookery, and bad grammar, predominate; where greasy cards are shuffled, and bad cigars are smoked of an evening, you might have found Ruth and her children."[154] Even the solace of a quiet deathbed was denied those who chose to reside in boardinghouses. In *Mabel Vaughan*, Mrs. Leroy lay dying "while doors banged loudly and hurried foot-steps tramped across the marble floors, and voices shouted from the halls below, and bells rang in angry rivalry from every quarter of the building, and heaven and

[151] Evans, *Resignation*, I, 21.
[152] Judson, *The Mysteries and Miseries of New York*, III, 98.
[153] Ingraham, *The Sunny South*, p. 489.   [154] Parton, *Ruth Hall*, p. 139.

earth seemed alike contentious . . . where an imprisoned soul sought to burst its tenements of clay. . . ."[155] Mrs. Hale's *Boarding Out* was devoted to a melancholy recital of the misfortunes suffered by the Barclay family as a result of their removal from a comfortable home to an apartment hotel. Domestic discord, dissipation, bankruptcy, and the death of their favorite child followed hard upon each other. Peace was restored only after the harassed family established a home of their own.[156] The hero of *Blonde and Brunette* offered a simple recipe for married happiness: avoid "in-laws" and "boardinghouses." "He preferred the Parisian garret, with the wife's own little *ménage,* however humble it might be, to the most fashionably splendid boarding-house in Gotham."[157] Mrs. Stahle needed but a few days to discover inconvenience and immorality. "I found it quite impossible to get anything I wanted . . . one is necessarily circumscribed in a boarding-house," she observed in *Rose Clark,* "the cellar may not be visited for coal, or the kitchen for water, if the landlady does not see fit to have the bells answered." These things might have been endured, but the landlady also happened to be "a vile procuress."[158] Husbands of high principles were eloquent upon evils of this kind. "For never, will I carry a bride of mine, to make her home in a fashionable hotel," vowed Ernest Linwood. "I would as soon plunge her in the roaring vortex on Norway's coast."[159]

Married life in the bedlam of a boardinghouse was, at least, married life. Divorce was raised to a worse eminence in the catalogue of domestic evils. "Like almost any other unperverted woman," wrote Mrs. Southworth in *Shannondale,* "she felt that any sort of a life *with* her husband, was better than any sort of a life *without* him.[160] Cooper numbered divorce laws as among the most hated of the "improvements" which threatened to destroy time-honored institutions. "Nowadays nothing is easier," he complained, "than to separate a man from

[155] M. S. Cummins, *Mabel Vaughan* (Boston, 1858), pp. 323-324.
[156] S. J. Hale, *Boarding Out* (New York, 1846), pp. 128-129.
[157] Burdett, *Blonde and Brunette,* p. 235.
[158] Parton, *Rose Clark,* p. 246.   [159] Hentz, *Ernest Linwood,* p. 232.
[160] E. D. E. N. Southworth, *Shannondale,* p. 141.

his wife, unless it be to obtain civic honours for a murderer."[161] The heroine of *Retribution* discovered to her dismay that her admired John Milton had penned a tract urging divorce. "But I do not admire Milton with all my former enthusiasm," she confessed, "since I find that he has written a work advocating polygamy, and defending divorce. Polygamy! Divorce! What spots upon the sun of his glory. Oh! no, no, no; I can not admire the great luminary now as formerly."[162] Although these novelists conceded reluctantly that the hour for loving sometimes did not coincide with the proper person to love, they refused to sanction divorce as a solution. "Whence can there come a power of divorce?" asked Hammond in John Neal's *Errata*. "There is no such power. A marriage, lawfully had, must be forever. . . ."[163] To those who objected that this might entail needless suffering, Miss Sedgwick was ready with a facile answer. "If he, who, ignorant of his pilot, goes to sea in a ship, unseaworthy and without ballast, deserves the wreck he meets, surely those who enter into the most sacred, complicated, and hazardous relation of life rashly," she replied, "deserve the chastisement they provoke."[164]

Family life was attacked from without by the temptations of city life and by divorce; it was also seriously threatened by even more insidious disturbers of domestic peace from within. Not the least of these was *the new woman* who was beginning to question the maxim that her place was in the home. "We now have women-poets, women-sentimentalists, women-statesmen, women-historians, women-preachers, and women-doctors, *et id omne genus*," bewailed a contributor to *Knickerbocker's* in 1855, "and the cry is, 'still they come.' "[165] Emancipated wives like Mrs. Grayson were disillusioning their husbands. "Domestic happiness! quiet of home!" she answered to his entreaties. "Why, my dear, these are old phrases—obsolete in

---

[161] *The Crater*, I, 30. Cooper's fear of the passage of unwise divorce legislation is also reflected in *The Ways of the Hour*, p. 28.
[162] E. D. E. N. Southworth, *Retribution*, p. 63.
[163] *Errata* (New York, 1823), II, 161.   [164] *Married or Single?* I, 18.
[165] *Knickerbocker's Magazine* (New York, 1855), XLV, 525.

this age of progress and refinement."[166] The new woman, however, was not entirely without her champions. Mrs. Kirkland ventured her opinion that "there is no telling a bookish woman anymore, even in her house-keeping. There are no more cobwebs in literary parlours than elsewhere."[167] Mrs. Hentz also hazarded the heretical view that while the home of the intellectual woman was likely to resemble "the eyrie of the eagle, lofty, but bleak," the nest of her old-fashioned sentimental sister, "though pleasant and downy in the sunshine, will furnish no shelter from the fierce storms and tempestuous winds of life."[168] What was needed, she observed to Gabriella, was a compromise. The sentimental generation was certainly familiar enough with such counsel.

Many were the flies which hovered over the domestic ointment. Bungling servants were among the most irritating of these. "Every house-keeper has experienced what is called *a breaking season,*" wrote a sufferer, "when the centre of gravitation seems shaken, as far as crockery is concerned."[169] Mrs. Ashley in *Elmwood* bore witness to the startling amount of damage in a short period. "Why, that cook has broken three seventy-cent pudding dishes, four large pitchers, ten pie plates and the handles off of three butter-boats, during the last six weeks," she charged, "to say nothing of the dishes she has *cracked.*"[170] China was the least valuable of the things broken; domestic tranquility was not so easily repaired. "It has been stated to me, confidentially," reported an amazed neighbor in *Letters to the Joneses,* "that you have had nineteen different cooks and thirteen chambermaids in your house during the past year."[171] Miss Packard found the situation grave enough to demand governmental interference and control. "It is not below the task of legislation, if legislation is a study of the order and happiness of a community," she remarked, "or if legisla-

[166] Lasselle, *The Belle of Washington,* p. 8.
[167] C. M. S. Kirkland, *A Book for the Home Circle* (New York, 1853), pp. 78-79.
[168] *Ernest Linwood,* p. 225.
[169] Packard, *Recollections of a Housekeeper,* p. 129.
[170] Mayfield, *Elmwood,* pp. 275-276.
[171] Holland, *Letters to the Joneses,* p. 86.

tors would have neat houses, good dinners, and smiling wives."[172] The servant problem, like so many other troubles for the housewife, was largely confined to the cities. Country-women ordered matters more satisfactorily. "I know what's to be done, and most help is no help to me," Mrs. Scudder boasted in *The Minister's Wooing*. "I want people to stand out of my way and let me get done. I've tried keeping a girl once or twice, and I never worked so hard in my life."[173]

Troublesome servants might be dismissed; vexatious mothers-in-law were not to be disposed of so easily. Mrs. Southworth, who created an extraordinarily wicked group of "in-laws" in her novels, devoted a full-length book to the subject. "It seems to me there might be some remedy for this evil," she wrote in *The Mother-in-Law*, "it seems to me that the brightness of the bride's morning should not thus be overcast—the evening of her parent's age not thus left desolate."[174] Many heroines shared the plight of Pauline in *Beulah*. "I love my husband; I would do anything on earth to make him happy, if we were left to ourselves," she sighed. "Oh, tell me what I ought to do to rid myself of this tormenting sister-in-law and father-in-law, and I may say, all of Ernest's kin."[175] The parents of newly married couples seemed to find their own happiness in meddling into the affairs of their children. A separate house did not protect Ruth Hall from her "in-laws" who promptly rented the house next door and when she tried to escape by moving, followed her from one neighborhood to another until they ruined her happiness.[176] Mrs. Southworth's facile solution of the problem was devised to enable harassed couples to avoid their "in-laws" and to have them, too! "There are seldom more than three generations on earth at the same time," she argued

---

[172] *Recollections of a House-keeper*, p. 155. The author further suggested a municipal steam-bar to solve the problem: "What a desideratum is a cooking-establishment, where families can be provided with prepared food . . . now the improvement in steam can give them [meals] hotter than from our own hearths." Cora Mayfield in *Elmwood* hailed a servants' training school as "the signal triumph for housekeepers of the nineteenth century."

[173] Stowe, *The Minister's Wooing*, p. 55.

[174] E. D. E. N. Southworth, *The Mother-in-Law*, p. 64.

[175] Evans, *Beulah*, p. 359.   [176] Parton, *Ruth Hall*, pp. 52 ff.

plausibly, "and it seems to me that houses might be built large enough to accommodate three generations. And how united a family would be then! What permanency, what security, what peace. . . ."[177]

Permanency, security, and peace are not precisely the words to describe a condition of life at the mercy of so many disrupting influences. The long gauntlet of advice through which those about to marry were forced to run was ominous enough in itself to recommend celibacy. Mrs. Gilman warned prospective wives that their future happiness might depend upon keeping clean the wicks of their oil lamps.[178] Other authors pointed to the dangers to domestic peace and personal health in the employment of wet nurses.[179] "I very much doubt," cautioned the author of *Resignation*, "if the nocturnal ball can be attended consistently with virtue or with happiness."[180] Miss Leslie wrote a novel to illustrate the folly of spending too much for pocket handkerchiefs.[181] Stepmothers were even more fatal in their influence than mothers-in-law. "If she were my child," vowed S. A. Southworth, "I'd sooner lay her in the grave, than place her in the hands of a step-mother."[182] *Mr. and Mrs. Woodbridge* was written to show how the road to divorce was paved by nagging and "the everlasting rubbing of petty annoyances."[183] To open a charge account was to close the door upon mutual confidence and love.[184] Ice-saloons, French pastry, and dressmakers invariably unbalanced mother's diet, the family budget, and the husband's temper. "Fanny Fern" recorded her disgust at the "spectacle of scores of ladies devouring, *ad infinitum,* brandy-drops, Roman punch, Charlotte Russe, pies, cakes, and ices; and sipping *parfait amour,* till their flushed

---

[177] *The Mother-in-Law*, pp. 64-65.

[178] *Recollections of a New England Bride and of a Southern Matron*, p. 348.

[179] This was a favorite subject with sentimentalists who insisted that mothers nurse their own children. See McIntosh, *Two Lives*, p. 293, and Pike, *Here and Hereafter*, pp. 360-361.   [180] Evans, *Resignation*, I, 271.

[181] E. Leslie, *Althea Vernon* (Philadelphia, 1838), p. 178.

[182] *Lawrence Monroe*, p. 17.

[183] E. Leslie, *Leonilla Lynmore*, and *Mr. and Mrs. Woodbridge* (Philadelphia, 1847), pp. 98-99. The latter story was published separately at Providence in 1841.

[184] Haven, *Out of Debt, Out of Danger*, p. 37.

cheeks and emancipated tongues prepared them to listen and reply to any amount of questionable nonsense from their attendant roué cavaliers."[185] Sylvester Judd found Parisian styles equally demoralizing. "Can anything exhibit a more 'hideous mien' than Fashion? Madame Laponte threatens a worse evil than Napoleon," he warned in *Margaret*. "She has actually invaded America, and thousands of females have fallen victims to her arts."[186]

One need go no further than the pages of Judd's own novel for the answer. Far more frightful than Fashion was the Seducer. Allow his heroine to describe him: "Scarlet coat, white breeches, Napoleon hat, sparkling black eyes, large black whiskers meeting under his chin, like a muskrat."[187] Permit his victim to tell her story: ". . . Raxman was base and unprincipled. I was horror-struck, stupefied at his conduct, I know not what, I must have fainted and fallen, I only remember being borne into the house. . . . Raxman fled. . . . My father . . . died soon of that disease with which his daughter will ere long follow him, a broken-heart. My mother, always of a delicate constitution . . . she too died. My sister became insane."[188] Differing only in details, this was the story repeated in countless novels. The nineteenth-century follower of Lovelace was able to add a few new tricks to his notorious repertory. Mormonism provided Richard Wilde with a novel approach. "The truth is, Maggie, I have had a vision," he told his victim. "It has been revealed to me what I must do. But before I tell you, you must promise me to be reconciled to the will of the Lord, as revealed by the Spirit to me."[189] The jargon of pseudo science was also made to serve the base purposes of villainy. Euston Hastings half convinced Evelyn that their "souls" might mingle "in a sentiment as tender, as profound, but less exacting, less selfish than love." "Do you forget," he asked, "there is now a chain between our souls by which the thoughts and feelings of each pass to the other with the quickness of the

[185] Parton, *Ruth Hall*, p. 157.
[186] *Margaret*, p. 444.
[187] *Ibid.*, p. 293.
[188] *Ibid.*, pp. 290-291.
[189] Fuller, *Mormon Wives*, p. 211.

electric flash?"[190] These glib advocates of "passional association" were, of course, only the more sophisticated of the in-
triguers. Less gifted seducers were successful enough, however,
with the time-tried ruses which Lovelace had employed. They
were aided by the unfortunate conditions which prevailed in
sweatshops and slums, although even the peaceful countryside
was not immune. Thus the remote hamlets of Maine were
blighted by the oily destroyer of innocence. "The last time I
came this way, a snake was creeping round among these very
flowers," bemoaned Jacob Strong upon his return to his old
homestead. "That snake left poison on everything it touched,
at least in this valley."[191] Few novels were launched without
at least one seducer to darken the pages. Mrs. Stowe yielded to
the convention in *The Minister's Wooing*. "It is one of the
saddest truths of this sad mystery of life," she wrote, "that
woman is, often, never so much an angel as just the moment
before she falls into an unsounded depth of perdition."[192] Nor
could Donald Grant Mitchell resist the temptation to use the
motif in his shadowy and sentimental *Dream Life*. But the
author was content to play gently and felicitously with his
subject, to sit back comfortably while the moth circled the
flame unsinged. All of the thrills of seduction are delectably
suggested without mention of their inconvenient consequences:
"At the first suspicion of his falsity, her dignity and virtue
shivered all his malice."[193] It is perhaps a fair commentary
upon this faded classic to note the absence of passion from a
theme which demanded it. One cannot have one's virtue and
a seduction, too. A reviewer in *Harper's* found in the work of
Mitchell "the most beautiful revelations that can be drawn
from the depths of a rich experience...."[194] But that experience
was limited to sentimental reveries before the snug hearth of a
complacent bachelor.

Carl Van Doren wrote wisely of the domestic novels written
in the sentimental years before the Civil War when he observed

[190] McIntosh, *Charms and Counter-charms*, pp. 82-83.
[191] Stephens, *Fashion and Famine*, p. 97.
[192] *The Minister's Wooing*, p. 232.   [193] *Dream Life*, p. 252.
[194] *Harper's Magazine* (New York, 1851), II, 281.

"that whereas the dime novels were consumed by boys, and meant for them, sentimental romances fell increasingly into the hands of girls—especially of girls molded and approved by American Victorianism." They were written in a tradition firmly established by *Charlotte Temple*. Their tearful classics, Susan Warner's *The Wide, Wide World* and Maria Cummins's *The Lamplighter*, followed the same facile sentimental formula. Each in its turn was hailed by an army of feminine readers as the eagerly awaited "great American novel." Authentic artists like Nathaniel Hawthorne might well ask about the mysterious appeal of these popular books which found their way into the hearts of so many readers and sold by the hundred thousand.

The answer is to be found, perhaps, in the reality of the aspirations which they voiced. It should be remembered, however, that with the possible exception of Mrs. Stowe, these novelists were not realists. They were gentle dreamers like Donald Grant Mitchell and George William Curtis; moralists and teachers like Mrs. Hale and Mrs. Child; sensationalists like Mrs. Stephens and Mrs. Southworth. In general, they were either too much above or too far below life to find the truth. The mirror which they held up to Nature was either concave or convex; the reflection was not that of life itself, but a distortion of it. Here are to be found the compensations in fiction for the coveted values life had failed to give them. Nowhere outside of their books could these women have encountered a delicacy so fastidious and a poetic justice so immutable. Nowhere beyond their pages could womanhood have survived with such glory the fiery ordeals of hot pursuit, hairbreadth escape, and uncomplaining endurance. It would, however, be uncritical to forget that despite their many impossible episodes, these domestic novels did succeed in presenting ideals which were cherished not only by many parents and teachers, but by their pupils and children as well. To the casual reader today, they represent something more than mere literary knickknacks or wax flowers under glass. Their yellowed pages reveal the aspirations and hopes, which in its earnest moments, a generation of readers strove to achieve.

V

STEPPING HEAVENWARD

Religious novels forsooth! Why, what do they teach but this—*this!*—
the very end and aim of all novels; namely, that after a certain portion of
suffering, trial and sorrow, marriage comes about,—marriage with the desired, accompanied by beauty, wealth, rank, etc. etc. *as the greatest earthly
good!* . . . As they are now managed, they are the most pernicious of all
books that appear. And why? Because under the name of religious truth,
we are taught only this, that the most perishable of earthly things are what
the evangelical should hope to be rewarded with, if they persevere through
all the temptations that beset their path. Religious novels indeed!

—John Neal,
Authorship, 1830.

THE SENTIMENTAL era was one of an intense and increasing
religious ferment. Although most men preferred political to
religious activity and willingly delegated the latter to their
wives, religion was too profoundly concerned with public issues
to escape connection with politics. Every temperance and abolition orator tried first of all to prove that his cause was backed
up by Holy Writ. More and more emphasis was being placed
upon the relation of religion to life and many matters funda-
mentally moral were calling imperiously for legislative action.
The restless thirties and forties were also pervaded by an intense individualism which bred strange sects and queer reforms;
emotionalism, moreover, ran rampant, feeding the revivals
and awakenings which "burnt over" large portions of the
country. Signs of interest in spiritual topics were noted everywhere. "On board the ferry-boat," observed John Neal, "they
found the people talking more about revivals, and awakenings,
and the wonderful conversions, and strange behavior of their
friends and acquaintances, than about business or stocks, or the
last European advices."[1] Impressed by the number of new
churches rising on every hand, the author of *Aristocracy* was
moved to declare that "amidst many contending sects, some

[1] *True Womanhood* (Boston, 1859), p. 359.

hypocrisy, and more enthusiasm, pure and vital religion never probably had so great an influence upon any nation."[2]

The jaunty optimism, easy equality, and ebullient self-confidence which swept Jacksonian democracy into the White House also helped to vote Calvinism out of the churches. This gloomy doctrine with its grim insistence that men were born in sin sounded strange at a time when every young shaver was being told he might become president. "The fashion of religion has changed, amazingly . . . since I was a boy," a recent convert testified in *Bubbleton Parish*. "I think some of you liberals have made an improvement,—for I never could see, even when a child, how religion was made any more attractive by hitching on so many scare-crows, and torture-chambers, and hell-flames, and such like."[3] Even stage-drivers were beginning to question the theory of total depravity which was made to appear a bit ridiculous by the innocent face of every baby. "That boy is a beauty . . . ," a coachman remarked of the heroine's child in *Rose Clark*. "I'm beat if any parson could call *him* totally depraved."[4] The old Calvinism, however, was too firmly intrenched to yield without a struggle to the rising tide of liberalism. "We are taught in our earliest years that men are by nature totally depraved," protested Sylvester Judd. "We are in effect instructed to believe every man a villain, a thief, a murderer, at heart; as mean, selfish, and malicious, in his secret conscious purpose. This is the cardinal doctrine of what passes under the name of Christianity. It is annually enforced by hundreds of thousands of discourses from Bishops and Clergy in every part of Christendom."[5]

These doughty defenders of Edwards's logic and Calvinistic dogma were handled roughly by sentimental novelists who proclaimed the excellence of human nature and gloried in the perfectibility of man. Such an upholder of the traditional orthodoxy was the Reverend Julian Rossiter in *Victoria*. "He was less a shepherd than a law-giver and judge . . . ," wrote Caroline Chesebro'. "He forgot, or seemed to forget, that the world

[2] C. R. A. Williams, *Aristocracy* (Providence, 1832), p. 94.

[3] E. W. Reynolds, *Records of the Bubbleton Parish* (Boston, 1854), p. 203.

[4] Parton, *Rose Clark*, p. 114.   [5] *Margaret*, p. 250.

had been redeemed. It was still lying under the darkness of the curse."⁶ The unlovely aspects of the old theology were almost invariably presented. Thus Orestes Brownson pictured a Calvinist pastor as devoting his energies, which were not inconsiderable, to avoiding his personal damnation. "So intent was he upon gaining this end, so eager was he after it," the author charged, "that he rudely dashed against the most sacred relations of private life, hurled husband against wife, wife against husband, parent against child, and child against parent, brother against sister, and sister against brother."⁷ When Mrs. Southworth's villains were not atheists they were very likely to be Calvinists. "All he saw and felt in his religion," she wrote of Adam Hawk, "was original sin, total depravity, the wrath of God. . . . He joyed to think of the final judgment, of the consuming wrath of an Almighty God, of the tremendous fall of the wicked, of the lake that burneth with fire and brimstone. . . ."⁸ In Gilman's fictitious *Memoirs of a New England Village Choir* there is a merry war waged between a Calvinist minister and his rebellious choir-leader who had strong Universalist "leanings." Whenever the good pastor's request for a "bloody" hymn was disregarded by the singers, he retaliated with an ominous prayer, "beginning at the fall, and going through the whole body of divinity . . . dwelling at much length and with peculiar emphasis on the most dreadful realities of the future world." "Of course," added the author, "during the ensuing week, the parish was in an uproar."⁹

Traditional Calvinism fared badly when examined by Yankee common sense and when tested by Yankee experience. "If, says I to myself, I am to be damned," argued the picaresque hero of *The Hypocrite,* "I can't alter my fate by anything I can do; and I therefore may as well be damned for 'a sheep as a lamb,' so I shall follow the bent of my mind, while I present a fair, sly surface to the world."¹⁰ Cooper's Captain Truck

⁶ *Victoria*, p. 122.
⁷ O. A. Brownson, *Charles Elwood* (Boston, 1840), p. 63.
⁸ E. D. E. N. Southworth, *Virginia and Magdalene*, p. 39.
⁹ Samuel Gilman, *Memoirs of a New England Village Choir* (Boston, 1834), p. 148. [First edition, 1829]
¹⁰ [Anon.,] *The Hypocrite* (New York, 1844), pp. 21-22.

brought his nautical logic to bear upon the tenet of predestination while he was waiting to be rescued from a wreck. "That doctrine makes an easy tide's way of life," he calmly reasoned, "for I see no great use in a man's carrying sail and jamming himself up in the wind, to claw off immoralities, when he knows he is to fetch up on them after all his pains. I have worked all sorts of traverses to get hold of this matter, and never could make anything of it. It is harder than logarithms."[11] Crackerbox theologians, speculatively contemplating red-hot stoves in village grocery stores, were fond of bothering the orthodox with doubts about everlasting torment. "For one I must say, my eyes have been opened; I ain't a going to be hood-winked any longer," Pottle announced to Deacon Hadlock in *Margaret*. "I do not believe God is a wrathful being, I do not believe he will keep us in red-hot Hell to all Eternity for what we do in this short life."[12] Conscientious churchgoers were often perplexed by the attempts of their minister to consign man to Hell by predestination and yet, as Fenn remarked, "to worry out barely enough freedom for a man to be decently damned on. . . ."[13] "One Sunday he tells us that God is the immediate efficient Author of every act of will," complained James to Mary Scudder in *The Minister's Wooing*, "the next he tells us that we are entire free agents. I see no sense in it, and can't take the trouble to put it together."[14]

It remained for Mrs. Stowe to present with an understanding sympathy something of the heroism and poetry in the last stand of Calvinism against the incursion of a more liberal theology. The noblest champion of them all, the unforgettable Dr. Samuel Hopkins in *The Minister's Wooing*, gave ample proof of that fine disinterested benevolence which sweetened the lives of many of the old Calvinists. Dr. Hopkins "regarded himself as devoted to the King Eternal," wrote Mrs. Stowe, "ready in His hands to be used to illustrate and build up an Eternal Commonwealth, either by being sacrificed as a lost

---

[11] *Homeward Bound*, II, 9.   [12] Judd, *Margaret*, p. 315.
[13] W. W. Fenn, "The Revolution Against the Standing Order," *The Religious History of New England* (Cambridge, Mass., 1917), p. 130.
[14] Stowe, *The Minister's Wooing*, pp. 72-73.

spirit or glorified as a redeemed one. . . . He who does not see a grand side to these strivings of the soul cannot understand one of the noblest capabilities of humanity."[15] As the daughter of the Reverend Lyman Beecher, Mrs. Stowe was not likely to forget that old-fashioned Calvinists frequently left their austerity in their pulpits; at home they were often the gentlest and most companionable of men. She knew, too, as did no other novelist of the period, the unselfishness of men willing to be damned for the glory of God. "These hard old New England divines were the poets of metaphysical philosophy, who built systems in an artistic fervor, and felt self exhale from beneath them as they rose into the higher regions of thought."[16] These were the eloquent words of one who knew and loved the dusky old Puritan world of her forefathers. One need not agree with Lowell, who placed *The Minister's Wooing* first among her novels, to yield to the power of the rare spell invoked by this tender romance with its delicate love story enacted against a patchwork of the sunshine and the shadow of the theology of an earlier day.

Although Dr. Hopkins's bleak dogmas were softened by the kindness of his heart which overflowed with Christian charity, Mrs. Stowe was well aware of the fact that his crabbed doctrines were doomed. "They differ from the New Testament as the living embrace of a friend does from his lifeless body, mapped out under the knife of the anatomical demonstrator," she declared, "every nerve and muscle is there, but to a sensitive spirit there is the very chill of death in the analysis."[17] Against the new faith in an indwelling divinity, the Calvinistic dogma which had debased man as a vile creature, had no weapons to defend itself. The pages of religious fiction glowed with apostrophes to the divine elements in man's nature. "God himself breathes into us the breath of spiritual life," Judd testified. "This divine afflatus animates the embryon existence. The spirit assumes a material frame-work which it must quit at last. Our souls coming from God return to him. We are ever-living as the Divinity himself."[18] The

---

[15] *Ibid.*, p. 24.
[16] *Ibid.*, p. 25.
[17] *Ibid.*, p. 339.
[18] *Margaret*, p. 243.

intuitive sanctions of Unitarianism were extolled in *Probus* by William Ware, who showed considerable dexterity in weaving Unitarian doctrines into the patterns of his historical narratives. "There are some natures, mother, by the gods so furnished and filled with all good desires and affections," Lucius told Portia, "that their religion is born with them and is in them. It matters little under what outward form and administration of truth they dwell; no system could injure them—none would greatly benefit. They are the family of God, by birth, and are never disinherited."[19] Ware, who was a Unitarian clergyman, has Piso describe a loving, not a wrathful, God: "God is a parent, exercising a providence over his creatures, regardless of none, loving as a parent all, who has created mankind not for his own amusement or glory, but that life and happiness might be diffused. . . ."[20] The author's desire to emphasize the human rather than the Divine nature of Christ led him to sketch the brothers and sisters of Jesus, "sitting or playing around" the dooryard of their dwelling.[21] Not content with this delightful domestic touch, Ware proceeded to burden the mother of Jesus with the usual evening cares of the housewife. "I marvel why my husband and sons come not," she complained to Julian. "It is the hour of supper."[22] Cheered by this intimate glimpse of the home life of the family of Jesus, Julian was not overcome by his first glimpse of the Saviour. "I saw that the language of his countenance was not that of an Angel, nor of a God," he reported later, "but of a man bound, like myself, by the closest ties to every one of the multitudes who thronged him."[23]

From the crumbling strongholds of orthodoxy came a few scattering counterblasts at the new liberalism. "There is Unitarianism," scoffed Eastman in *Aunt Phillis's Cabin*, "that faith would undermine the perfect structure of the Christian religion; that says Christ is a man. . . ."[24] The inability of hide-

[19] *Probus* (New York, 1838), I, 17. Later published as *Aurelian* (New York, 1848).

[20] *Ibid.*, I, 147.   [21] *Julian* (New York, 1841), II, 178.

[22] *Ibid.*, II, 180.   [23] *Ibid.*, II, 325.

[24] *Aunt Phillis's Cabin*, p. 136. Because of its warm social sympathies and the conspicuous part played by its leaders in the Abolition movement, Unitarianism re-

bound conservatives to comprehend the position of liberals who broke with the old order was amusingly indicated in Curtis's *Trumps*. Nancy gave her impressions of a sermon by Dr. Channing to a humorless old deacon. "Have you ever heard him?" she asked Abel Newt. "It seems he is very famous in his own sect, who are infidels, or deists, or pollywogs, or atheists— I don't know which it is. I believe they preach mere morality, and read essays instead of sermons."[25] Augusta Jane Evans paid her respects icily to Theodore Parker in *Beulah,* where the heroine is represented as seeking comfort in Parker's *Discourses*. "Poor famishing soul!" sympathized the author. "What chaff she eagerly devoured. In her anxious haste, she paused not to perceive that the attempted refutations of Christianity contained objections more gross and incomprehensible than the doctrine assailed."[26] Ralph Waldo Emerson was linked with Parker to make a notorious pair of crackbrains. "They mock earnest, inquiring minds with their refined infinitesimal, homœopathic 'developments' of deity," Beulah was warned. "Metaphysical wolves in Socratic cloaks. Oh, they have much to answer for! 'Spring of Philosophy!' ha! ha! they have made a frog-pond of it, in which to launch their flimsy, painted toy-barks . . . Emerson's atheistic fatalism is enough to unhinge human reason. . . . As for Parker, a careful perusal of his works was enough to disgust me."[27] Orestes Brownson found Trinitarianism and Unitarianism both wide of the mark. "The Trinitarian contends for the Deity of the Son and Spirit, and in doing this he overlooks to some extent the fact of God's unity," he protested in *Charles Elwood*. "The Unitarian . . . looks so steadily on this, that he fails to see that this one God exists as a trinity."[28]

The emphasis upon the humanity rather than the divinity of Christ provoked a debate which was carried over into re-

ceived scant respect below Mason and Dixon's line. "Why, it is hardly tolerated at the South," exclaimed the author of this proslavery novel.

[25] G. W. Curtis, *Trumps* (New York, 1861), p. 50. Published serially in *Harper's Weekly Magazine* (April 9, 1859, to Jan. 21, 1860).

[26] *Beulah*, pp. 339-340.

[27] *Ibid.*, pp. 366-367.   [28] *Charles Elwood*, p. 248.

ligious fiction. "Christianity is everything or it is nothing—it is divine, or it is nothing . . . ," reasoned the author of *Letters to the Joneses.* "Is it necessary that I should argue to you the transcendent worth, the divine origin, or the grand claims of that religion which made an angel of your mother, and transformed the little room in which she died into heaven's gateway?"[29] Joseph Holt Ingraham, an Episcopal clergyman, dedicated his once immensely popular *The Prince of the House of David* to the task of establishing the divinity of Christ. The author, who used the epistolary method, frequently resorted to the tactics of a trained debater in summing up his evidence from time to time during the progress of a bulky correspondence. "Now, my dear father," wrote Adina from Jerusalem, "let me sum up the evidences that Jesus is the Messiah. First, his presentation in the Temple. . . . Secondly, the star which led the wise men to Bethlehem. Thirdly, their adoration of him in his cradle. Fourthly, the testimony of John the Baptist. Fifthly, the voice of God at his baptism. Sixthly, the descent of the Holy Ghost upon him in the form of a dove. Seventhly, his miracle at Cana of Galilee."[30] Fenimore Cooper regarded the denial of Christ's divinity as "a species of infidelity that is getting to be so widely spread in America as no longer to work in secret, but which lifts its head boldly among us, claiming openly to belong to one of the numerous sects of the land."[31] The love story, which succeeded in warming only slightly the Antarctic atmosphere of *The Sea Lions,* is largely concerned with the heroine's struggle between her love for Gardiner and her unwillingness to marry a man unconvinced of Christ's divinity. "Mary had reason to think that Roswell Gardiner denied the divinity of Christ, while he professed to honour and defer to him as a man far elevated above all other men, and as one whose blood purchased the redemption of his race!"[32] Credit for the hero's conversion was due to that salty Kennebunk seaman, Stimson, who knew his Bible as minutely as his Bowditch. Stoutly maintaining the divinity and glory of

[29] Holland, *Letters to the Joneses,* p. 73.
[30] *The Prince of the House of David* (New York, 1855), pp. 160-161.
[31] *The Sea Lions,* I, 26.   [32] *Ibid.*

Christ in a series of interminable discussions as his boat drifted perilously through storms and ice-fields, Stimson finally set Gardiner thinking in the direction which led to his earthly happiness with Mary and to the salvation of his immortal soul.[33] The clinching argument advanced by this theological tar was that of "the improbability of the apostles' inventing that which would seem to be opposed to all men's notions and prejudices. . . ." It was "this novel idea," wrote Cooper, that struck Gardiner "more forcibly than the argument adduced from the acquiescence of the Redeemer in his own divinity."[34] The problems raised by the mystery of the Godhead were frequently discussed in Cooper's romances. In *The Oak Openings,* the simple reverence of the Indians was cited as the proper attitude for civilized men. "It is worthy of being observed," he noted, "that not one of these savages raised any hollow objections to the incarnation of the Son of the Great Spirit, as would have been the case with so many civilized men. . . . It is when we begin to assume the airs of philosophy, and to fancy, because we know a little, that the whole book of knowledge is within our grasp, that men become sceptics."[35]

William Ellery Channing's reverence for human nature and his exaltation of the wide influence exerted by the power of virtue alarmed the orthodox who insisted that morality without religion was not enough. "Excellent, but not sufficient," replied the author of *The Fortune Hunter.* "To be truly good, he must neither break moral nor divine laws—and that, from love of goodness, which is from love of God."[36] Mary Pratt in *The Sea Lions* was only one of many heroines who told their suitors that moral excellence without the seal of religion was a poor guaranty for good conduct. Thus Anna warned the moral Hartley in *The Three Eras of a Woman's Life:* "In fact, unless our actions are regulated by Divine laws, our morality

<hr>

[33] Stimson's persistence may be seen by a glance at the number of pages devoted to his homilies on this subject: 138, 223-224, 226-227, 244-245, 252-254, 262, 267, 269-270, 283, 312, 346, 371-372, 380, 382, 413.

[34] *Ibid.,* II, 141. [35] Cooper, *The Oak Openings,* II, 137.

[36] A. C. Mowatt, *The Fortune Hunter,* p. 49.

has but a slender base to stand upon—is, in fact, only an assumed and not a real morality."[37] Mrs. Hale scouted the "false humanitarianism" of those "philosophers and reformers—so-called—of both sexes, who put their trust in humanity alone." —"we may admire their genius and enthusiasm—," she conceded, "but we cannot recognize them as Christian philanthropists."[38] Nor was that Stoic fortitude which emanated from "mere morality" to be compared with Christian resignation in the face of suffering. When Mr. Percy praised Elizabeth's "firmness," his wife sharply corrected him. "It rather, I think, merits the name of resignation," she replied, "for it seems to me that far from being the result of indifference to evil, it is the effect of a sweet submission to the will of the heavenly Father, under all the trials, which, in his unerring wisdom, he has seen it good to appoint for her."[39] Maria McIntosh had little patience with philosophers who praised pagan morality. "In their whole spirit—in Paganism, self was deified," she charged in *Charms and Counter-charms*. "A man was brave and patriotic,—he despised pain, he achieved difficult tasks, and suppressed or annihilated giant evils, because in so doing he gained honor—he exalted *himself*. In Christianity, we live not unto ourselves, but unto Him. . . ."[40] Augusta Evans's *Inez*, which was written when the author was but sixteen years old, and *Beulah*, which enjoyed a sale of twenty-one thousand copies, are both concerned with the sterility of moral philosophy unaccompanied by religion. In the earlier novel, Dr. Bryant confessed to the heroine, "For a time I found delight in intellectual pursuits, but soon wearied of what failed to bring real comfort in hours of trial."[41] The heroine of *Beulah*, after turning in disgust from the pages of Carlyle, Emerson, and Parker, arrived at a judgment of philosophy which the author printed as a motto on the title page: "She can teach us to hear of the calamities of others with magnanimity; but it is religion only that can teach us to bear our own with resignation."

[37] Arthur, *The Three Eras of a Woman's Life*, p. 148.
[38] *Northwood*, pp. 393-394.   [39] Evans, *Resignation*, II, 100-101.
[40] *Charms and Counter-charms*, pp. 370-371.
[41] A. J. Evans, *Inez* (New York, n.d.), p. 224. [First edition, 1855]

The old Calvinistic doctrines, cold as a meeting-house in January, had starved the emotions. "Reason! Reason! that is the real soul-destroyer!" exclaimed Brownson in *Charles Elwood*. "I cannot reason on religion; I hold it too sacred . . . I cannot mistake my feelings."[42] When a crisis in his own life forced him to sample the comfort afforded by the theology which he had been preaching, the Reverend Mr. Rossiter found scant solace. "Many years, a score of them," wrote Caroline Chesebro' in *Victoria*, "he had been dealing with abstractions, for in his studies and his creed he had left out the human element. . . . No matter what his creed was, his heart did not endorse it—it was not the loved disciple's Christianity."[43] "A good heart is, after all, your best philosopher," counseled Mrs. Stephens in *The Old Homestead*.[44] She taught her heroines to admit no other guide for their conduct. Maria Cummins shared this distrust of religion without emotion. In *El Fureidis*, she has Havilah refuse the suit of the wealthy Meredith because his faith was not rooted in his feelings. "He has a scholar's cold faith in Scripture; and an artist's worship of beauty, and a poet's dream of truth," she admitted, "but who can trust the stream which has no living fountain, the fruit which is hollow at the core, the spirit which is not linked to the Highest?"[45] Little Gertie, the sainted heroine of *The Lamplighter*, appealed to her disillusioned father to renew his faith. "I know of no religion but that of the heart," she reassured him.[46] Beulah also found that intellectual inquiry was an arid substitute for the "heart convictions" of childhood. "In lieu of the holy faith of my girlhood," she declared, "it gives me but dim, doubtful conjecture, cold metaphysical abstractions, intangible shadows that flit along my path, and lure me on to deeper morasses."[47] Camp meetings and revivals were welcomed by some novelists as affording a much needed outlet for the starved religious feelings. "The religious world had become all but dead, the church had lost nearly all sense of its mission . . . ," Brownson wrote in

---

[42] *Charles Elwood*, p. 78.
[43] *Victoria*, p. 309.   [44] *The Old Homestead*, p. 69.
[45] M. Cummins, *El Fureidis* (Boston, 1860), p. 128.
[46] Cummins, *The Lamplighter*, p. 382.   [47] Evans, *Beulah*, pp. 437-438.

defense of the warmly emotional Baptists and Methodists. "Something was necessary to awaken the slumbering con- science, to rescue man from the all-absorbing selfishness and worldly mindedness which had become so universal. . . ."[48] The same author found an easy explanation for female piety. "Women are easily affected in revival seasons," he stated. "They are creatures of sentiment rather than of reason, and are therefore much addicted to piety."[49] The dangers of excessive emotionalism, however, did not go unchallenged. "The trouble seems to be that we get religious feeling without acquiring evangelical principle," bravely warned Richard Edney, who was speaking at a perfervid revival meeting. "It is a glow- worm religion, that fails by day-light, and disappears in the glare of occupation. It is a parlor religion, that shifts its dress and loses its temper when it goes into the kitchen. The pursuit of salvation in the midst of excitement is like gunning in a strong wind; you cannot distinguish your game, nor steady your sight."[50]

Equally freighted with danger was the new attitude to nature. Before the impact of the romantic revolution upon the religion of New England, natural phenomena had been com- monly regarded as setting up a barrier between God and man. Transcendentalism had changed all that. Emerson's famous essay in 1836 had proclaimed eloquently that nature is a book in which men might read the workings of the mind of God. The transcendental heroine of Judd's *Margaret* found it im- possible to speak of nature without excess. She found God's presence everywhere. "All that is now about us is his, and he in it," she rhapsodized; "the beauty of the forest is the tincture of his beneficence, the breeze is the respiration of his mercy, the box-berries and mosses are his, the rocks and roots, the dancing shadows, the green breaks into the blue sky are his creation, the fair whole of color, perfume, and form, the in- describable sweet sensation that wells in our breasts, are his gift and his presence in the gift, they are the figures woven into

[48] *Charles Elwood*, p. 35.
[49] *Ibid.*, pp. 29-30.　　　　　　　　[50] Judd, *Richard Edney*, p. 177.

the tapestry that girths the Universe, the fragrance that fills the vinaigrette of Creation. Through all and in all pierces his spirit, that blows through us like the wind."[51] Guy Hartwell, an "advanced thinker" in *Beulah*, belonged to the popular new nature cult. "Truly thou art my mother, dear old earth! I feel that I am indeed nearly allied to thy divine beauty!" he cried rapturously. "Starry nights, and whispering winds, and fragrant flowers! yea, and even the breath of the tempest! all, all are parts of my being."[52] All those who prided themselves upon their sensibilities were attuned to what Susan Warner called "the fine but exquisite analogies of things material with things spiritual,—those *harmonies of Nature*, to which, talk as they will, all other ears are deaf!"[53] These nature-addicts aspired to an infinite haziness in which the pleasurable sensations varied directly with the fuzziness of the horizon. Thus Gabriella "loved to ramble alone, till she felt herself involved in the soft haziness of thought, which was to the soul what the blue mistiness was to the distant hills."[54] Borland, an exponent of the new religion which he called "Nature Harmonia," preached his gospel until he undermined the faith of the orthodox village pastor and set the entire community in an uproar. "Live in entire unity with nature," he exhorted, "and you will comprehend all things. Addressing yourself to the great idea, you will find an employment for every power of your intellect. . . . Yes! it tends all to one ultimate idea. That idea is the perfection of harmony, in other words, of Nature."[55] Communing with nature became a favorite form of self-indulgence. "Every breath which sighed through the emerald boughs seemed to sweep a sympathetic chord in her soul," the author wrote of Beulah, "and she raised her arms towards the trees as though she longed to clasp the mighty musical box of nature to her heart."[56]

Beulah was destined to learn, however, that this seductive form of worship was unable to satisfy the soul. "To what did

[51] *Margaret*, p. 242.
[53] *Queechy*, II, 214.
[55] Chesebro', *The Children of Light*, pp. 266-268.
[56] Evans, *Beulah*, pp. 16-17.

[52] Evans, *Beulah*, pp. 61-62.
[54] Hentz, *Ernest Linwood*, p. 73.

she, on bended knees, send up passionate supplications? To nature? To heroes?" asked the author. "These were the new deities. She could not pray; all grew dark. . . . The landmarks of earlier years were swept away; the beacon light of Calvary had sunk below her horizon."[57] J. G. Holland entertained wholesome doubts about the honesty of those exquisites who boasted of holding communion with their Maker in the woods and fields. "They know that they never worship God in the fields, and that they would be frightened at the thought of any actual communion with Him," he objected in *Letters to the Joneses*. "All this talk disgusts me, for I know that there is no sincerity in it."[58] Others, such as Caroline Chesebro', feared that the religion of nature gave a dangerous sanction to the passions. "Beautiful ideas they were which he took into his heart, and cherished for their beauty's sake," she wrote of a new convert to the cult. "But they were not, with him, the fixed laws of inner life, immutable rules for the regulation of his ways."[59] Augusta Evans came forward with a compromise which took into account the dangers of pantheism without denying the pleasures of pastoralism. "There is an ardent love of nature, as far removed from gross materialism or subtle pantheism on one hand, as from stupid inappreciation on the other," she wrote in *Beulah*. "While every sane and earnest mind must turn, disgusted and humiliated, from the senseless rant which resolves all divinity into materialistic elements, it may safely be proclaimed that genuine aesthetics is a mighty channel, through which the love and adoration of Almighty God enters the human soul."[60]

Not even Augusta Evans had any objection to the worship of flowers. Whether they were dancing in the breeze, or pressed between the pages of a book to recall in tranquility the perfumed memory of the time, the place, and the lady—flowers might be adored with perfect safety. Not to love them was the unpardonable sin. "Volumes with regard to her character were expressed in that simple phrase, 'Not love flowers!' " remarked

---

[57] *Ibid.*, p. 250.
[59] *The Children of Light*, p. 262.
[58] *Letters to the Joneses*, p. 118.
[60] *Beulah*, pp. 266-267.

Mrs. Hentz in *Rena*. "Those rainbows of earth, gilt with the seven-fold beams of heaven, proclaiming the covenant mercy of God, his tenderness and love, these smiles of creation so bright and radiant . . . those unfallen children of paradise. . . . Not love flowers! Alas for the young heart that conceives a sentiment like this!"[61] Alas, indeed! For Stella, who had uttered this damning admission, was not present at the distribution of rewards and blessings in the final chapter. Of quite another sort was the pure Eoline. "It is too little to say that Eoline loved flowers—she idolized them," the author noted with approval. "They were to her, living, breathing, animated beings. They talked to her with their balmy breath; as they bent their graceful stems and green leaves in the wind, they seemed to woo her caresses, and she longed to fold them in her arms, and hold them against her heart."[62] Wealthy heroines usually had conservatories next to their boudoirs. Gabriella not only enjoyed a private glass "kiosk" full of perpetual blooms, but she also saw to it that her guests lived in an atmosphere of flowers. "Our rooms were warmed by furnaces," a visitor reported. "In mine, the heat came up through an exquisite Etruscan vase, covered with flowers, which seemed to emit odor as well as warmth, and threw the illusion of Spring over the chilliness and gloom of Winter."[63] Evelyn Beresford's parents built her an indoor arboretum which was the envy and delight of her sentimental friends: "She had flown to the glass doors, and was gazing with delight upon roses and acacias and jessamines and orange-trees full of bloom, among which birds were flying almost as free and singing quite as merrily as in their native woods."[64] Less opulent parents found wallpaper and carpets economical substitutes for conservatories. "Everything around her was pure white," related the author of *The Old Homestead*, "but the walls were covered with clustering roses, and the carpet under her feet glowed out with flowers like the turf in a forest-glade."[65]

[61] *Rena*, p. 152.
[62] Hentz, *Eoline*, p. 30.   [63] Hentz, *Ernest Linwood*, p. 247.
[64] McIntosh, *Charms and Counter-charms*, p. 43.
[65] Stephens, *The Old Homestead*, p. 283. Reserved for special praise was the

Flowers also provided these novelists with their favorite source of imagery. "Viola, of Summerfield!" announced Mrs. Southworth at the threshold of *Shannondale*. "The most fair and fragile looking human flower that ever bloomed its day in the parterres of a palace conservatory!"[66] What, after all, was a teacher but a gardener of souls? "I consider myself an humble florist in the garden of my Lord," Miss Manly told her pupils in *Eoline*, "cultivating for His glory these intellectual and moral flowers which shall bloom in immortal beauty, when low in dust shall fade the blossoms of Magnolia Vale."[67] With commendable consistency, Miss Manly modestly described herself as "the full-blown rose" among her tender buds! Mrs. Child would have been helpless, without the aid of flowers, to depict the plight of a fair English lady sighing amid the alien storms of bleak New England. "What was she now?" she asked in *Hobomok*. "A lily weighed down by the pitiless pelting of the storm; a violet shedding its soft, rich perfume on bleakness and desolation; a plant which had been fostered and cherished with mild sunshine and gentle dews, removed at once from the hot-house to the desert, and left to unfold its delicate leaves beneath the darkness of the lowering storm."[68] Floral metaphors also served neatly to make clear the intimate relationships enjoyed by a happy family. "True, dear one, we are linked together," the head of the household remarked to his wife. "Yet as is the oak to the vine which clings around it, am I to you; as the budding rose which starts from the sod beneath, is our child to us both."[69] Sylvester Judd hesitated only for a moment when he was asked to define a novel. "A Tale is not like a house, except in its door-plate, the title-page . . .," he admitted judiciously. "It is rather like a rose, the sum of the qualities of which are visible at a glance; albeit it will repay

---

carpet in the home of the Seldens in Mrs. Holmes's *The English Orphans* (New York, 1855). "The design of the Brussels carpet was exquisitely beautiful," the author wrote, "and the roses upon it looked as if freshly plucked from the parent stalk."

[66] E. D. E. N. Southworth, *Shannondale*, p. 4.

[67] Hentz, *Eoline*, p. 260.

[68] *Hobomok*, p. 98.

[69] Judson, *The Mysteries and Miseries of New York*, II, 6.

minute attention, and affords material for prolonged enjoyment."[70]

The moral exhalations of flowers were of most interest to religious novelists. "Oh, what a blessed thing flowers are!" exclaimed Augusta Evans. "They have been well styled, 'God's undertones of encouragement to the children of earth.' "[71] "I have thought that wildflowers might be the alphabet of the angels," Mrs. Child wrote in *The Rebels*, "whereby they write on hills and fields mysterious truths, which it is not given our fallen nature to understand."[72] Zana, in *The Heiress of Greenhurst*, boasted that she had no difficulty in deciphering the enchanting language. "I never felt lonely when flowers were my companions," she declared. "They seemed to me like a beautiful alphabet, which God had given, that I might fashion out with them the mystic language of my own heart."[73] The hero of *The Wide, Wide World* disclosed to Ellen the secret of his skill in translating floral messages. "It is written as plainly to me in their delicate painting and sweet breath and curious structure, as in the very pages of the Bible," he said confidently, but added with modesty, "though no doubt without the Bible I could not read the flowers."[74] Wise lovers knew that they were never more persuasive than when they discoursed of the sentiment of the flowers. When he called upon Alice Montrose, Robert "spoke of the sentiment always associated with certain flowers," Maria McIntosh wrote approvingly, "and of the singular universality of such associations, and he repeated to her allusions to the rose in the old English poets, and in the Latin and the Greek, translating, of course, the two last. . . ."[75] Model heroes were well versed in the moral and religious connotations of flowers. John Humphreys edified Ellen with a homily on the white camellia. "It reminds me of what I ought to be—and of what I shall be if I ever see Heaven," he expounded. "It seems to me the emblem of a sinless pure

[70] *Richard Edney*, p. v.   [71] *Beulah*, p. 218.
[72] L. M. Child, *The Rebels* (Boston, 1850), p. 257.
[73] Stephens, *The Heiress of Greenhurst*, p. 199.
[74] Warner, *The Wide, Wide World*, II, 228.
[75] *The Lofty and the Lowly*, II, 188.

spirit,—looking up in fearless spotlessness."[76] He was equally eloquent on the daphne. "It is like the fragrance that Christian society sometimes leaves upon the spirit," he explained, "when it is just what it ought to be."[77] Although the flowers breathed a many-hued language, they all spoke the same message of decay and glorious rebirth. "I envy not him who can look coldly on a blade shooting from its unsightly seed into verdure," declared Mrs. Gilman, "the sacred and startling emblem of that mortal which is to put on immortality."[78]

Spring blossoms and their autumnal decay thus inevitably suggested the most vital of all problems faced by the religious novelists. "One idea haunted her," wrote Augusta Evans of Beulah, "aside from revelation, what proof had she that unlike those moldering flowers, her spirit should never die?"[79] Readers of Mrs. Child's *Philothea*, a romance of Greek life, may have been somewhat startled to receive reassurance on this capital point by the granddaughter of Anaxagoras. "With quiet earnestness," Philothea replied: "Lady, the simple fact that the human soul has ever *thought* of another world, is sufficient proof that there is one; for how can an idea be formed by mortals, unless it has first existed in the divine mind?"[80] This facile solution was offered in many novels. "It is contrary to common sense to suppose that we could receive such a thought if it were not a truth," asserted Hungerford in *The Old Plantation*. "We cannot conceive of any thing as existing a hint of which is not given by something that exists."[81] What passed at the time for science was also hailed as proof of the existence of the immortal soul. "In cases of natural or induced somnambulism—of which thousands of instances are daily occurring around us—the body is deprived of all sensation, and the material senses are completely closed," announced the author of *The Fortune Hunter*. "Yet the soul feels, thinks, wills, and internally acts. It perceives, by means of spiritual senses, and

[76] Warner, *The Wide, Wide World*, II, 37.
[77] *Ibid.*, II, 228.
[78] C. Gilman, *Recollections of a Southern Matron* (New York, 1838), p. 261.
[79] *Beulah*, p. 155.   [80] *Philothea*, p. 27.
[81] J. Hungerford, *The Old Plantation*, p. 281.

in some states has intercourse with spirits, distances are annihilated, and the spiritual vision perceives objects, too far removed to be visible to the keenest natural sight."[82]

Considerable disagreement existed upon the exact shape or form of what Mrs. Southworth called "the soul of my soul—the sensorium of my spirit—that part of me which shall be immortal."[83] Arria Walton was reasonably confident that the soul would "assume the form of a human being." If not, she asked, what's a Heaven for? "If our spirits were but ether, how could they, in another world, exercise the faculties which they have enjoyed here—and what would existence be without those faculties?"[84] Mrs. Gilman took quite the opposite view. "It is my favorite idea," she wrote, "that 'we shall all be changed,' spiritually as well as physically. The world has been more bright to me than to many, but I have no wish to carry away any of its recollections. . . . I hope for a butterfly transition—a change from this headaching and heartaching scene to a bright and God-sunned atmosphere."[85] The author of *The Black Gauntlet* considered "corporeal resurrection" among "the most captivating ideas held out in the Bible. . . . For what sublime genius could bear the idea of having his soul housed for eternity, in any other than his own individual body?"[86] An exceedingly awkward point was raised by Dr. Adams in respect to the souls of children. The doctor admitted that analogy seemed to favor the idea of children "growing up" in Heaven, but that most mothers hoped their offspring would remain young until they were permitted to join them in the other world. ". . . but some people seem to think that we are to be re-constituted into families, in Heaven," he stated in *Agnes,* "and that parents will gather their children about them, and have what they call happy homes. Therefore they like the thought of infants and young children remaining such."[87] He wisely left the question open.

[82] Mowatt, *The Fortune Hunter*, p. 65.
[83] E. D. E. N. Southworth, *Shannondale*, p. 102.
[84] Mowatt, *The Fortune Hunter*, p. 20.
[85] *Recollections of a Southern Matron*, p. 186.
[86] Mrs. M. H. Schoolcraft, *The Black Gauntlet*, pp. 453-454.
[87] N. Adams, *Agnes* (Boston, 1857), p. 60.

The most popular proof of the immortality of the soul was to be found in the scenes attending the death of a Christian. "I would have you see him," wrote the author of *Monaldi*, "for the death of a Christian—the death in hope—has no parallel in sublimity on our earth."[88] All doubts disappeared at the death-bed of little Mary in *Virginia and Magdalene*. "It is better than a thousand learned discourses on the Evidences of Christianity . . . ," a witness testified, "never did I feel immortality as now."[89] The death of children furnished unanswerable proof to Mrs. Southworth: "It makes immortality, Heaven, certain, because necessary; and necessary, because just."[90] Dying Christians invariably remained conscious and eloquent to the end, dispensing cheer and hope to the watchers. "O, *it is sweet to die!* I love to think that I was born to prepare for this hour!" the stricken Lucy Otis told her family. "Can this be death? O, how bright does eternity appear!"[91] Cornelia Dale's last words made her mourners envy her. "To me, death is a lovely word—one of the fairest in the firmament of language," she reassured her sobbing friends. "'Tis the sweet moon-lit night which precedes the bridal morn of life immortal. Old age is the true altar, and death is the venerable priest who weds us to a fairer world above."[92] The approach of dissolution usually brought with it a conviction of the shallowness of earthly joys. "You know very little, indeed, of the world, if you think it is a place so pleasant," fifteen-year-old Hope Rossiter informed those who had come to bid her farewell. "To depart is far better. To many people the hour when they die is the happiest hour of all."[93] Ernest Linwood's miraculous recovery after all hope had been abandoned enabled him to discuss his "last moments" with some authority. "I have been on the confines of the spirit world, my mother," he testified, "so near as to see myself by the light it reflected. Death is the solar microscope of life. It shows a hideous mass, where all seemed fair and

---

[88] Washington Allston, *Monaldi* (Boston, 1841), p. 251.
[89] E. D. E. N. Southworth, *Virginia and Magdalene*, p. 36.
[90] *The Discarded Daughter*, II, 21.
[91] M. D. Weston, *The Weldron Family* (Providence, 1848), p. 80.
[92] Tator, *Brother Jonathan's Cottage*, p. 182.
[93] Chesebro', *Victoria*, p. 159.

pure."[94] A religious novel without at least one deathbed is as rare as an historical romance without a battle. Authors exploited this rich source of sentimental appeal and Christian teaching; canny publishers, moreover, knew that a moral novel was no better than its death scenes. "The death-scenes are inimitable," boasted Appleton's advertisement of *Juno Clifford* in 1856.[95] In the wealth of its deathbed tableaux, *Resignation* achieved what is, perhaps, a record. This melancholy tale which chronicled the last moments of fifty-seven of the dramatis personae must have satisfied the most exacting taste. Since infant mortality was high, a dearth of characters finally brought the story to an end. *Resignation,* indeed, was an appropriate title for a work which averaged at least one demise in every ten pages.[96]

In describing the phenomena of dissolution, novelists may have found useful the researches conducted by Andrew Jackson Davis, clairvoyant, who claimed the power of projecting his vision through space. His account of a death scene in *The Great Harmonia,* published in 1850, provided tempting material for religious fiction. "The spirit rose at right angles over the head or brain of the deserted body," he reported with scientific exactness. "But immediately previous to the final dissolution of the relationship that had for so many years subsisted between the two spiritual and material bodies, I saw— playing energetically between the feet of the elevated spiritual body and the head of the prostrate physical body—a bright stream of vital electricity." Watchers at deathbeds frequently noted phenomena of this kind. "Instances of such preternatural assurance—," declared a witness of Miss Arlington's death in *Bubbleton Parish,* "sometimes accompanied by exclamations of ecstatic delight—have fallen under the observation of all who are familiar with Christian departures. . . . Here, we see

[94] Hentz, *Ernest Linwood,* p. 461.

[95] Quoted from the publisher's blurb printed in Susan Warner's *The Hills of the Shatemuc* (New York, 1856).

[96] Miss Evans did not append a table of vital statistics, but a hasty count indicates that old age claimed the largest number with sixteen victims; undiagnosed ailments accounted for fifteen others; consumption wasted away eight lives; ills of childhood, storms at sea, duels, fits, and military disasters complete the casualties.

the soul rising, august, into its native element—unscathed by death or time. . . ."[97] The ascension of Monaldi's soul seemed visible to an attendant. "This is not the mere crumbling of a mortal body," he declared, ". . . for it seemed as if I could see his soul raying through his eyes. . . ."[98] For the "vital electricity" which Davis had described as playing so energetically at the moment the soul passed into the invisible world, novelists found the rays of the setting sun a convenient substitute. "I feel that my spirit could be borne to heaven on a beam of light," the failing Ella told her mother. "And my dear mamma, do not be startled, if as the sunlight fades from earth this coming eve, my soul should take its departure to that realm where no shadow of night ever comes."[99]

The rays of the setting sun, although on occasion the rising sun served just as well, flooded these death chambers with their radiant promises of life-everlasting. Practiced readers soon learn to become wary of particularly spectacular sunsets; they are infallible prophecies that the death-rattle cannot be far behind. Dissolution promptly followed the appearance of the first ray in *Ruth Hall*. "One beam penetrated the little window, hovering like a halo over Daisy's sunny head," wrote "Fanny Fern." "A quick, convulsive start, and with one wild cry (as the little throat filled to suffocation), the fair white arms were tossed aloft, then dropped powerless on the bed of Death!"[100] Usually effects were not managed quite so abruptly. Little Fanny was given time to exclaim: "Oh! is it not beautiful! Don't you hear? And look! oh, look! and my mother, too! Oh! it is too bright for such as I!" The rest was silence and a benediction by J. R. Gilmore, the author. "The heavenly gates had opened to her! She had caught a vision of the better land!" he concluded. "Then a low sound rattled in her throat, and she passed away, just as the last rays of the winter sun streamed through the low window. One of its bright beams rested on her face, and lingered there till we laid

[97] Reynolds, *Records of the Bubbleton Parish*, p. 289.
[98] Allston, *Monaldi*, p. 253.
[99] Lasselle, *The Belle of Washington*, p. 118.
[100] Parton, *Ruth Hall*, p. 84.

her away forever."[101] Even those who had fallen into a coma were momentarily revived by the setting sun. "She continued in a lethargic state during the remainder of the day," observed the author of *Resignation,* who arrived at something like proficiency in varying the details of her fifty-seven death scenes, "but when the departed sun reflected his lingering rays on the scenery of evening; and all nature rested in the sweetness of her tranquility, as if smiling on the peaceful moments of a Christian's death; she unclosed her eyes."[102]

Children were encouraged to contemplate "the rosy-golden track that led across the stream toward the sunset." "It was pleasant to me to indulge the fancy," the hero recollected in *The Old Plantation,* "that that brilliant track was the path trod by the angels in passing to and fro between heaven and earth."[103] It was more than a mere fancy, however, to the dying Bernard Watt in *Minnie Hermon.* "He turned his face to the sun, and a smile, sweeter than sunlight, came over the wasted and bloodless lips," a friend recounted. "Upon that golden pathway the little one was smiling back upon kindred angels in Heaven!"[104] Little Eva trailed her clouds of glory for some time before the fatal evening. "It was late in the afternoon, and the rays of the sun formed a kind of glory behind her," wrote Mrs. Stowe, "as she came forward in her white dress, with her golden hair and glowing cheeks, her eyes unnaturally bright. . . ."[105] Chapters XXVI and XXVII, which were devoted to an account of Eva's last moments, are too well known to require further comment here. The scenic effects in the stage versions certainly went far to make good Uncle Tom's prediction that "when that ar blessed child goes into the kingdom, they'll open the door so wide, we'll all get a look in at the glory. . . ."[106]

---

[101] *My Southern Friends* (New York, 1863), pp. 39-40.

[102] Sarah Evans, *Resignation,* I, 183. Before she *unclosed* them, however, she had time to shout, "O Grave! where is thy victory? O Death! where is thy sting?" *Unclosed* is an elegant variation worth noting. The author used it sparingly, a restraint not often shown in these novels, and in this instance remarkable considering the many opportunities her subject afforded.

[103] Hungerford, *The Old Plantation,* p. 54.

[104] Brown, *Minnie Hermon,* p. 196.

[105] *Uncle Tom's Cabin,* II, 85.   [106] *Ibid.,* II, 110.

A glimpse of glory was denied to few of the souls whose deaths were related in religious fiction. "Heaven is before me! Its portals are open!" shouted the doomed Littlefield in *Mapleton*. "The beams of glory, shining through, fall direct on my soul!"[107] Jonathan was able to discern some of the details of the heavenly landscape: "It seemed inviting to his feet. Celestial flowers bloomed with fadeless beauty and deathless perfume on either side. Spiritual fountains refreshed his vision, and spiritual rainbows spanned them; while a light unearthly pervaded all things, and displayed their truest beauty."[108] Visions of such beauty were cited to account for the fact that dying Christians invariably wore an expression of serenity. "Winnie's face," observed the author of *The Hills of the Shatemuc*, "looked as though it might have been the prison of a released angel."[109] Mrs. Stowe had the same to tell of Susan in *Dred*. "The soul, though sunk below the horizon of existence," she wrote, "had thrown back a twilight upon the face radiant as that of the evening heavens."[110] The novelists preferred less debatable evidence than the occult works of Davis and his fellow practitioners of "philosophico-theology" to substantiate their accounts of the phenomena attending dissolution. Mrs. Southworth comforted those who had not actually seen the souls of their dear ones take their upward flight because, as she explained in *Lawrence Monroe*, "their eyes were blind with weeping, and their spirits fainting with their heavy loss."[111] Dr. Adams assured those about to die that their first view of the new glory would not be too dazzling or painful to eyes which had been accustomed to the light of common day. "Neither are we to suppose that heaven breaks upon the senses of the spirit with such an overpowering brightness, as to excite confusion and pain," he stated in *Catharine*. "No doubt the revelation is gradual and most pleasant. Perhaps the celestial city appears at first in the distance . . . and from the convoy of

---

[107] Church, *Mapleton*, p. 364.
[108] Tator, *Brother Jonathan's Cottage*, p. 228.
[109] Warner, *The Hills of the Shatemuc*, p. 356.
[110] *Dred*, I, 132.
[111] S. A. Southworth, *Lawrence Monroe*, p. 365.

ministering angels, such information and instructions are received as prepare it for the full vision of heaven."[112]

Religious fiction would have presented something less than a complete record of the spiritual interests of the age had it failed to reflect a concern about the skepticism which threatened the church from outside. Every village had its infidel who delighted to perplex the parson with questions out of Tom Paine or from the "higher criticism." A young pastor in *Charles Elwood* was made to wilt before the new historical criticism of the Bible. "The ancient historian who would fill his history with marvels would by no means be held in so high respect even by yourself," a freethinker charged, "as one who confined his faith to the simple, the ordinary, the natural. His faith in marvels, omens, oracles, prodigies, you would regard as an impeachment of his judgment. Why not do the same in regard to the Bible historians?"[113] Germany had come to supplant France as the hotbed of infidelity. "I shall spend some time in Germany," the hero of *Hoboken* told his mother, "where these questions are dissected with merciless precision." The worried mother retaliated by stowing away in her son's luggage copies of the Bible, the Prayer Book, Butler's *Analogy*, and Paley's *Evidences*.[114] Mrs. Linwood's heart also sank when she was informed that Ernest wished to finish his studies at Göttingen. "She looked at him with an anxious, questioning glance," wrote Mrs. Hentz, and put a Bible in his trunk as an antidote against German heresies.[115] Strauss's *Life of Jesus* affected many young minds as it did that of Harry Lennox. "This work is the most learned, searching, powerful, and suc-

[112] *Catharine* (Boston, 1859), pp. 70-71. Dr. Adams also found consolation in the improved designs of coffins. "Their shape is not in seeming mockery of the rigid, swathed body," he noted in *Agnes*. "The broken lines and angles of the old coffin are drawn into continuous lines; they look like other things. . . . Within, they are prepared with a pearly white lining, the inside of the lid is draped in the same way; the name is on the inside; and a lock and key supplant the remorseless screws and screw-driver." These and other refinements enabled a bereaved father to console his wife by saying: "A more beautiful sight probably was never beheld than your dear little boy in his coffin." See *Agnes*, pp. 15, 102-103.

[113] Brownson, *Charles Elwood*, p. 24.

[114] Theodore S. Fay, *Hoboken* (New York, 1843), I, 181-182.

[115] *Ernest Linwood*, p. 109.

cessful attack ever made on Christianity," he concluded after a first reading, "and has been justly considered an important event in ecclesiastical history."[116] Although Lennox studied his mother's Bible dutifully, he was unimpressed: "He had read a curious historical monument of ancient credulity, palmed upon mankind when there was no press, and descended to the present time in some odd way, which he remembered Gibbon had admirably explained, though he did not recall exactly how."[117] What the Bible had failed to do was accomplished by a serious attack of brain fever which brought this freethinker to a dependence upon supernatural aid and finally persuaded him that his mother's religion was best.

These novels include few instances of female skepticism. As Cooper observed in *The Sea Lions,* "Few men relish infidelity in a woman, whose proper sphere would seem to be in believing and in worshiping and not in caviling, or in splitting straws on matters of faith."[118] Isa was an exception. She resolutely spurned her pastor's advice to free herself "of every distracting thought" by accepting the dogma of the church. "I do not desire rest, or peace, or quiet, or tranquility, if that is only to be gained by cessation of thought," she replied bravely. "Much would I prefer fighting my way out into a clearer light."[119] Young ladies who betrayed the slightest interest in "higher criticism" were warned of the consequences of agnosticism. "Beulah, do you want to be just what I am?" asked Hartwell, an unhappy skeptic. "Without belief in any creed! hopeless of eternity as of life? Do you want to be like me? If not, keep your hands off my books!"[120] When heroines were unable to confute the subtle propositions advanced by unbelievers they were told not to be discouraged. "It's such a beautiful thing to *know,* just by believing," Reuben reassured Faith in *Say and Seal.* "And then whatever people say or do, and if we can't find a word to answer them, we *know* down in our hearts, that the Bible is true. And so 'by faith we stand.' "[121]

[116] Fay, *Hoboken,* II, 162.   [117] *Ibid.,* II, 83.   [118] *The Sea Lions,* I, 214.
[119] Caroline Chesebro', *Isa* (New York, 1852), p. 60.
[120] Evans, *Beulah,* p. 153.
[121] Susan and A. B. Warner, *Say and Seal,* II, 262.

Few heroines were content to stand by their faith passively; they marched against the forces of infidelity with the zeal of missionaries. "It is part of the sailing orders of every Christian to speak every other vessel that he can," counseled the authors.[122] Fleda's conversion of Guy Carleton attested to the persuasiveness of these fair evangelists. After years of study and travel here and abroad had failed to convince Carleton of the existence of the slightest shred of evidence for a rational belief in God, little Fleda needed only to point to the setting sun. "Who made that, Mr. Carleton?" she asked significantly. Immediate and unconditional surrender followed. "A slight arrow may find the joint in the armour before which many weightier shafts have fallen powerless," exulted the author of *Queechy*. "Mr. Carleton was an unbeliever no more from that time."[123] Orestes Brownson added his garland of praise to those bestowed upon the influence and example of Christian womanhood. " 'O, there is a God!' spoken by the sweet lips of eighteen, by her we love and hope in a few days to call our own by the most intimate and sacred of ties—," he wrote in *Charles Elwood*, "it goes well nigh to melt even the atheist."[124] The hardened criminal hired to kidnap Lilla Hart was prepared for everything except his victim's piety. "Lilla took her Bible and read to me, and prayed with me," he said in accounting for his conversion, "and the fear of the Lord came over me then. I went upon my knees for the first time in my life...."[125] Little Natalie's specialty was the regeneration of Indians and Negroes. A single lesson was sufficient to win Quedy, a Nantucket redskin, who died blessing his teacher: "Me love Great Spirit; Great Spirit so good to send his little white-face to tell me how to get home." Black Vingo had the same message in a different, but equally unauthentic dialect: "Ah! bress de Lord, but it am good as a small bible to hear dat chile talk."[126] Heroines of different temperaments achieved their goals by differ-

---

[122] *Ibid.*, I, 134.

[123] Susan Warner, *Queechy*, I, 164.   [124] *Charles Elwood*, p. 29.

[125] C. Burdett, *Lilla Hart* (New York, 1846), p. 151. Lilla also converted the villain who had hired the kidnapper. See *ibid.*, pp. 189-191.

[126] E. V. Hallett, *Natalie* (Andover, 1858), p. 49.

ent methods. "She influenced you like a sedative," explained Mrs. Southworth. "The most beneficial mesmeric influence emanated from the presence of Susan Somerville."[127] Others worked more feverishly. "She lived, as it were, in a perpetual brainfever," Augusta Evans wrote of Beulah's missionary endeavours, "and her physical frame suffered proportionably."[128] Whether it was as a sedative or as an elixir, these evangelists were equally successful. Infidelity had no weapons strong enough to cope with their blandishments.

Second only to the inroads of infidelity was the disturbance caused by sectarian controversies. "Are not sects, and shades of sects, springing up among us on every side," complained Fenimore Cooper, "until the struggle between parsons is getting to be not who shall aid in making most Christians, but who shall gather into his fold most sectarians?"[129] The intense individualism of the period and the ease with which divergent elements within a denomination were able to separate to form new sects gave rise to considerable bitterness. Things had reached such a pass in 1842 that Dr. Adams asked anxiously, "Shall the morning of the Millennium break upon the church, and find the different divisions of her hosts embattled amongst themselves?"[130] Too many Americans, willing to try anything once, resembled Cooper's "Commodore of Otsego" who had an enlightening, if somewhat checkered, denominational history. "I was born an Episcopalian, if one can say so," he told Captain Truck, "but was converted to Presbyterianism at twenty. I stuck to this denomination about five years, when I thought I would try the Baptists, having got to be fond of the water, by this time. At thirty-two I fished a while with the Methodists; since which conversion, I have chosen to worship God pretty much by myself, out here on the lake."[131] Cooper's distrust of sects was a part of his deep-seated antipathy to social levelers and Jacksonian Democrats just as his staunch Episcopalianism was an accompaniment of his love for the old

[127] E. D. E. N. Southworth, *The Mother-in-Law*, p. 20.
[128] *Beulah*, p. 384.
[129] *The Chainbearer* (New York, 1845), I, 187.
[130] *The Baptized Child*, p. viii.   [131] *Home As Found*, II, 77.

landed aristocracy. In *The Wing-and-Wing* he maintained "that the American, who has lived long enough to witness the summersets that have been thrown in the practices and creeds of most of the modern sects of his own country, within the last quarter of a century, would come to have something like a suitable respect for the more stable and venerable divisions of the Christian world."[132] Particularly distasteful were those who held the liturgy to be alien to democratic institutions. Mark Woolston, the hero of *The Crater,* "was too much behind the curtain to be the dupe of any pretending claims to sudden inspirations, and well knew that every sect had its liturgy, though only half-a-dozen have the honesty to print them."[133]

Although all sects had come to stand equal before the law, popular opinion was quick to recognize their social differences and to give each one its place in the social scale. "One must be a little cautious where one goes to Church, now-a-days," Margaret was warned by her host in Boston, "it is rather delicate business. One's character is apt to suffer. I should be sorry to have you make a misstep."[134] M. J. Holmes's account of the denominational and social levels in *Meadowbrook* was typical of many towns described in religious fiction: "First, there was Laurel Hill, famed as the residence of certain families who were styled *proud* and *aristocratic*—to say nothing of their being *Episcopalians,* which last fact was by some regarded as the main cause of their haughtiness. Next came the 'Centre,' with its group of red houses, and its single spire, so tall . . . it scarce needed the lettering over the entrance to tell the stranger that *Presbyterians* worshipped there. Lastly came Flattville, by far the largest village in Rockland, and the home of all the *isms* in the known world."[135] Most popular in the new settlements along the Western frontier was Methodism. William Gilmore Simms paid his respects to the circuit riders who followed the population as it moved westward. In *Guy Rivers*

---

[132] *The Wing-and-Wing* (Philadelphia, 1842), I, 147.
[133] *The Crater,* II, 141.
[134] Judd, *Margaret* (rev. ed.; Boston, 1871), p. 316.
[135] *Meadowbrook,* p. 185.

he declared that they "may confidently claim to have done more, and with motives as little questionable as any, toward the spread of civilization, good habits, and a proper morality, with the great mass, than all other known sects put together."[136] Methodist doctrines of free will and free grace were admirably suited to the optimism and emotionalism of the times. "It's all true, and there's only one denomination who are sincere in what they profess, and that's the Methodist," testified an enthusiast in *Meadowbrook*. "They carry their religion into their whole life, while the Episcopalians, Presbyterians, and Baptists sit on different sides of the fence, and quarrel like fun about High Church and Low, Old School and New, close communion and open communion, and all that sort of thing. . . . I shall be a roaring Methodist, and ride the Circuit at once!"[137] The sincerity and simplicity of Methodist worship attracted many converts to whom the services of other denominations seemed coldly formal. Thus the simplehearted black John apologized for his apostasy. "I wasn't allus a herrytic," he explained in *Cousin Maude*, "but was as good a 'Piscopal as St. George ever had."[138] The rapid spread of Methodism and the Methodist system of licensing "lay" or local preachers were not always the subjects of panegyrics. At least one author feared the establishment of a Wesleyan "ecclesiastical tyranny." A Methodist preacher who seduced one of his parishioners at a camp meeting and later murdered his victim provided most of the villainy in *Fall River*, a lurid tale by Mrs. C. R. A. Williams. The only effect these revolting crimes had upon the congregation was to prompt them to save their pastor's neck by sharking up no less than one hundred and sixty witnesses ready to discredit the state's evidence by perjured testimony. In her Preface, the author expressed a desire to correct "that idolatrous regard for ministers, for preachers of the gospel, which at the present day is a scandal. . . ."[139] Lowest in the so-

---

[136] *Guy Rivers* (New York, 1859), p. 141. [First edition, 1834] The ministry of the Methodists was, of course, by no means confined to the frontier. Interesting accounts of revival meetings in a Methodist chapel on St. John Street in New York City appear in Sedgwick's *Clarence* and in Curtis's *Trumps*.

[137] Holmes, *Meadowbrook*, p. 145.   [138] Holmes, *Cousin Maude*, p. 33.

[139] C. R. A. Williams, *Fall River* (Providence, 1832), p. vi.

cial scale were the Roman Catholics. Mrs. Elliott, who had been accustomed to identify Catholicism with immigrants congregated in the large cities along our Eastern seaboard, found to her amazement that the best families in France were Catholics! In *Two Lives* she has her daughter Grace married to a Marquis by an Episcopal bishop because of "her own prejudices, which represented Romanism as the faith, in America, of the lower classes, amongst which only she had known it."[140]

Roman Catholicism enjoyed a rapid growth in the thirties and forties. This expansion, greatly augmented by the increase in Irish immigration after 1845, enabled the Roman Catholic Church to gain adherents in greater numbers than any Protestant denomination. With few exceptions, however, when novelists wrote of religion they meant only the Protestant religion, just as when they referred to the Bible they had in mind the King James Version. Ithuel Bolt was a bit under the weather at the time, but his account of the position of Catholicism in the United States would have been approved by the great majority of his fellow Protestants. "Look here, Signore," he told the vice-governatore in *The Wing-and-Wing*, "we don't call your ceremonies, and images, and robes, and ringing of bells, and bowing and scraping, a religion at all. . . ."[141] Indeed, as the historian of the sentimental generation has observed, many officials "had a vague but decided impression that Christianity of the Protestant brand was part of the common law of America." C. C. Pise, a militantly Catholic novelist, complained that his church was maligned everywhere. "This is the language of some of the most distinguished men," he protested in *Letters to Ada*. "You find it in almost every book of travels, every romance, every geography, every history;— from the heavy and elaborated folio down to the flying tract, and simple primer."[142] In *Father Rowland* he charged that the public schools taught anti-Romanism. "There is hardly a primer, or an elementary book of instruction, that has not some

[140] McIntosh, *Two Lives*, p. 248.
[141] Cooper, *The Wing-and-Wing*, I, 58.
[142] *Letters to Ada* (New York, 1834), p. 18.

or other disingenuous attack on the Catholic Religion," he declared. "Even *Peter Parley,* a little work intended to leave deep impressions on the mind of childhood, does not forget to insult the whole community of Roman Catholics, in his remarks on Italy."[143] The lowest of the isms enjoyed a status of respectability when compared with the odium with which Catholicism was regarded. "You may turn Moravian, Socinian, Unitarian, any thing . . . and not much will be said about it," Pise remarked sadly, "but become a Catholic, and there is a general excitement."[144] In his three pro-Catholic novels: *Father Clement, Letters to Ada,* and *Father Rowland,* the slender narratives meander aimlessly through mazes of doctrinal discussion. Pise made the most of the undignified sectarian squabbles of the Protestants: "The Episcopalian contends that he is right, and appeals to the Bible. The Presbyterian contends that he is right, and appeals to the Bible. The Methodist contends that he is right; the Baptist that he is right; the Quaker that he is right; the Unitarian that he is right; and all appeal to the Bible. The Bible is silent, and the ardour and tumult of controversy still continue."[145] The author introduced his heroines as the innocent victims of Protestant propaganda. He subjected them to a deluge of dissertations upon transubstantiation, purgatory, the intercession of the saints, relics, and absolution until every prejudice was dispelled and the last doubt satisfied. In this task of instruction, Father Rowland had an eloquent ally in Moses, a converted Negro slave, whose exemplary character and skill in dialectic finally persuaded Virginia to become a Roman Catholic. " 'Tis dat which was not made by any man, massa; now you see de Lutheran religion was made by Luther, massa; and de Protestant by Henry de eight, massa; and de Methodist by some oder man, massa," argued this ebon evangelist. As for Catholicism, Moses asserted that it was founded "By a God-man. It was gwying on a long time before de time of de reformation."[146]

Although the startling growth of the Romanist faith in the

---

[143] *Father Rowland* (Baltimore, 1831), p. 55. [First edition, 1829]
[144] *Letters to Ada,* p. 46.
[145] *Father Rowland,* p. 75.   [146] *Ibid.,* p. 143.

United States alarmed most Protestant novelists, Fenimore Cooper saw in it a happy augury. "All this shows a tendency towards that great conmingling of believers," he predicted in *The Oak Openings,* "which is doubtless to precede the final fusion of sects, and the predicted end."[147] The success of popular revival meetings offered additional encouragement to a friend of Christian unity in *True Womanhood.* "I have seen with my own eyes," he marveled, "Presbyterians, Quakers, Baptists, Jews, and Methodists, and scores of desperate men, who, but a little time before, had been the terror of Philadelphia, all praying together, and all in earnest...."[148] Even the apologists for Roman Catholicism showed a willingness to make compromises in order to help achieve the ideal of a universal Christian brotherhood. The converted hero of the pro-Catholic *Ralphton* urged the adoption of an Americanized brand of Romanism devoid of all objectionable pomp and pageantry.[149] Timothy Flint, a sturdy Protestant, confessed that he was sick of charges and countercharges. "There is enough that is common to every form of Christian faith and profession," he asserted in *Francis Berrian,* "to unite us in deeds of beneficence and feelings of charity."[150] The need of an entirely new religious foundation to embrace all faiths was proclaimed by Orestes Brownson. "I have no fault to find with catholicism ... ," he admitted. "But at the epoch of the Reformation it had finished its work ... and since then it has been a mere cumberer of the ground." Protestant denominations fared no better. "But the new institution is not yet found," he lamented, "nor has any one of the numerous sects now extant, its nucleus even."[151] Sylvester Judd announced his solution in *Margaret.* In this novel he described the establishment of Christ Church, which he hastened to explain was a Holy, but not a Roman Catholic Church. It was devised to attract men of all faiths and to reconcile the irreconcilables. Armenians, Russians, Greeks, Jews, Mohammedans, and Hindoos were among those who came to worship and remained to join. The greatest triumph of all deserves to be given in the

[147] *The Oak Openings* (New York, 1848), I, 211.
[148] Neal, *True Womanhood,* p. 139.   [149] Brisbane, *Ralphton,* p. 198.
[150] *Francis Berrian,* II, 254.   [151] *Charles Elwood,* p. 110.

words of the minister of the new Christian society: "Roman Cardinal and Greek Patriarch slept in the same bed; an event, Mr. Evelyn said, that had probably not happened since the year 1054. . . ."[152]

A last word about these religious novels should be written in that spirit of Christian charity and tolerance which their pages so frequently sought to invoke. It certainly would be uncharitable, if not uncritical, to stress too seriously the limitations of works which appeared with so many prefatory protestations of humility and incompetence. "I do not send it forth as a work of art, and I have not studied to conform to the established laws of the species of composition to which it may seem to belong," apologized Brownson disarmingly.[153] The apologia for *Natalie* was designed to melt the critics: "If anything of interest be found . . . it is well,—and should any be led to take up their Cross in meekness and humility, searching out the path that leads the wanderer home, it is indeed well."[154] In face of hopes so pious and pleas so disarming, reviewers were content to label these novels as "chaste" or "pure" or "elevating" or "moral" or "religious" and to neglect all other considerations. "Goodish books are written in great numbers by people who write with good motives and incompetent brains . . . ," objected the author of *Letters to the Joneses,* "but good motives alone never made a good book."[155]

Perhaps contemporary critics realized the folly of objecting to the strange and wonderful devices by which wrong was invariably worsted and virtue ultimately rewarded. Accident and chance, after all, were hardly recognized by novelists who ascribed their miracles of plotting to the daily intervention of Providence in the affairs of man. "I believe . . . that the words *accident* and *chance,* should be banished from the lexicon of the christian," maintained the heroine of *Resignation.* "The Bible certainly teaches us that incidents apparently unimportant

---

[152] *Margaret,* p. 427.

[153] *Charles Elwood,* p. v. The love story of the hero and Elizabeth is smothered under religious exhortations. Brownson seems to have forgotten about her fate until the very last line. "Pardon me," he concluded. "I have planted wild flowers on her grave and watered them with my tears."

[154] Hallett, *Natalie,* p. [v].   [155] Holland, *Letters to the Joneses,* p. 220.

are regarded by God:—how then can we doubt, that events affecting the happiness of beings destined for immortality, are directed . . . by the infinitely wise and benevolent Governor of the universe. . . ."[156] Although most critics chose to be silent before plots engineered by Providence, other novelists sometimes found themselves unable to refrain from commenting upon the lack of reality in religious fiction. "But, who ever talks in actual life as your religious people do in novels?" asked Pike in *Here and Hereafter*.[157] "And not only do elderly people preach, in the fictions of these well-intentioned caterers for youth," protested Mrs. Kirkland, "but even children utter homilies to each other, and to their parents, such as no child ever attempted, unless it might be Joseph Surface in his boyhood."[158]

The gravest indictment of these novels is their essential falsity to life. Too often their pages inculcated a prudential morality baited with attractive promises of comfortable material rewards. The religious life was fully guaranteed to pay substantial dividends in this world, here and now. If these promised payments in earthly goods were unaccountably deferred, the heavenly compensations were made to sound no less solid and material; celestial mansions were fully equipped with all modern conveniences. A passage expressing John Neal's indignation at such specious claims was printed at the head of this chapter. It is fitting that this same critic be permitted to have the last word. His question is one which must have troubled the minds of many readers of these novels as they closed the covers upon a last chapter happiness confined, alas, to sentimental, religious fiction: "Why do they not portray the young and lovely separated, and *forever,* from what they love; and supported nevertheless by their piety, their earnest and faithful religion; or coupled for life with the wicked and persecuted, and yet bearing their lot in marriage, as none but those who really deserve the name of the religious of the earth could bear it?"

[156] Sarah Evans, *Resignation*, II, 203-204.
[157] F. W. Pike, *Here and Hereafter*, p. 273.
[158] *A Book for the Home Circle*, p. 30.

VI

THE SENTIMENTAL COMPROMISE

The central experiment of the generation had been toward the reconciliation of unlikes—the humanitarian philosophy of enlightenment, perfectibility, democracy, beside the philosophy of acquisition, laissez-faire,
gratuitous benevolence. Under this aegis people had played, very earnestly,
many variants of a game which may be called Effects without Consequences. Religion without humility. Sensuality without smut. Laissez-
faire without oppression. Benevolence without sacrifice. Little Latin and
less tears. Salvation without pangs. Administration without statesmanship.
Femininity without feminism. Food, and a cupboard undepleted. Bricks
without straw. . . .
                    —E. D. Branch, *The Sentimental Years, 1836-1860.*

THE GENERATION which revealed itself in this abundant outpouring of sentimental novels was destined to witness stirring
scenes in a great national drama. Historians have done full
justice to the breath-taking events which were set in motion by
the brash triumph of Andrew Jackson, and which came to an
end in the *Sturm und Drang* of the Civil War. Few periods in
history have been packed with elements so diverse and dynamic. The rise of the common man on the wings of the new
democracy, the conquest of a continent, the voice of the West
imperiously demanding to be heard in the councils of state,
the widening breach between the planting and the commercial
interest culminating in the victory of industrialism—these were
but a few of the turbulent factors which added to the growing
pains of an adolescent society. It was an era in which the sweep
of powerful economic forces brought panics and prosperity and
laid the foundations of vast private fortunes. Rapid technological advances carried in their wake unemployment, poverty,
exploitation of labor, and widespread unrest. The generation
learned to know the consequences of the "speed-up" in production methods and the effects of the "walk-out" and the strike.
It was an age seething with movements and reforms: Millerism
and Mormonism, Bloomerism and Transcendentalism, Tem-

perance and Abolition. It was an epoch abounding in prodigies and paradoxes: anesthetics and animal magnetism, electric telegraphy and mesmerism, P. T. Barnum and Ralph Waldo Emerson, mass movements and individualism, Lowell factories and Brook Farm, *Godey's Lady's Book* and *Leaves of Grass,* the dime novel and *The Dial.* The national arena was thronged with a motley assembly: John Jacob Astor and Thoreau, "Fanny Fern" and Margaret Fuller, the Fox Sisters and Louis Agassiz, Professors Orson Fowler and Longfellow, Sam Houston and Henry Ward Beecher, Bronson Alcott and Horace Mann. Pervading everything was an exuberant optimism, as jaunty and as expansive as the frontier. The air was electric with hope and expectancy. Millerites eagerly awaited the Day of Judgment, and Perfectionists confidently scanned the horizon for a glimpse of the morning star of the Millennium. Few were the eyes discerning enough to descry the gathering storm clouds of the irrepressible conflict.

Least of all were the sentimental novelists fitted to enlighten their readers as to the real nature of their civilization. They winced before the realities of this raucous period in which were being fashioned the sinews of a new nation. Imbued with a lyric faith in the perfectibility of man, they regarded the America of their own day as a mere vestibule to Utopia. They preferred to dwell in a cozy cloudland of sentiment, secure in a haven of dreams. "Cares cannot come into this dreamland where I live. They sink with the dying street noise, and vanish with the embers of my fire." Thus Donald Grant Mitchell in his *Reveries of a Bachelor* sounded the graceful notes to which the sentimentalists beat their retreat. He touched the tender stops of the same popular theme of escape in *Dream Life.* With angry protests over the Fugitive Slave Law jangling in his ears, Mitchell retired to a farm in his Connecticut Xanadu where he fondled the fleecy cloud drifts of feeling that eternally floated upon "the great over-arching sky of thought." "I like to be rid of them all in this midsummer's day," he wrote of the feverish cares of the fifties. "I like to steep my soul in a sea of quiet, with nothing floating past me as I lie moored to my thought, but the perfume of flowers, and soaring birds, and shadows of clouds." In *Prue and I,* another cherished classic of the generation, George William Curtis savored the luxuries of a roseate world viewed through the spectacles of sentiment. The amiable Prue counted it as her chief blessing that her consort was not compelled to wear "the glasses of truth." The unfortunate Titbottom, whose spectacles were unrouged by sentiment, found them to be a sorry boon; they revealed too many sharp, unupholstered facts. "I longed to enjoy the luxury of ignorant feeling, to love without knowing," he confessed sadly, "to float like a leaf upon the eddies of life, drifted now to a sunny point, now to a solemn shade—now over glittering ripples, now over gleaming calms, —and not to determined ports, a trim vessel with an inexorable rudder." This mood so felicitously evoked by Mitchell and Curtis was in exquisite harmony with popular taste. *Prue and I* was saluted by some enthusiastic critics as the long overdue "great American novel." *Reveries of a Bachelor,* published in 1850, was pirated in fifty editions. More than a million copies were sold in authorized printings. Lulled into a comfortable complacency by soporifics such as these, society drifted pleasantly toward the edge of the whirlpool.

In *Letters and Leadership,* Mr. Van Wyck Brooks has written acutely of the failure of much of our literature to motivate the American scene and to impregnate it with meaning because that literature too often emanated from a national mind sealed against experience. His indictment applies with peculiar force to the writings of the sentimental novelists. They were escapists, artfully evading the experiences of their own day from which letters derive much of their strength. They fed the national complacency by shrouding the actualities of American life in the flattering mists of sentimental optimism. "Phrases take the place of deeds, sentiments those of facts, and grimaces those of benevolent looks," charged Fenimore Cooper in *The Sea Lions.* "How weak we are!" complained Caroline Chesebro' in *The Children of Light.* "We are so afraid of real things and earnest lives—so contented with shams and shows—so willing to put up with the intolerable cant of scribes, pharisees and hypocrites! This forever wishing, and never, by any mistake, doing!" Everywhere in popular fiction there was a tendency to idealize or to shy away from what Mitchell has disparagingly called the "definite, sharp business" of reality. In their aversion to stubborn facts, the sentimentalists resembled Jasper in *The Linwoods*. "He had an instinctive dislike of definitions, as they in Scriptures, who loved darkness, had to light," declared Miss Sedgwick. "He was fond of enveloping his meaning in shadowy analogies, which, like the moon, often led astray, with a beautiful but imperfect and illusive light." Bathed in the refulgent rays of sentiment, even the most barren aspects of the American landscape were thus gilded and transfigured; white democracy and black slavery, when seen through this fuzzy haze, appeared to be comfortably compatible.

At a time when things were in the saddle, and America was in the midst of a boastful materialism, the sentimentalists felt a need of enveloping the new industrial order in an aura of approval. Accepting without critical scrutiny the sanctions of the philosophy of acquisition, they dangled the tempting bait of material prosperity before the eyes of every reader. "Fortune almost literally knocks at every man's door, and the tide is sure to flow, and in many instances, reflow past the dwellings of all," Bickley promised in *The Aristocrat*. Drugged with the opiate of materialism, these writers succumbed without a struggle to the national acquisitiveness. Seldom have novelists been so thoroughly at the mercy of contemporaneity. The public table laden with lavish gifts is barred only to the vicious, boasted Miss Leslie in *Althea Vernon;* every industrious mechanic is on the certain road to plenty. "The prizes are open to all, and they fall with equal favour," corroborated Miss Sedgwick in *The Poor Rich Man and the Rich Poor Man.* "The poor family of this generation is the rich family of the next." Agreeable optimism was a popular ameliorative. "It is an almost invariable truth," proclaimed Lee in *The Contrast,* "that a man in this country, can obtain any place for which he is properly qualified." Aroused at "the mechanical philosophy" of materialism which enshrined greed as a virtue and stultified the aspirations of the human spirit, Emerson scouted the prevailing optimism of its jaunty apologists. "And all of us apologize when we ought not, and congratulate ourselves when we ought not," he lamented in his journal in 1839.

Unmindful of warnings such as this, the sentimental novelists persisted in their mission of putting their contemporaries on extremely pleasant terms with themselves. "In the laboring class, property is a sign of good morals," announced Catharine Sedgwick. "In this country nobody sinks into deep poverty, except by some vice, directly or indirectly." This same facile apologist further declared that "In all our widespread country there is very little necessary poverty. In New England *none* that is not the result of vice and disease." A footnote offered pleasant assurance that the same enviable conditions obtained in New York City, where only the sinful were poor. Timothy Shay Arthur found economics to be a benevolent, not a dismal, science, in which the laws of supply and demand benignly obeyed the dictates of a convenient morality. "If, in a particular branch of business, there should occur a surplus of labor," he observed cheerfully in *The Way to Prosper,* "those who are most skillful, and are at the same time, sober and industrious, will be those who will find employment; while the lazy, drunken, or bad workmen, will be driven off to other and less profitable callings." Over the swift rise of capitalistic industrialism was thrown the glamorous veil of individual freedom and initiative. "You will become exactly what you choose to make yourself. . . . Everything is possible, in any place where Providence has put you," asserted Susan Warner in *The Hills of the Shatemuc.* Mrs. Sarah Hale admitted that increased competitive pressures and new industrial techniques had resulted in some poverty, but found ample compensation in the independence and freedom of American laborers. These redeeming factors, she stated in *Northwood,* distinguish "the poorest of our free citizens from the peasantry of every other country in the world." In America of the fabulous forties every prospect pleased and only foreigners were vile. "We have no *low* in American society," remarked the author of *The Hypocrite*. The few ignorant and vicious exceptions were, for the most part, immigrants and these, he added complacently, were rapidly being reformed in our penitentiaries and state prisons.

The darker aspects of the new industrialism were either blithely ignored or bathed in the warm glow of optimism. Country lads seeking their fortunes found every mill town a veritable Paradise. "The factories appeared like an abode of enchantment," Judd wrote of his young hero in *Richard Edney*, "and the sight revived his heart, and gave him a pleasant impression of the city, as much as a splendid church, or a sunny park of trees, or fine gardens would have done." The operatives were represented as happy and content. Richard "envied the girls, some of whom he knew, who, through that troubled winter night, were tending their looms as in the warmth, beauty, and quietness of a summer-day." Those who protested at the shameless exploitation of laborers were advised not to ponder too seriously over social maladjustments. "It is all very fair," Lee argued in *The Contrast*. "The rich pay their money to the poor, and in process of time, the poor, if they are industrious, grow rich." Miss Sedgwick expressed her indignation at the outcries sometimes heard against rich men. "Providence has bound the rich and poor by one chain," she had a capitalist declare in *The Poor Rich Man*. "Their interests are the same. If there were none of these hateful rich people," she asked, "who, think you, would build hospitals, and provide asylums for orphans, and for the deaf and dumb, and the blind?" The mercantile economy was endowed with the patriarchal ideals of the benevolent squirearchy which had dignified the life of an earlier generation. "The merchant of today is happier than was Columbus, or Drake, or Vespucius, or Raleigh, or Gilbert," averred Elizabeth Oakes Smith in *The Newsboy*, "for he holds in his good iron safe the wealth of a principality. . . . The chivalry of the olden time, the soul of a Bayard and a Raleigh, have been reproduced." He was, moveover, cited as the only true missionary of civilization.

"He hears of famine, and oppression and suffering, and he waits no tardy movements of government, but a ship is freighted with the surplus products of an over-flowing soil, and away goes the American ship, wafted by the benedictions of thousands." If mercantile philanthropists seemed to show more zeal in dispatching succor to the remote places of the earth than to their needy neighbors at home, they merely afford one more instance of the failure of sentimental reformers to take themselves in hand before setting out to improve the world at large. Fashionable women who refused to pay a living wage to their seamstresses also eased their consciences by engaging in flattering humanitarian enterprises. "I sometimes think there is more kindness to the poor than there is justice," objected an underpaid worker in *Three Experiments in Living.* "The ladies are very good in getting up societies and fairs to help us; but they very often seem unwilling to pay us the full price of our labor. If they would *pay* us well, and *give* us less, it would be better for us." With sentimentalists, however, charity rarely began at home.

In their desire to represent human beings, not as they are, but as we should like to have them, the sentimental novelists almost invariably crowned their heroes' careers with worldly riches. The "success story" was immensely popular with a generation of readers who believed that every boy had an equal chance to become president. The saga of Benjamin Franklin strolling through Philadelphia with his rolls of bread under his arm, and the same Franklin, the idol of a brilliant circle at Versailles, was repeated in every household. Horace Courtenay, the ambitious hero of *The Cabin and the Parlor,* "had read of so many, who, like him, had started friendless boys, yet had finally won opulence and station, that he never, for a moment, doubted of success." Longfellow had provided a stirring motto for these aspiring youths whose lexicons contained no such word as *fail.* "I have written *Excelsior* on my banner," boasted Eugene in *Beulah,* "and I intend, like that noble youth, to press forward over every obstacle, mounting at every step, until I, too, stand on the highest pinnacle . . . I feel as if I should like to see Mr. Longfellow, to tell him how I thank him for having written it." Two avenues to riches were open to every boy, according to the author of the *New England Village Choir:* "The one was, to become a clerk of some wholesale or retail merchant in Boston, and the other, to pass through a college." Novelists usually were careful to clear the tracks and to give ambition the right of way. Benjamin Nelson in *The Weldron Family* found it was an easy leap from apprentice to partner: "Being an excellent book-keeper, and proving himself worthy of confidence by his strict integrity and unremitting attention to business, he had not been two years in the mercantile house in which he first engaged, ere he was taken into partnership by his employer." Typical of these success stories was Frederick Thomas's *Clinton Bradshaw* in which the hero advanced rapidly from law school to Congress without a serious setback in his career. The world seemed to be an easy oyster for fictional heroes to pry open. They invariably found pearls. Fenimore Cooper protested vainly at such sentimental mythmaking. "Success may be said to be certain," he wrote ironically in *Afloat and Ashore.* "I like the notion of beginning with nothing, it is so American!"

This sentimentalizing of reality is to be found at every point at which these novelists touched life. They wrote in a perpetual twilight of compromise and repression. Theirs was the captivating game of sporting decorously with indecency, of obscene thinking and strait-laced doing. Like Nora in Mrs. Hentz's *Robert Graham,* they laid the flattering unction to their souls that "It is not the *feeling* passion, but indulging it, that constitutes a sin." They betrayed a sniggering interest in sensuality without violating the merest punctilio of the moral proprieties. They were prudish Peeping Toms in a world of conventionally shaded windows; their lush modesty was nicely calculated to produce something between a smirk and a blush. "Well, there, as I live, was the prettiest *chambre à coucher* imaginable," exulted the author of *Blonde and Brunette* at the sight of a bridal suite. "The curtains were rich white silk damask looped with silver, the coverlet of white merino embroidered, the pillows and sheets trimmed with real Brussels." After reveling at length in other decorous details, Burdett revealed himself as a master in the tantalizing art of knowing just where to stop. There are those who are sensitive, he wrote solicitously, upon "approaching too near the awful secrets of wedlock." Edward Judson, known to a vast underworld of fiction readers as "Ned Buntline," delighted to conduct moral slumming excursions in his own novels. In *The Mysteries and Miseries of New York,* he introduced his hero to a bevy of prostitutes who were disporting themselves on "splendid ottomans." "You will find quite a variety," boasted the madame. "We have blondes and brunettes. The creole of the South; the lily of the Central States; and the snow-drop of the North." This and countless similar scenes served admirably to gratify prurient curiosity and to point an obvious moral. "Reader, we will not linger here in this garden of corruption," Judson wrote piously. "This is a book in which we have pledged ourselves not to write one line that we would not lay before a young sister's eye." There was probably no period in American history at which an ankle was so exciting, observed a recent historian of the era. The novelists made the most of it. "It is a confounded pretty foot," exclaimed a daring admirer in *Ruth Hall.* "I always put my coat on in the front entry, about the time she goes up stairs, to get a peep at it." Modesty without decency, love without sex, affection without passion— these were the prudish ingredients with which the sentimentalists worked. If any of them was ever tempted to call a spade a spade, he succeeded in resisting the impulse.

Much of the teaching in religious fiction was softened to an easy compliance with the universal desire for comfort and cheerfulness. In *Authorship,* John Neal scoffed at the widespread popularity of religious novels with their lessons heavily gilded with promises of durable material rewards. The church has "no god but gold," charged Samuel Judah in *The Buccaneers.* Fashionable sermons were as comfortably cushioned as the most expensive pews. A new minister in *Bubbleton Parish* was warned against preaching "practical sermons." "Our people generally prefer to have their pastor set forth the principles of the gospel in a forcible and attractive manner, instead of indulging in direct allusions, which are apt to irritate the feelings," advised a friendly parishioner. "It grieves them to see a minister disregard the apostolic method, and discuss in the pulpit irritating themes, such as can only mar the peace of a congregation, and disturb the unity of Christian sentiment." George William Curtis in *Potiphar Papers* described the readiness of the clergy to fill their sermons with the sonorous irrelevancies dear to the hearts of sentimentalists. "The cloth is very hard upon Cain, and completely routs the erring Kings of Judah," he noted. "The Spanish Inquisition, too, gets frightful knocks, and there is much eloquent exhortation to preach the gospel in the interior of Siam." Southern divines who were too honest to attempt to justify slavery by Scriptural authority took refuge in the safe doctrines of moderation and moral suasion. "I can but preach the gospel, teach the people the great law of love to God and man, and leave that to do the work gradually," concluded a pastor in *Honor*. "I say little about slavery, but much about justice and charity to all." To the underprivileged, the church urged the virtues of Christian resignation and the beauties of meek poverty. To wealthy communicants, she guaranteed salvation without pangs: "If you feel any wish to enter Heaven, just pave the way there by charity. It is the best road that I can point out to you, and has bridges in it, that will carry you over a multitude of sins." The Reverend Josiah Gilbert Holland found it difficult to believe that a good businessman could be "a very bad man." "Men who have exacted the last fraction of a cent with one hand, in the way of business," he submitted in his *Letters to the Joneses,* "have disbursed thousands of dollars with the other, in the way of charity." The sentimental pilgrim's progress to the Celestial City was made attractive by liberal stop-over privileges in Vanity Fair. There was abundant assurance, too, that even that pleasantly wicked city would, somehow or other, ultimately be washed clean with tears.

The most conspicuous failure of the sentimentalists was

their inability to solve the irrepressible problem of slavery. Certainly they tried hard enough. All their cherished weapons: pleasant escape, artful dodging, cunning evasion, and comfortable compromise were brought to bear upon it without avail. Slavery stubbornly refused "to vanish like a dream" as Hawthorne had predicted it might if it were only unmolested. "But come, we will compromise—compromise cuts all the gordian knots now-a-days," urged an optimist in Miss Sedgwick's *Married or Single?* This was the sovereign specific in the pharmacopoeia of the sentimentalists, and they prescribed it confidently. For their facile faith in its powers there seemed to be ample warrant in the tactics of the nation's lawmakers. Had not repeated applications of this soothing emollient allayed the bothersome eruptions of this malady in 1787, 1820, 1833, and 1850? Surely, it might succeed once again. Slavery was an evil, to be sure, but one too subtly woven into the warp and woof of our existence to be handled rigorously. "It is a dark thread," admitted Caroline Lee Hentz in *Marcus Warland,* "but as it winds along, it gleams with bright and silvery lustre, and some of the most beautiful lights and shades of the texture are owing to the blending of these sable filaments." Were not slaves the best of domestic servants, their ebon faces shining in the glory of subserviency? Were they not happier singing spirituals by their cabin doors under the Southern moon than they would have been chanting cannibalistic war songs in darkest Africa? Had the annals of Christian benevolence anything to show more fair than the sight of a planter's wife tenderly nursing a sick old granny whose wool had grown white in her mistress's service? Were not planters carrying out God's own providence in acquainting the race of Ham with the consolations of the Gospel? What were a few short years in Louisiana rice fields to the priceless boon of eternal freedom in Beulah Land? Had not New Englanders quite enough to do to ameliorate the conditions of their own white slaves in the textile mills? Would Uncle Tom have been more comfortable in a miserable "company house" in Lawrence or Lowell than in his honeysuckle-embowered cabin in the genial Southland?

Did millowners cheerfully pamper their aged operatives in their twilight years with inexhaustible fried chicken and endless holidays of sunny idleness? Slavery by any other name would be far from hideous. Was it not, after all, merely an evangelical course in compulsory manual training and Christianity, mercifully designed for a benighted race whose souls could be reclaimed by no other means? These were the questions being asked by sentimentalists on both sides of Mason and Dixon's line. Nor were the abolitionists more eager to put their own houses in order before they set out to reform those of their neighbors. In attacking the plantation system they closed their eyes to the factory system, and to the exploitative basis of their own raw industrialism in which they confused wage labor with free labor. As Parrington has observed, it was the familiar story of the kettle and the pot. Blinded by sectional economic interests, each side saw only half the truth. "They beheld the mote in a brother's eye, but considered not the beam that was in their own."

It would be uncritical to assume that the bombardment of Fort Sumter demolished the stronghold of the sentimentalists. Not unlike Major Anderson and his Union forces, they evacuated their position with colors flying and with drums beating. In the age of critical realism which followed the Civil War, they continued to recruit their readers from those who persisted in clinging to myths, who refused to recognize reality, and who sought in fiction an escape rather than a challenge. Lutestring enthusiasts are not peculiar to any age, although they found in the first generation of the American middle class a comfortable habitat. Worse than uncritical, moreover, would be the easy assumption that these sentimental novels never rang true, that they sprang from impulses which were wholly false, and that they failed to reflect the aspirations quietly cherished in thousands of hearts. The enlarged heart of sentimentality is a disease to which those who readily respond to the appeal of human nature are peculiarly susceptible. It is the excess of a virtue, the perversion of an ideal. No student of our national letters can escape the conviction that ours is an idealistic literature, fired with a passion for justice, liberty, and brotherhood. The failure of the sentimental compromise should teach our critics that theirs is the task of guiding the creative spirit to face squarely the realities of American life without losing its high ideals. Although an unwitting one, this is the most important lesson these faded favorites of an earlier generation have for us today.

Bibliography

BIBLIOGRAPHY

The primary sources for this study have been the novels themselves. I have indicated in the footnotes the date and place of publication of each novel upon its first mention in the text; sources of the passages quoted from the fiction have been cited in the notes. The Index contains every title to which reference has been made throughout the book. Bibliographies, literary histories, and special studies are listed in the general bibliography. For the early novels I consulted the bibliographies in the useful pioneer studies of Mr. Wegelin and Dr. Loshe. I also had the privilege of reading the manuscripts of Dr. Finch's Yale dissertation, *The Beginnings of the American Novel, 1789-1798,* and Dr. Hunt's bibliographical study, *Le Roman Américain, 1830-1850.* In my search for the novels discussed in the chapter on slavery fiction I used M. N. Work's *Bibliography of the Negro.* The extensive temperance collection in the New York Public Library provided me with most of the titles considered in the chapter on cold-water fiction. Of the early subscription libraries, I found the New York Society Library and the Mercantile Library of New York the most useful. Indispensable to students of American fiction are the valuable collections in the Library of Congress, the American Antiquarian Society, the Harvard College Library, and the New York Public Library.

The need of a scholarly bibliography of early American fiction with an accurate census locating copies in the various libraries throughout the country has been met happily by the publication of the bibliography of Mr. Lyle H. Wright, of the staff of the Henry E. Huntington Library and Art Gallery, San Marino, California. This eminently useful work includes the titles of novels and separately published short stories by Americans, beginning with Francis Hopkinson's *A Pretty Story* (1774) and extending to 1850.

General Works and Literary Histories

BAKER, E. A. *The History of the English Novel.* Vol. IV, *Intellectual Realism: From Richardson to Sterne.* London, 1930. Vol. V, *The Novel of Sentiment and the Gothic Romance.* London, 1934.

BEARD, CHARLES A. AND MARY R. *The Rise of American Civilization.* New York, 1927.

BENSON, M. S. *Women in Eighteenth Century America.* New York, 1935.

BERNBAUM, E. *The Drama of Sensibility: A Sketch of the History of English Sentimental Comedy and Tragedy, 1696-1780.* Boston, 1915.

BLACK, F. G. *The Epistolary Novel in the Late Eighteenth Century.* Eugene, Oregon, 1940.

BRANCH, E. D. *The Sentimental Years, 1836-1860.* New York, 1934.

BROOKS, VAN WYCK. *The Flowering of New England, 1815-1865.* New York, 1936.

COLE, A. C. *The Irrepressible Conflict, 1850-1865.* New York, 1934.

FAIRCHILD, H. N. *The Noble Savage: A Study in Romantic Naturalism.* New York, 1928.

FISH, C. R. *The Rise of the Common Man, 1830-1850.* New York, 1935.

HEILMAN, R. B. *America in English Fiction: 1760-1800.* Baton Rouge, 1937.

HERTZLER, J. O. *The History of Utopian Thought.* New York, 1923.

MINNIGERODE, M. *The Fabulous Forties, 1840-1850.* New York, 1924.

PARRINGTON, V. L. *The Romantic Revolution in America, 1800-1860.* New York, 1930.

PATTEE, F. L. *The First Century of American Literature, 1770-1870.* New York, 1935.

————. *The Feminine Fifties.* New York, 1940.

RICHARDSON, L. N. *A History of Early American Magazines, 1741-1789.* New York, 1931.

SWEET, W. W. *The Story of Religions in America.* New York, 1930.

THOMPSON, R. *American Literary Annuals & Gift Books, 1825-1865.* New York, 1936.

TOMPKINS, J. M. S. *The Popular Novel in England, 1770-1800.* London, 1932.

WECTER, D. *The Saga of American Society: A Record of Social Aspiration, 1607-1937.* New York, 1937.

WRIGHT, W. F. *Sensibility in English Prose Fiction, 1760-1814: A Reinterpretation.* Urbana, Ill., 1937. "Illinois Studies in Language and Literature," XXII, Nos. 3-4.

Bibliographies and Histories of American Fiction

DUNLAP, G. A. *The City in the American Novel, 1789-1900.* Philadelphia, 1934. Bibliography, pp. 176-183.

FINCH, E. D. *The Beginnings of the American Novel, 1789-1798.* An unpublished Yale dissertation.

FLORY, C. R. *Economic Criticism in American Fiction, 1792-1900.* Philadelphia, 1936. Bibliography, pp. 245-257.

HUNT, T. *Le Roman Américain, 1830-1850. Avec une Bibliographie des Romans.* Paris, 1937. Bibliography, pp. 183-216.

JOHNSON, J. G. *Southern Fiction Prior to 1860.* Charlottesville, 1909.

LOSHE, L. D. *The Early American Novel.* New York, 1907 and 1930. Bibliography, pp. 106-124.

QUINN, A. H. *American Fiction: An Historical and Critical Survey.* New York, 1936.

RUSK, R. L. *The Literature of the Middle Western Frontier.* 2. vols. New York, 1925 and 1926. Bibliography of fiction in Vol. II, pp. 351-353.

VAN DOREN, C. *The American Novel.* New York, 1921; Revised ed., 1940.

WEGELIN, O. *Early American Fiction.* Stanford, 1902; Revised ed., New York, 1913; 1929.

WRIGHT, L. H. *American Fiction, 1774-1850: A Contribution toward a Bibliography.* San Marino, Calif., 1939.

Biographies and Special Studies

ADKINS, N. F. "An Early American Story of Utopia," *Colophon,* New Series, I (1935), 123-132.

BABBITT, I. "Two Types of Humanitarians: Bacon and Rousseau," *Literature and the American College* (Boston and New York, 1908), 32-71.

BIRKHEAD, E. "Sentiment and Sensibility in the Eighteenth Century English Novel," *Essays and Studies,* XI (1925), 92-116.

BLACK, F. G. "The Technique of Letter Fiction in English from 1740 to 1800," *Harvard Studies and Notes in Philology and Literature,* XV (1933), 291-312.

BOAS, F. S. "Richardson's Novels and Their Influence," *Essays and Studies,* II (1911), 36-70.

BOLTON, C. K. "Circulating Libraries in Boston, 1765-1865," *Publications of the Colonial Society of Massachusetts* (Boston, 1910), XI, 196-207.

——. *The Elizabeth Whitman Mystery.* Peabody, Mass., 1912.

BRADSHER, E. L. *Mathew Carey: Editor, Author, and Publisher.* New York, 1912.

BRAYLEY, A. W. "The Real Author of *The Power of Sympathy*," *Bostonian,* I (1894), 224.

BROWN, H. R. "Elements of Sensibility in *The Massachusetts Magazine*," *American Literature,* I (1929), 286-296.

——. "Richardson and Sterne in *The Massachusetts Magazine*," *New England Quarterly,* V (1932), 65-82.

——. "Sensibility in Eighteenth-Century American Drama," *American Literature,* IV (1932), 47-60.

——. "The Great American Novel," *American Literature,* VII (1935), 1-14.

CHARVAT, W. *The Origins of American Critical Thought, 1810-1835.* Philadelphia, 1936.

CROSS, W. L. *The Life and Times of Laurence Sterne.* New Haven, 1935.

DALL, C. H. *The Romance of the Association; or, One Last Glimpse of Charlotte Temple and Eliza Wharton.* Cambridge, 1875.

DEXTER, F. B. "The Manuscripts of Jonathan Edwards," *Proceedings of the Massachusetts Historical Society* (Cambridge, 1901), XV (Second Series), 2-16.

DOWNS, B. W. *Richardson.* London, 1928.

ELLIS, M. "The Author of the First American Novel," *American Literature,* IV (1933), 359-368.

FATOUT, P. "Yarning in the Fifties," *American Scholar,* III (1934), 281-293.

FENN, W. W. "The Revolt Against the Standing Order," *The Religious History of New England* (Cambridge, 1917), pp. 77-133.

FIELD, V. B. *Constantia: A Study of the Life and Works of Judith Sargent Murray, 1751-1820.* Orono, 1931. "University of Maine Studies," Second Series, No. 17.

FLITCROFT, J. E. *Daniel Pierce Thompson: The Novelist of Vermont.* Cambridge, Mass., 1929.

GAINES, F. P. *The Southern Plantation.* New York, 1924.

GILBERTSON, C. *Harriet Beecher Stowe.* New York, 1937.

GROWOLL, A., *Book-trade Bibliography in the United States in the XIXth Century*. New York, 1898.

HALLENBECK, C. T. "A Colonial Reading List from the Union Library of Hatboro, Pennsylvania," *Pennsylvania Magazine of History and Biography*, LVI (1932), 289-340.

JENKINS, W. S. *Pro-Slavery Thought in the Old South*. Chapel Hill, 1935.

KELLOGG, T. L. *The Life and Work of John Davis, 1774-1853*. Orono, 1924. "University of Maine Studies," Second Series, No. 1.

KENNEDY, J. E. *George Watterston: Novelist, Metropolitan Author, and Critic*. Washington, D. C., 1933.

KRAUS, M. "Slavery Reform in the Eighteenth Century: An Aspect of Transatlantic Cooperation," *Pennsylvania Magazine of History and Biography*, LX (1936), 53-66.

KRUTCH, J. W. *Five Masters*. New York, 1930.

LONG, O. W. "English Translations of Goethe's Werther," *Journal of English and Germanic Philology*, XIV (1915), 169-203.

McDOWELL, T. "Sensibility in Eighteenth Century American Novel," *Studies in Philology*, XXIV (1927), 383-402.

——. "Last Words of a Sentimental Heroine," *American Literature*, IV (1932), 174-177.

——. "An American Robinson Crusoe," *American Literature*, I (1929), 307-309.

McKILLOP, A. D. *Samuel Richardson, Printer and Novelist*. Chapel Hill, 1936.

MAYNADIER, G. H. *The First American Novelist?* Cambridge, 1940.

MORE, P. E. "Religious Grounds of Humanitarianism," *Shelburne Essays, First Series* (New York and London, 1907), pp. 225-253.

ORIANS, G. H. "Censure of Fiction in American Romances and Magazines, 1789-1810," *Publications of the Modern Language Association of America*, LII (1937), 195-214.

PENDLETON, E. AND ELLIS, M. *Philenia: The Life and Works of Sarah Wentworth Morton*. Orono, 1931. "University of Maine Studies," Second Series, No. 20.

RADDIN, G. G., JR. *An Early New York Library of Fiction*. New York, 1940.

SHURTER, R. L. "Mrs. Hannah Webster Foster and the Early American Novel," *American Literature*, IV (1932), 306-308.

SMALL, M. R. *Charlotte Ramsay Lennox*. New Haven, 1935.

378 BIBLIOGRAPHY

SPILLER, R. E. *Fenimore Cooper: Critic of His Times*. New York, 1931.

STEARNS, B.-M. "Before *Godey's*," *American Literature*, II (1939), 248-255.

TANDY, J. "Pro-Slavery Propaganda in American Fiction in the Fifties," *South Atlantic Quarterly*, XXI (1922), 41-51, 170-178.

THOMPSON, H. W. *A Scottish Man of Feeling*. . . . Oxford, 1931.

TUPPER, F. "Royall Tyler, Man of Law and Man of Letters," *Proceedings of the Vermont Historical Society* (1928), pp. 65-101.

TURNER, L. D. *Anti-Slavery Sentiment in American Literature Prior to 1865*. Washington, D. C., 1929.

VAIL, R. W. G. *Susanna Haswell Rowson, the Author of Charlotte Temple, a Bibliographical Study*. Worcester, 1933.

VIOLETTE, A. G. *Economic Feminism in American Literature Prior to 1848*. Orono, 1925. "University of Maine Studies," Second Series, No. 2.

WARNER, A. B. *Susan Warner*. New York, 1904.

WRIGHT, L. H. "A Statistical Survey of American Fiction, 1774-1850," *Huntington Library Quarterly*, II (1938-1939), 309-318.

Diaries, Memoirs, Letters, Tracts, Travels, Etc.

ADAMS, H. *A Memoir of Miss Hannah Adams*. Boston, 1832.

ARMES, E. (ed.). *Nancy Shippen, Her Journal Book; the International Romance of a Young Lady of Fashion of Philadelphia with Letters to Her and About Her*. Philadelphia, 1935.

BENSON, A. B. (ed.). *America of the Fifties: Letters of Fredrika Bremer*. New York, 1924.

BENNETT, J. *Letters to a Young Lady on a Variety of Useful and Interesting Subjects*. . . . Hartford, 1791.

BRISSOT DE WARVILLE, J. P. *New Travels in the United States of America*. . . . London, 1794.

BROWN, C. B. *Alcuin: A Dialogue*. New York, 1798.

BURTON, J. *Lectures on Female Education and Manners*. New York, 1794.

CHASTELLUX, FRANÇOIS JEAN DE. *Travels in North America in the Years 1780, 1781, and 1782*. London, 1787.

CHINARD, G. (ed.). *The Literary Bible of Thomas Jefferson*. Baltimore, 1928.

DAVIES, S. *Religion and Patriotism: The Constituents of a Good Soldier.* Philadelphia, 1755.

DAVIS, J. *Travels of Four Years and a Half in the United States of America.* . . . London, 1803.

DENNIE, J. *The Lay Preacher; or, Short Sermons for Idle Readers.* Walpole, N. H., 1796.

DUCHÉ, J. *Observations on a Variety of Subjects.* Philadelphia, 1744.

DWIGHT, T. *Travels in New-England and New-York.* . . . New Haven, 1821-1822.

EARLE, A. M. (ed.). *The Diary of Anna Green Winslow.* Boston, 1894.

FISHER, J. (ed.). "The Journal of Esther Burr," *New England Quarterly,* III (1930), 296-315.

FORD, P. L. (ed.). *The Writings of Thomas Jefferson.* New York and London, 1892-1899.

GRAYDON, A. *Memoirs of a Life.* Harrisburg, 1811.

GREGORY, J. *A Father's Legacy to his Daughters.* New York, 1775.

HART, A. B. (ed.). *Hamilton's Itinerarium being a Narrative of a Journey.* . . . St. Louis, 1907.

HOSMER, J. K. (ed.). *Winthrop's Journal: 1630-1649.* New York, 1908.

KENNEDY, J. P. (ed.). *Memoirs of the Life of William Wirt.* Philadelphia, 1850.

KEEP, A. B. *History of the New York Society Library.* New York, 1908.

MACDONALD, F. W. *The Journal of the Rev. John Wesley.* London and New York, n.d.

POND, J. S. *Bradford, a New England Academy.* Boston, 1930.

SHIPPEN, J. *Observations on Novel Reading.* Philadelphia, 1792.

SKEEL, E. E. F. (ed.). *Mason Locke Weems: His Works and Ways.* New York, 1929.

SMYTHE, A. H. (ed.). *The Writings of Benjamin Franklin.* New York and London, 1905.

TICKNOR, C. *Hawthorne and His Publisher.* Boston, 1913.

TRUMBULL, J. *The Poetical Works of John Trumbull.* Hartford, 1820.

WARD, G. A. (ed.). *Journal and Letters of the Late Samuel Curwen.* New York, 1842.

WEBSTER, N. *A Collection of Essays and Fugitive Writings on Moral, Historical, Political and Literary Subjects.* Boston, 1790.

WHITTIER, J. G. (ed.). *Letters of Lydia Maria Child, with a Biographical Introduction.* Boston, 1883.

WILLIAMS, J. R. (ed.). *Journals and Letters* [of Philip Vickers Fithian], *1767-1774.* Princeton, 1900.

Index

INDEX